ASS 2. Contains material originally published in magazine form as KICK-ASS 2 #1-7. First printing 2012. ISBN# 978-0-7851-5245-3. Published by MARVEL WORLDWIDE, INC., a subsidiary of MARVEL
TAINMENT, LLC. OFFICE OF PUBLICATION: 135 West 50th Street, New York, NY 10020. Copyright © 2010, 2011 and 2012 Mark Millar and John S. Romita. All rights reserved. $24.99 per copy in the U.S. and $27.99
ada (GST #R127032852); Canadian Agreement #40668537. KICK-ASS, the Kick-Ass logo, and all characters and content herein and the likenesses thereof are trademarks of Mark Millar and John S. Romita, unless
ise expressly noted. The events and characters presented are intended as fiction. Any similarity to real events or to persons living or dead is purely coincidental. This work may not be reproduced, except in small
nts for journalistic or review purposes, without permission of the authors. ICON and the Icon logo are trademarks of Marvel Characters, Inc. **Printed in the U.S.A.** ALAN FINE, EVP - Office of the President, Marvel
vide, Inc. and EVP & CMO Marvel Characters B.V.; DAN BUCKLEY, Publisher & President - Print, Animation & Digital Divisions; JOE QUESADA, Chief Creative Officer; TOM BREVOORT, SVP of Publishing; DAVID BOGART,
Operations & Procurement, Publishing; RUWAN JAYATILLEKE, SVP & Associate Publisher, Publishing; C.B. CEBULSKI, SVP of Creator & Content Development; DAVID GABRIEL, SVP of Publishing Sales & Circulation;
EL PASCIULLO, SVP of Brand Planning & Communications; JIM O'KEEFE, VP of Operations & Logistics; DAN CARR, Executive Director of Publishing Technology; SUSAN CRESPI, Editorial Operations Manager; ALEX
ES, Publishing Operations Manager; STAN LEE, Chairman Emeritus. For information regarding advertising in Marvel Comics or on Marvel.com, please contact John Dokes, SVP Integrated Sales and Marketing, at
@marvel.com. For Marvel subscription inquiries, please call 800-217-9158. **Manufactured between 4/16/2012 and 5/14/2012 by R.R. DONNELLEY INC., SALEM, VA, USA.**

KICK-ASS 2

Writer & Co-Creator
MARK MILLAR

Penciler & Co-Creator
JOHN ROMITA JR.

Inker & Tones
TOM PALMER

Colorist (Issues #1-5 & #7)
DEAN WHITE
with MICHAEL KELLEHER

Colorist (Issue #6)
DAN BROWN

Letterer
CHRIS ELIOPOULOS
with CLAYTON COWLES

Editor
AUBREY SITTERSON
with JOHN BARBER AND CORY LEVINE

Collection Editor: AUBREY SITTERSON
Book Designer: SPRING HOTELING
Senior Vice President of Sales: DAVID GABRIEL
SVP of Business Affairs & Talent Management: DAVID BOGART

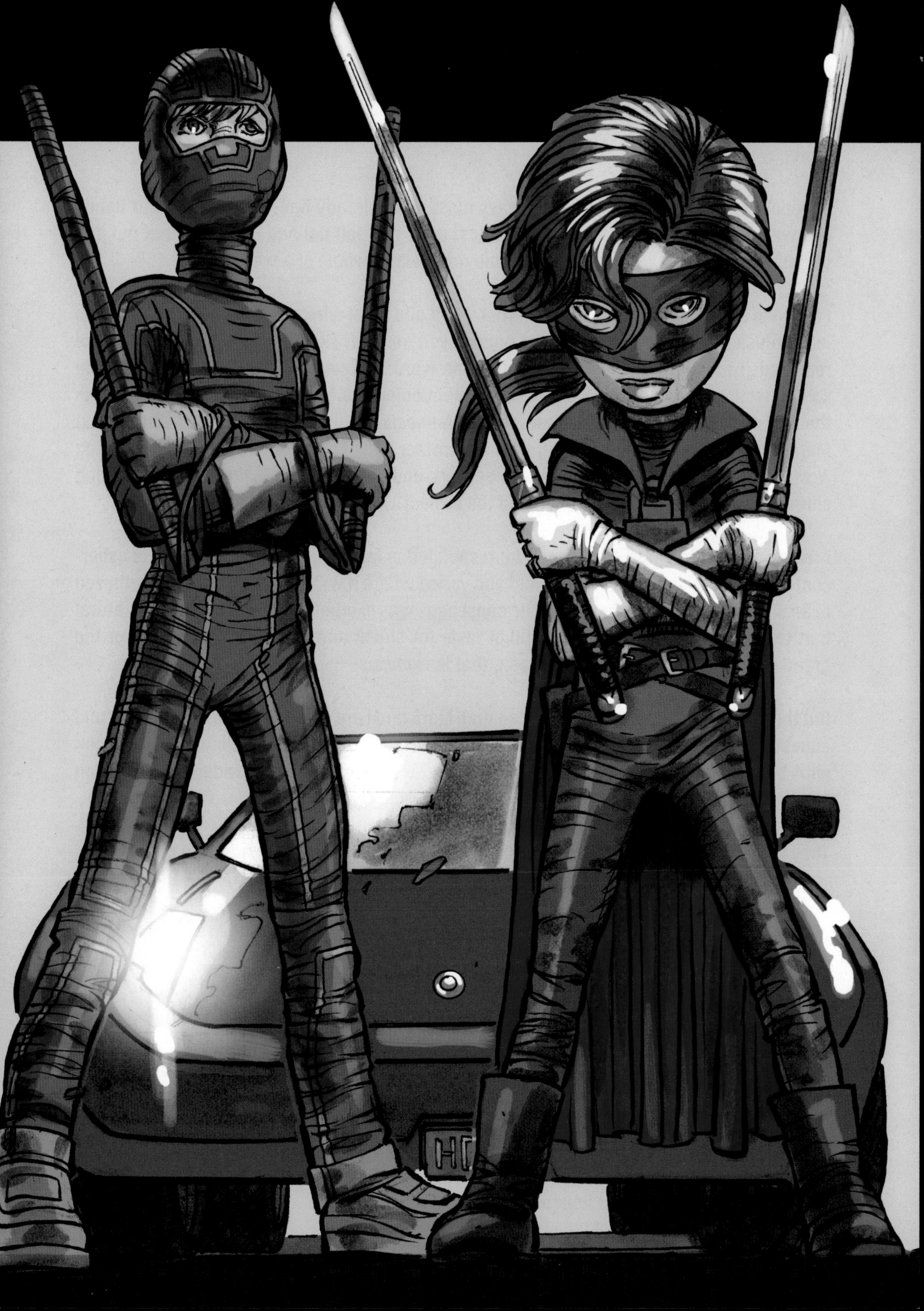

Hey fucker.

Let's face facts, you're one of these fucking fetishistic "fanboy" jerkoffs who secretly wishes that *he* could be Dave Lizewski, beating the shit out of muggers, gangbangers and mob heavies with those akimbo batons as a comely, prepubescent Hit Girl slashes and burns by your side.

It's cool. <u>Me too</u>. I mean good money says most of us already have our dicks in our hands and we're not even out of the intro… but just pace yourself pal and don't pop that nut just yet 'cuz what follows in these pages is one great white *whale* of a wank.

I suppose some basic backstory is in order. Mark and I met where folks not living in an igloo in Bumfuck, Antarctica tend to meet nowadays… online. Twitter to be precise. Someone reposted (I fucking flat-out refuse to use the word *'Retweet'* for fear that my balls will spontaneously detonate) a Millar passage mentioning his love of *The A-Team* as well as the fact that he had named a character in *Nemesis* "Carnahan" after yours truly. What Mark didn't know, was that I, along with my brother Matt, had been charged with adapting *Nemesis* for Fox but it had all gone sideways under the stewardship of this conniving shithead who singlehandedly torpedoed the project… for the time being.

I reached out to Mark on Twitter and he responded, a fast friendship formed and its cyber-content was reprinted on websites vast and varied where it was poured over and scrutinized at an almost forensic fucking level. <u>The consensus was excitement</u>. It seemed totally natural that two like-minded lads with a mutual taste for shock and awe should team up for the grand guignol-like assault on good taste that is *Nemesis*.

But the bond goes quite a bit deeper than that. Mark and I are of both shared ethnic stock and ancestral discord. We're displaced modern day Celts from a long bloodline chock-a-block with bludgeonings and beheadings. Our forefathers fought Viking invaders on forgotten shores, losing their women, their land and finally, <u>their minds</u>.

They were *The Fraternity Of The Fucked…* and we are their proud descendants.

In keeping that spirit alive and ablaze with wanton bloodlust, my Scottish chum (despite the arrival of another Millar heir and him being dry as a 90-year-old nun's snatch in honor of lent) has nevertheless managed to purge his most putrid cranial pools; the brackish backwaters of the brain where traditional narratives get gang-raped by roid-raging, beer-bellied, gore-soaked gargantuans… to give you sonsabitches yet *another* magnum opus.

In *Kick-Ass 2*, Millar and creative cohort John Romita, Jr. have hotwired the elevator of their frayed mental state to plunge you, fair reader, deeper down into the dripping sub-basement of his perfectly *pitch-black* psychosis. There are no headlamps to light the way down here my lovelies… only the stink of sulfur and suppressed rage. Their off-brand of storytelling is *exactly* the type of perversely, unprintable shit that A.) <u>I love</u> and B.) Affords a battalion's worth of shrinks beachfront homes and Bel Air addresses.

In short, <u>it's a shit-ton of fun</u>.

What you're about to embark on is a true tour de force and the *Kick-Ass* team is in full command of their craft; master illusionists who have perfected the legerdemain of the lewd and vicious, the loathsome and the vile. Blending humor, emotion, sorrow, pain and regret while supercharging the stakes and never forsaking the spirit of what *Kick-Ass* ultimately is: A kid with a ridiculously outsized dream, who dared to make it a reality… <u>and did</u>.

Gone is the rank teenage ennui of the original and in its place a superheroic dystopia. Dave Lizewski has come to terms with what being a famous public figure is. Larger than life is harder than hell when you're still in high school but growing pains, like a brand new patch of pubes, is par for the course and Dave's willingness to throw himself headlong into shitstorm after shitstorm reconfirms his unbreakable conviction to the ethos of his alter ego, *Kick-Ass*.

Pushing him ruthlessly along in his journey is the former Red Mist, now rechristened "The Motherfucker." Chris Genovese is no more. The soul-patched nihilist that now inhabits his form thinks nothing of laying waste to an entire suburb for shits and grins or assassinating a sidewalk full of school kids for sport. This "Motherfucker" is the sneering embodiment of society's mindless, amoral masochism.

Rounding out the trifecta is that sweet, chocolate-covered little claymore mine formerly known as "Hit-Girl." Ironically, it's young Mindy Macready that provides the most unlikely moral core for our story. Resigned to a quiet life in relative seclusion with her adopted parents, she reluctantly returns to the mask only when all seems lost to once again embrace her god-given gifts as a taker of unholy souls, a death machine in overdrive, a living, breathing, <u>paean to pain</u>.

So, with appetites whetted and palms slicked, sit back and have at it kids. What follows is a nightmarish, nuclear meltdown of a mindfuck, lovingly cooked up in the shared mental meth lab of Mark Millar and John Romita, Jr.

Enjoy… *cocksuckers!*

Joe Carnahan
Los Angeles,
March, 2012

ONE

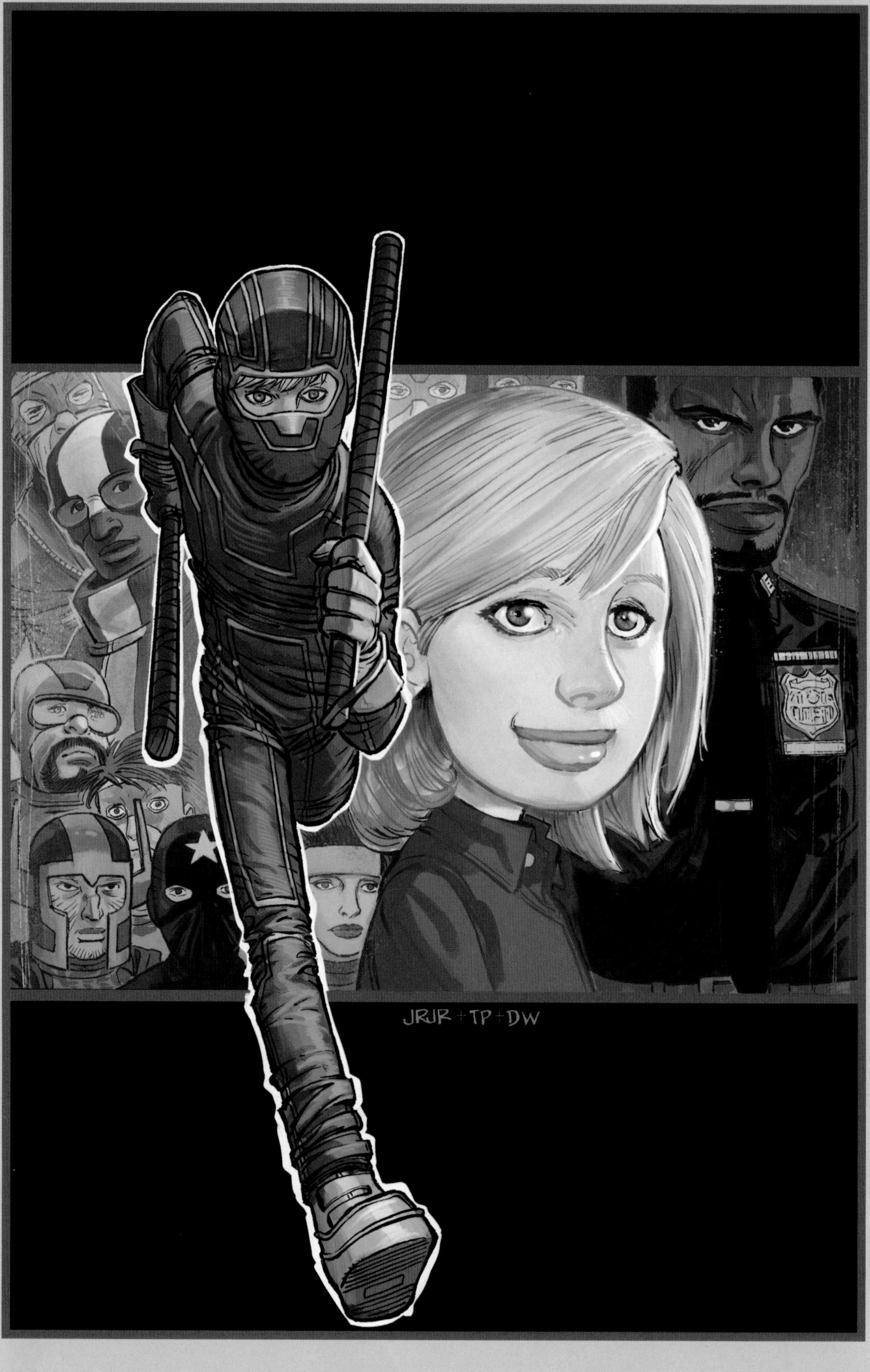
JRJR + TP + DW

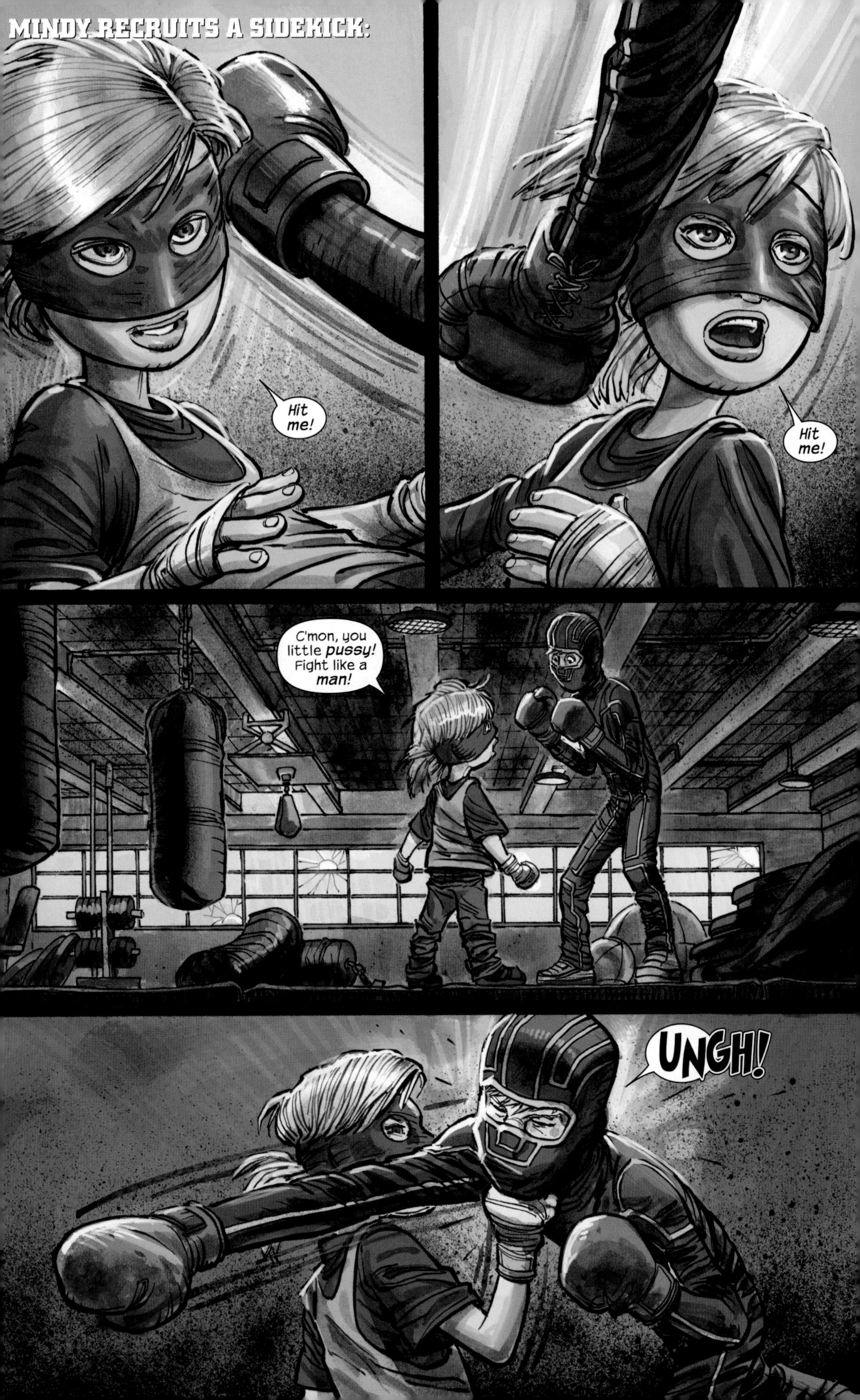
MINDY RECRUITS A SIDEKICK:
Hit me!
Hit me!
C'mon, you little *pussy*! Fight like a *man*!
UNGH!

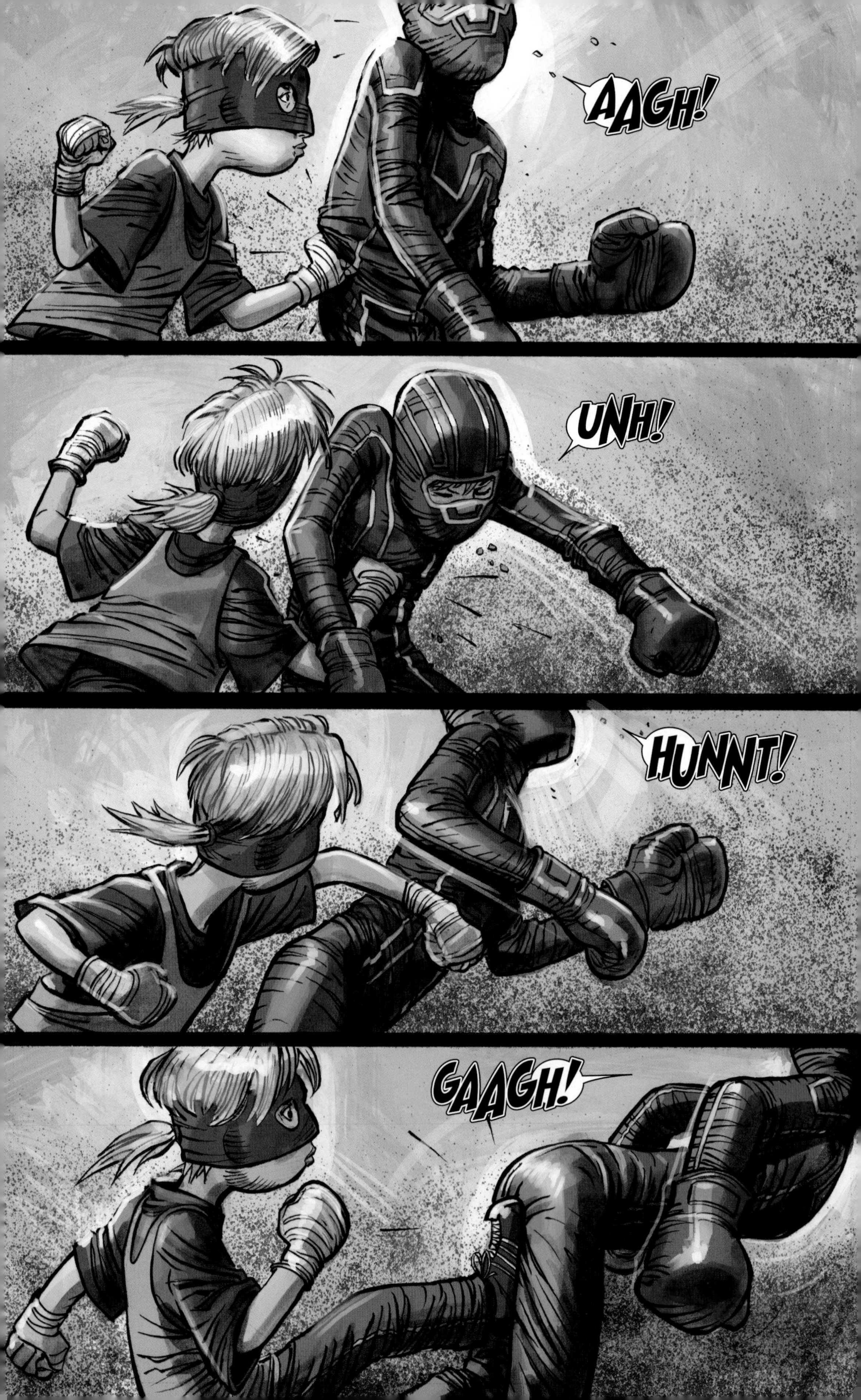
AAGH!
UNH!
HUNNT!
GAAGH!

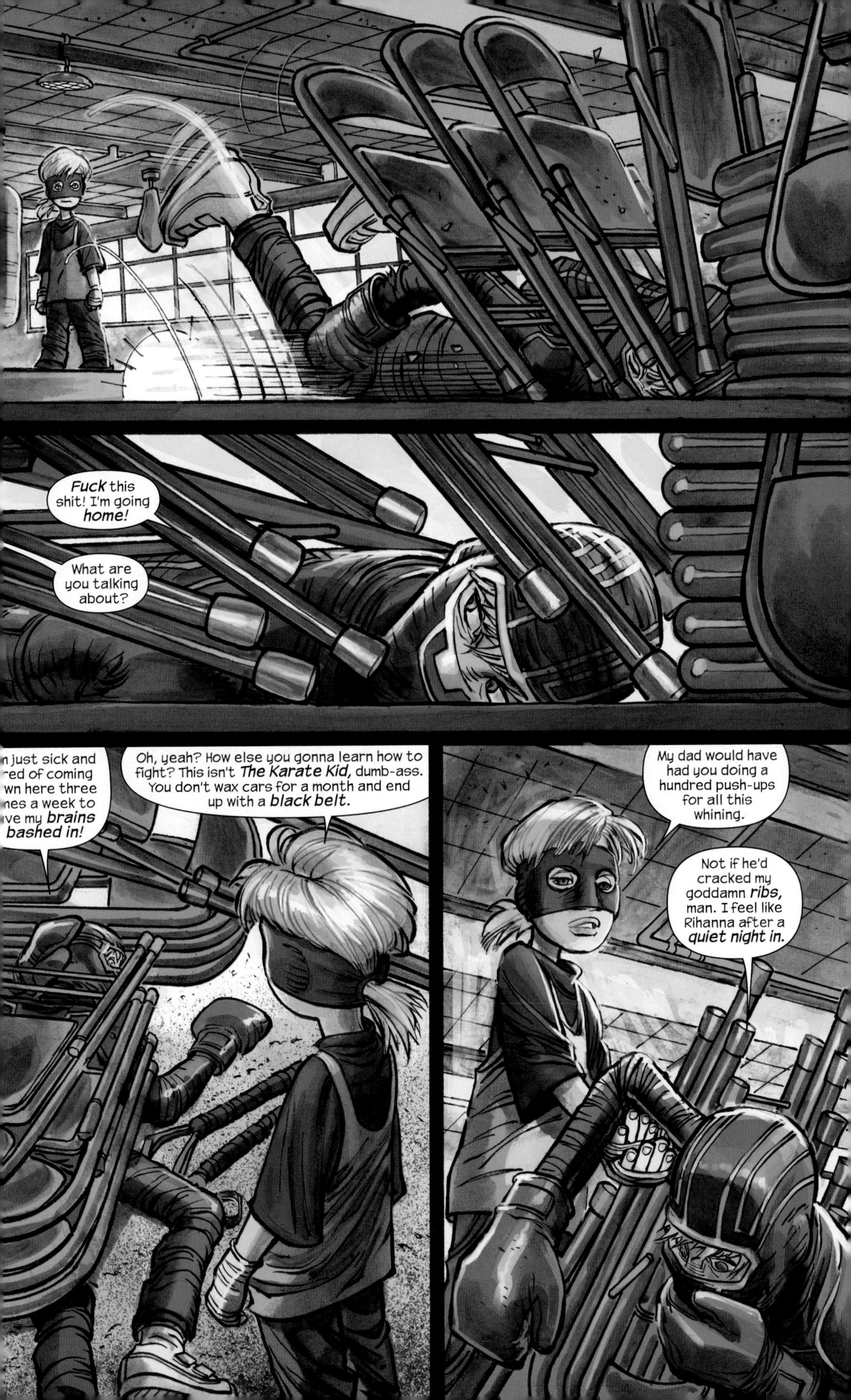

Fuck this shit! I'm going *home!*
What are you talking about?
n just sick and red of coming wn here three nes a week to ve my *brains bashed in!*
Oh, yeah? How else you gonna learn how to fight? This isn't *The Karate Kid,* dumb-ass. You don't wax cars for a month and end up with a *black belt.*
My dad would have had you doing a hundred push-ups for all this whining.
Not if he'd cracked my goddamn *ribs,* man. I feel like Rihanna after a *quiet night in.*

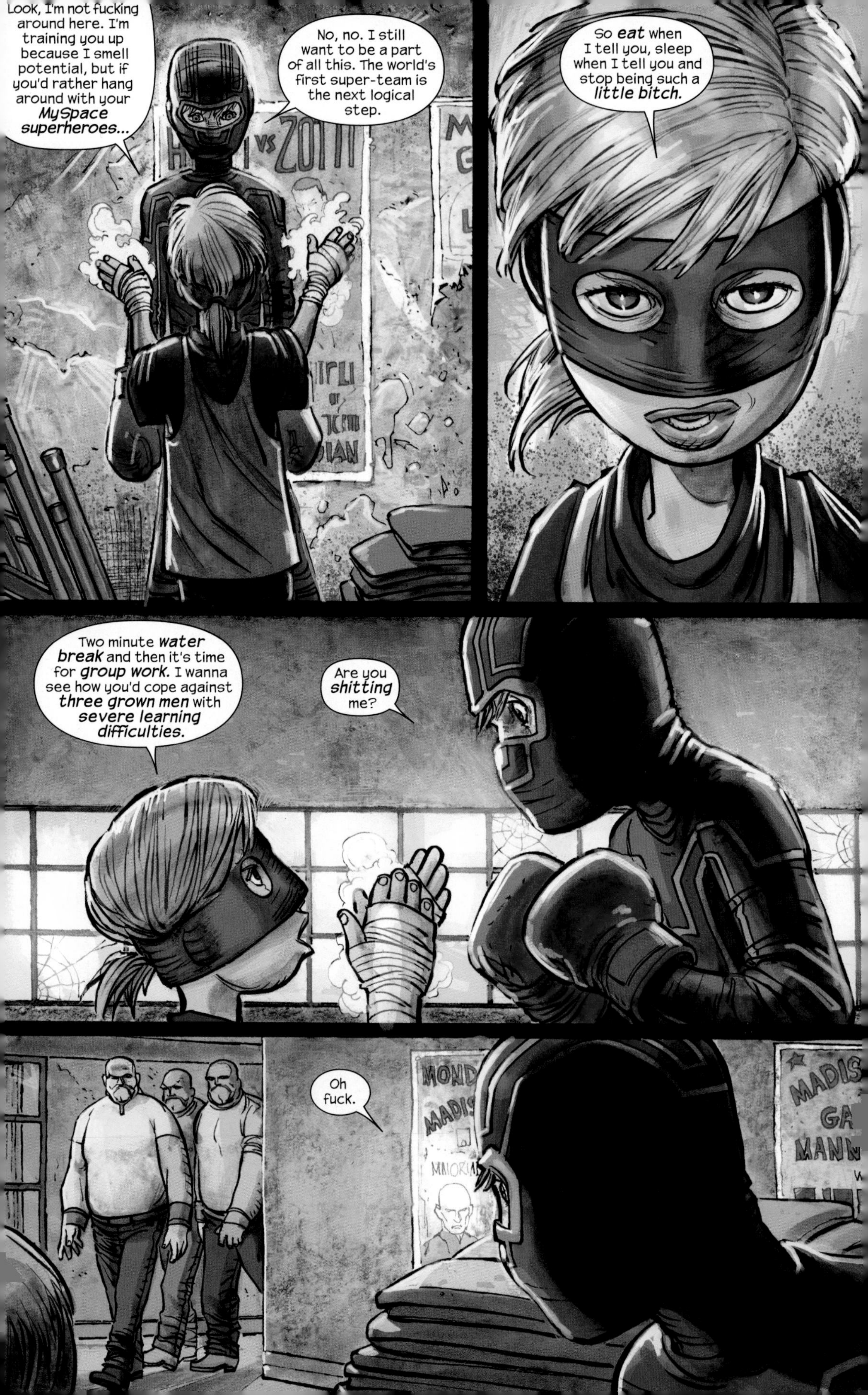
Look, I'm not fucking around here. I'm training you up because I smell potential, but if you'd rather hang around with your MySpace superheroes...
No, no. I still want to be a part of all this. The world's first super-team is the next logical step.
So eat when I tell you, sleep when I tell you and stop being such a little bitch.
Two minute water break and then it's time for group work. I wanna see how you'd cope against three grown men with severe learning difficulties.
Are you shitting me?
Oh fuck.

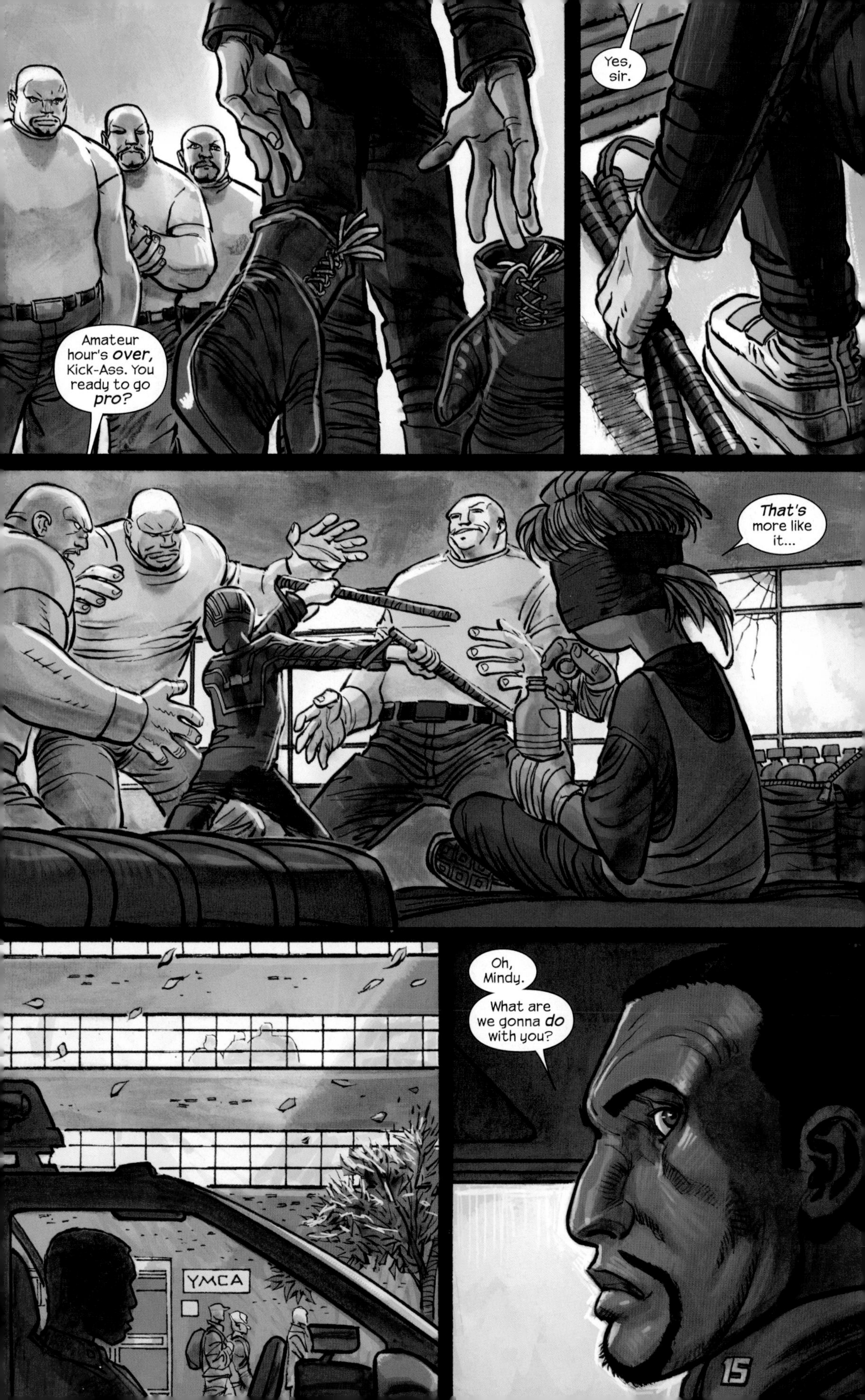
Amateur hour's *over,* Kick-Ass. You ready to go *pro?*
Yes, sir.
That's more like it...
YMCA
Oh, Mindy.
What are we gonna *do* with you?

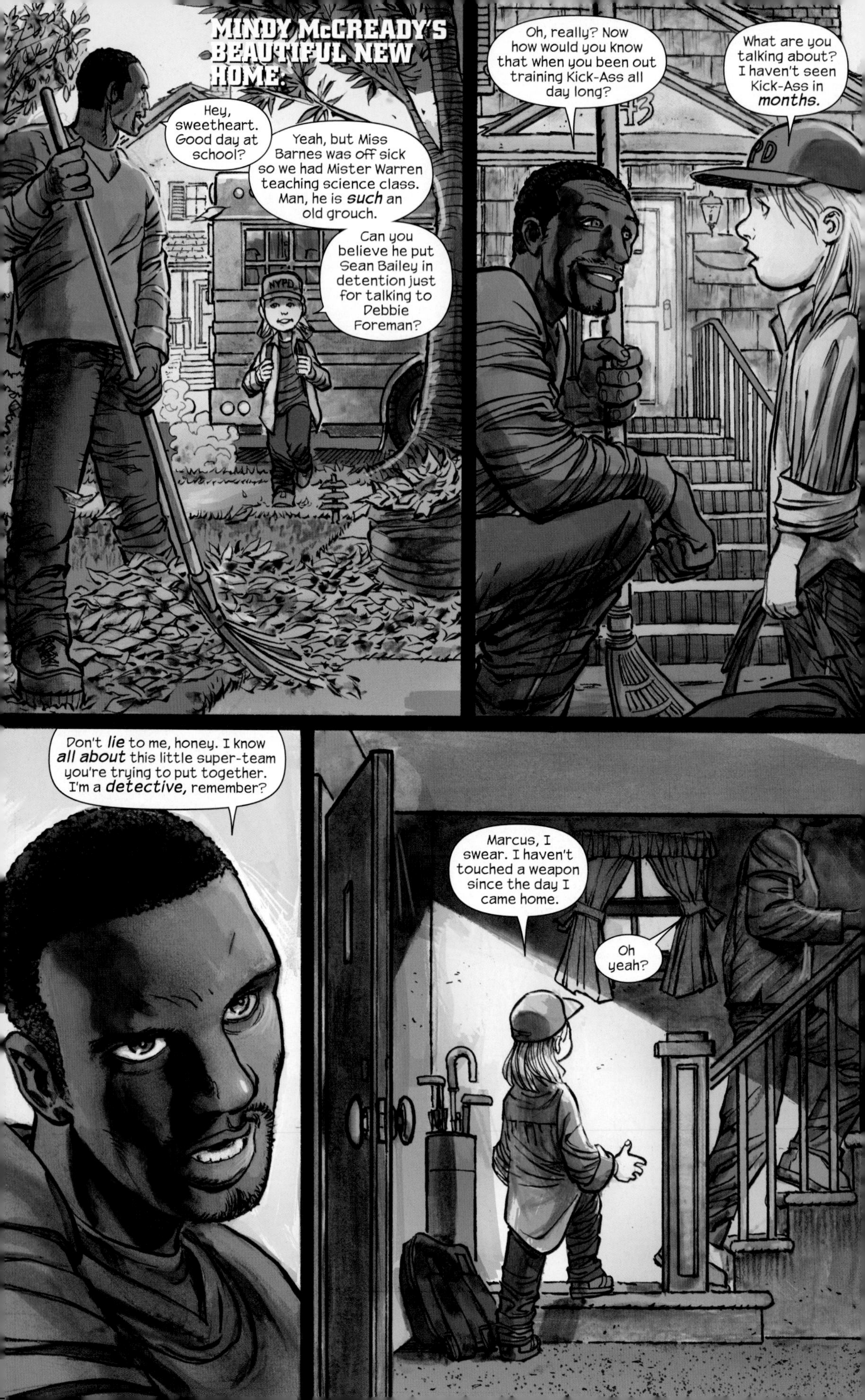
MINDY McCREADY'S BEAUTIFUL NEW HOME:
Hey, sweetheart. Good day at school?
Yeah, but Miss Barnes was off sick so we had Mister Warren teaching science class. Man, he is *such* an old grouch.
Can you believe he put Sean Bailey in detention just for talking to Debbie Foreman?
NYPD
Oh, really? Now how would you know that when you been out training Kick-Ass all day long?
What are you talking about? I haven't seen Kick-Ass in *months.*
Don't *lie* to me, honey. I know *all about* this little super-team you're trying to put together. I'm a *detective,* remember?
Marcus, I swear. I haven't touched a weapon since the day I came home.
Oh yeah?

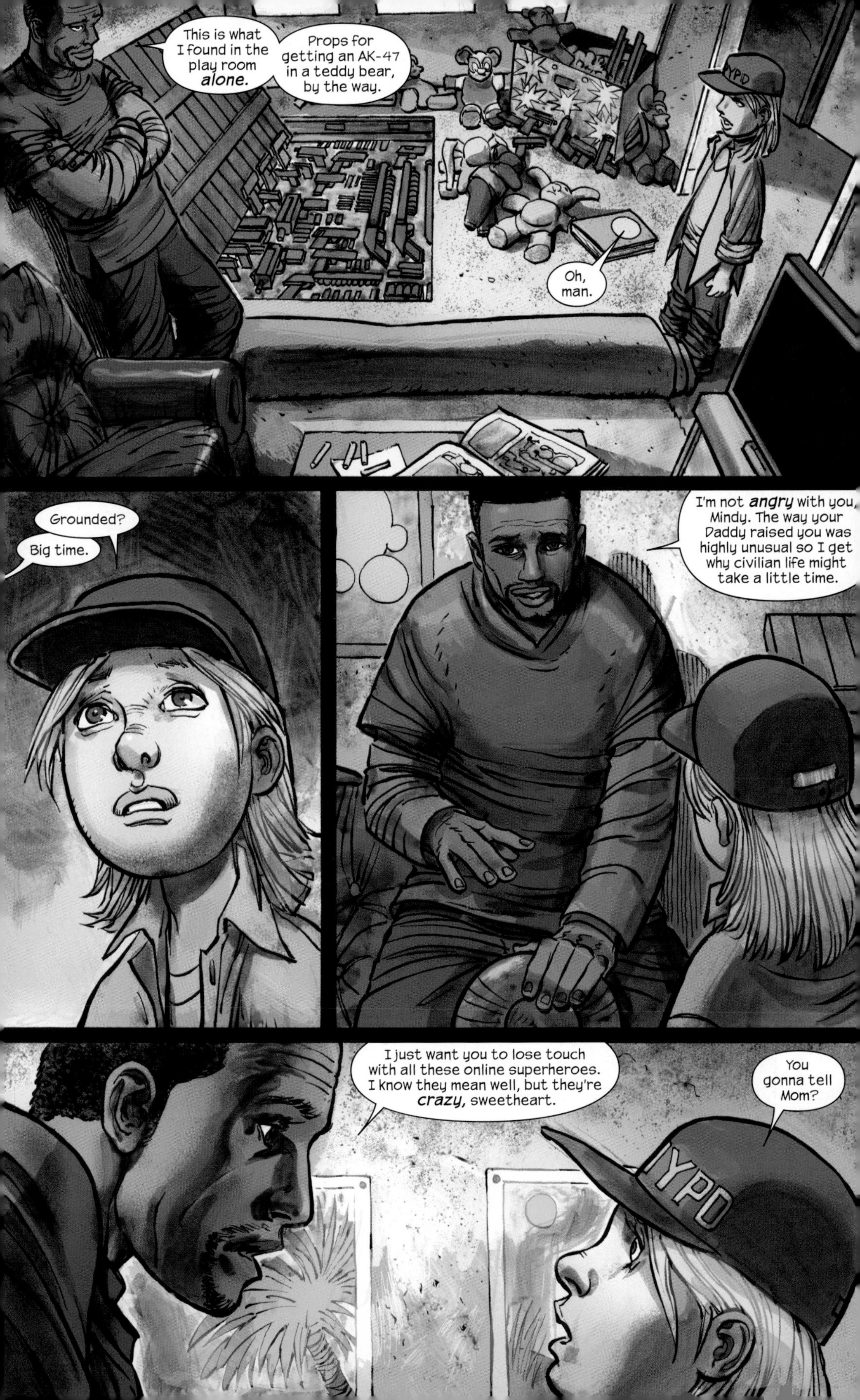
This is what I found in the play room alone.
Props for getting an AK-47 in a teddy bear, by the way.
Oh, man.
Grounded?
Big time.
I'm not angry with you, Mindy. The way your Daddy raised you was highly unusual so I get why civilian life might take a little time.
I just want you to lose touch with all these online superheroes. I know they mean well, but they're crazy, sweetheart.
You gonna tell Mom?
NYPD

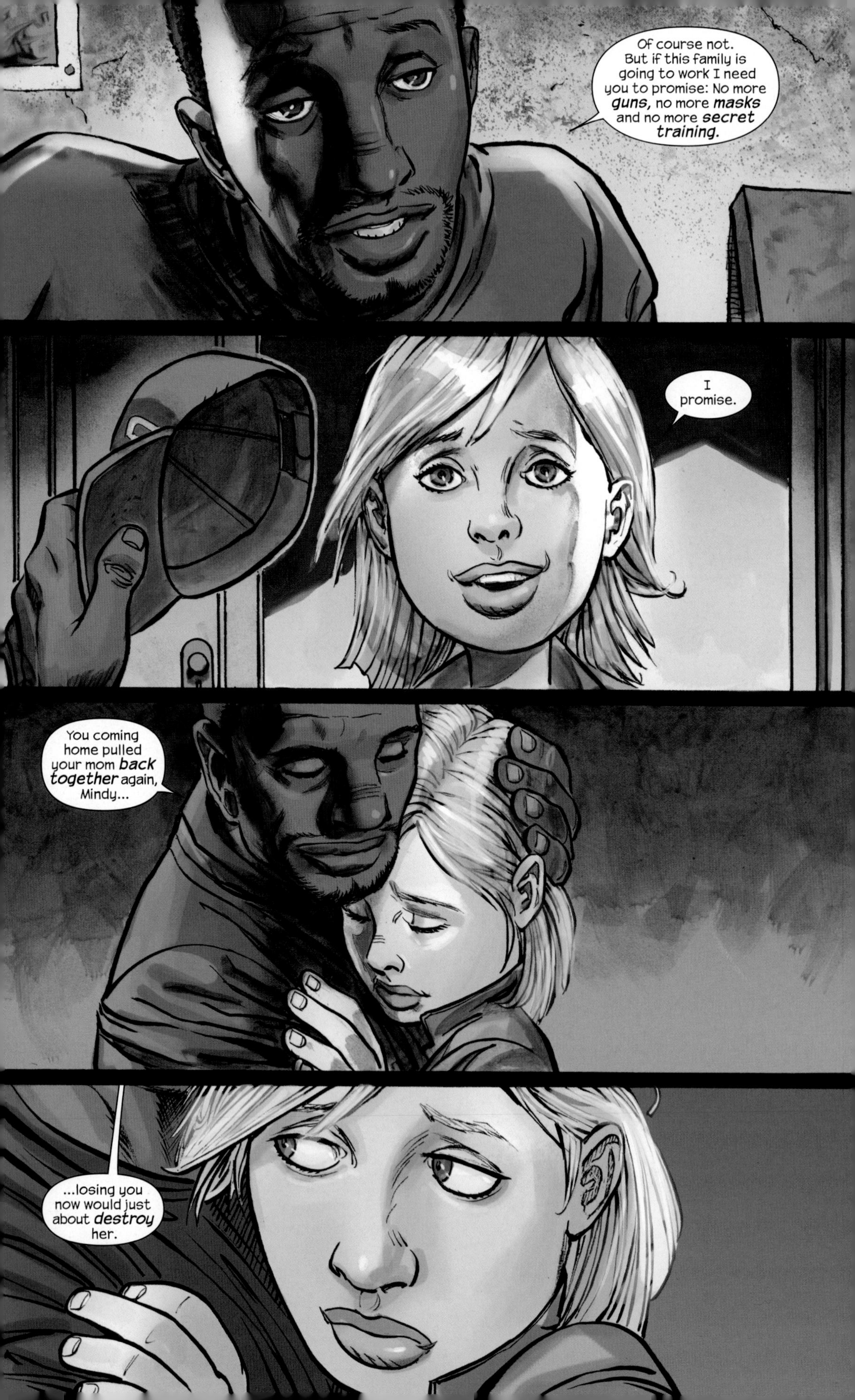
Of course not. But if this family is going to work I need you to promise: No more *guns,* no more *masks* and no more *secret training.*
I promise.
You coming home pulled your mom *back together* again, Mindy...
...losing you now would just about *destroy* her.

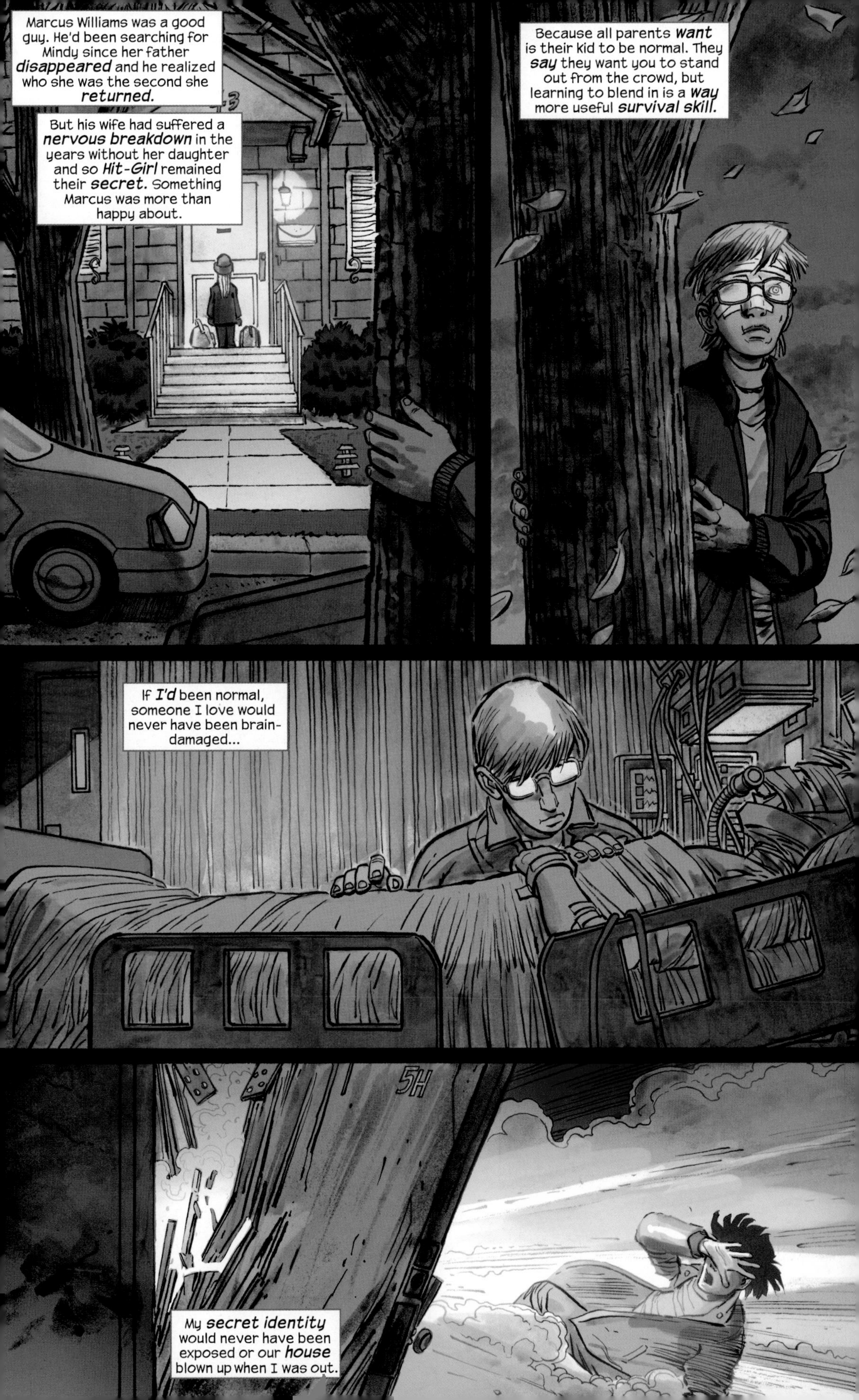
Marcus Williams was a good guy. He'd been searching for Mindy since her father disappeared and he realized who she was the second she returned.
But his wife had suffered a nervous breakdown in the years without her daughter and so Hit-Girl remained their secret. Something Marcus was more than happy about.
Because all parents want is their kid to be normal. They say they want you to stand out from the crowd, but learning to blend in is a way more useful survival skill.
If I'd been normal, someone I love would never have been brain-damaged...
5H
My secret identity would never have been exposed or our house blown up when I was out.

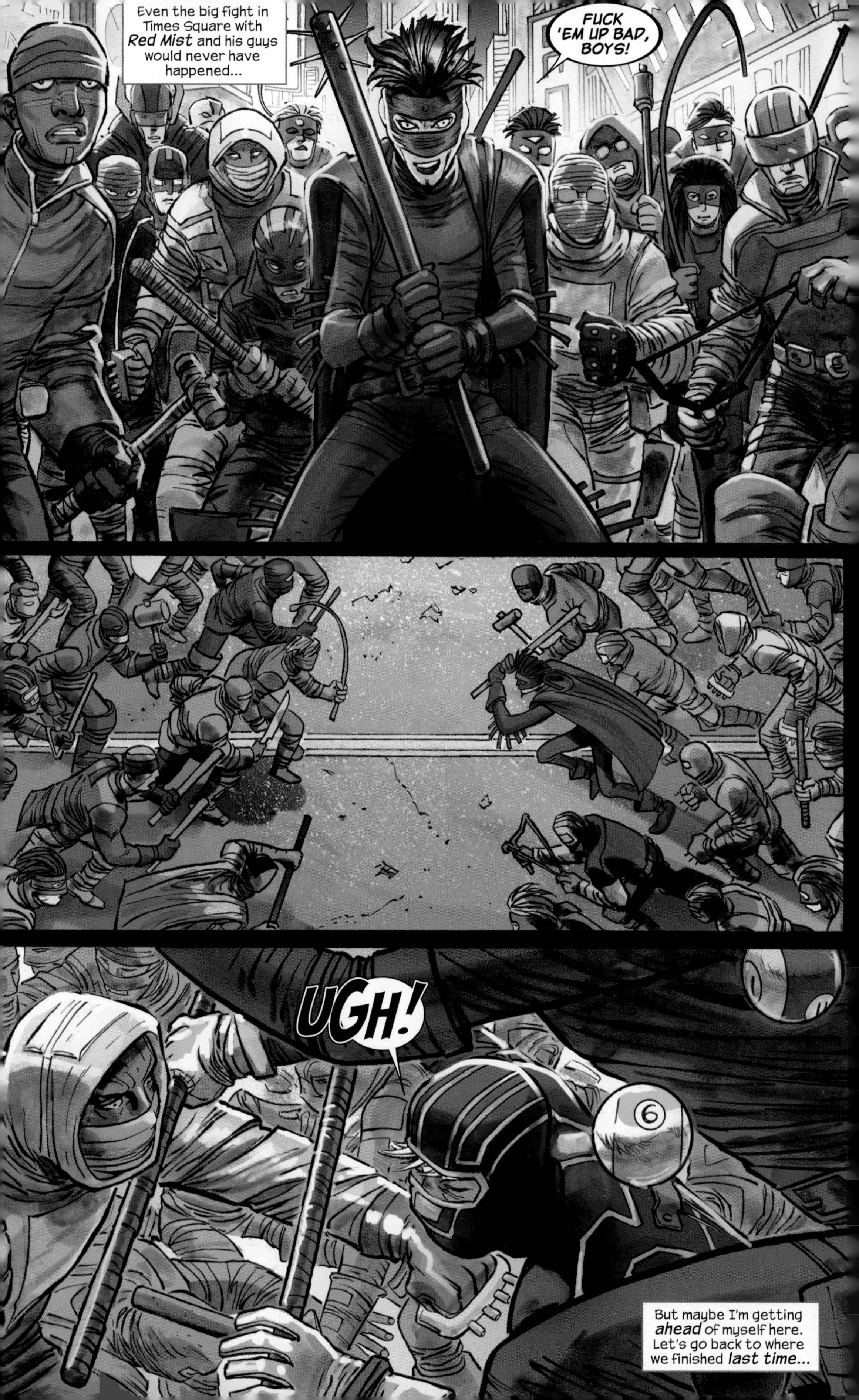
Even the big fight in Times Square with Red Mist and his guys would never have happened...
FUCK 'EM UP BAD, BOYS!
UGH!
But maybe I'm getting ahead of myself here. Let's go back to where we finished last time...

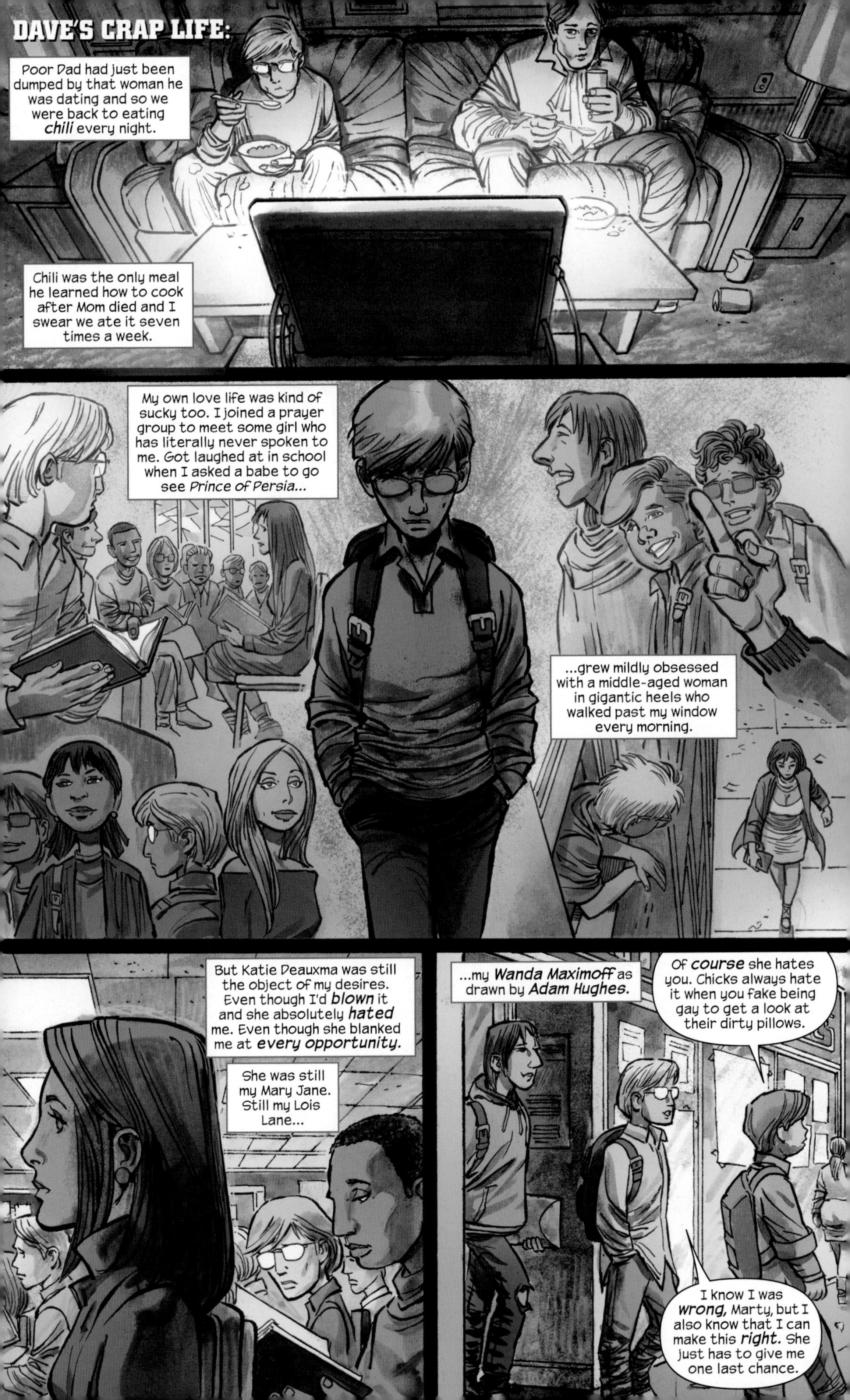
DAVE'S CRAP LIFE:
Poor Dad had just been dumped by that woman he was dating and so we were back to eating chili every night.
Chili was the only meal he learned how to cook after Mom died and I swear we ate it seven times a week.
My own love life was kind of sucky too. I joined a prayer group to meet some girl who has literally never spoken to me. Got laughed at in school when I asked a babe to go see Prince of Persia...
...grew mildly obsessed with a middle-aged woman in gigantic heels who walked past my window every morning.
But Katie Deauxma was still the object of my desires. Even though I'd blown it and she absolutely hated me. Even though she blanked me at every opportunity.
She was still my Mary Jane. Still my Lois Lane...
...my Wanda Maximoff as drawn by Adam Hughes.
Of course she hates you. Chicks always hate it when you fake being gay to get a look at their dirty pillows.
I know I was wrong, Marty, but I also know that I can make this right. She just has to give me one last chance.

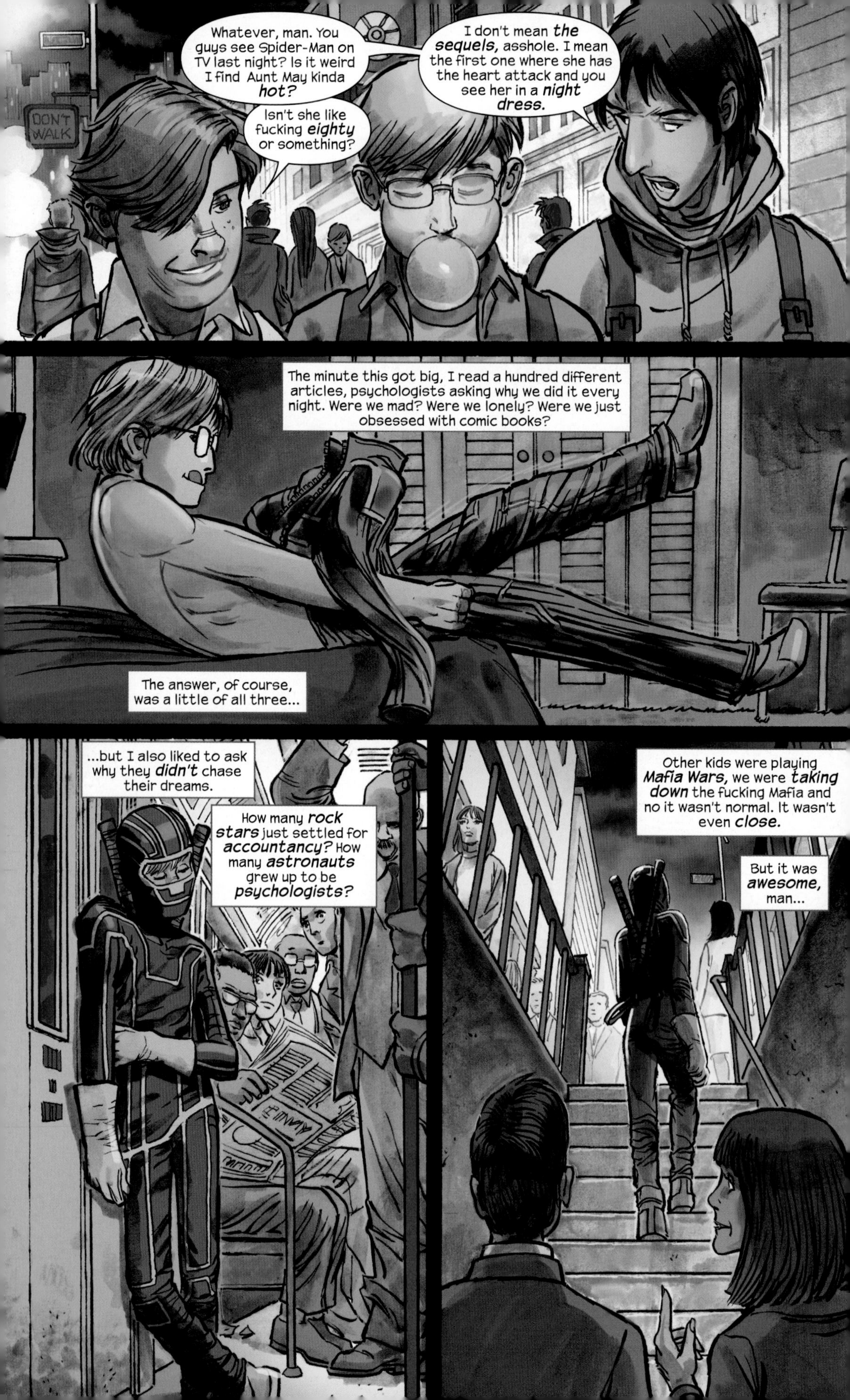

DON'T WALK
Whatever, man. You guys see Spider-Man on TV last night? Is it weird I find Aunt May kinda hot?
Isn't she like fucking eighty or something?
I don't mean the sequels, asshole. I mean the first one where she has the heart attack and you see her in a night dress.
The minute this got big, I read a hundred different articles, psychologists asking why we did it every night. Were we mad? Were we lonely? Were we just obsessed with comic books?
The answer, of course, was a little of all three...
...but I also liked to ask why they didn't chase their dreams.
How many rock stars just settled for accountancy? How many astronauts grew up to be psychologists?
Other kids were playing Mafia Wars, we were taking down the fucking Mafia and no it wasn't normal. It wasn't even close.
But it was awesome, man...

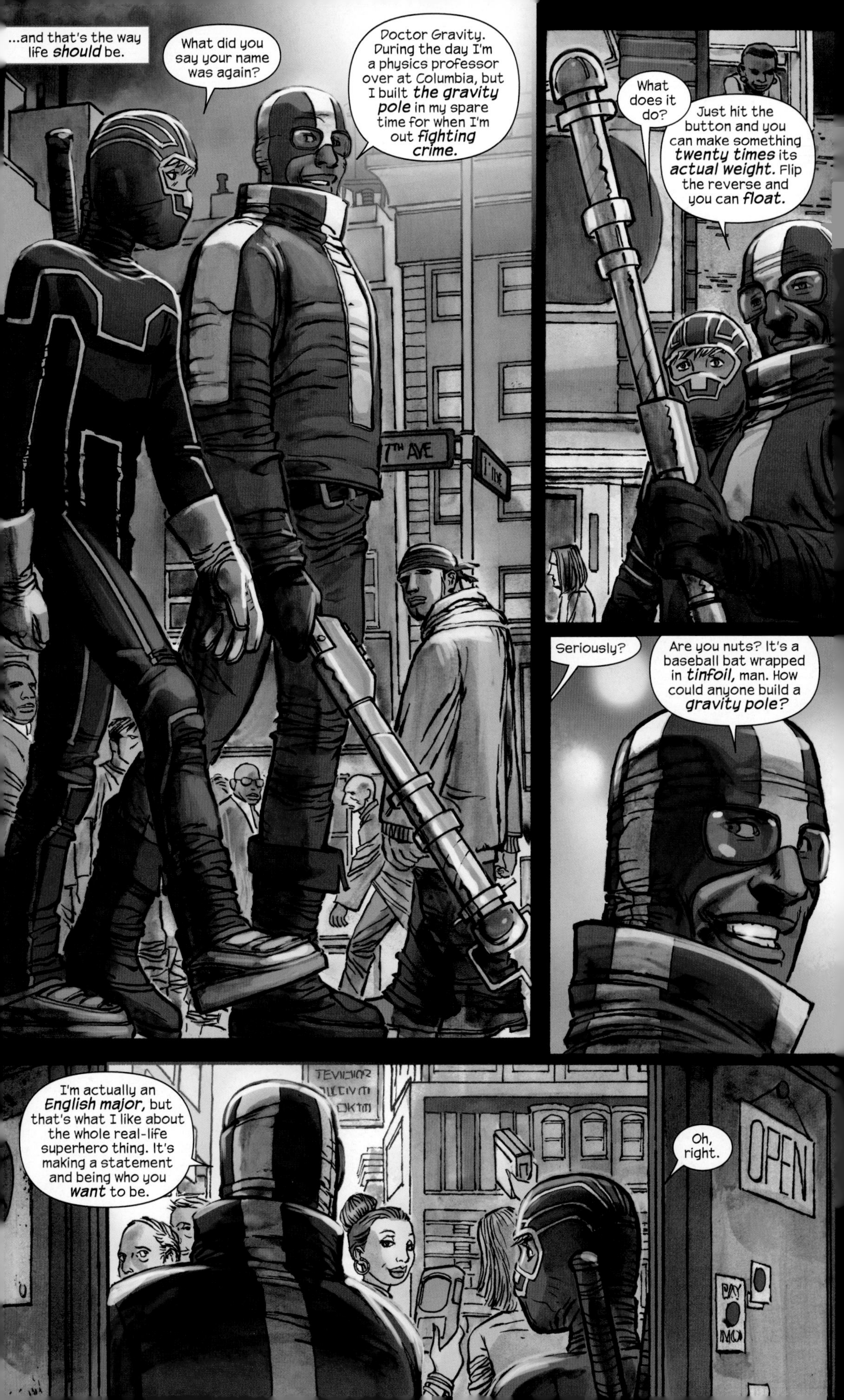
...and that's the way life *should* be.
What did you say your name was again?
Doctor Gravity. During the day I'm a physics professor over at Columbia, but I built *the gravity pole* in my spare time for when I'm out *fighting crime.*
7TH AVE
What does it do?
Just hit the button and you can make something *twenty times* its *actual weight.* Flip the reverse and you can *float.*
Seriously?
Are you nuts? It's a baseball bat wrapped in *tinfoil,* man. How could anyone build a *gravity pole?*
I'm actually an *English major,* but that's what I like about the whole real-life superhero thing. It's making a statement and being who you *want* to be.
Oh, right.
OPEN

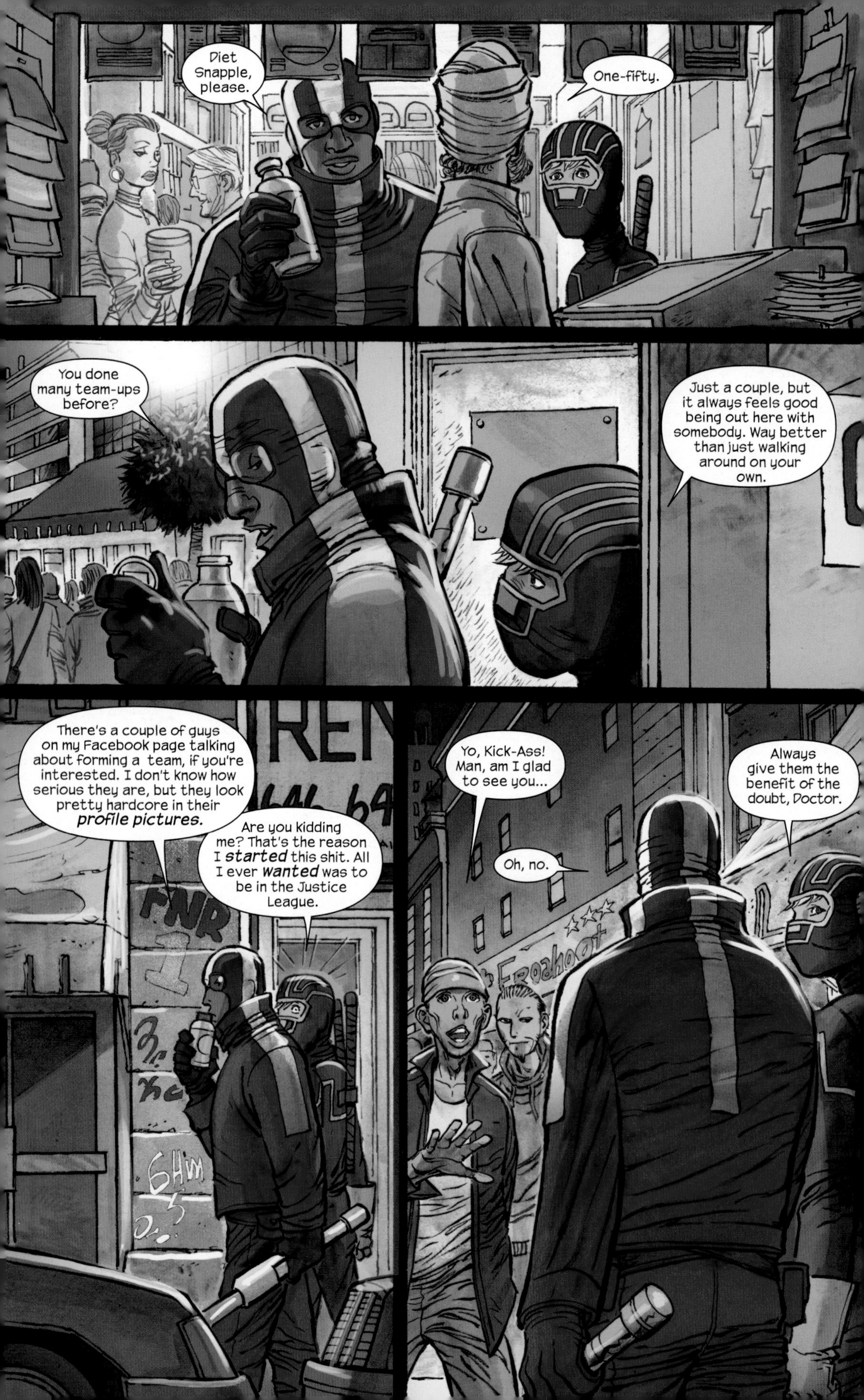
Diet Snapple, please.
One-fifty.
You done many team-ups before?
Just a couple, but it always feels good being out here with somebody. Way better than just walking around on your own.
There's a couple of guys on my Facebook page talking about forming a team, if you're interested. I don't know how serious they are, but they look pretty hardcore in their *profile pictures.*
Are you kidding me? That's the reason I *started* this shit. All I ever *wanted* was to be in the Justice League.
Yo, Kick-Ass! Man, am I glad to see you...
Oh, no.
Always give them the benefit of the doubt, Doctor.

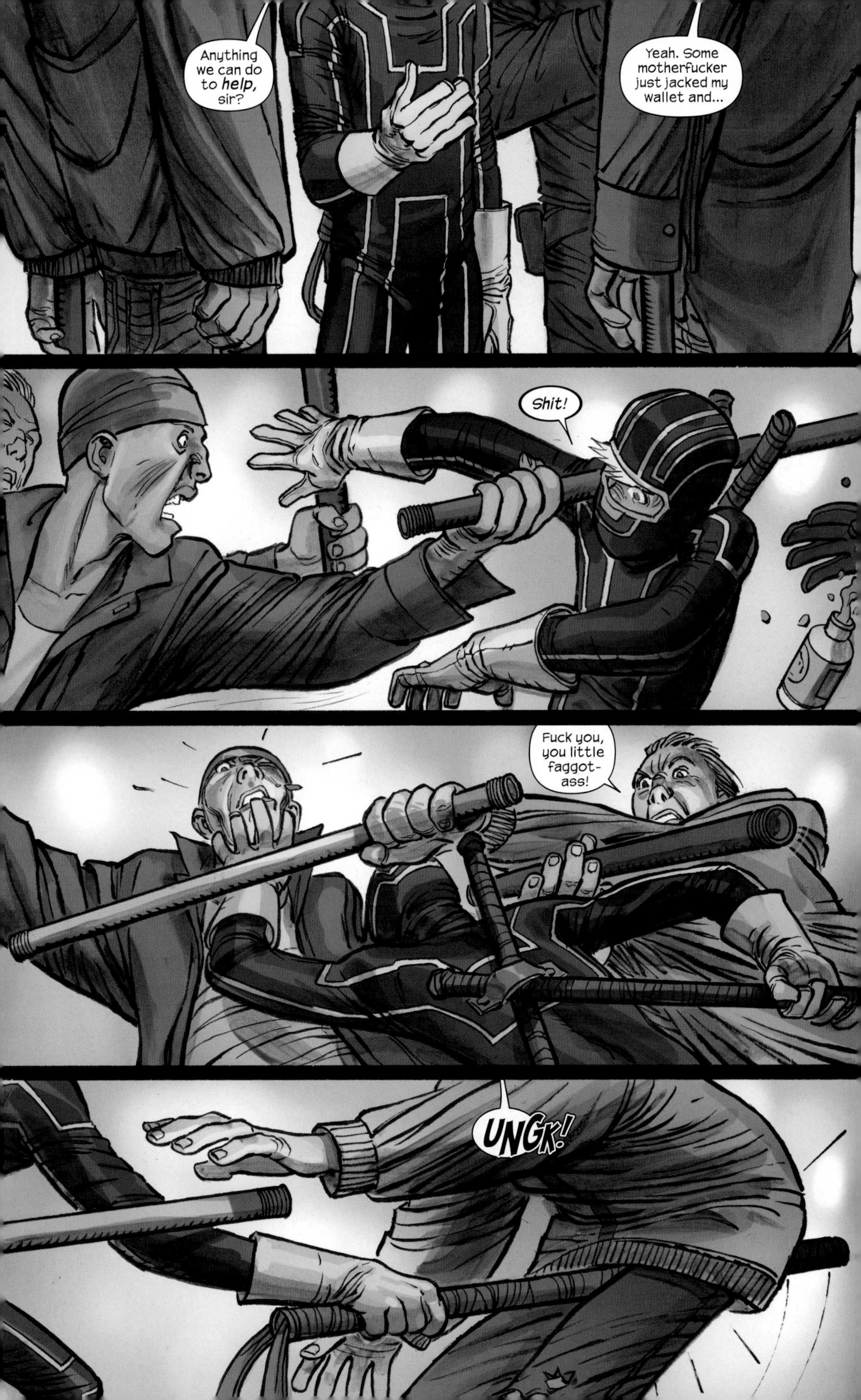
Anything we can do to *help,* sir?
Yeah. Some motherfucker just jacked my wallet and...
Shit!
Fuck you, you little faggot-ass!
UNGK!

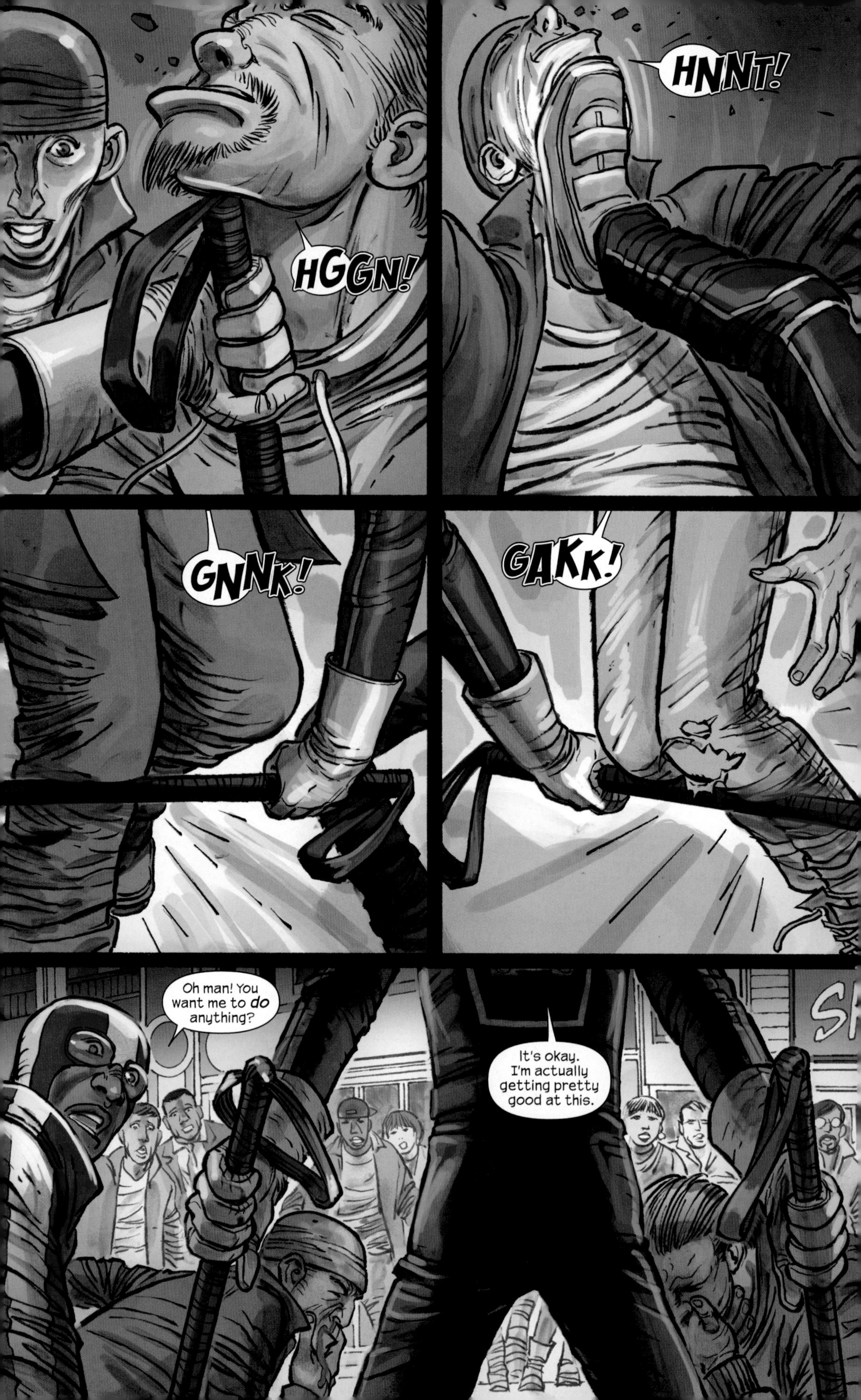
HGGN!
HNNT!
GNNK!
GAKK!
Oh man! You want me to do anything?
It's okay. I'm actually getting pretty good at this.

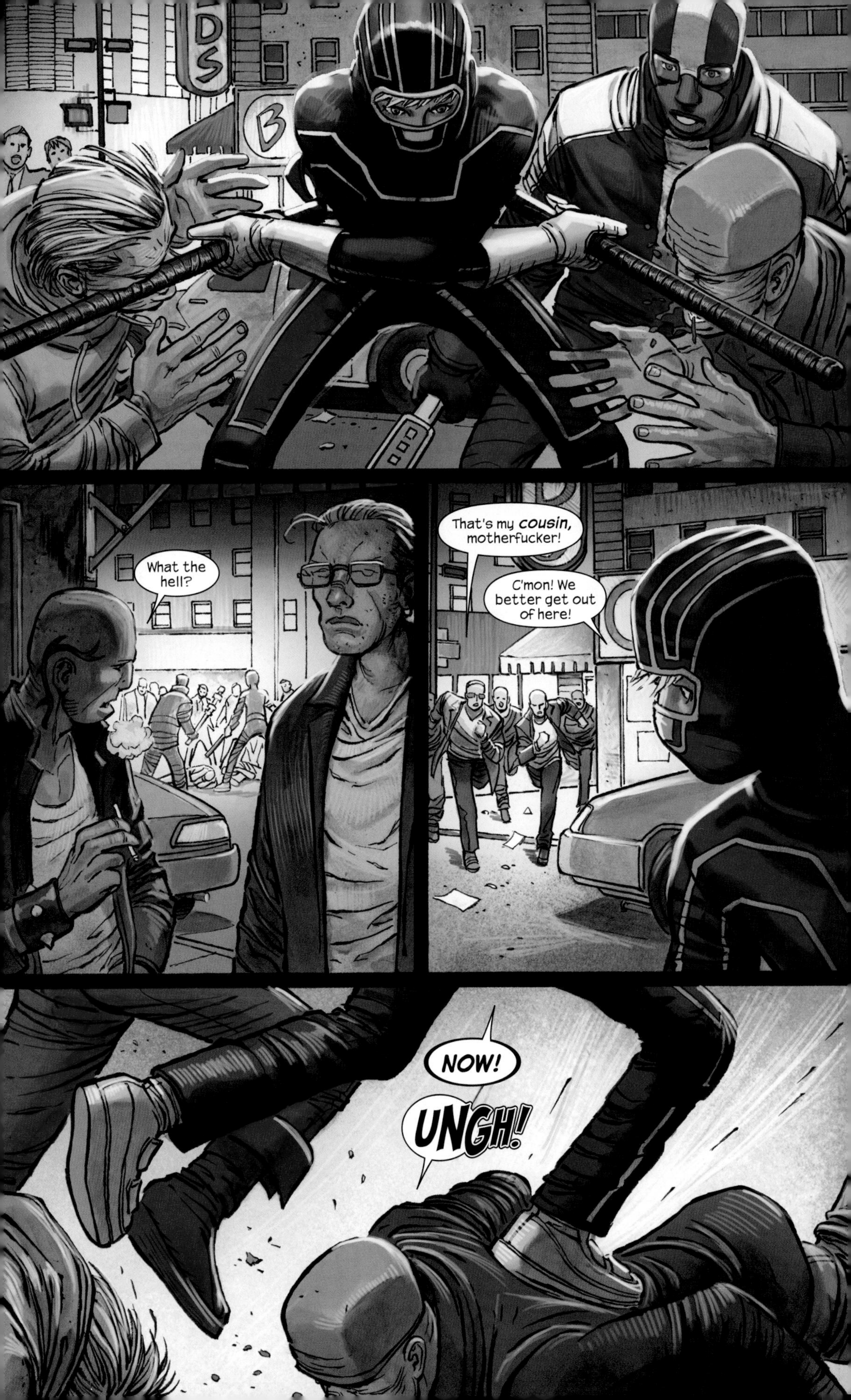
What the hell?
That's my cousin, motherfucker!
C'mon! We better get out of here!
NOW!
UNGH!

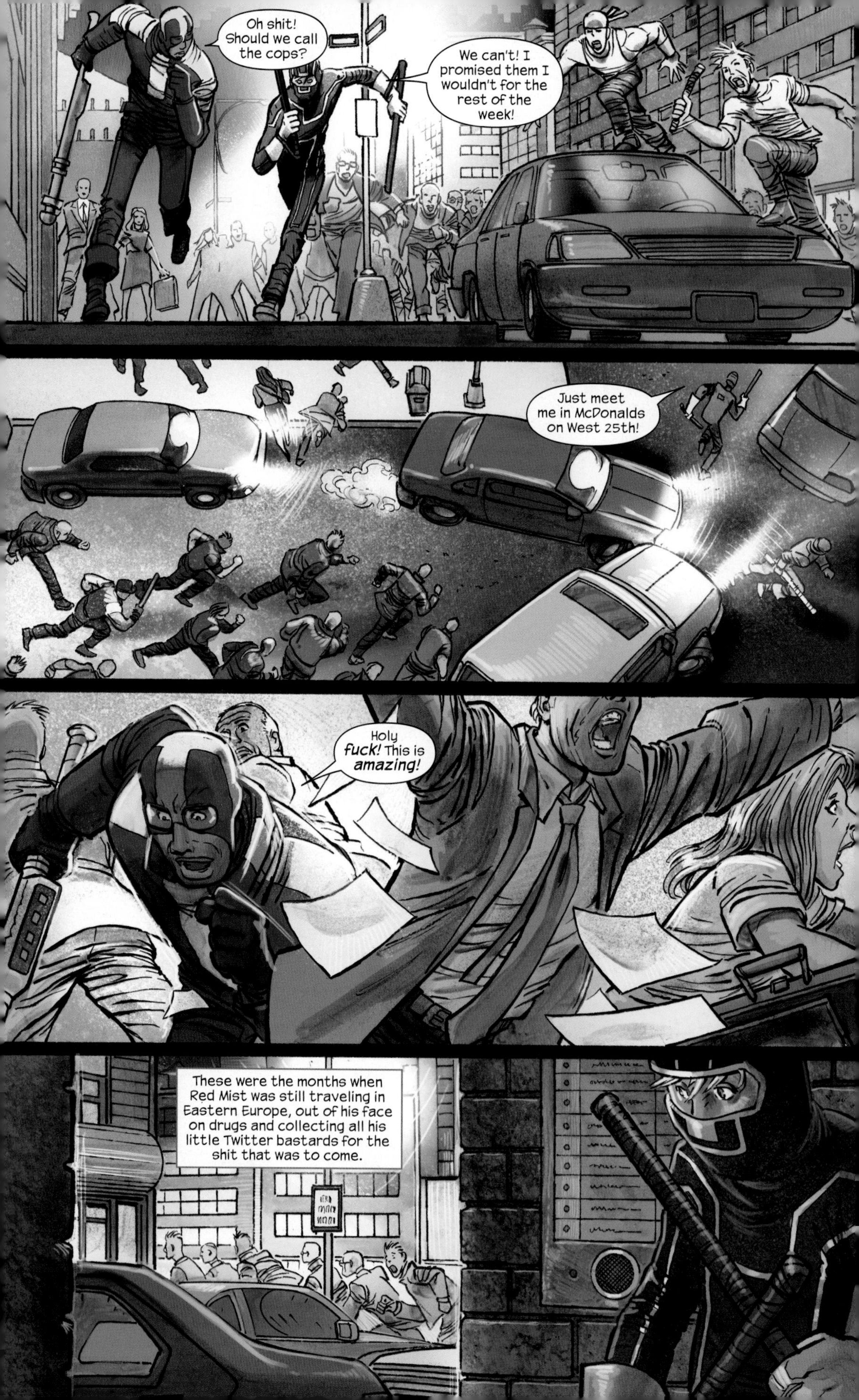
Oh shit! Should we call the cops?
We can't! I promised them I wouldn't for the rest of the week!
Just meet me in McDonalds on West 25th!
Holy fuck! This is amazing!
These were the months when Red Mist was still traveling in Eastern Europe, out of his face on drugs and collecting all his little Twitter bastards for the shit that was to come.

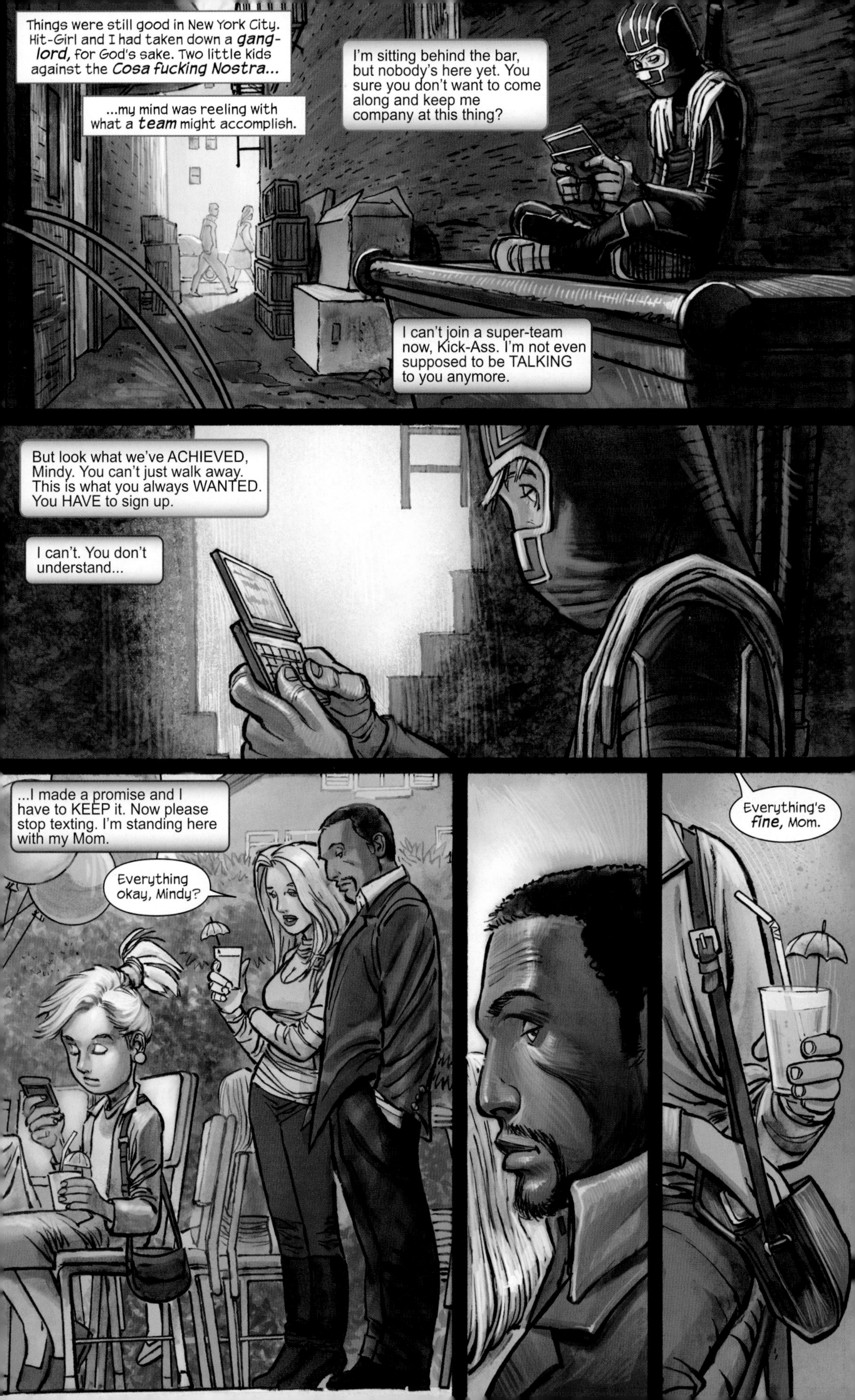

Things were still good in New York City. Hit-Girl and I had taken down a gang-lord, for God's sake. Two little kids against the Cosa fucking Nostra...
...my mind was reeling with what a team might accomplish.
I'm sitting behind the bar, but nobody's here yet. You sure you don't want to come along and keep me company at this thing?
I can't join a super-team now, Kick-Ass. I'm not even supposed to be TALKING to you anymore.
But look what we've ACHIEVED, Mindy. You can't just walk away. This is what you always WANTED. You HAVE to sign up.
I can't. You don't understand...
...I made a promise and I have to KEEP it. Now please stop texting. I'm standing here with my Mom.
Everything okay, Mindy?
Everything's fine, Mom.

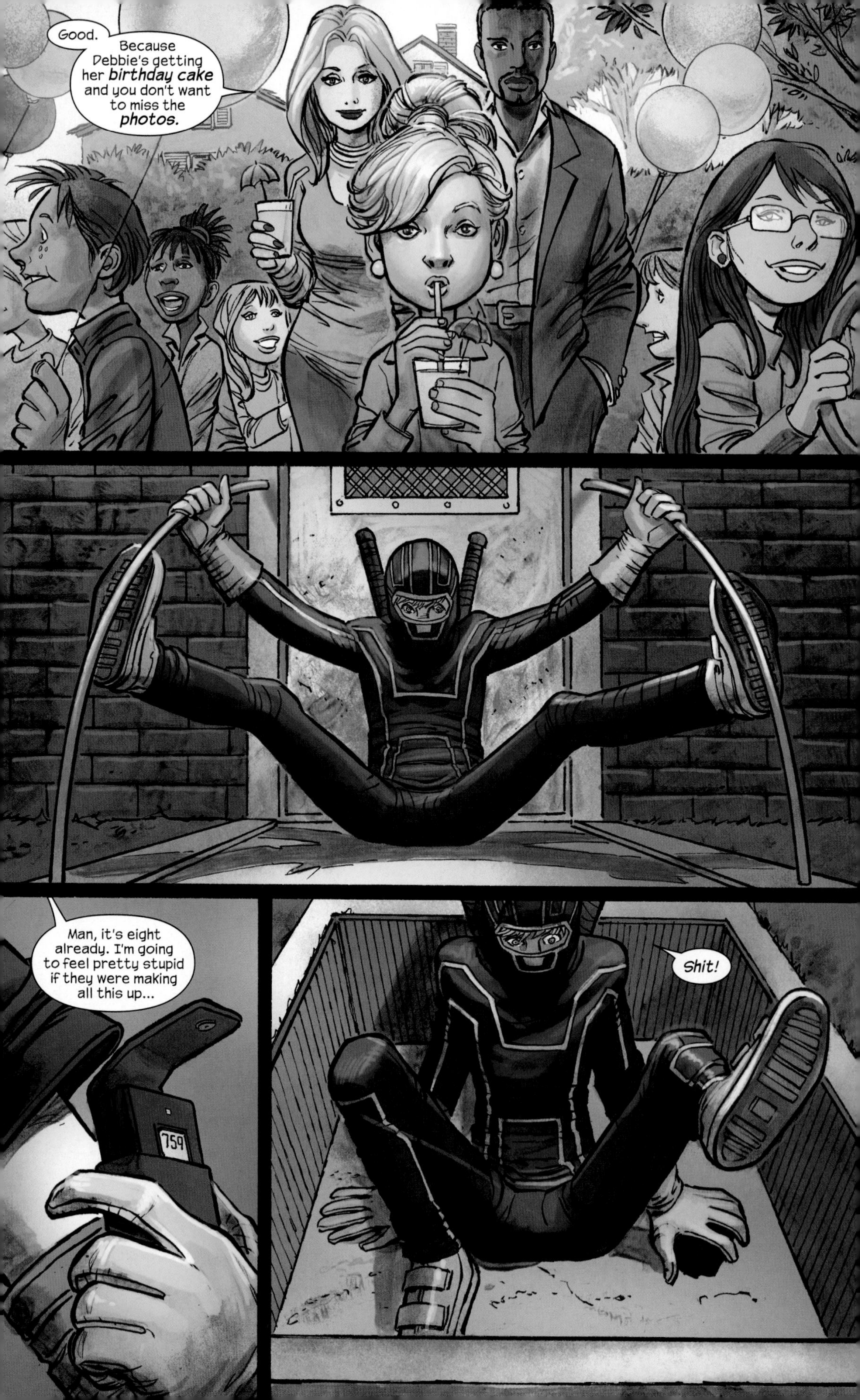
Good.
Because Debbie's getting her *birthday cake* and you don't want to miss the *photos.*
Man, it's eight already. I'm going to feel pretty stupid if they were making all this up...
759
Shit!

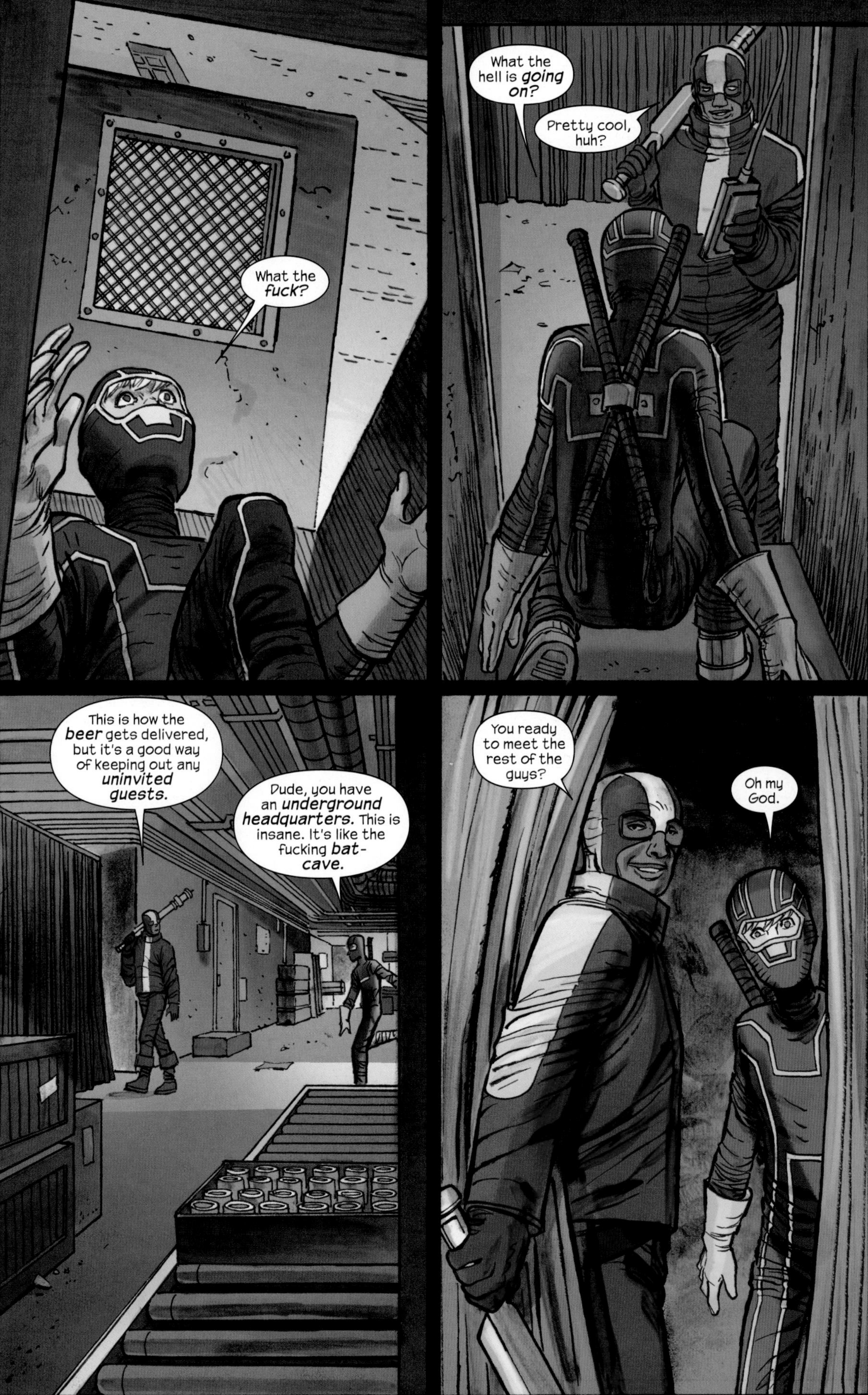
What the fuck?
What the hell is going on?
Pretty cool, huh?
This is how the beer gets delivered, but it's a good way of keeping out any uninvited guests.
Dude, you have an underground headquarters. This is insane. It's like the fucking bat-cave.
You ready to meet the rest of the guys?
Oh my God.

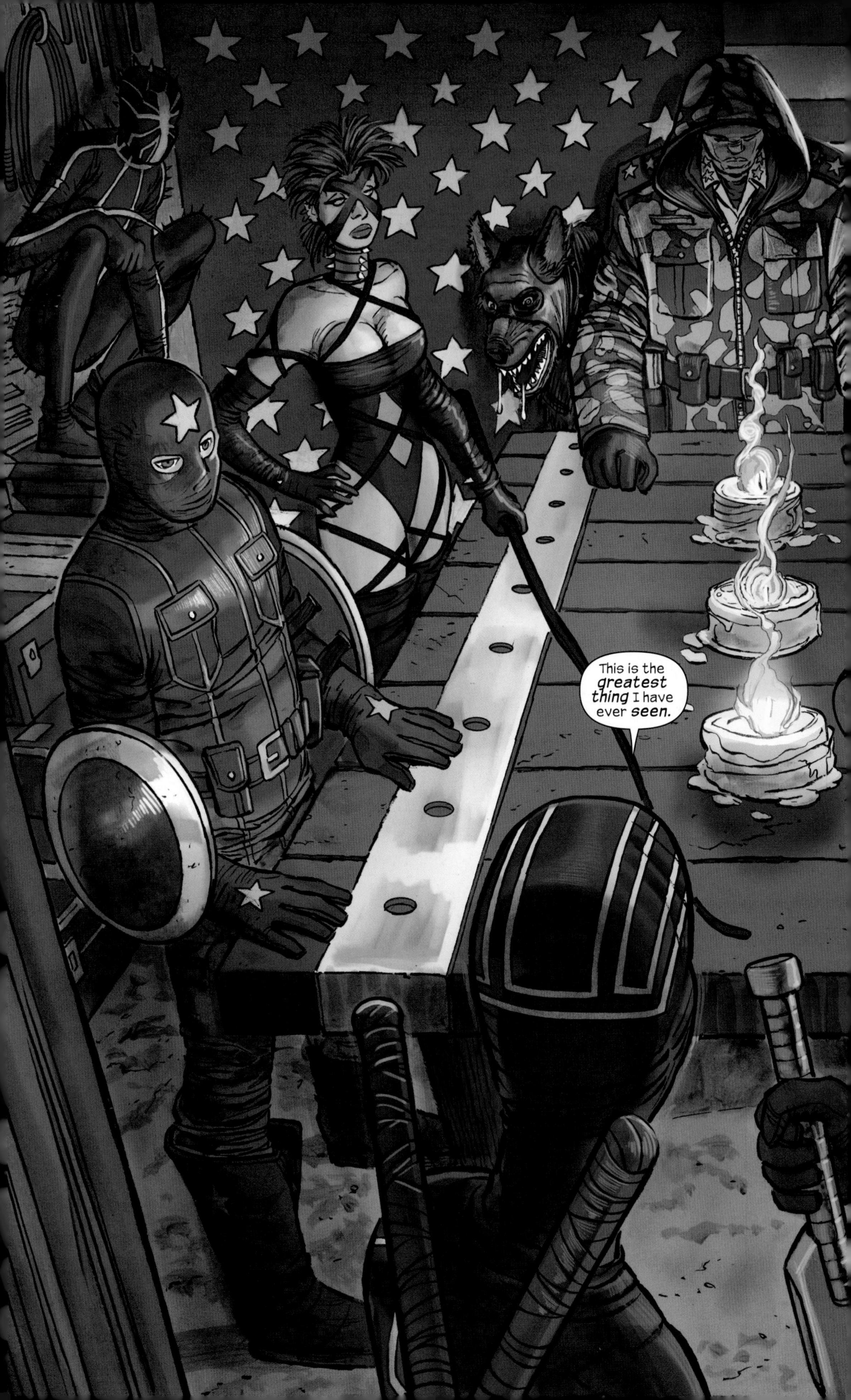
This is the *greatest thing* I have ever *seen.*

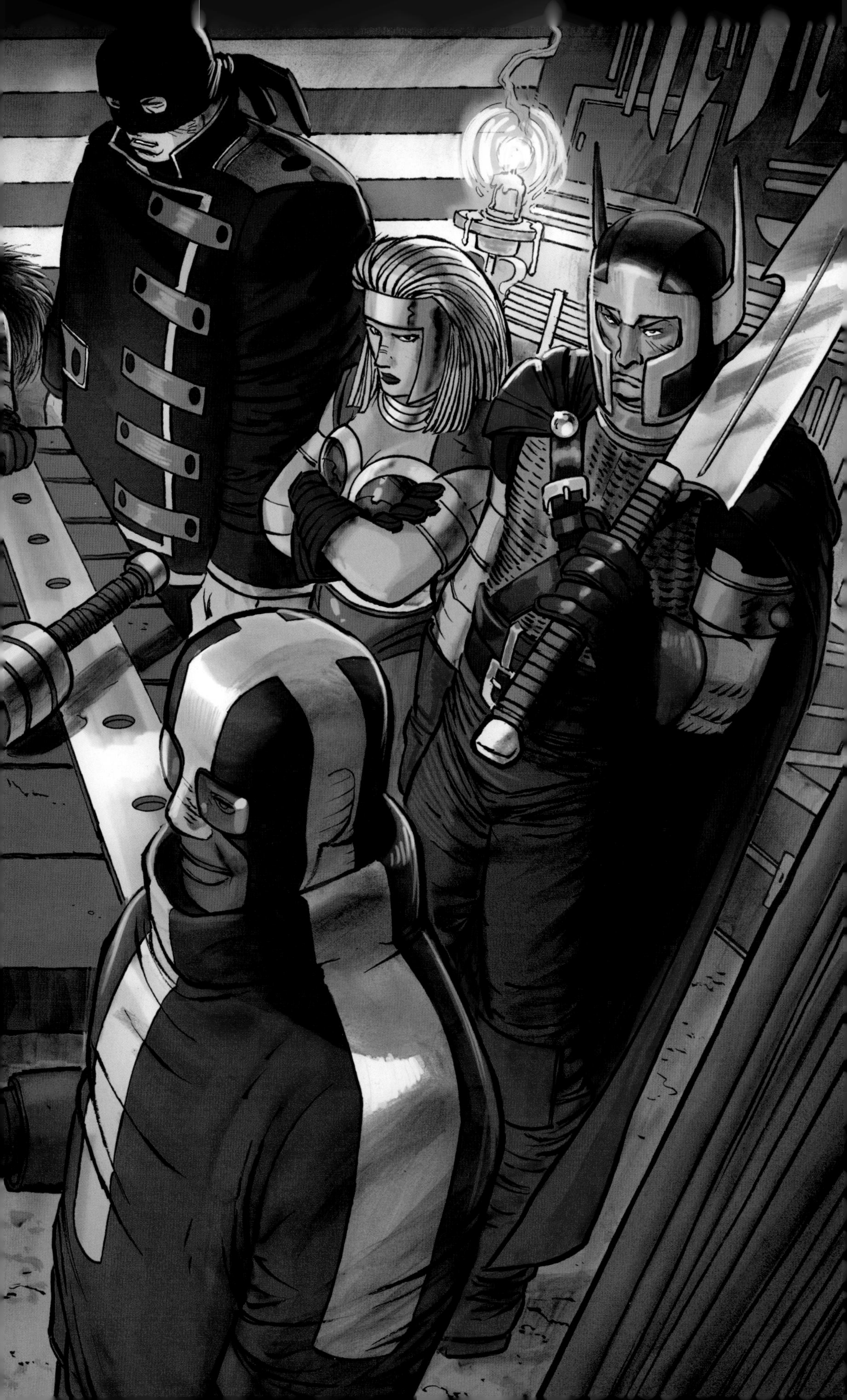

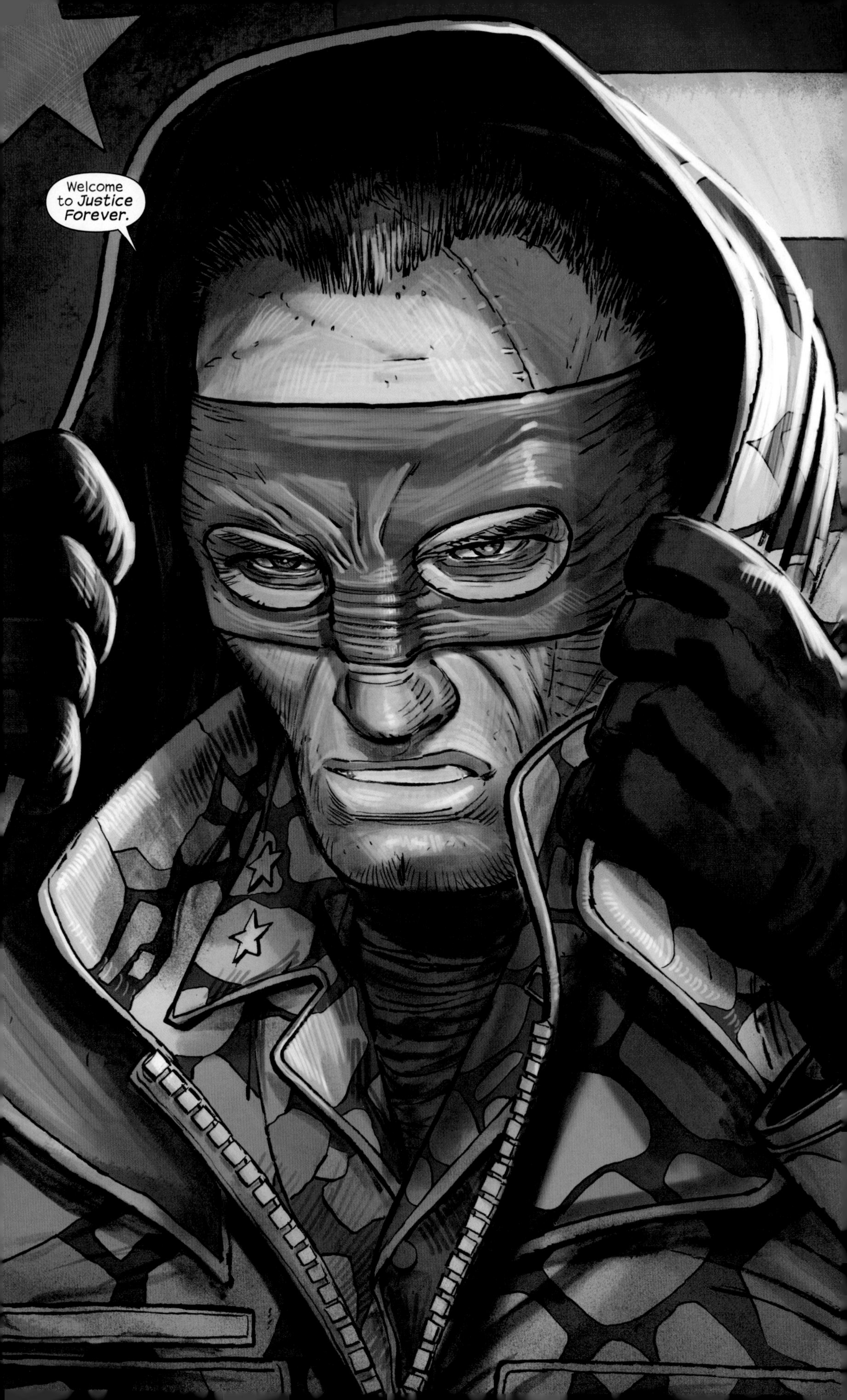
Welcome to *Justice Forever.*

TWO

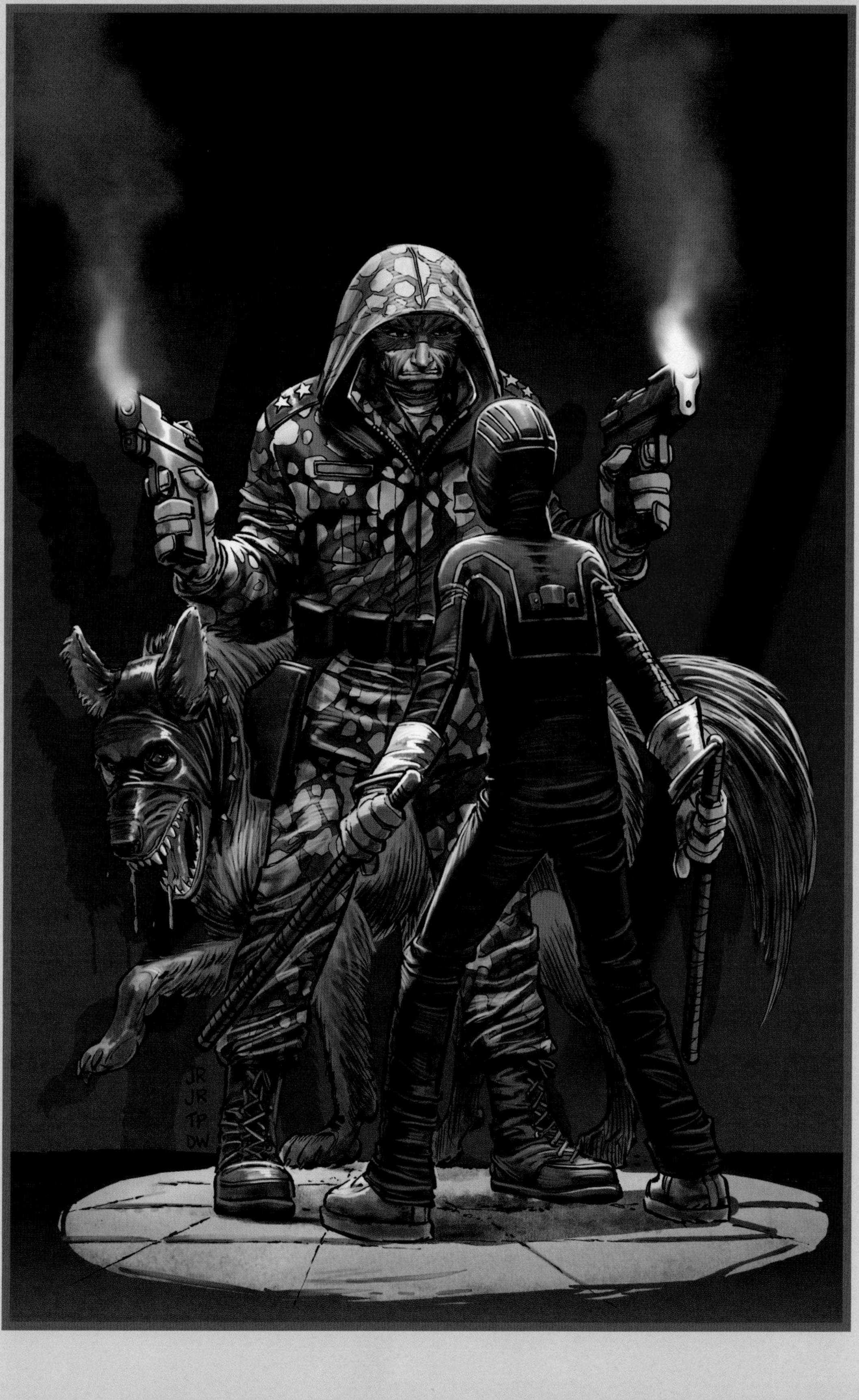
JR JR TP DW

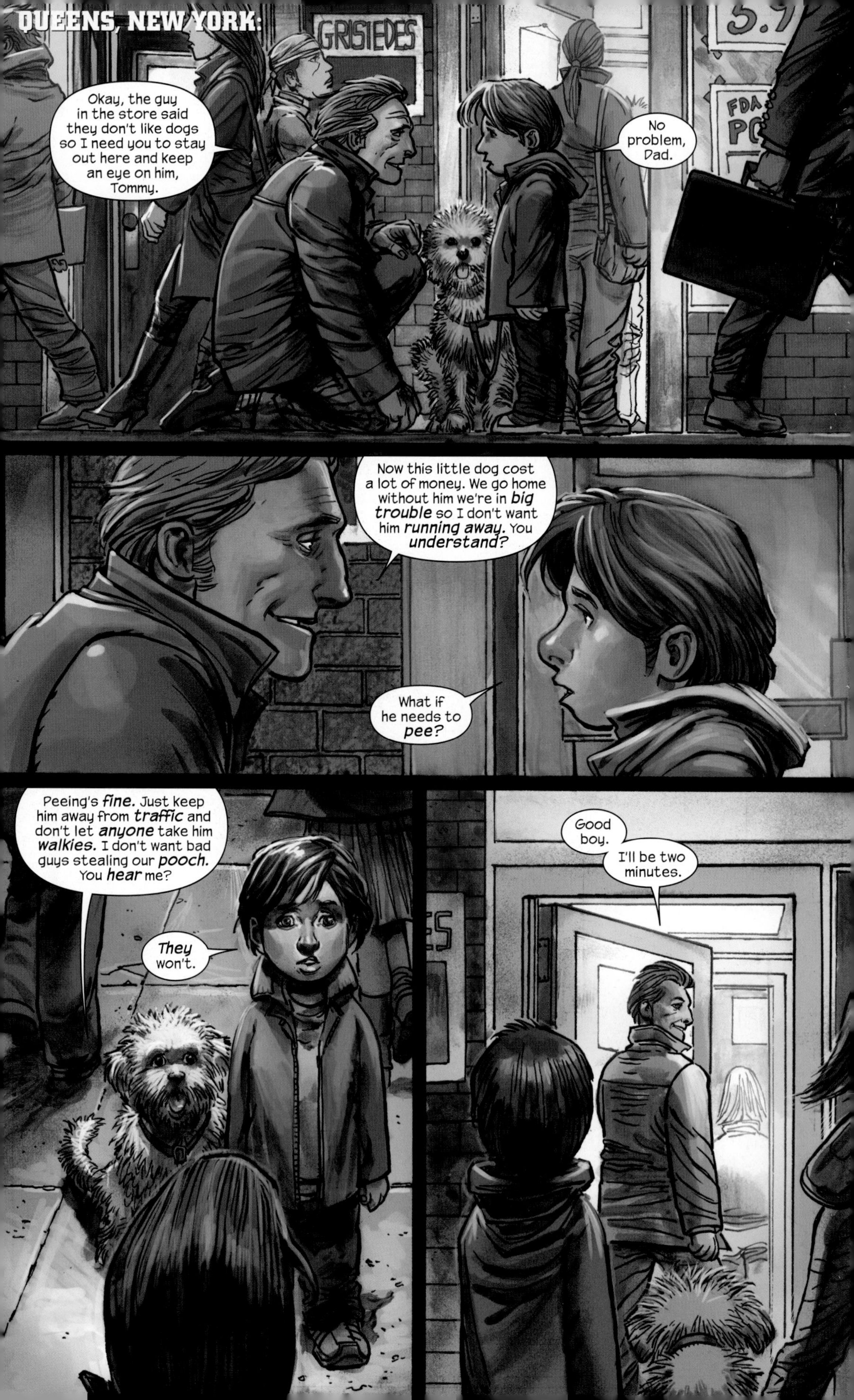
QUEENS, NEW YORK:
GRISTEDES
Okay, the guy in the store said they don't like dogs so I need you to stay out here and keep an eye on him, Tommy.
No problem, Dad.
Now this little dog cost a lot of money. We go home without him we're in big trouble so I don't want him running away. You understand?
What if he needs to pee?
Peeing's fine. Just keep him away from traffic and don't let anyone take him walkies. I don't want bad guys stealing our pooch. You hear me?
They won't.
Good boy.
I'll be two minutes.

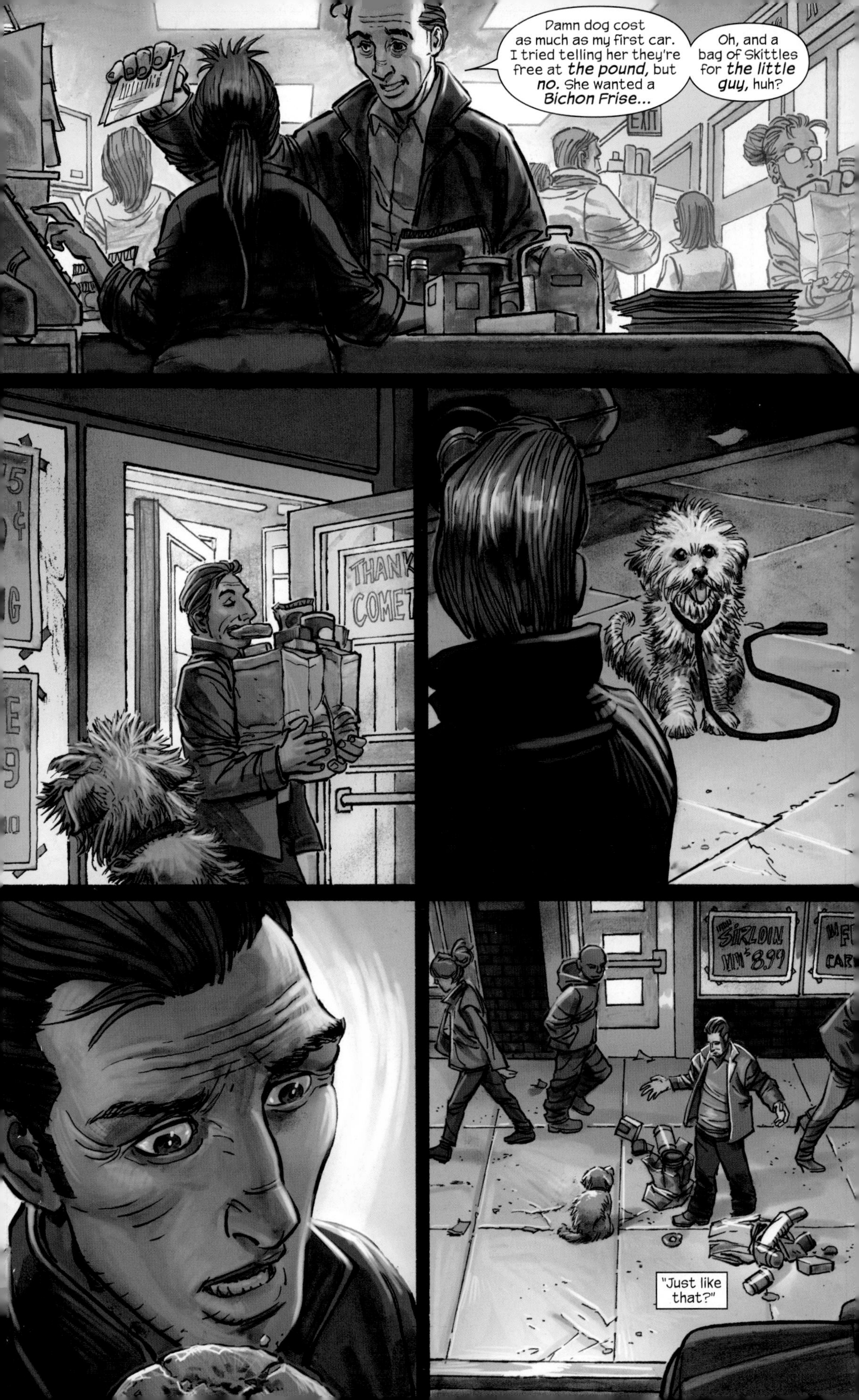
Damn dog cost as much as my first car. I tried telling her they're free at *the pound,* but *no.* She wanted a *Bichon Frise...*
Oh, and a bag of Skittles for *the little guy,* huh?
EXIT
THANK
COMET
SIRLOIN
8.99
"Just like that?"

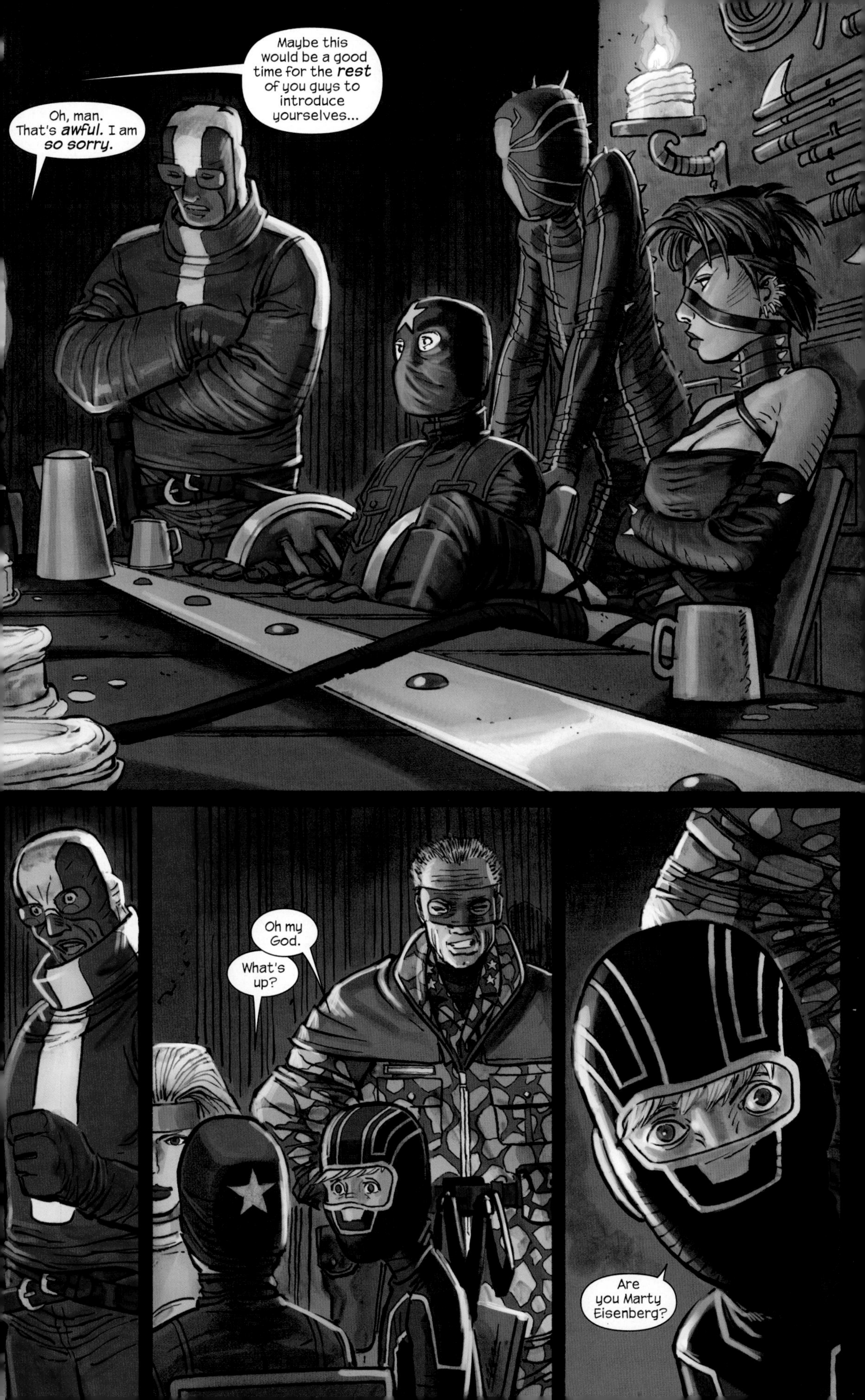
Oh, man. That's awful. I am so sorry.
Maybe this would be a good time for the rest of you guys to introduce yourselves...
Oh my God.
What's up?
Are you Marty Eisenberg?

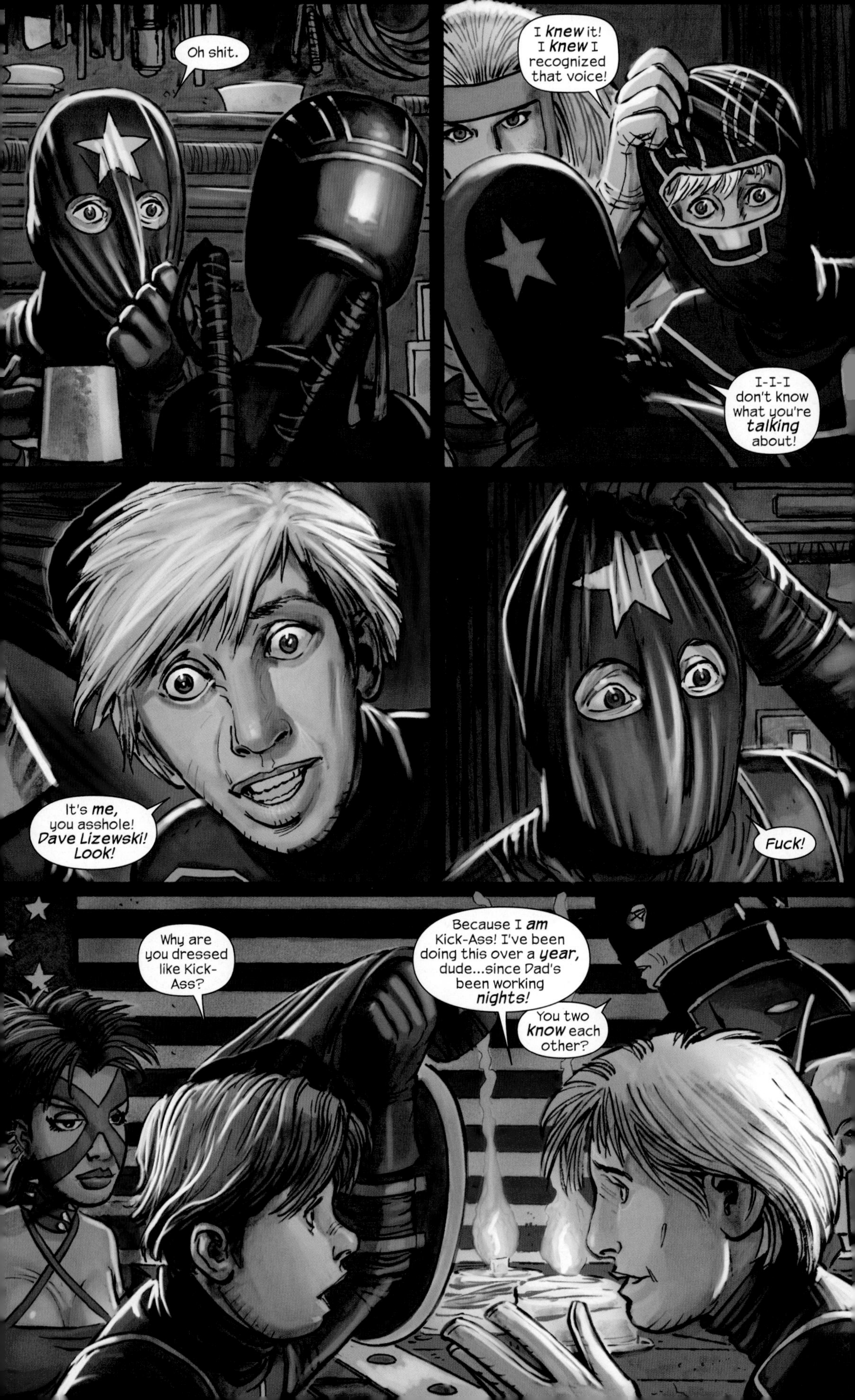
Oh shit.
I *knew* it! I *knew* I recognized that voice!
I-I-I don't know what you're *talking* about!
It's *me,* you asshole! *Dave Lizewski! Look!*
Fuck!
Why are you dressed like Kick-Ass?
Because I *am* Kick-Ass! I've been doing this over a *year,* dude...since Dad's been working *nights!*
You two *know* each other?

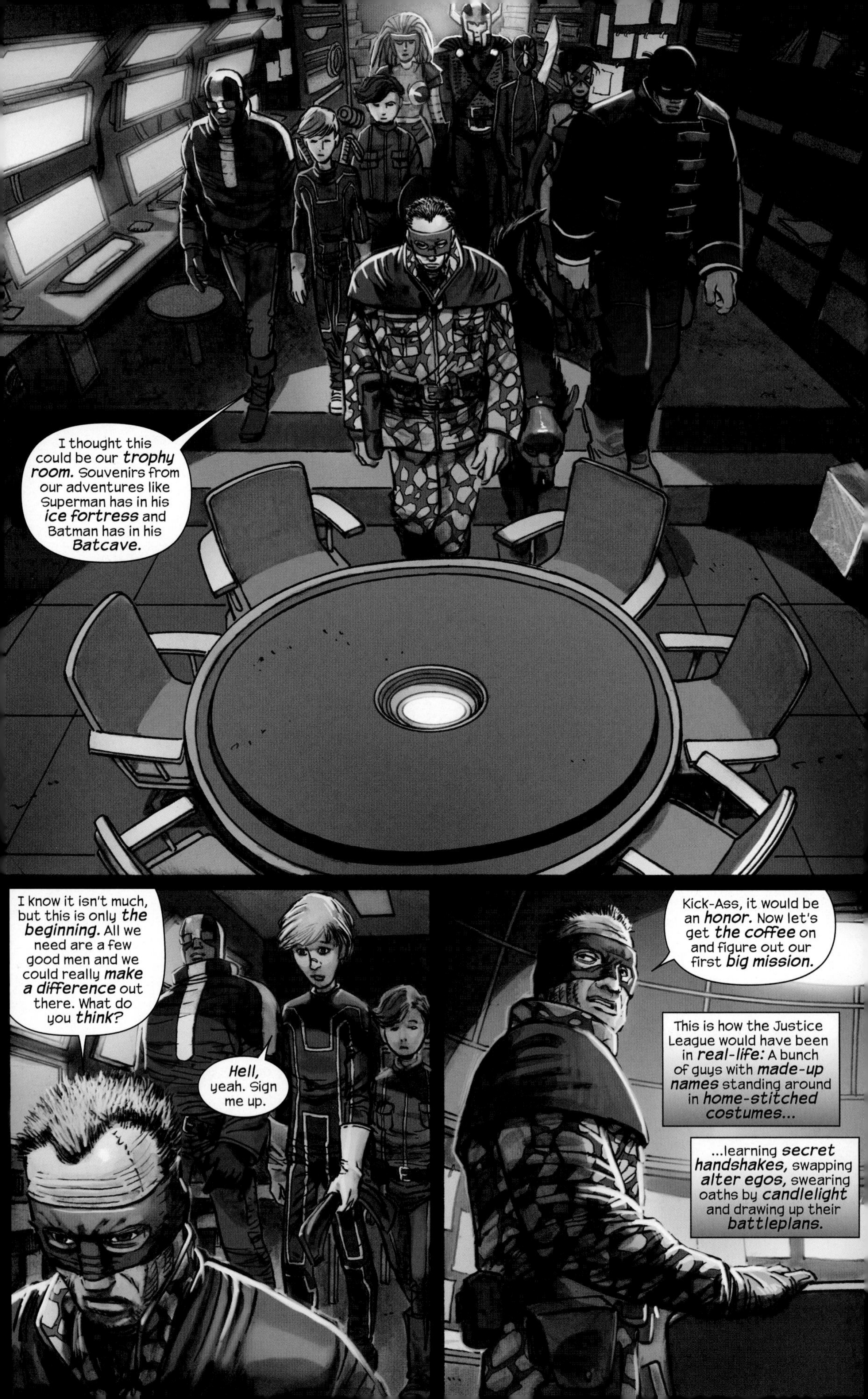
I thought this could be our *trophy room.* Souvenirs from our adventures like Superman has in his *ice fortress* and Batman has in his *Batcave.*
I know it isn't much, but this is only *the beginning.* All we need are a few good men and we could really *make a difference* out there. What do you *think?*
Hell, yeah. Sign me up.
Kick-Ass, it would be an *honor.* Now let's get *the coffee* on and figure out our first *big mission.*
This is how the Justice League would have been in *real-life:* A bunch of guys with *made-up names* standing around in *home-stitched costumes...*
...learning *secret handshakes,* swapping *alter egos,* swearing oaths by *candlelight* and drawing up their *battleplans.*

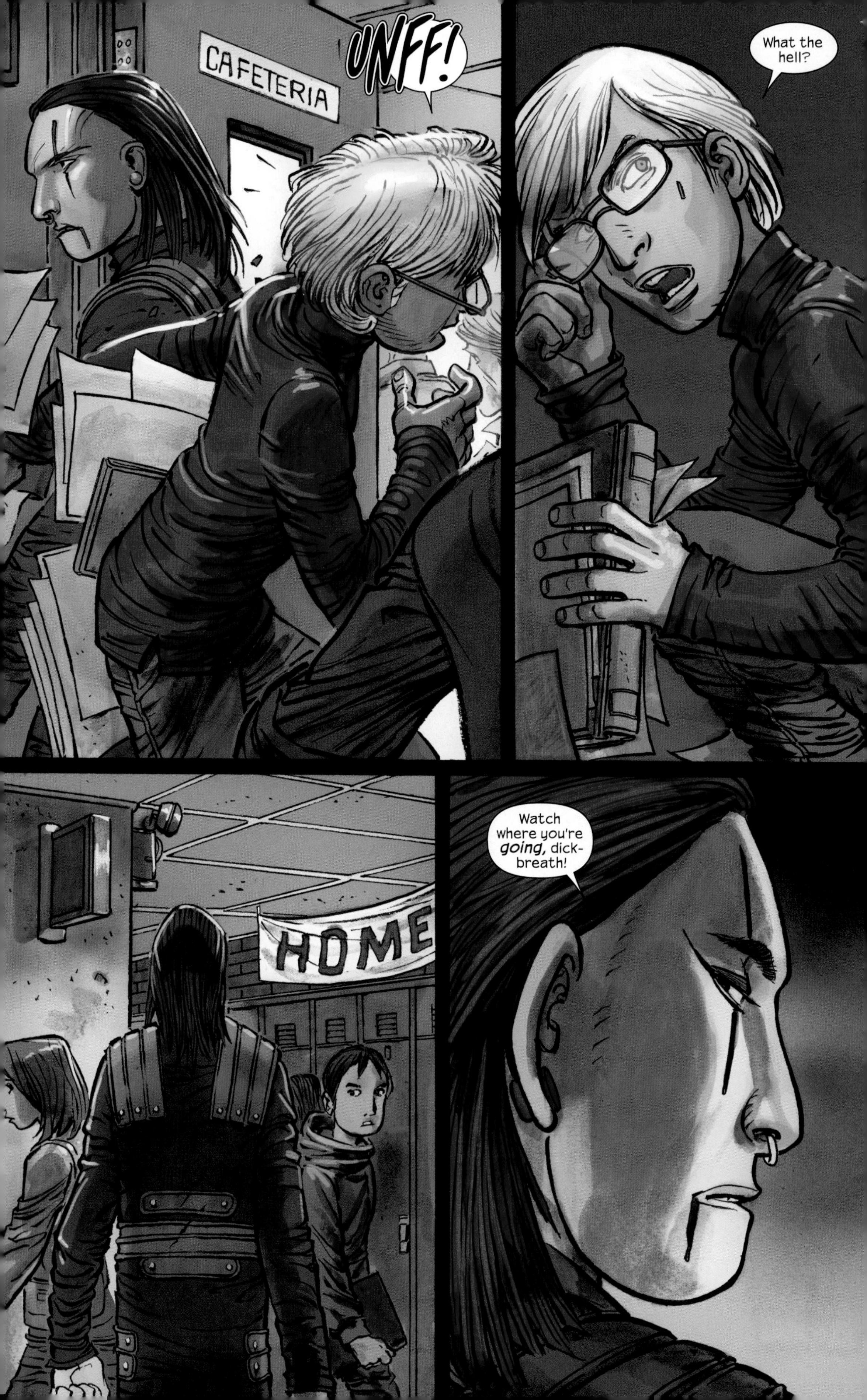
CAFETERIA
UNFF!
What the hell?
HOME
Watch where you're *going,* dick-breath!

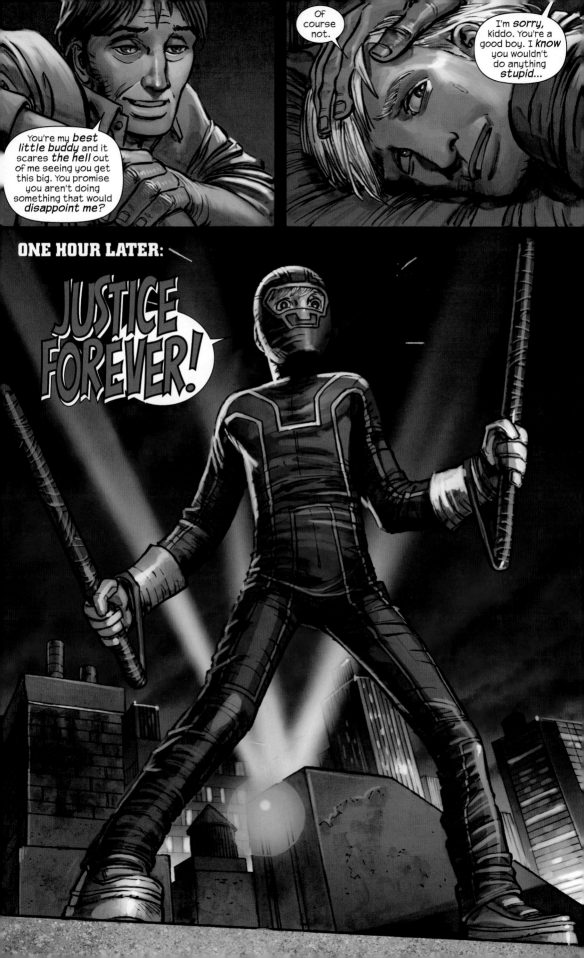

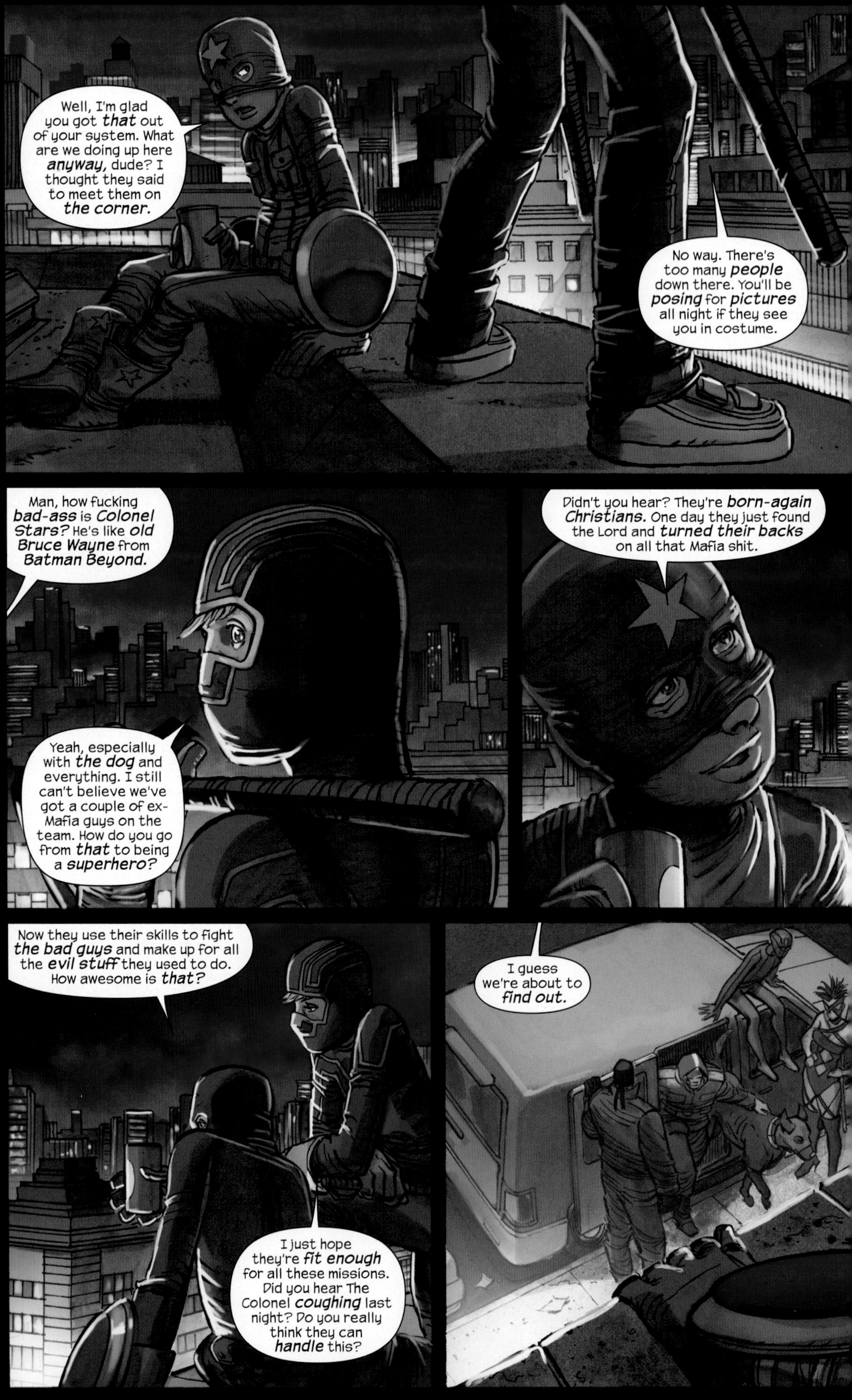
Well, I'm glad you got *that* out of your system. What are we doing up here *anyway,* dude? I thought they said to meet them on *the corner.*
No way. There's too many *people* down there. You'll be *posing* for *pictures* all night if they see you in costume.
Man, how fucking *bad-ass* is *Colonel Stars?* He's like *old Bruce Wayne* from *Batman Beyond.*
Yeah, especially with *the dog* and everything. I still can't believe we've got a couple of ex-Mafia guys on the team. How do you go from *that* to being a *superhero?*
Didn't you hear? They're *born-again Christians.* One day they just found the Lord and *turned their backs* on all that Mafia shit.
Now they use their skills to fight *the bad guys* and make up for all the *evil stuff* they used to do. How awesome is *that?*
I just hope they're *fit enough* for all these missions. Did you hear The Colonel *coughing* last night? Do you really think they can *handle* this?
I guess we're about to *find out.*

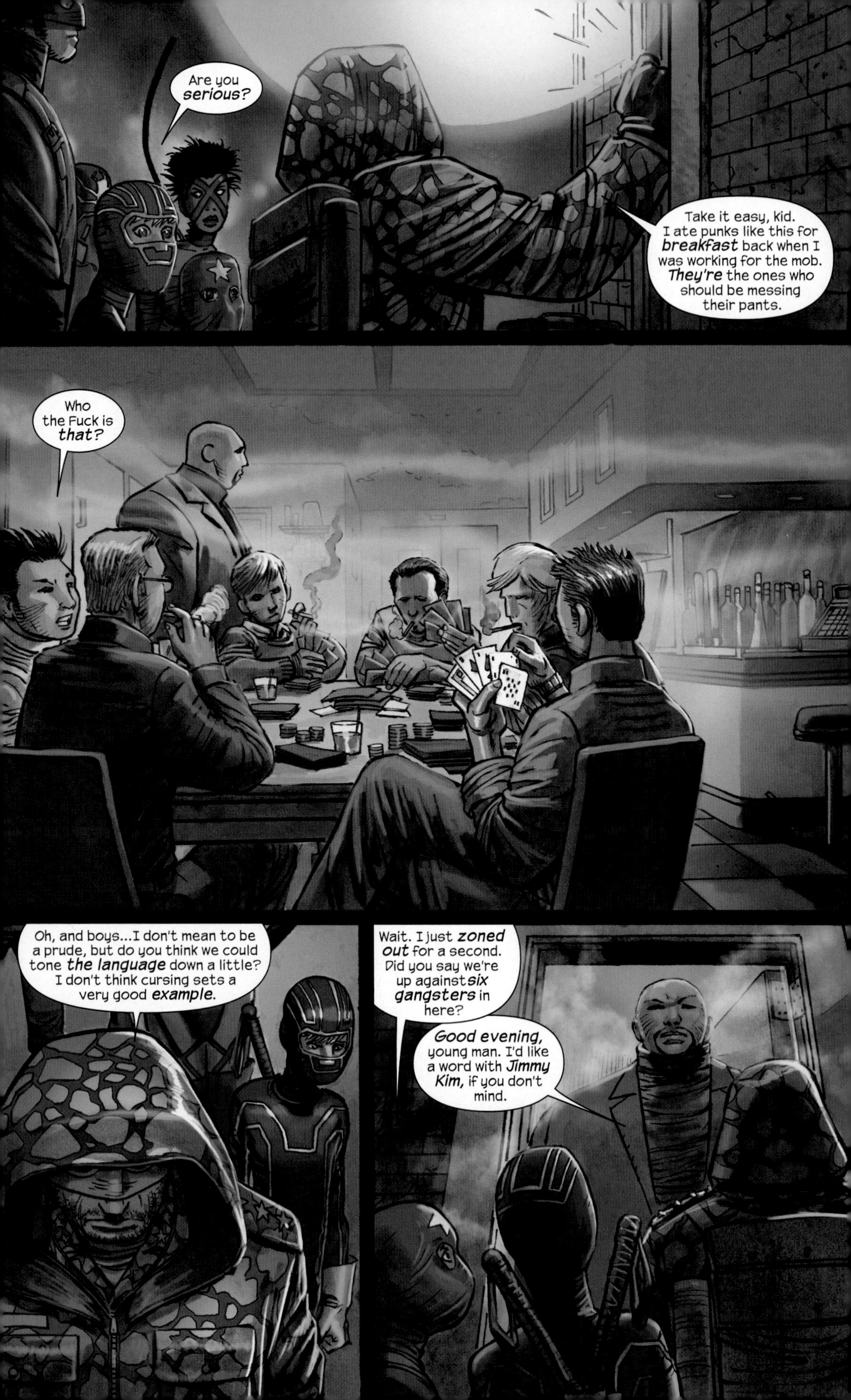

Are you serious?
Take it easy, kid. I ate punks like this for breakfast back when I was working for the mob. They're the ones who should be messing their pants.
Who the Fuck is that?
Oh, and boys...I don't mean to be a prude, but do you think we could tone the language down a little? I don't think cursing sets a very good example.
Wait. I just zoned out for a second. Did you say we're up against six gangsters in here?
Good evening, young man. I'd like a word with Jimmy Kim, if you don't mind.

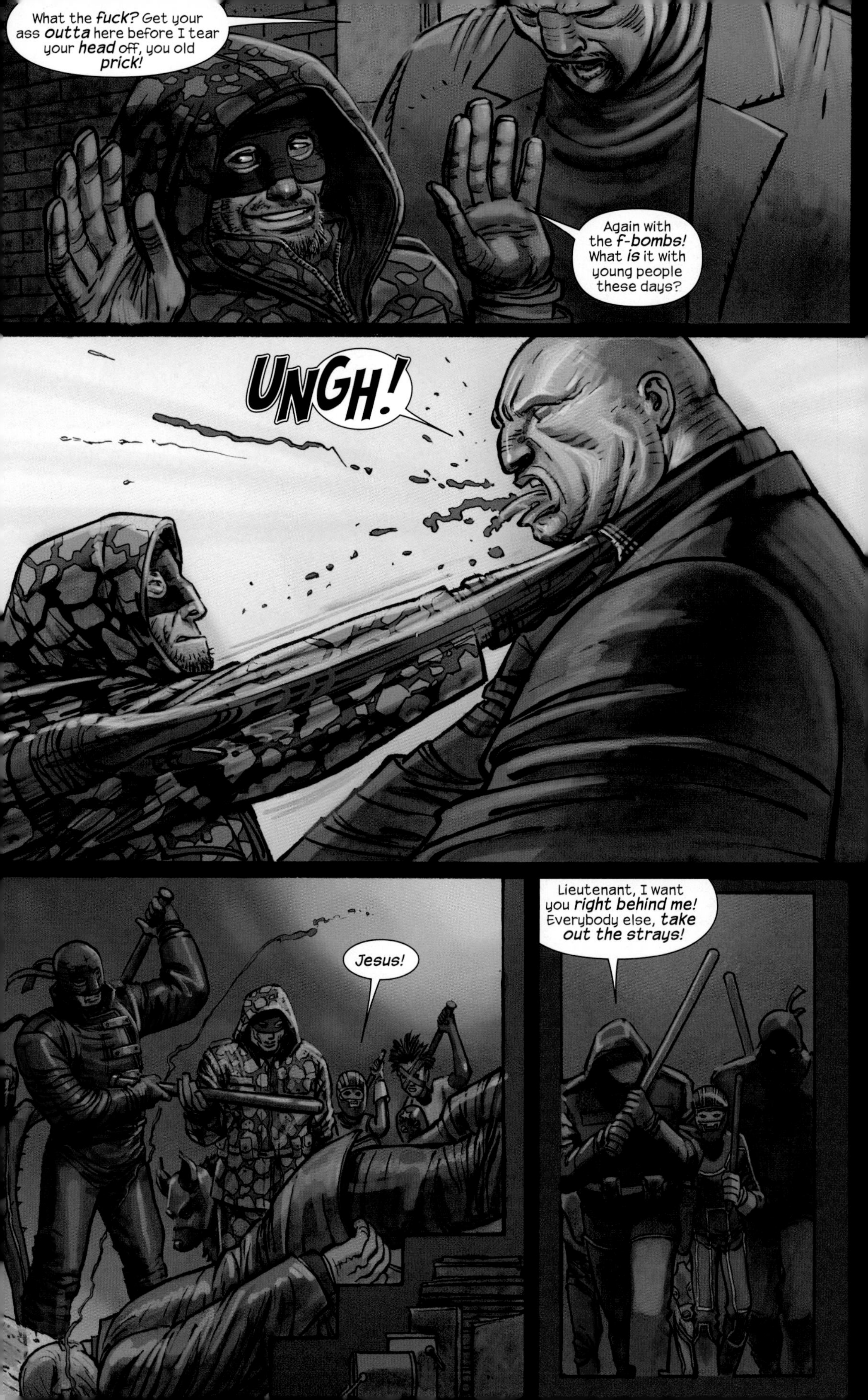
What the *fuck?* Get your ass *outta* here before I tear your *head* off, you old *prick!*
Again with the *f-bombs!* What *is* it with young people these days?
UNGH!
Jesus!
Lieutenant, I want you *right behind me!* Everybody else, *take out the strays!*

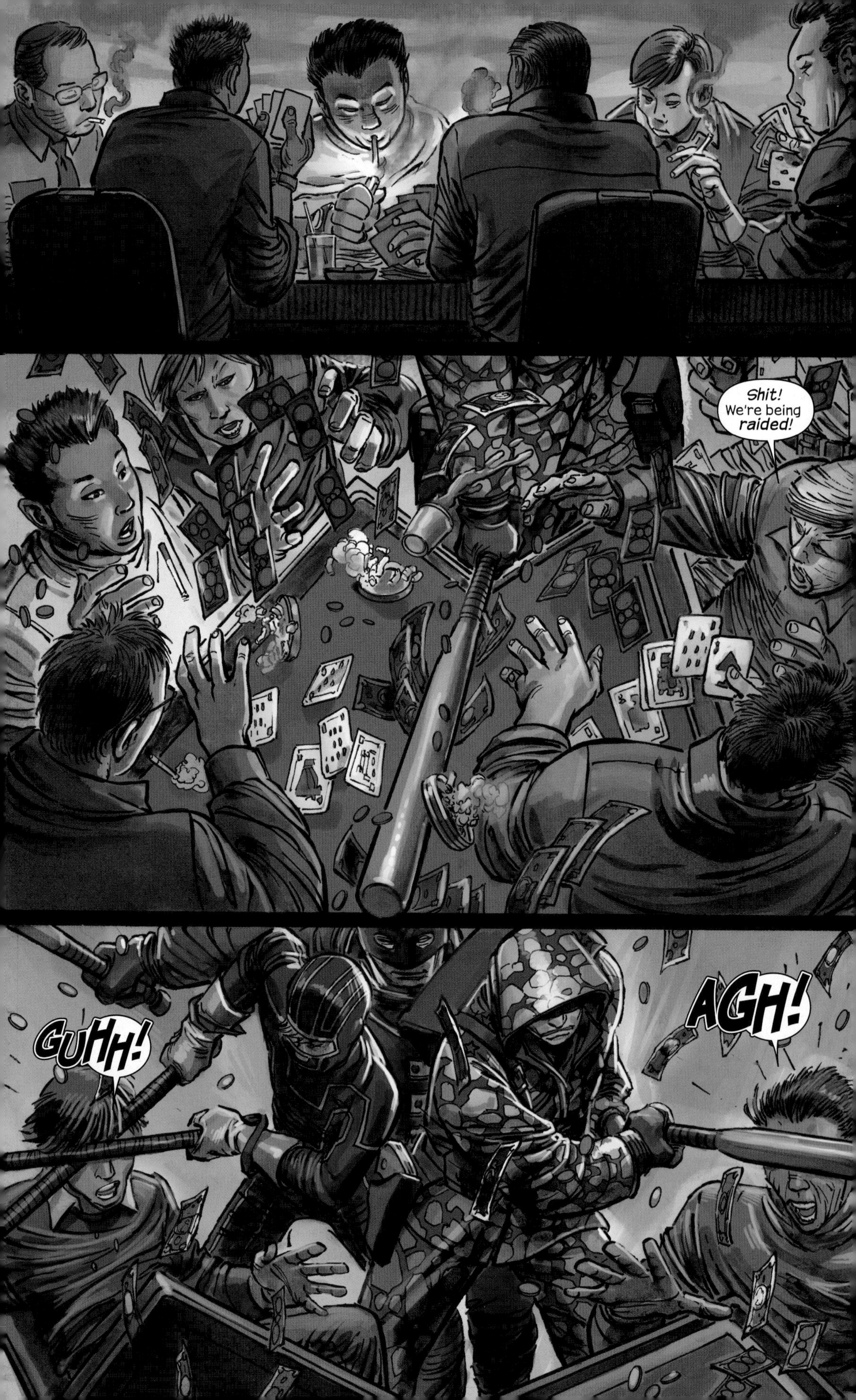
Shit! We're being raided!
GUHH!
AGH!

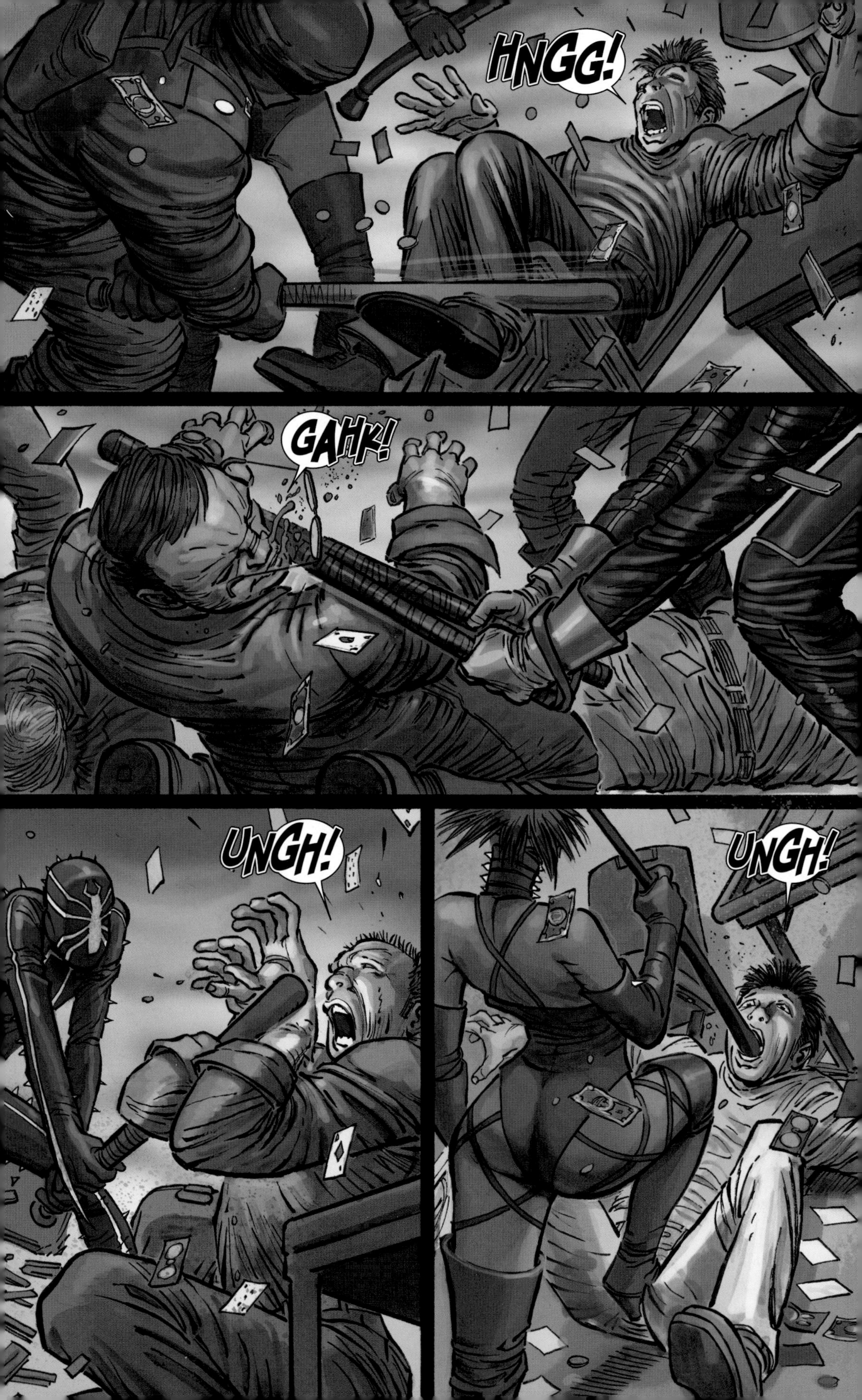
HNGG!
GAHK!
UNGH!
UNGH!

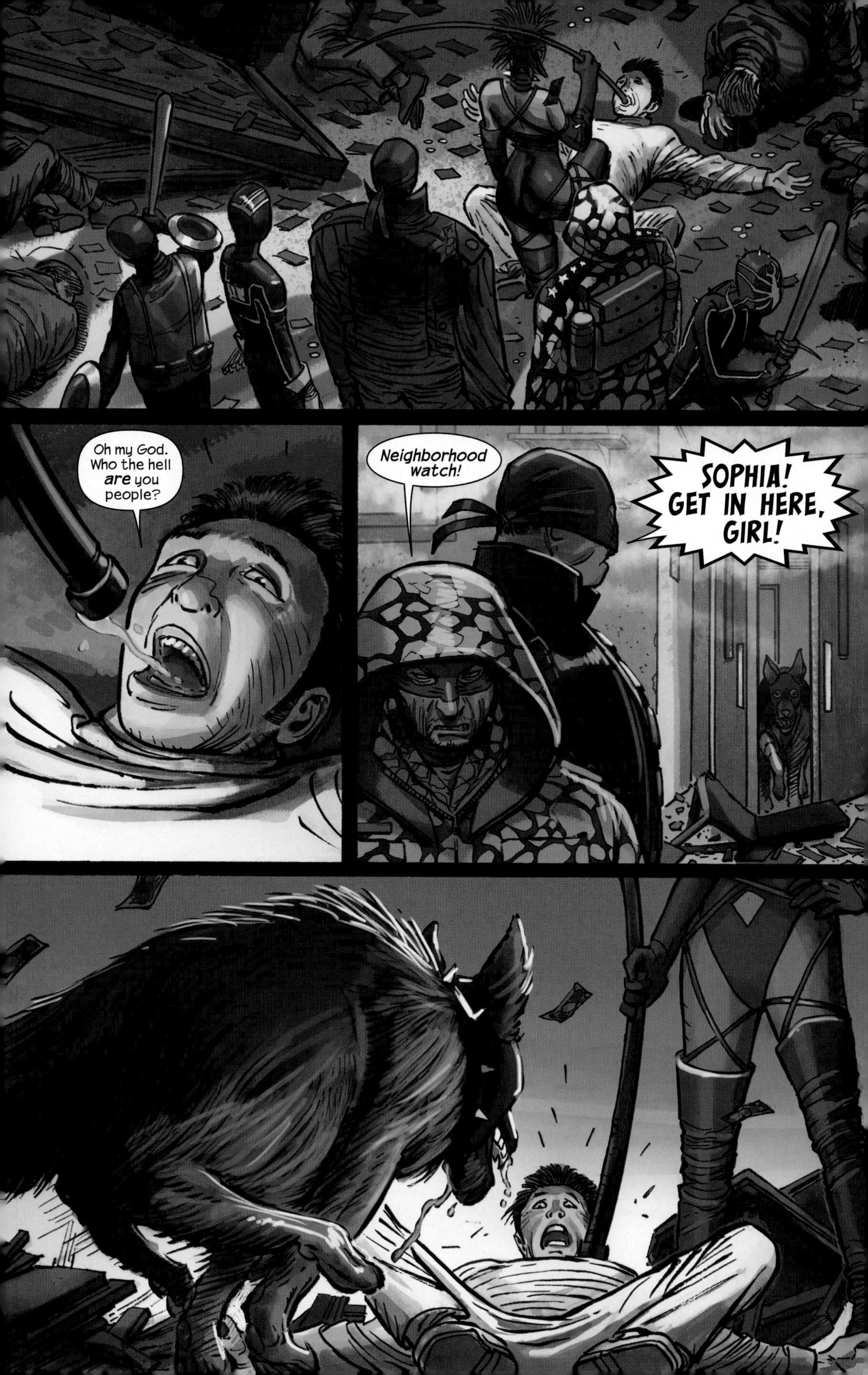
Oh my God. Who the hell are you people?
Neighborhood watch!
SOPHIA! GET IN HERE, GIRL!

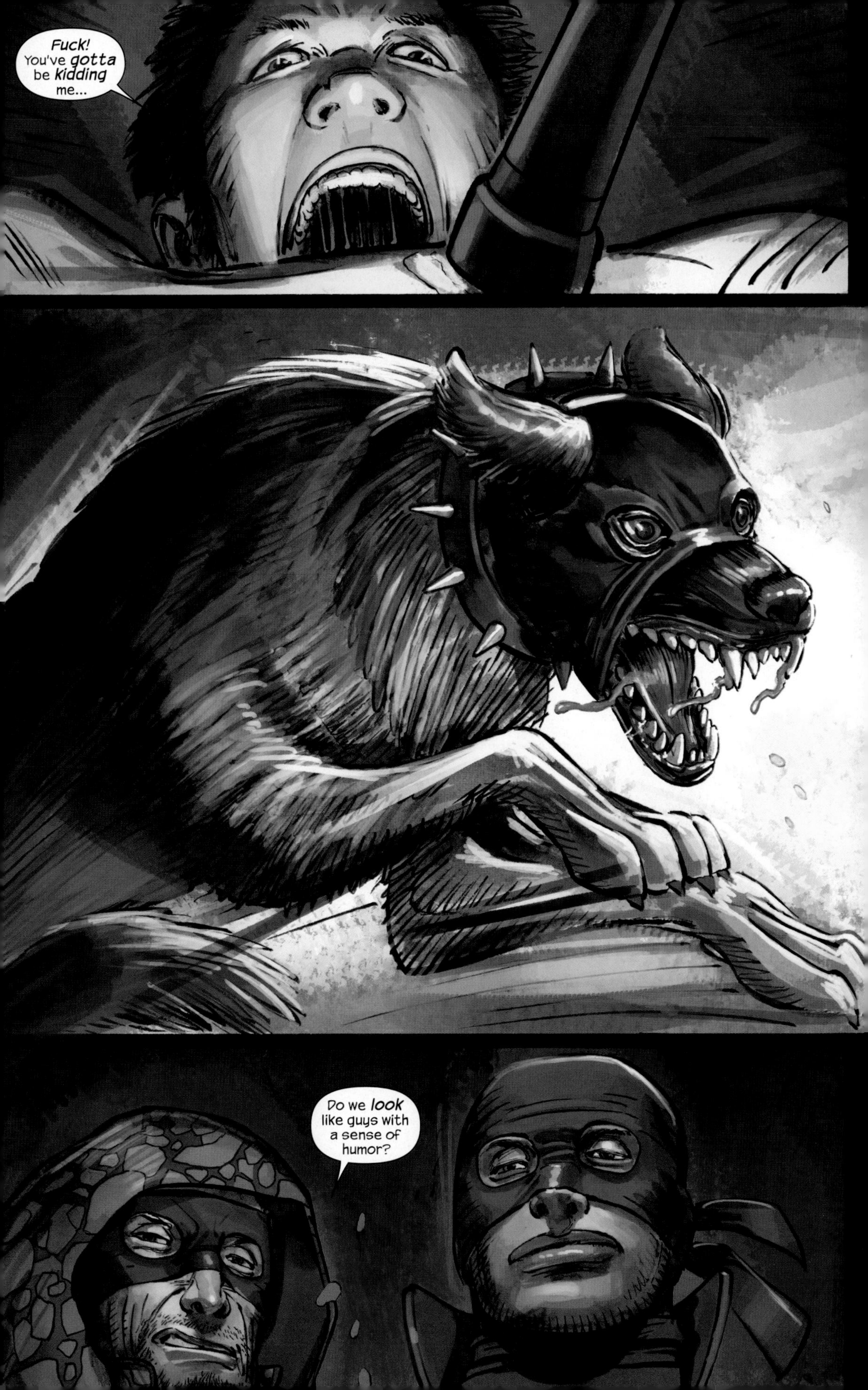
Fuck! You've gotta be kidding me...
Do we look like guys with a sense of humor?

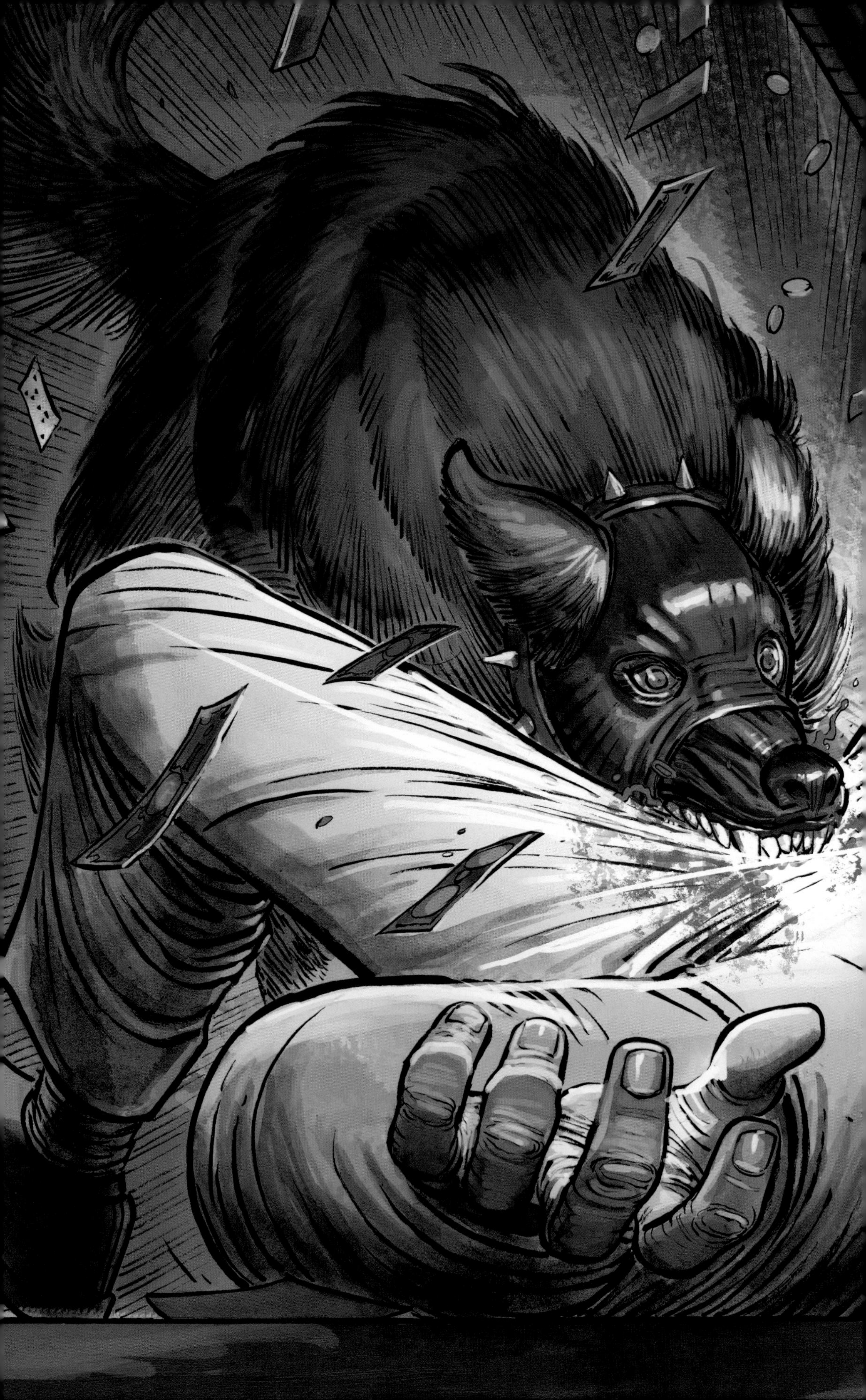

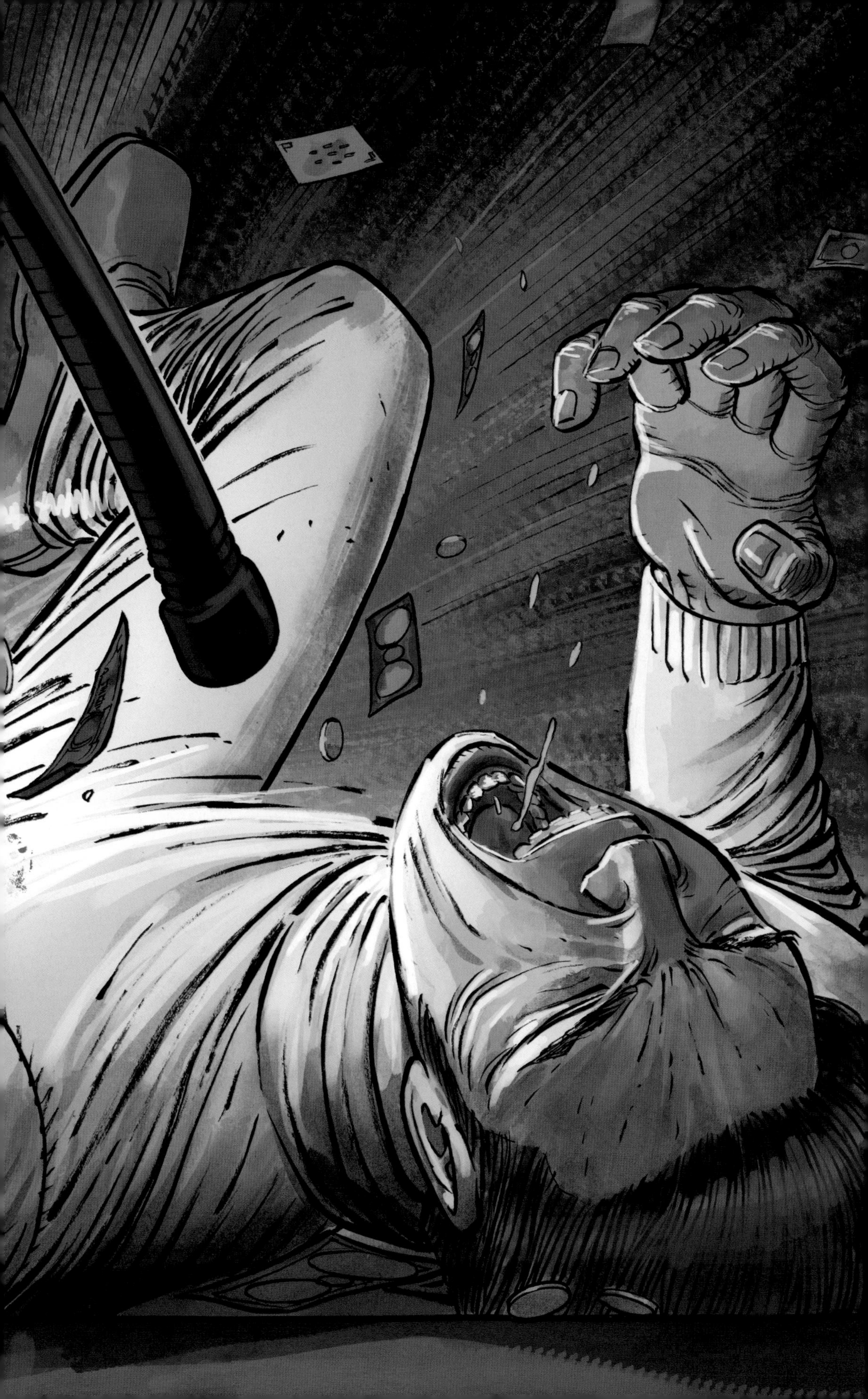

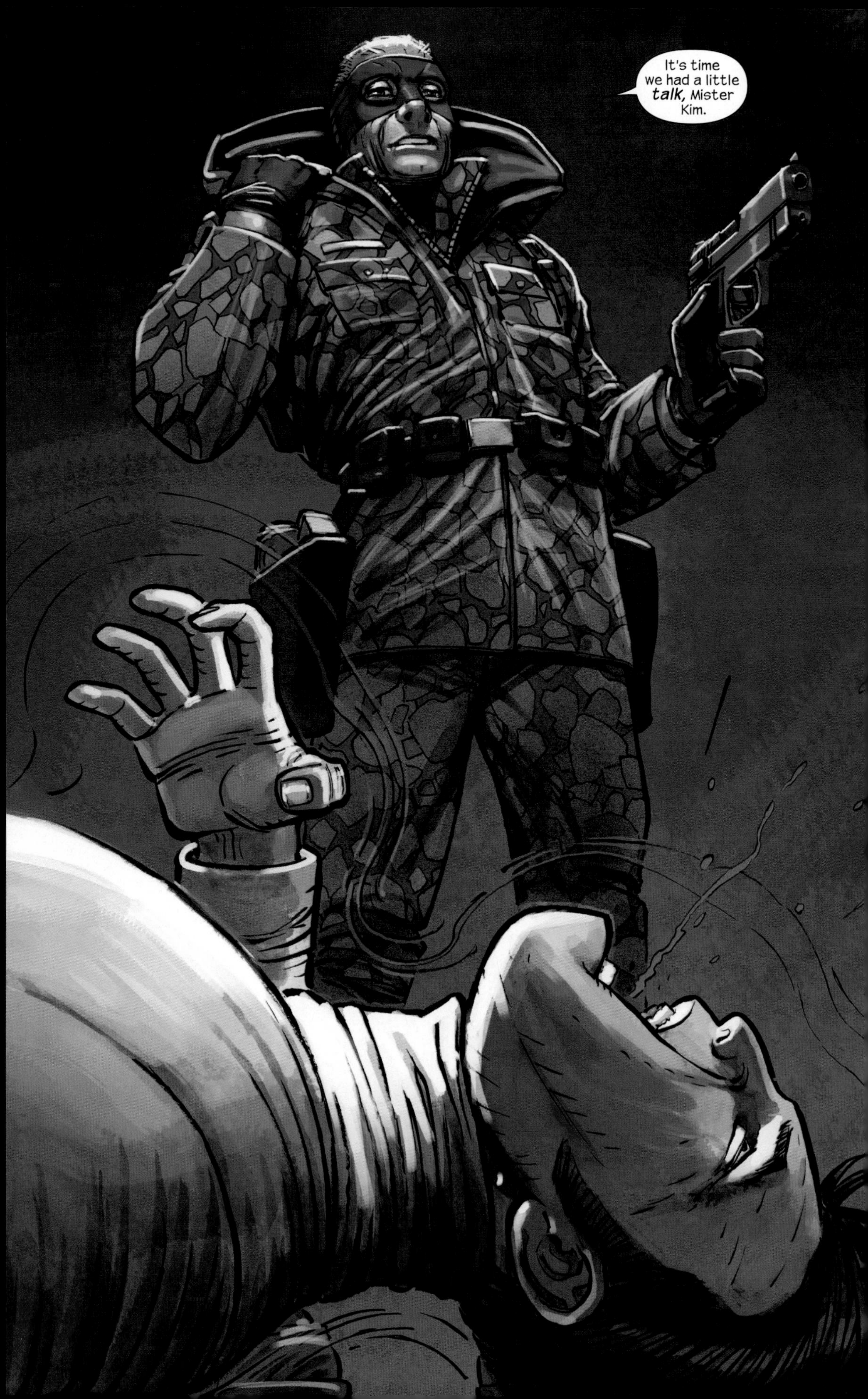
It's time we had a little *talk,* Mister Kim.

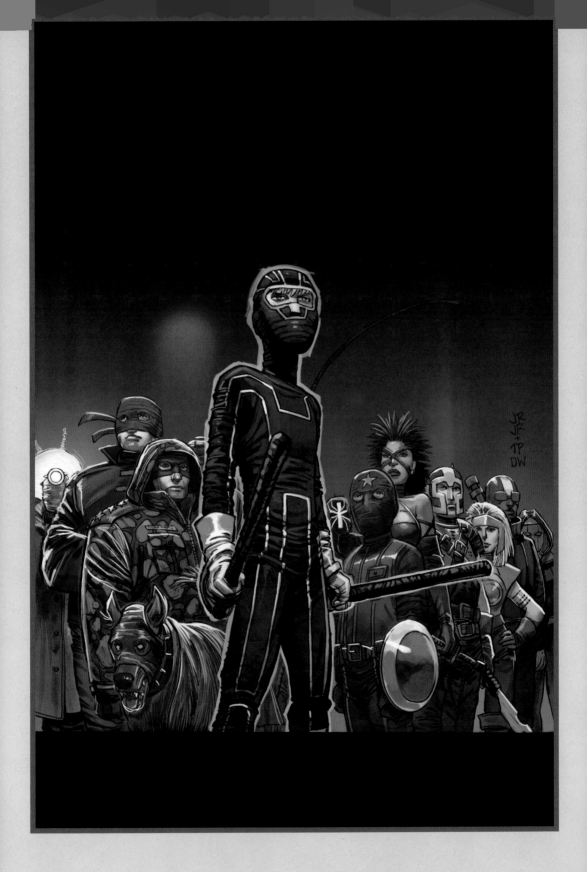

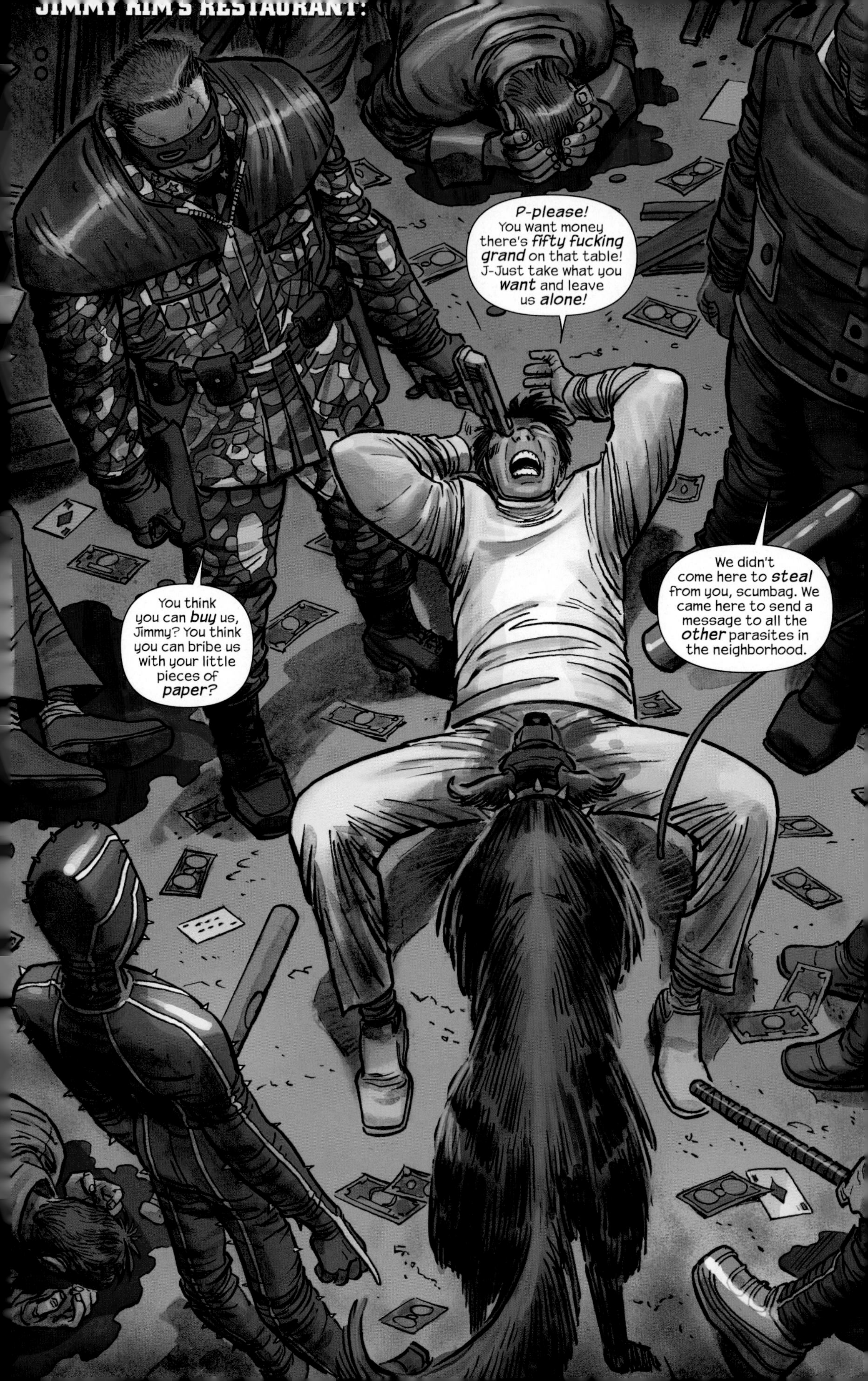
JIMMY KIM'S RESTAURANT:
P-please! You want money there's *fifty fucking grand* on that table! J-Just take what you *want* and leave us *alone!*
You think you can *buy* us, Jimmy? You think you can bribe us with your little pieces of *paper?*
We didn't come here to *steal* from you, scumbag. We came here to send a message to all the *other* parasites in the neighborhood.

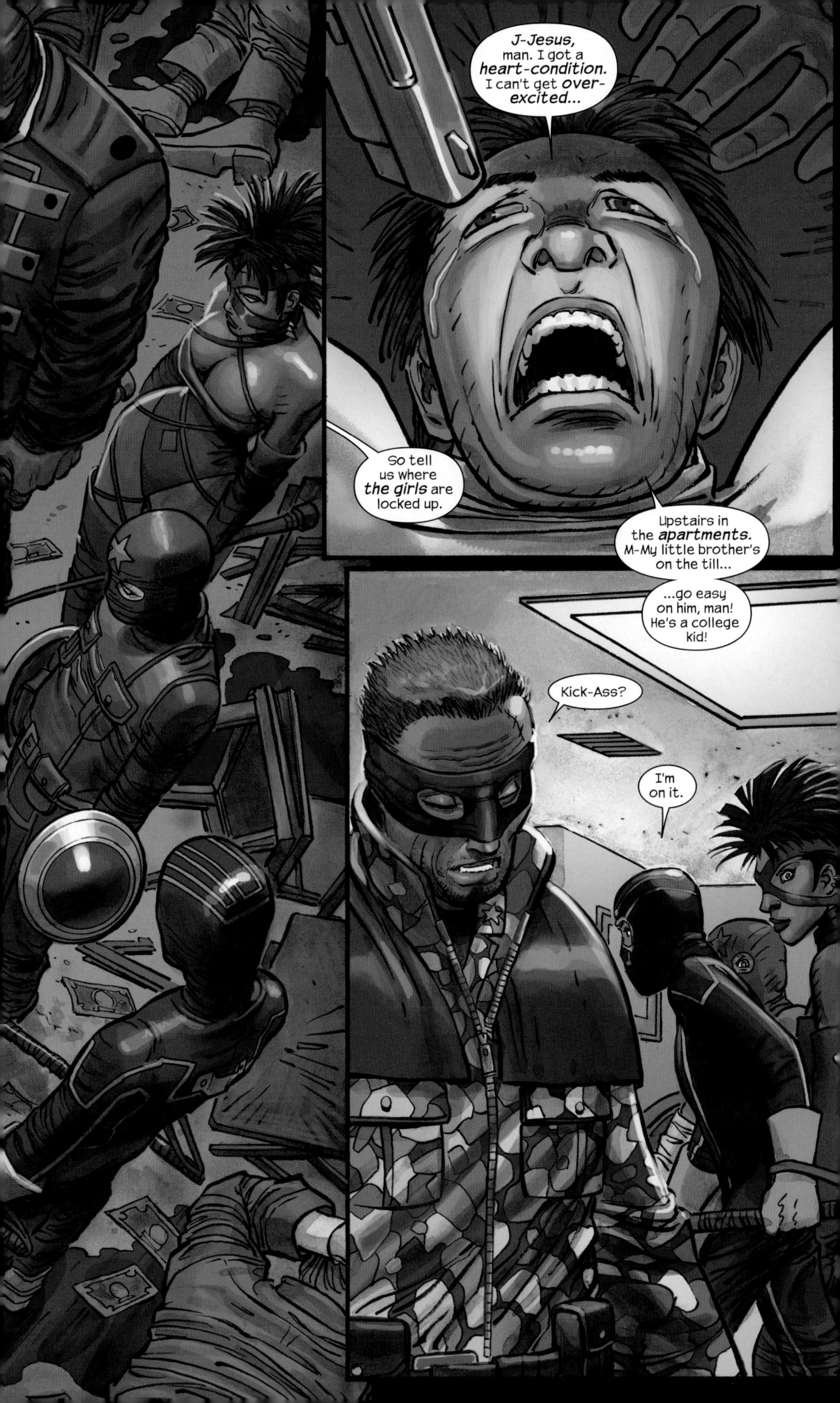
J-Jesus, man. I got a heart-condition. I can't get over-excited...
So tell us where the girls are locked up.
Upstairs in the apartments. M-My little brother's on the till...
...go easy on him, man! He's a college kid!
Kick-Ass?
I'm on it.

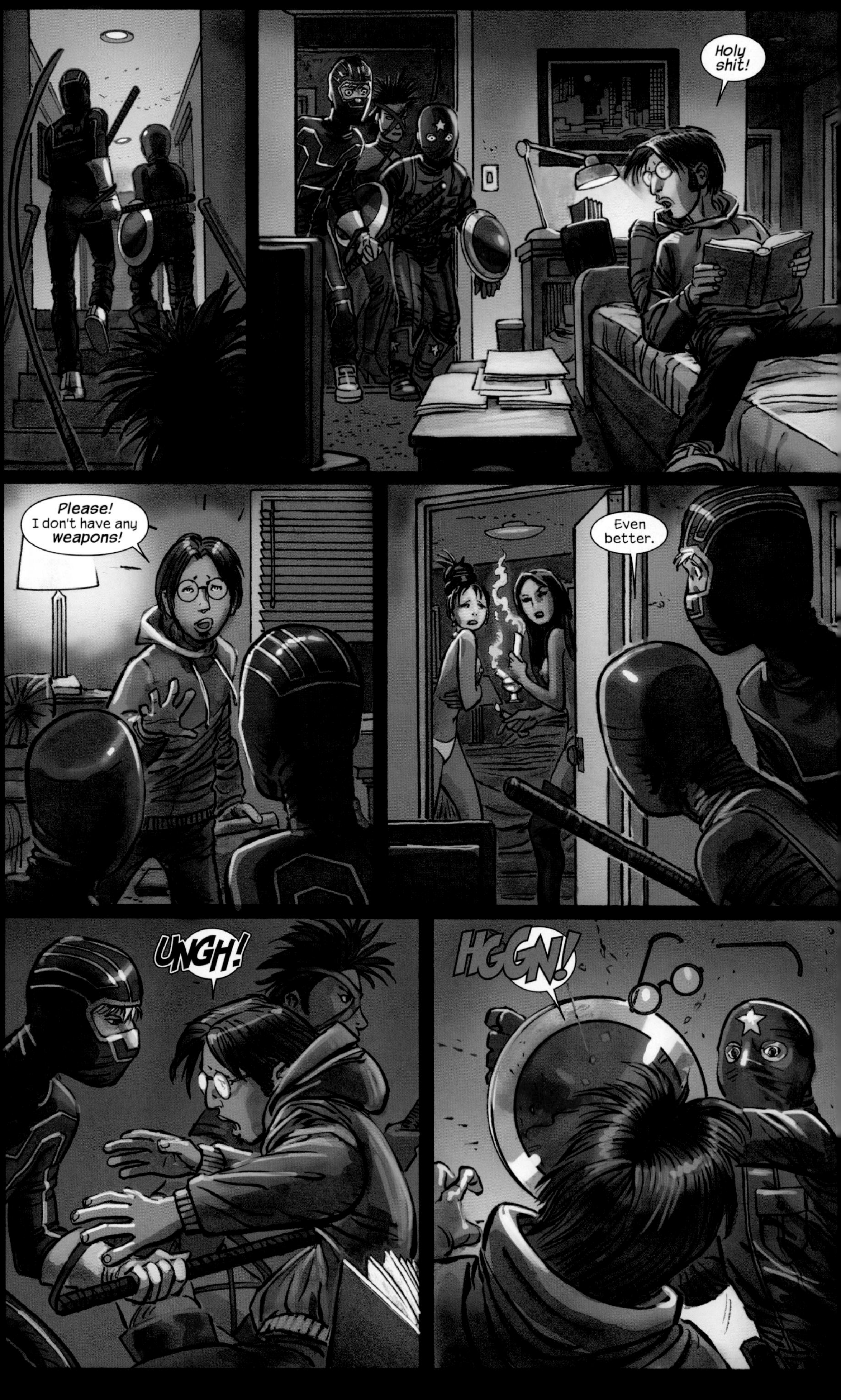
Holy shit!
Please! I don't have any weapons!
Even better.
UNGH!
HGGN!

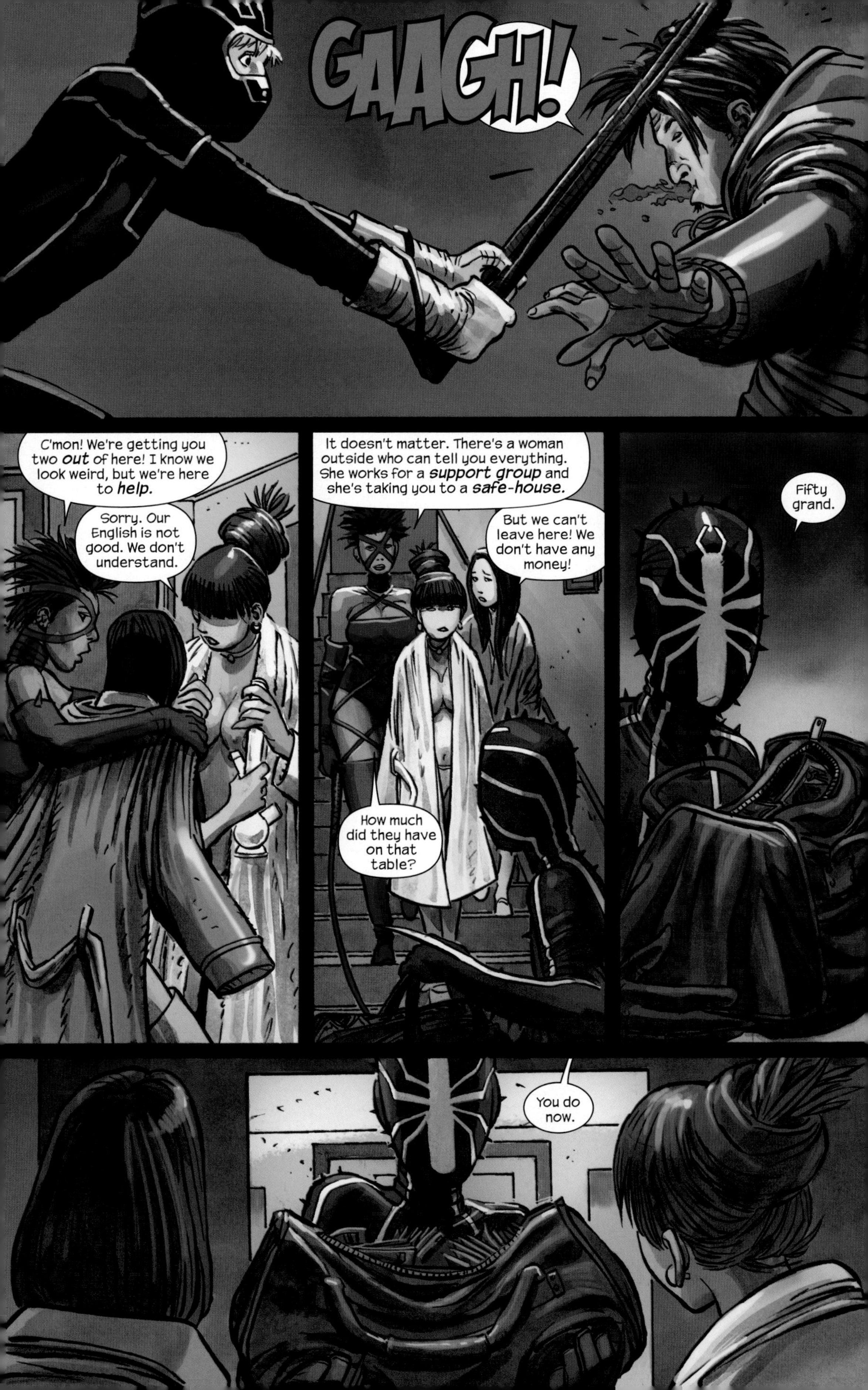
GAAGH!
C'mon! We're getting you two out of here! I know we look weird, but we're here to help.
Sorry. Our English is not good. We don't understand.
It doesn't matter. There's a woman outside who can tell you everything. She works for a support group and she's taking you to a safe-house.
But we can't leave here! We don't have any money!
How much did they have on that table?
Fifty grand.
You do now.

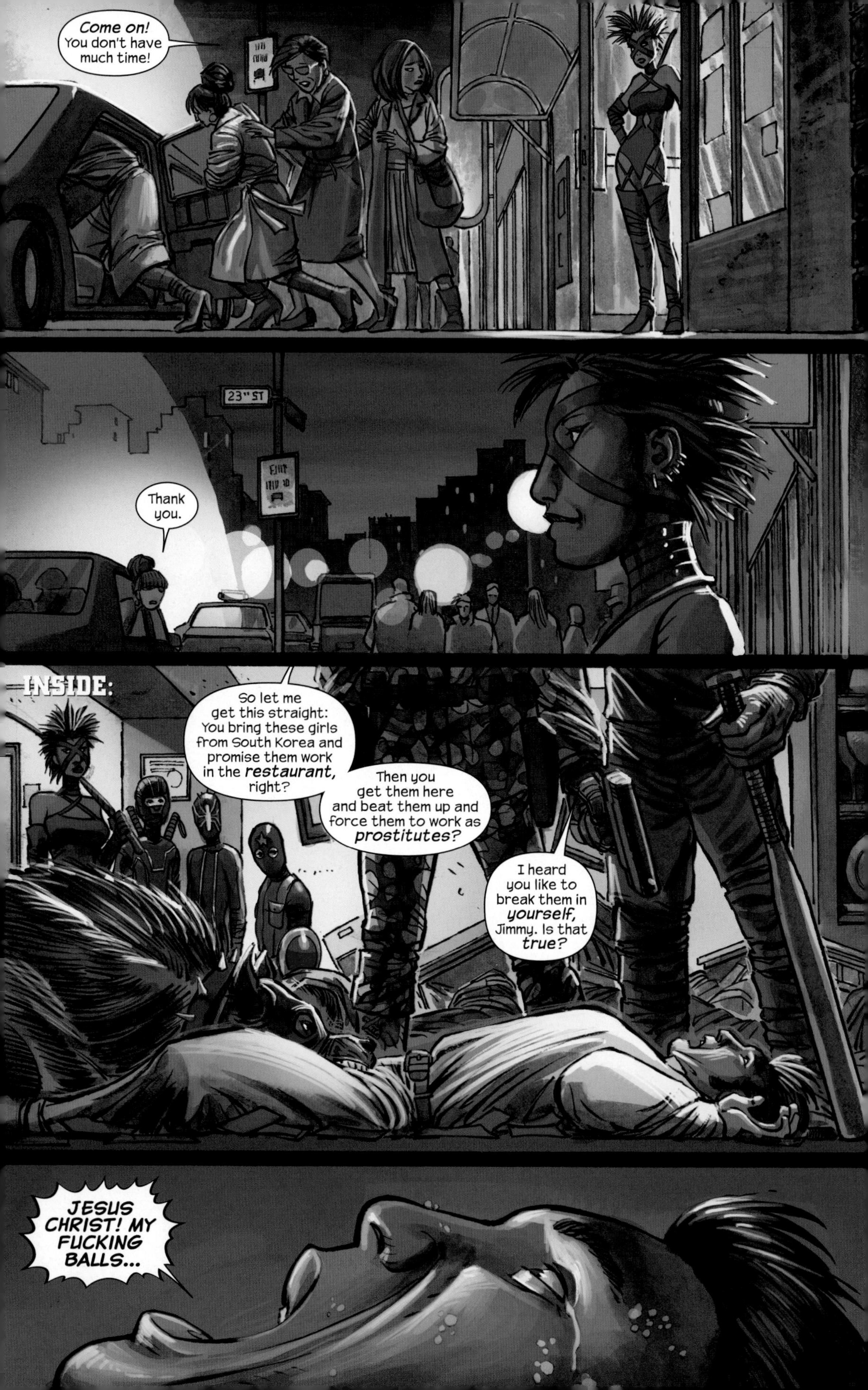
Come on! You don't have much time!
Thank you.
INSIDE:
So let me get this straight: You bring these girls from South Korea and promise them work in the *restaurant,* right?
Then you get them here and beat them up and force them to work as *prostitutes?*
I heard you like to break them in *yourself,* Jimmy. Is that *true?*
JESUS CHRIST! MY FUCKING BALLS...

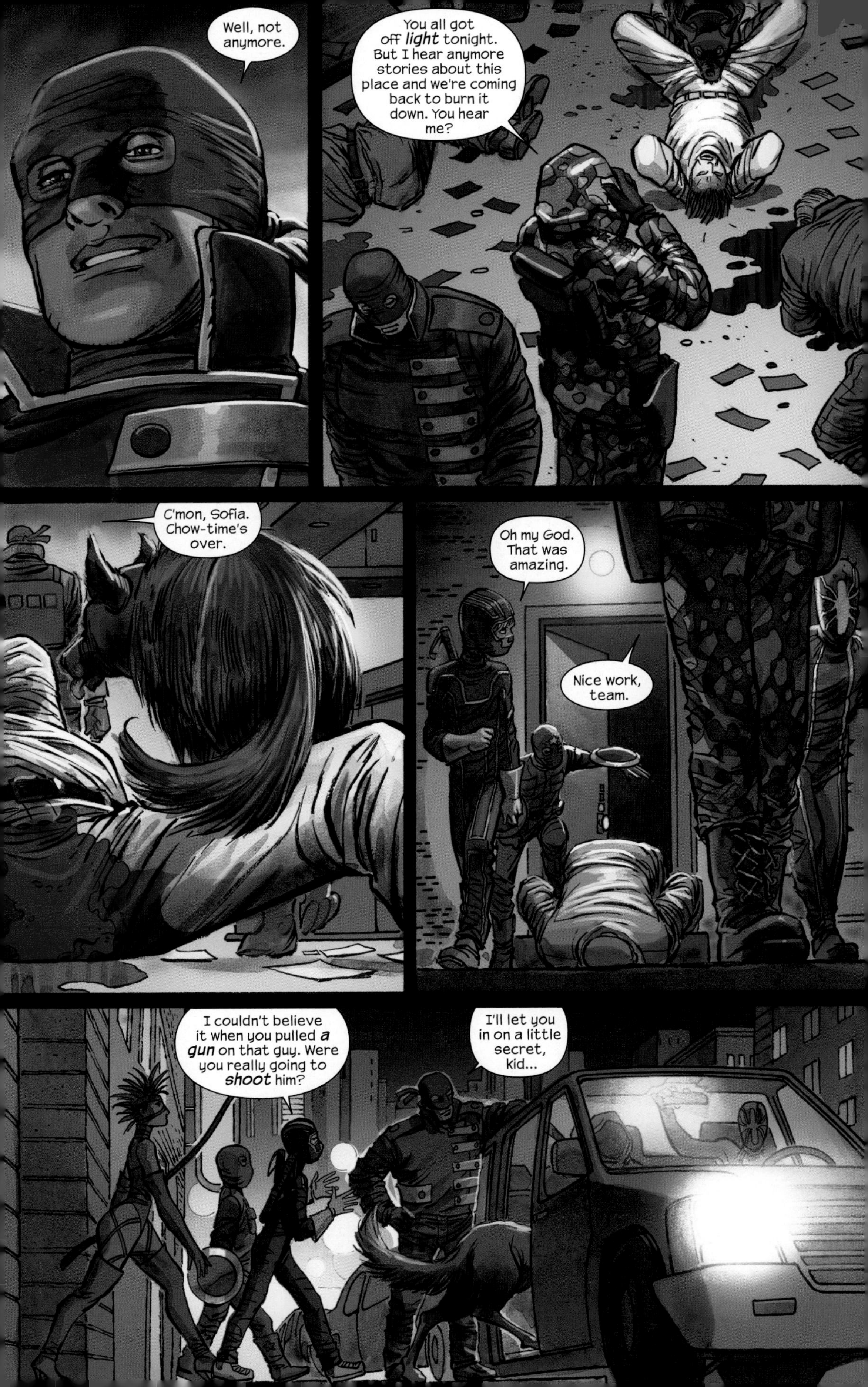
Well, not anymore.
You all got off light tonight. But I hear anymore stories about this place and we're coming back to burn it down. You hear me?
C'mon, Sofia. Chow-time's over.
Oh my God. That was amazing.
Nice work, team.
I couldn't believe it when you pulled a gun on that guy. Were you really going to shoot him?
I'll let you in on a little secret, kid...

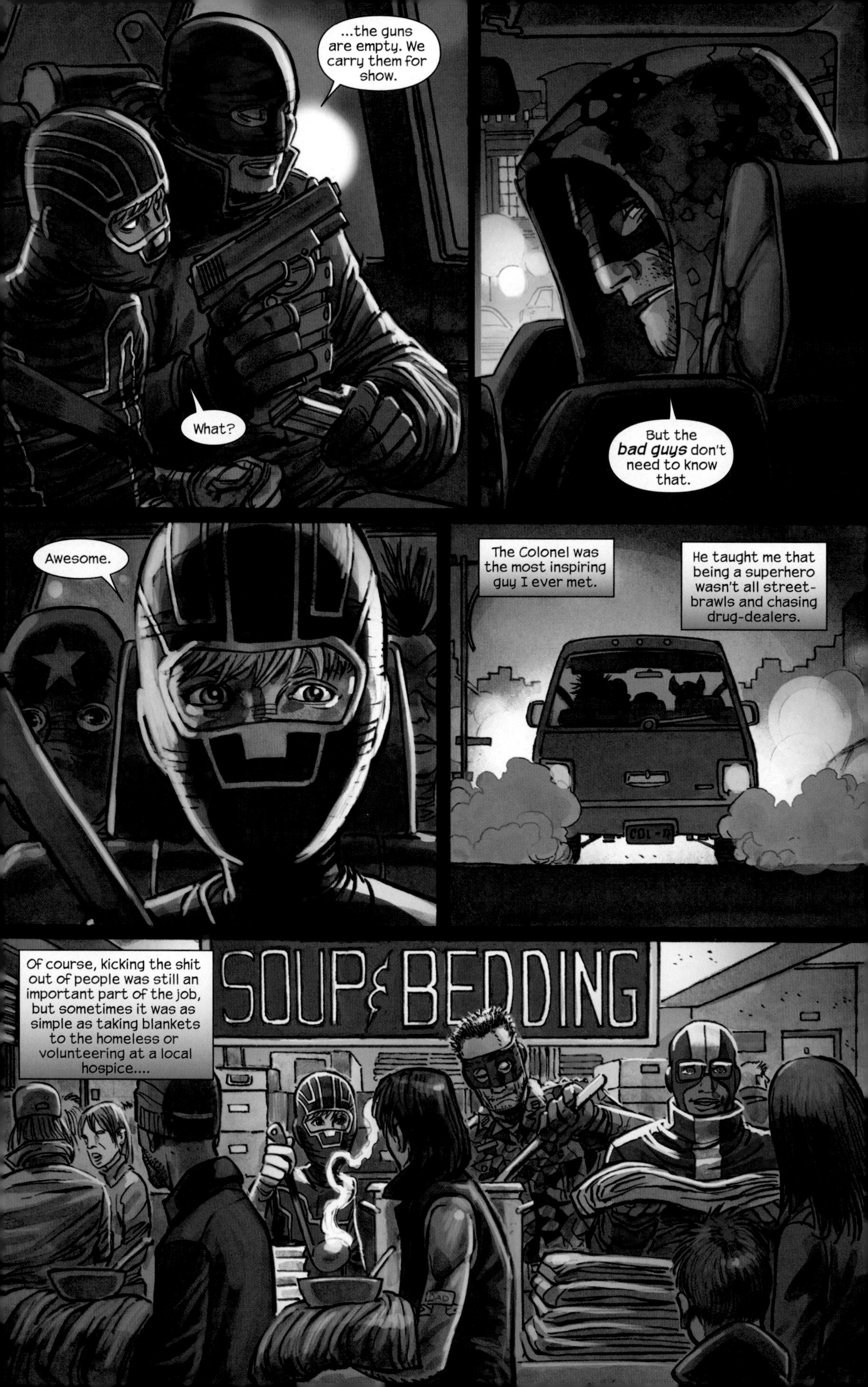
...the guns are empty. We carry them for show.
What?
But the bad guys don't need to know that.
Awesome.
The Colonel was the most inspiring guy I ever met.
He taught me that being a superhero wasn't all street-brawls and chasing drug-dealers.
Of course, kicking the shit out of people was still an important part of the job, but sometimes it was as simple as taking blankets to the homeless or volunteering at a local hospice....
SOUP & BEDDING

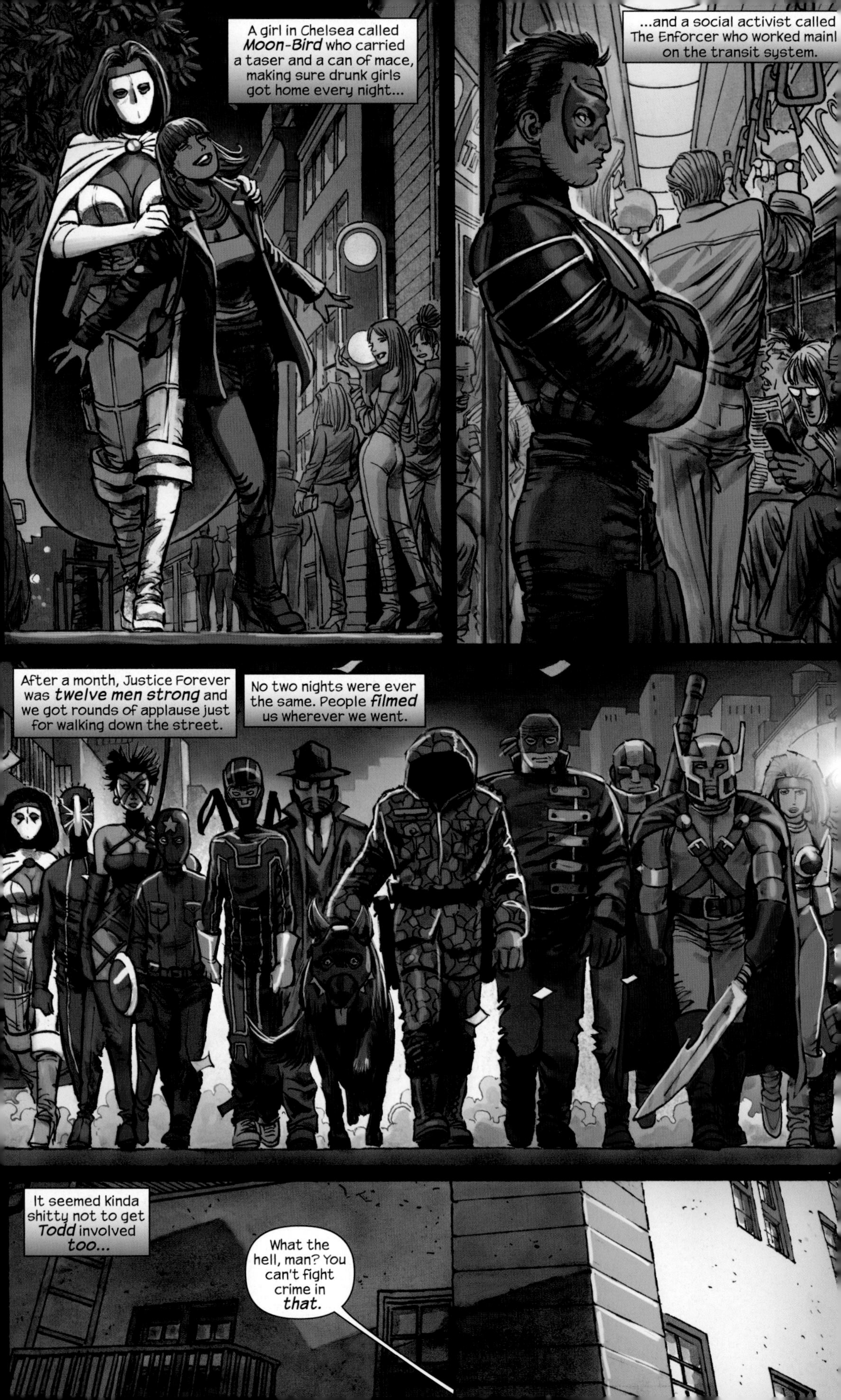
A girl in Chelsea called Moon-Bird who carried a taser and a can of mace, making sure drunk girls got home every night...
...and a social activist called The Enforcer who worked mainl on the transit system.
After a month, Justice Forever was twelve men strong and we got rounds of applause just for walking down the street.
No two nights were ever the same. People filmed us wherever we went.
It seemed kinda shitty not to get Todd involved too...
What the hell, man? You can't fight crime in that.

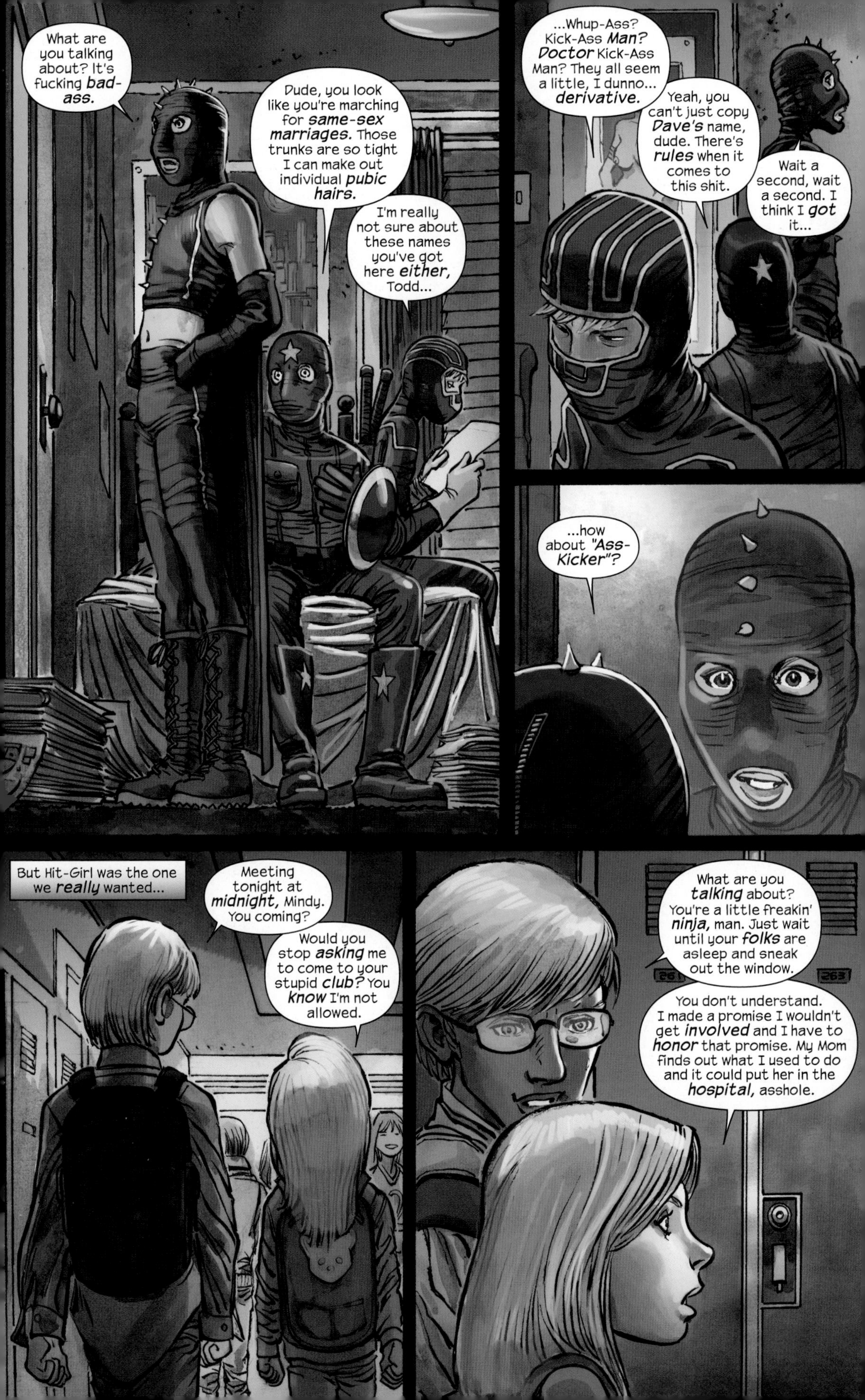
What are you talking about? It's fucking *bad-ass.*
Dude, you look like you're marching for *same-sex marriages.* Those trunks are so tight I can make out individual *pubic hairs.*
I'm really not sure about these names you've got here *either,* Todd...
...Whup-Ass? Kick-Ass *Man? Doctor* Kick-Ass Man? They all seem a little, I dunno... *derivative.*
Yeah, you can't just copy *Dave's* name, dude. There's *rules* when it comes to this shit.
Wait a second, wait a second. I think I *got* it...
...how about *"Ass-Kicker"?*
But Hit-Girl was the one we *really* wanted...
Meeting tonight at *midnight,* Mindy. You coming?
Would you stop *asking* me to come to your stupid *club?* You *know* I'm not allowed.
What are you *talking* about? You're a little freakin' *ninja,* man. Just wait until your *folks* are asleep and sneak out the window.
You don't understand. I made a promise I wouldn't get *involved* and I have to *honor* that promise. My Mom finds out what I used to do and it could put her in the *hospital,* asshole.

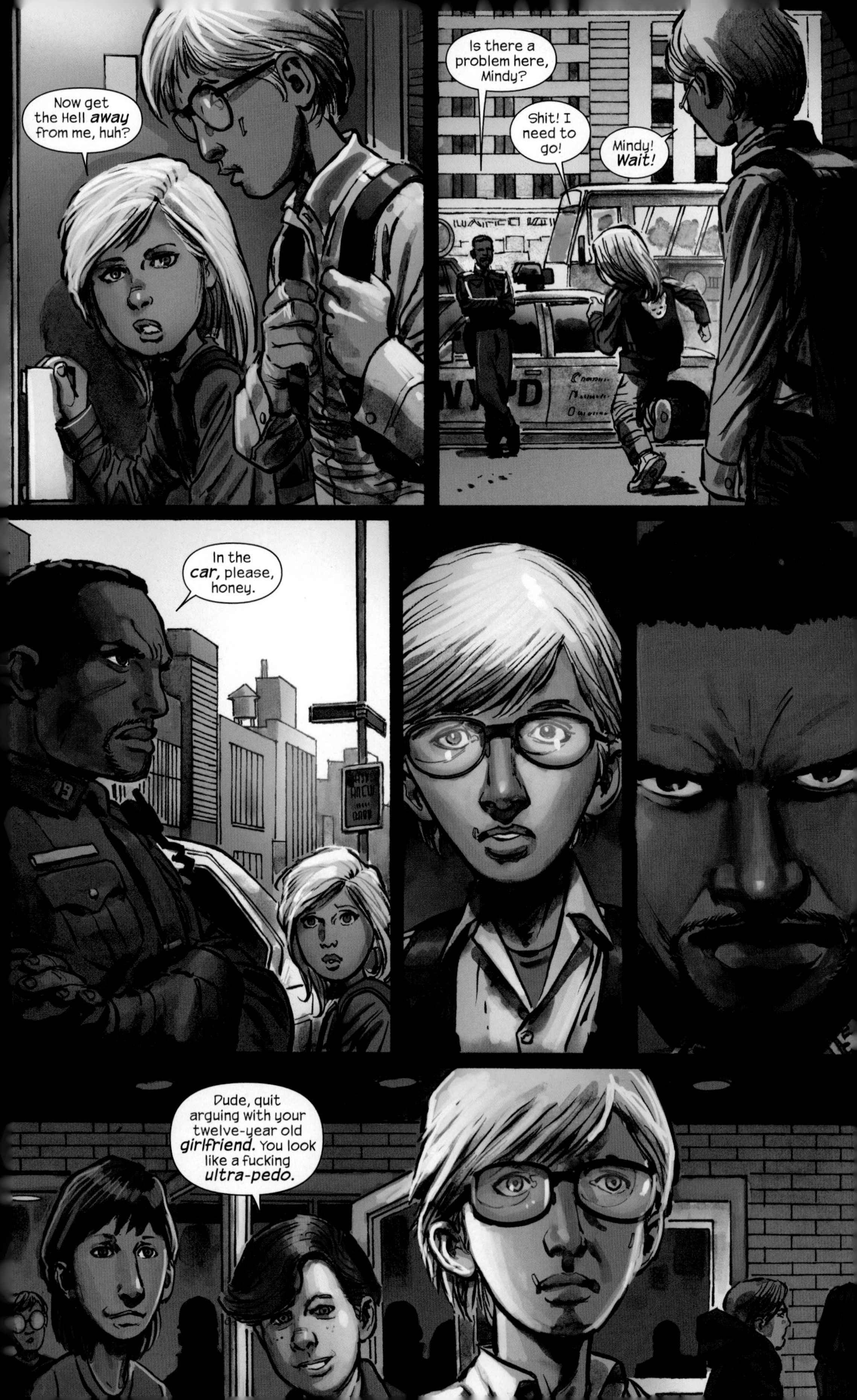
Now get the Hell *away* from me, huh?
Is there a problem here, Mindy?
Shit! I need to go!
Mindy! *Wait!*
NYPD
In the *car,* please, honey.
Dude, quit arguing with your twelve-year old *girlfriend.* You look like a fucking *ultra-pedo.*

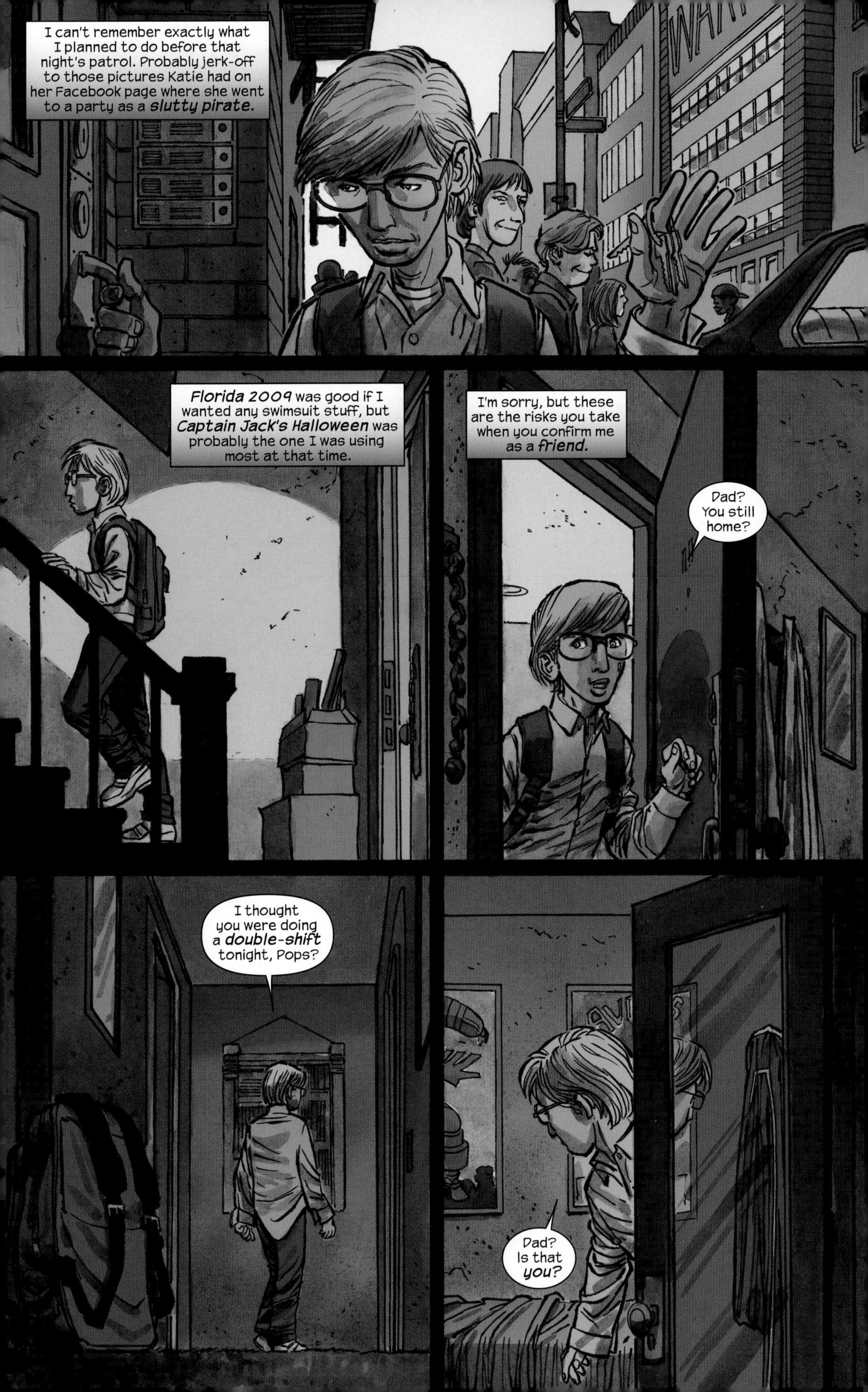
I can't remember exactly what I planned to do before that night's patrol. Probably jerk-off to those pictures Katie had on her Facebook page where she went to a party as a *slutty pirate.*
Florida 2009 was good if I wanted any swimsuit stuff, but *Captain Jack's Halloween* was probably the one I was using most at that time.
I'm sorry, but these are the risks you take when you confirm me as a *friend.*
Dad? You still home?
I thought you were doing a *double-shift* tonight, Pops?
Dad? Is that *you?*

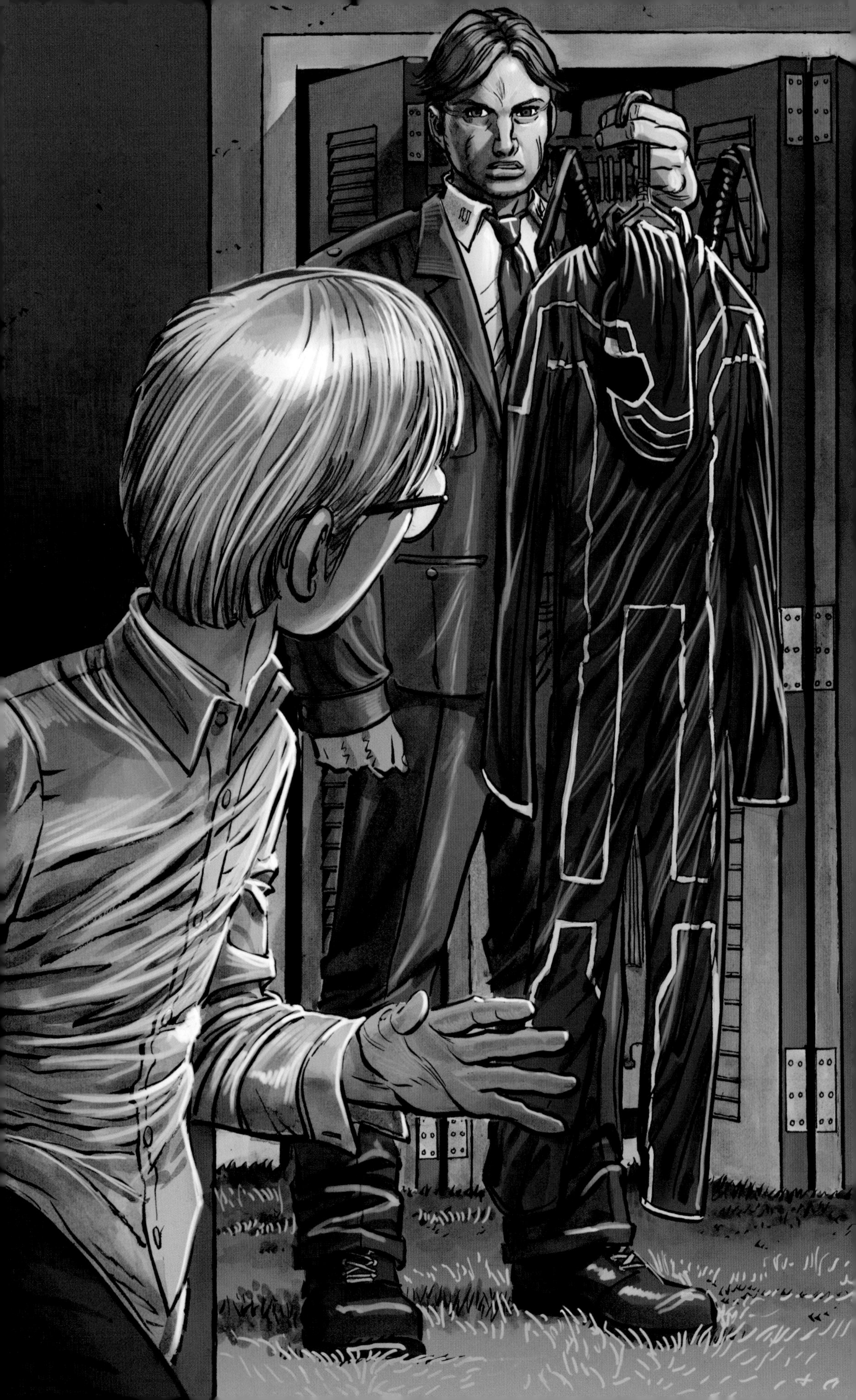

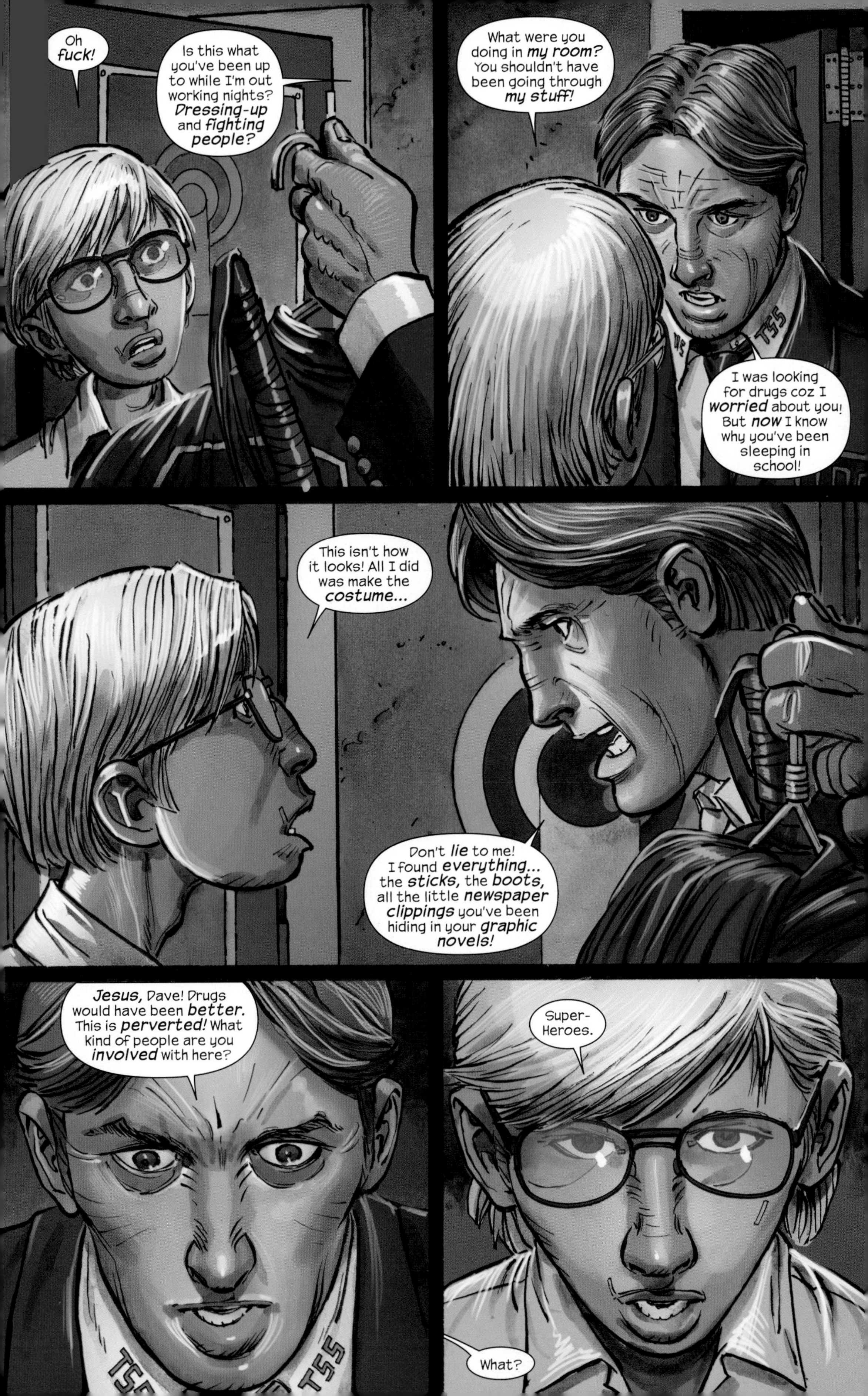
Oh fuck!
Is this what you've been up to while I'm out working nights? Dressing-up and fighting people?
What were you doing in my room? You shouldn't have been going through my stuff!
I was looking for drugs coz I worried about you! But now I know why you've been sleeping in school!
This isn't how it looks! All I did was make the costume...
Don't lie to me! I found everything... the sticks, the boots, all the little newspaper clippings you've been hiding in your graphic novels!
Jesus, Dave! Drugs would have been better. This is perverted! What kind of people are you involved with here?
Super-Heroes.
What?

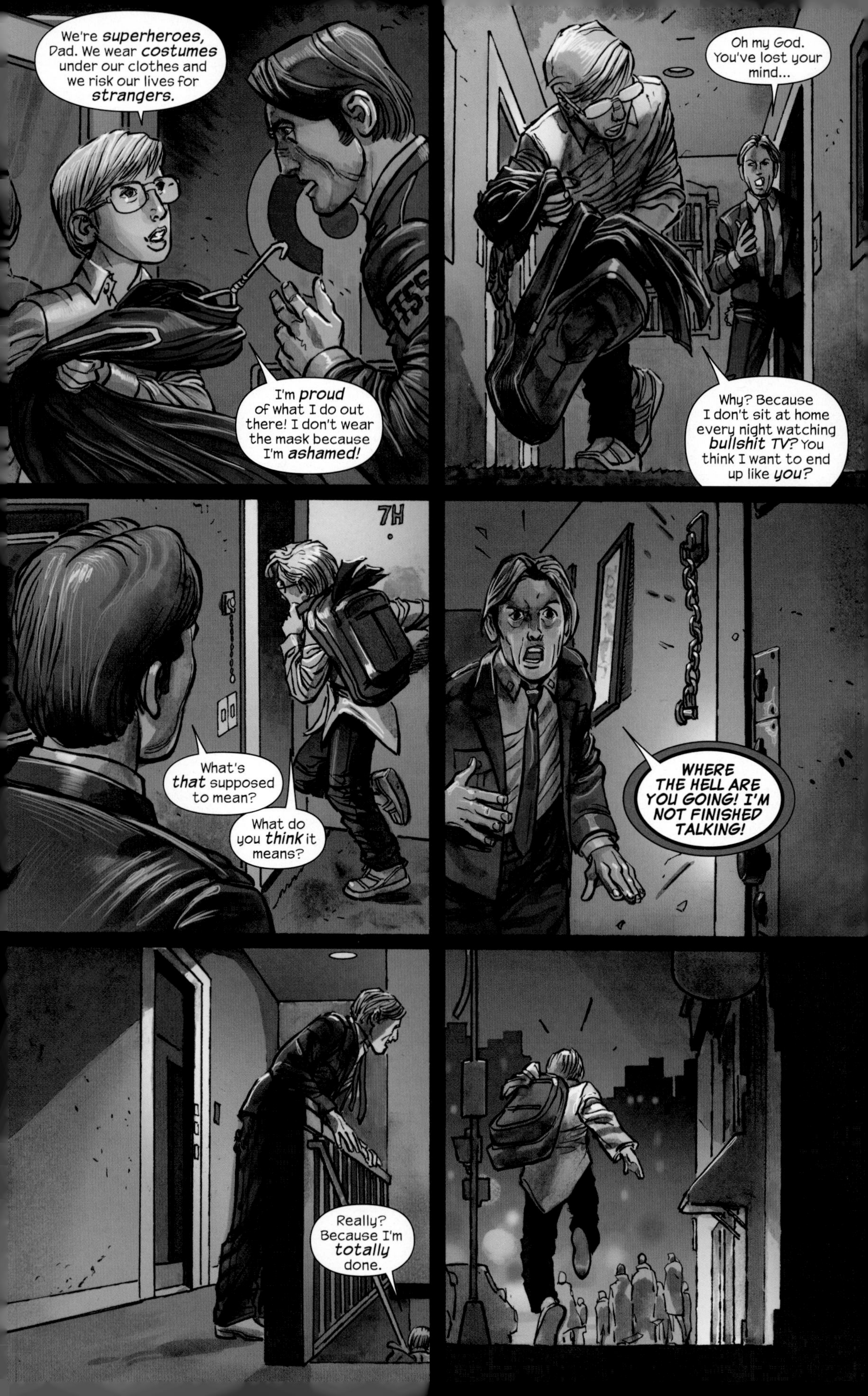
We're superheroes, Dad. We wear costumes under our clothes and we risk our lives for strangers.
I'm proud of what I do out there! I don't wear the mask because I'm ashamed!
Oh my God. You've lost your mind...
Why? Because I don't sit at home every night watching bullshit TV? You think I want to end up like you?
7H
What's that supposed to mean?
What do you think it means?
WHERE THE HELL ARE YOU GOING! I'M NOT FINISHED TALKING!
Really? Because I'm totally done.

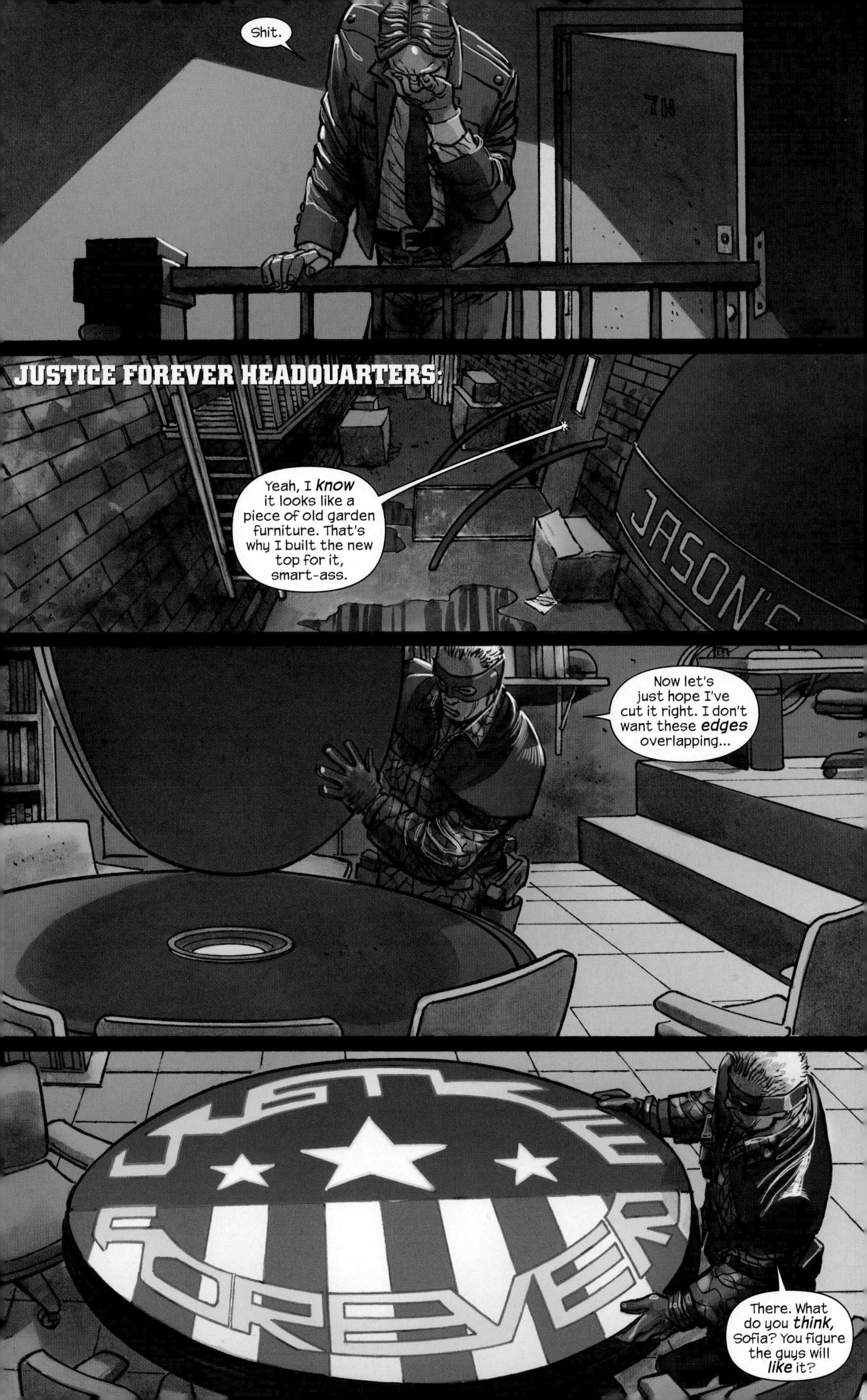
Shit.
7H
JUSTICE FOREVER HEADQUARTERS:
Yeah, I *know* it looks like a piece of old garden furniture. That's why I built the new top for it, smart-ass.
JASON'S
Now let's just hope I've cut it right. I don't want these *edges* overlapping...
FOREVER
There. What do you *think,* Sofia? You figure the guys will *like* it?

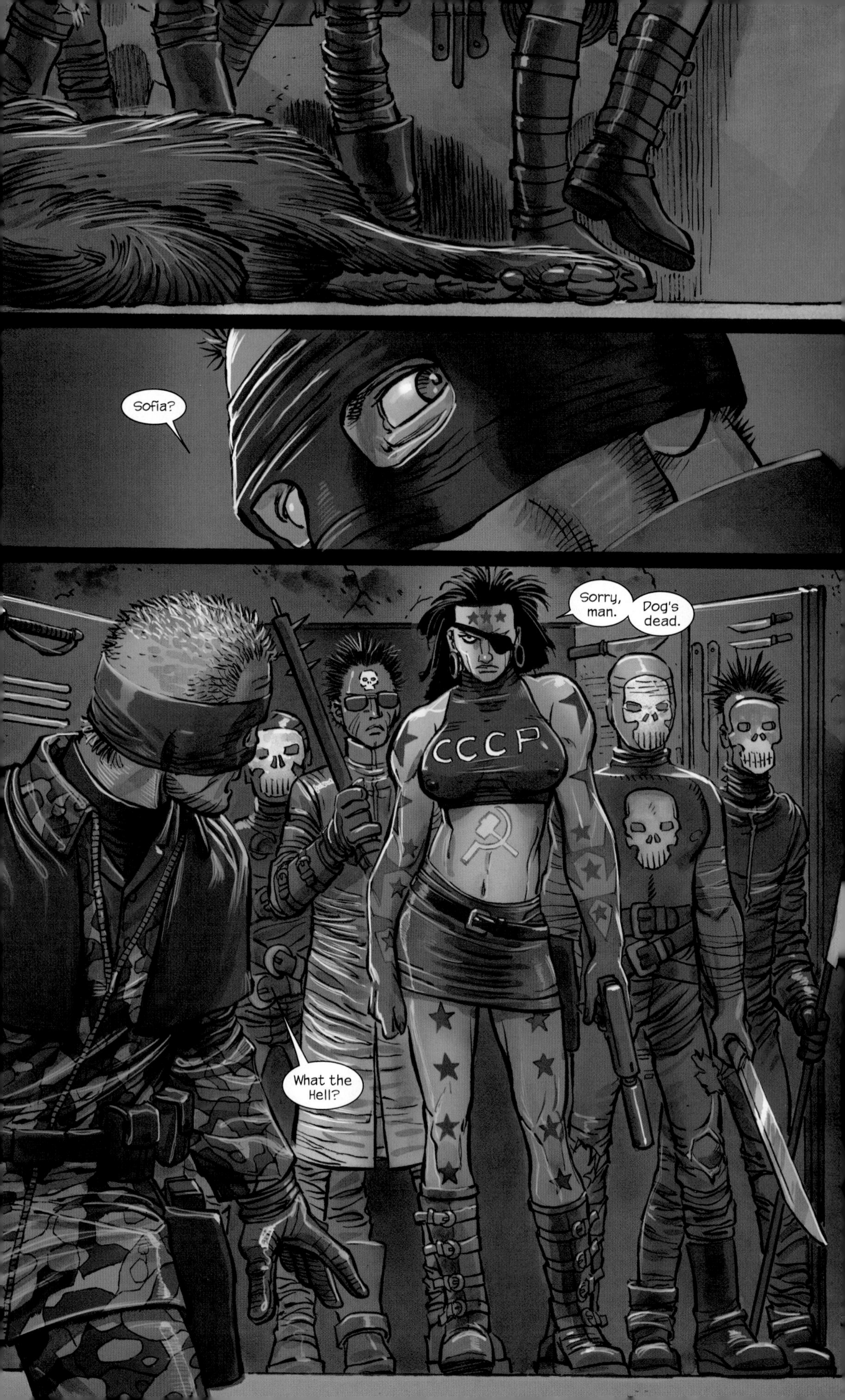
Sofia?
Sorry, man.
Dog's dead.
What the Hell?
CCCP

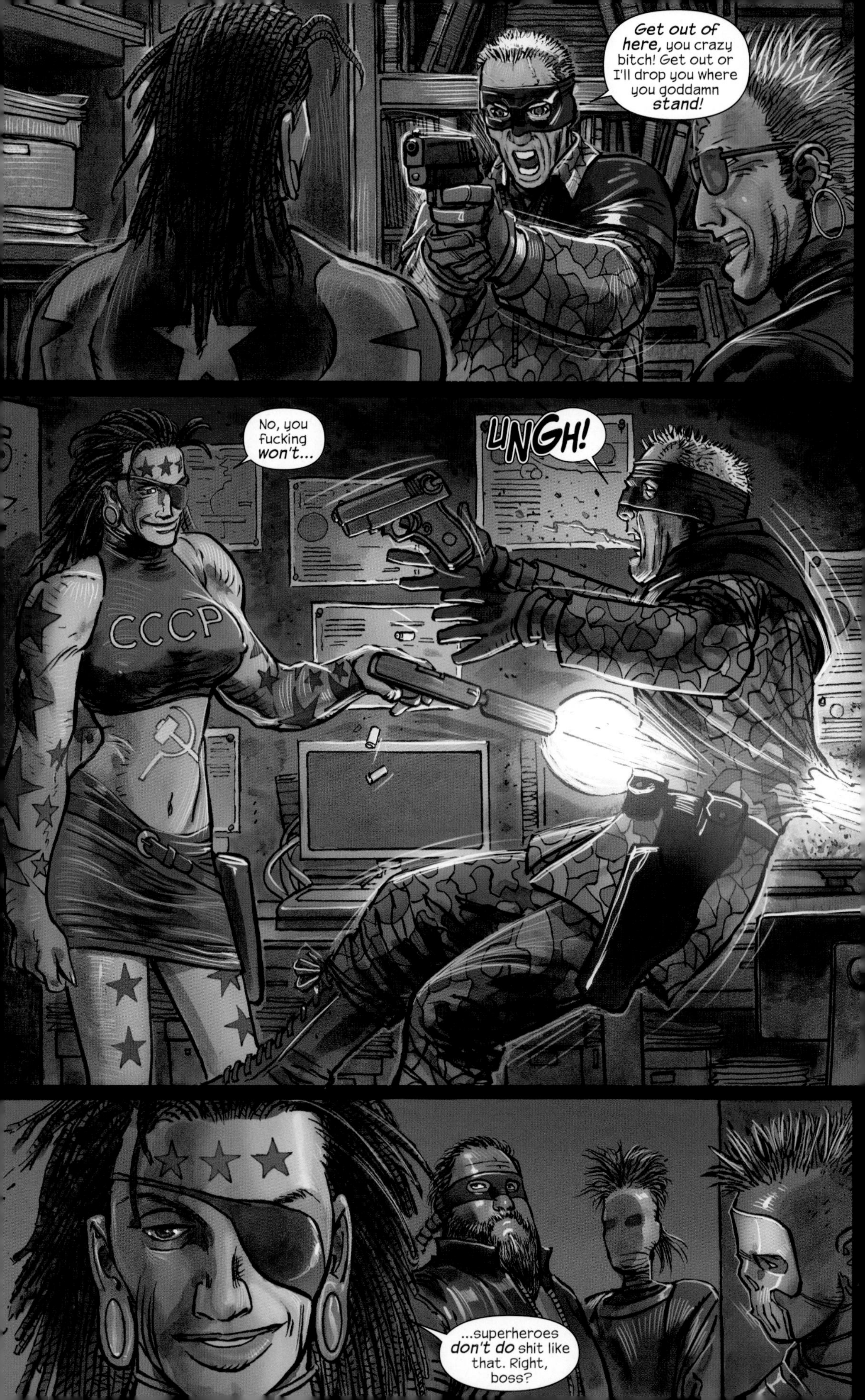
Get out of here, you crazy bitch! Get out or I'll drop you where you goddamn stand!
No, you fucking won't...
UNGH!
CCCP
...superheroes don't do shit like that. Right, boss?

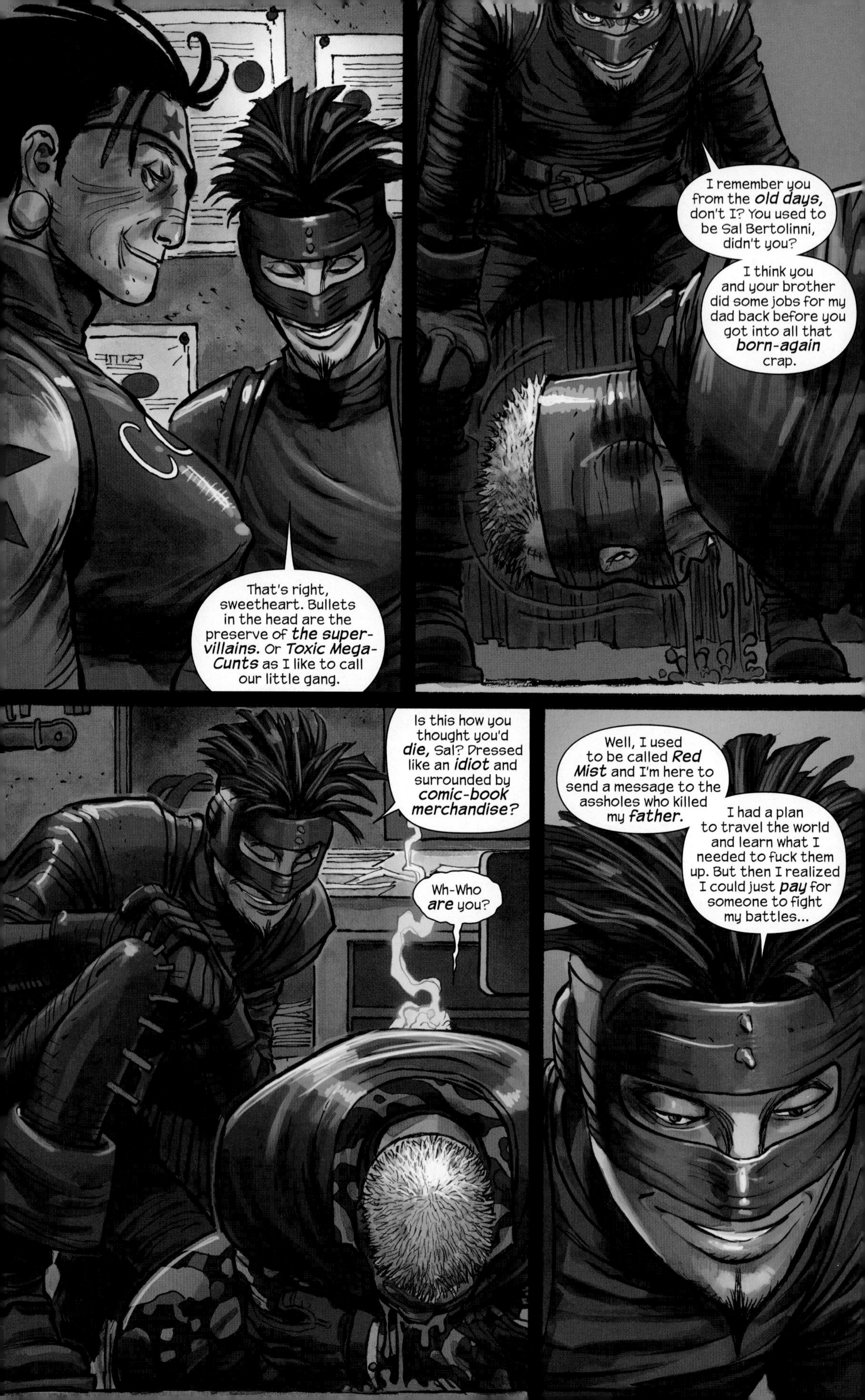
That's right, sweetheart. Bullets in the head are the preserve of the super-villains. Or Toxic Mega-Cunts as I like to call our little gang.
I remember you from the old days, don't I? You used to be Sal Bertolinni, didn't you?
I think you and your brother did some jobs for my dad back before you got into all that born-again crap.
Is this how you thought you'd die, Sal? Dressed like an idiot and surrounded by comic-book merchandise?
Wh-Who are you?
Well, I used to be called Red Mist and I'm here to send a message to the assholes who killed my father.
I had a plan to travel the world and learn what I needed to fuck them up. But then I realized I could just pay for someone to fight my battles...

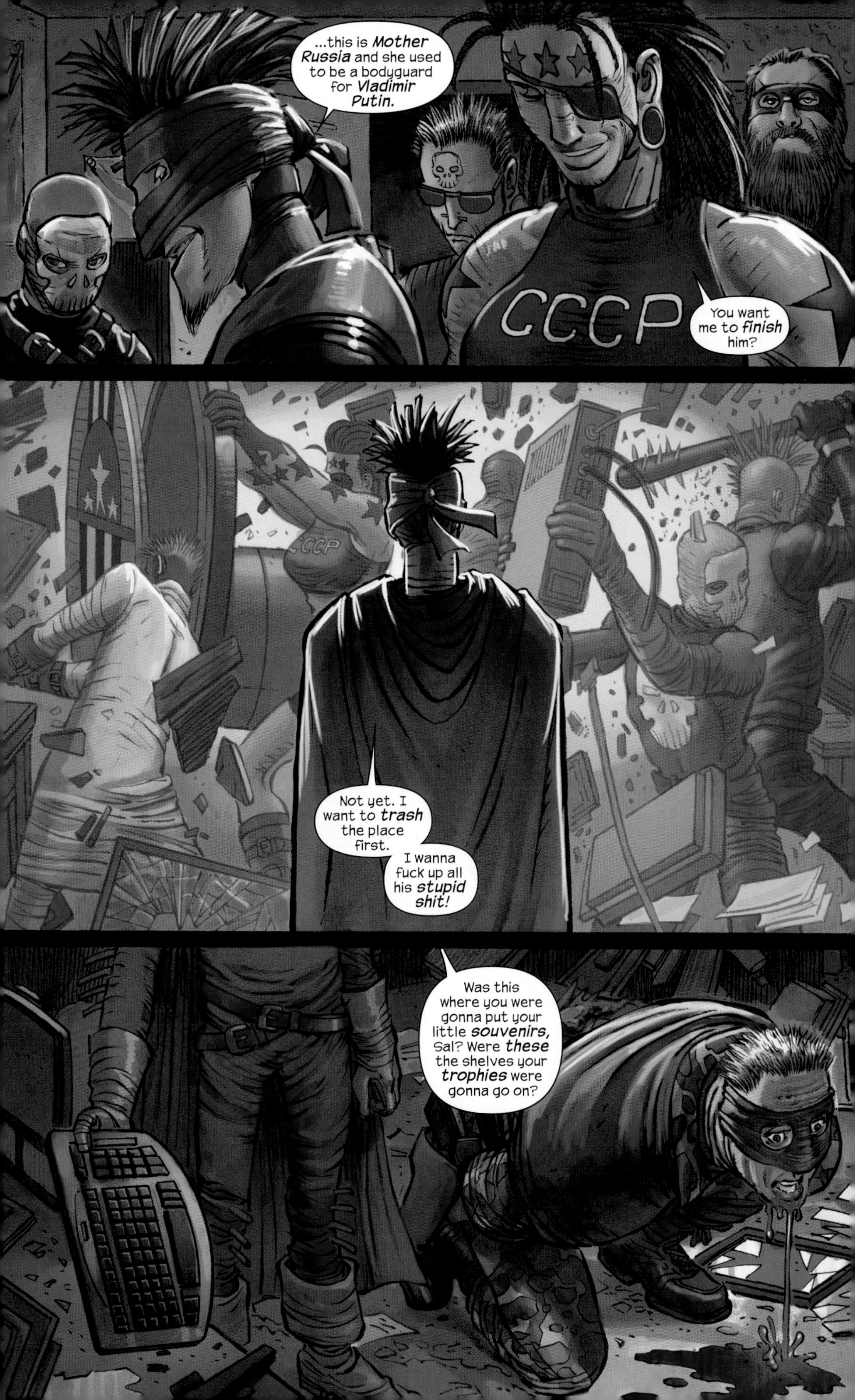
...this is *Mother Russia* and she used to be a bodyguard for *Vladimir Putin.*
CCCP
You want me to *finish* him?
CCCP
Not yet. I want to *trash* the place first.
I wanna fuck up all his *stupid shit!*
Was this where you were gonna put your little *souvenirs,* Sal? Were *these* the shelves your *trophies* were gonna go on?

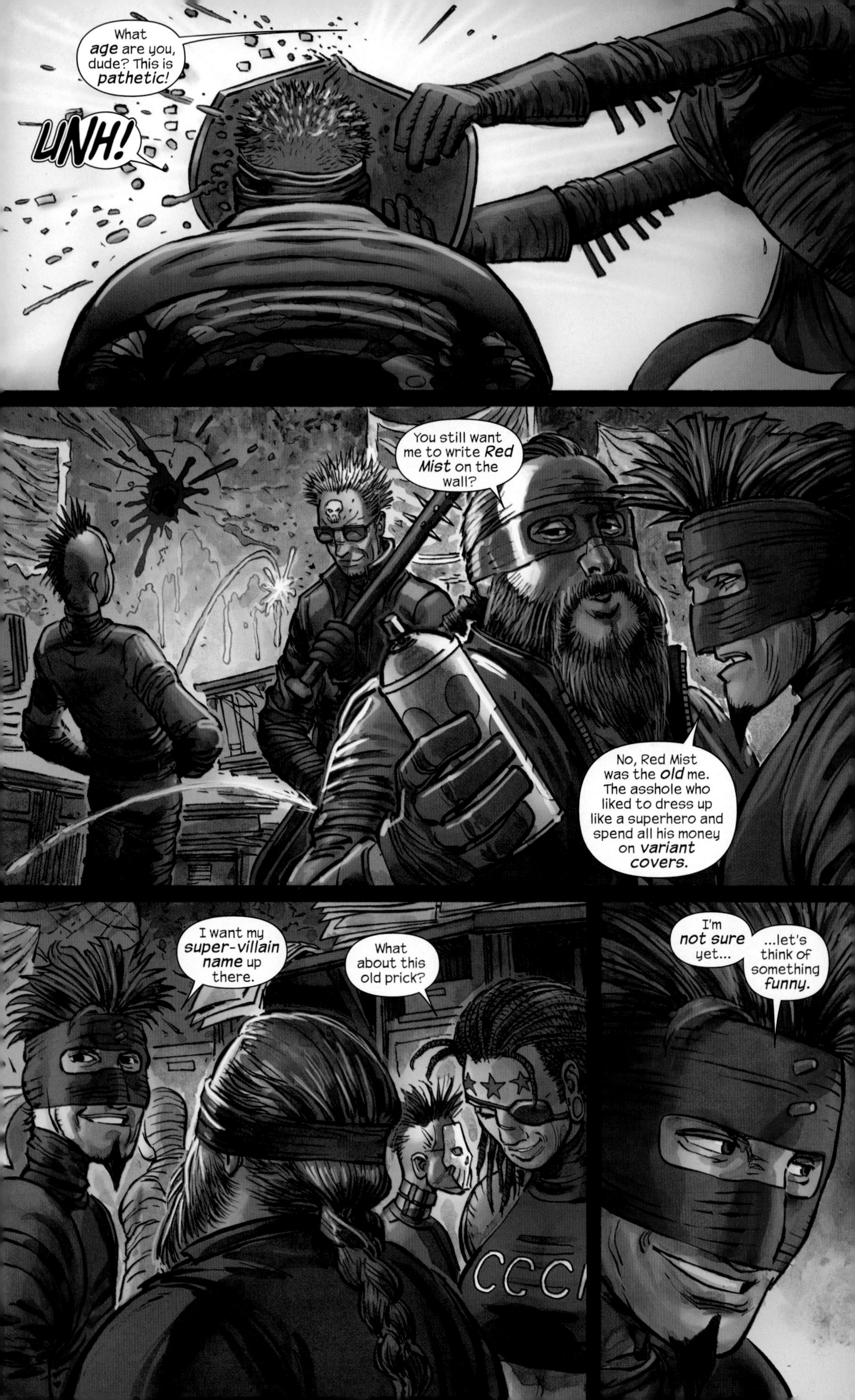
What age are you, dude? This is pathetic!
UNH!
You still want me to write Red Mist on the wall?
No, Red Mist was the old me. The asshole who liked to dress up like a superhero and spend all his money on variant covers.
I want my super-villain name up there.
What about this old prick?
CCCP
I'm not sure yet...
...let's think of something funny.

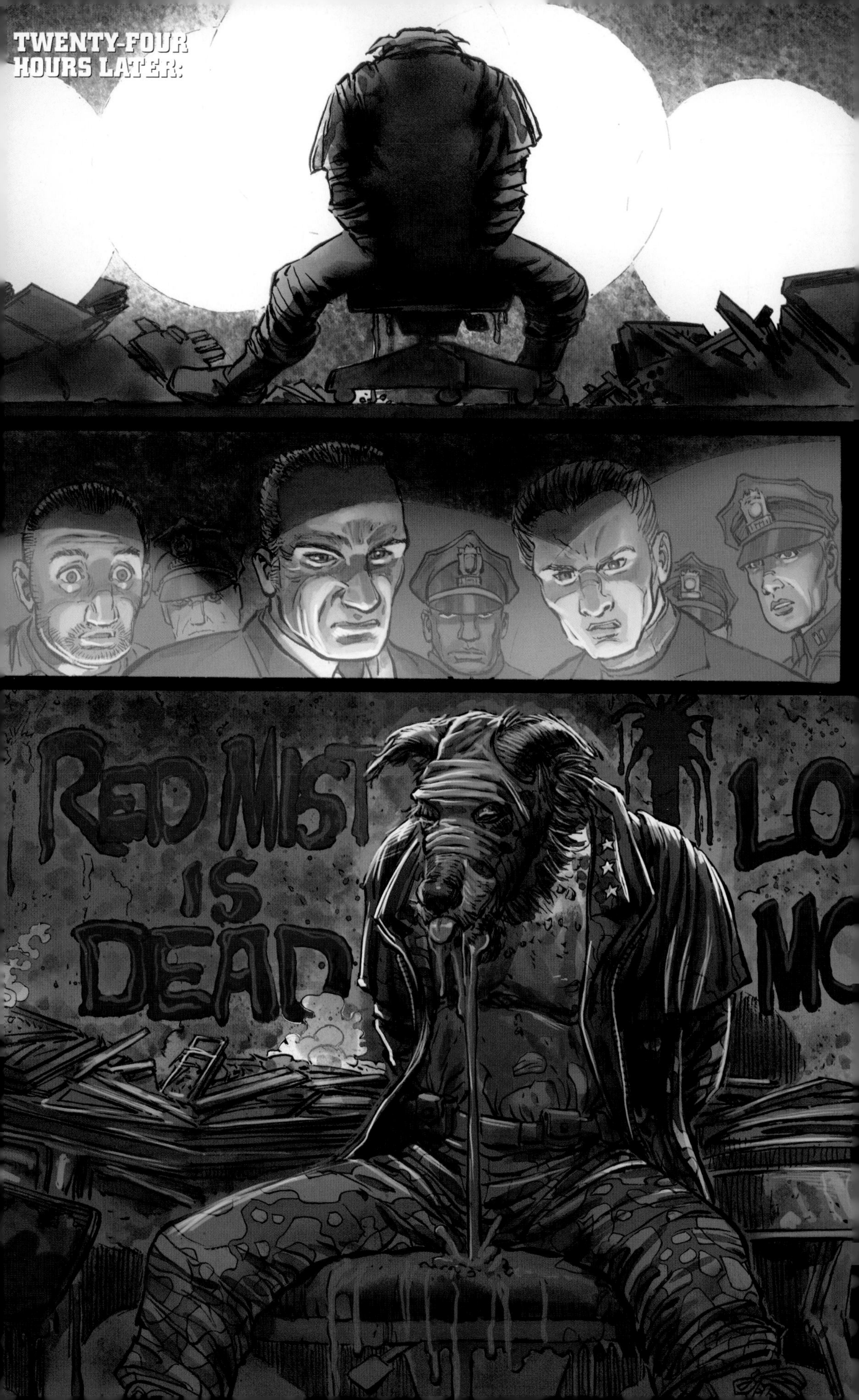
TWENTY-FOUR HOURS LATER:
RED MIST IS DEAD

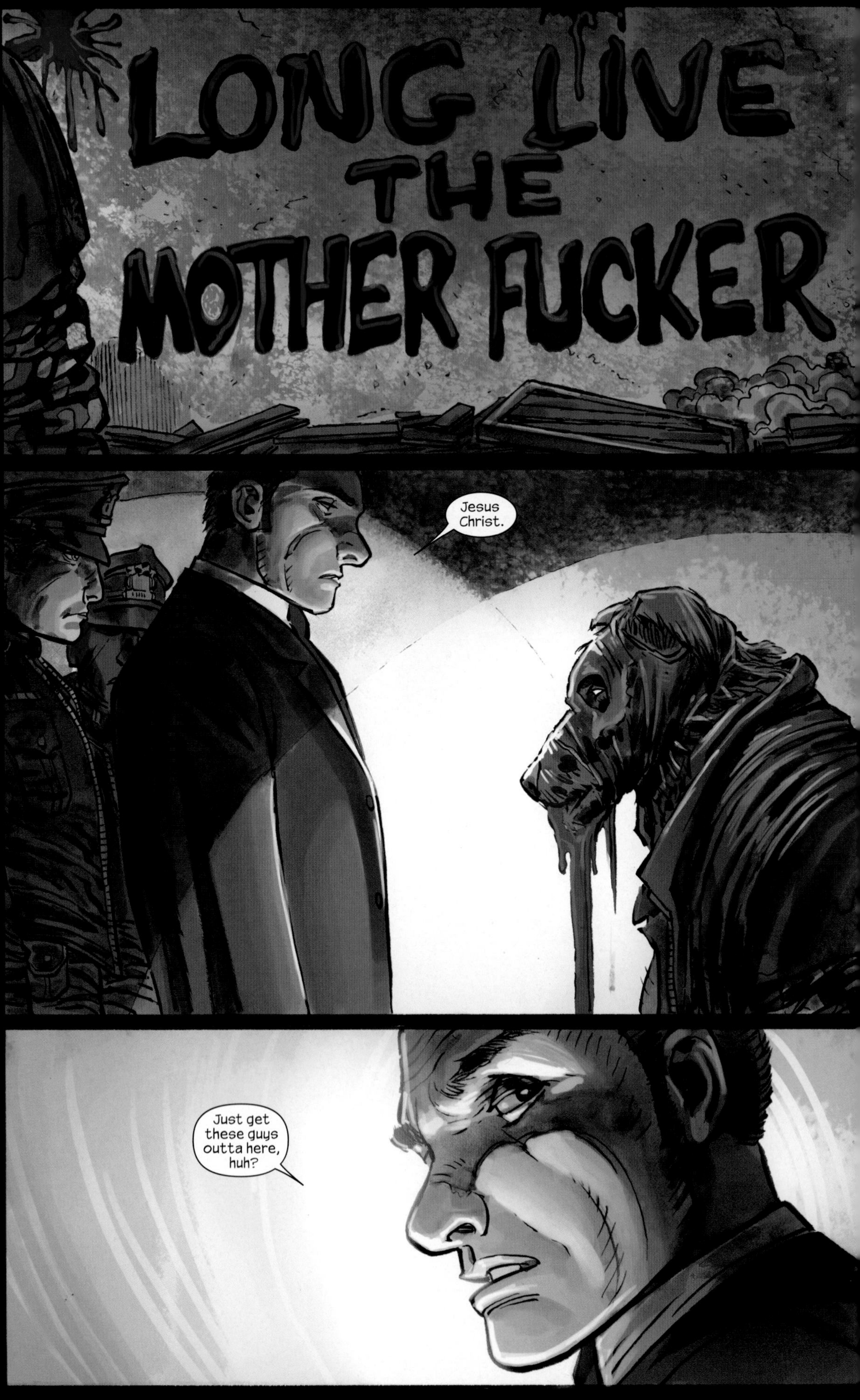
LONG LIVE THE MOTHER FUCKER
Jesus Christ.
Just get these guys outta here, huh?

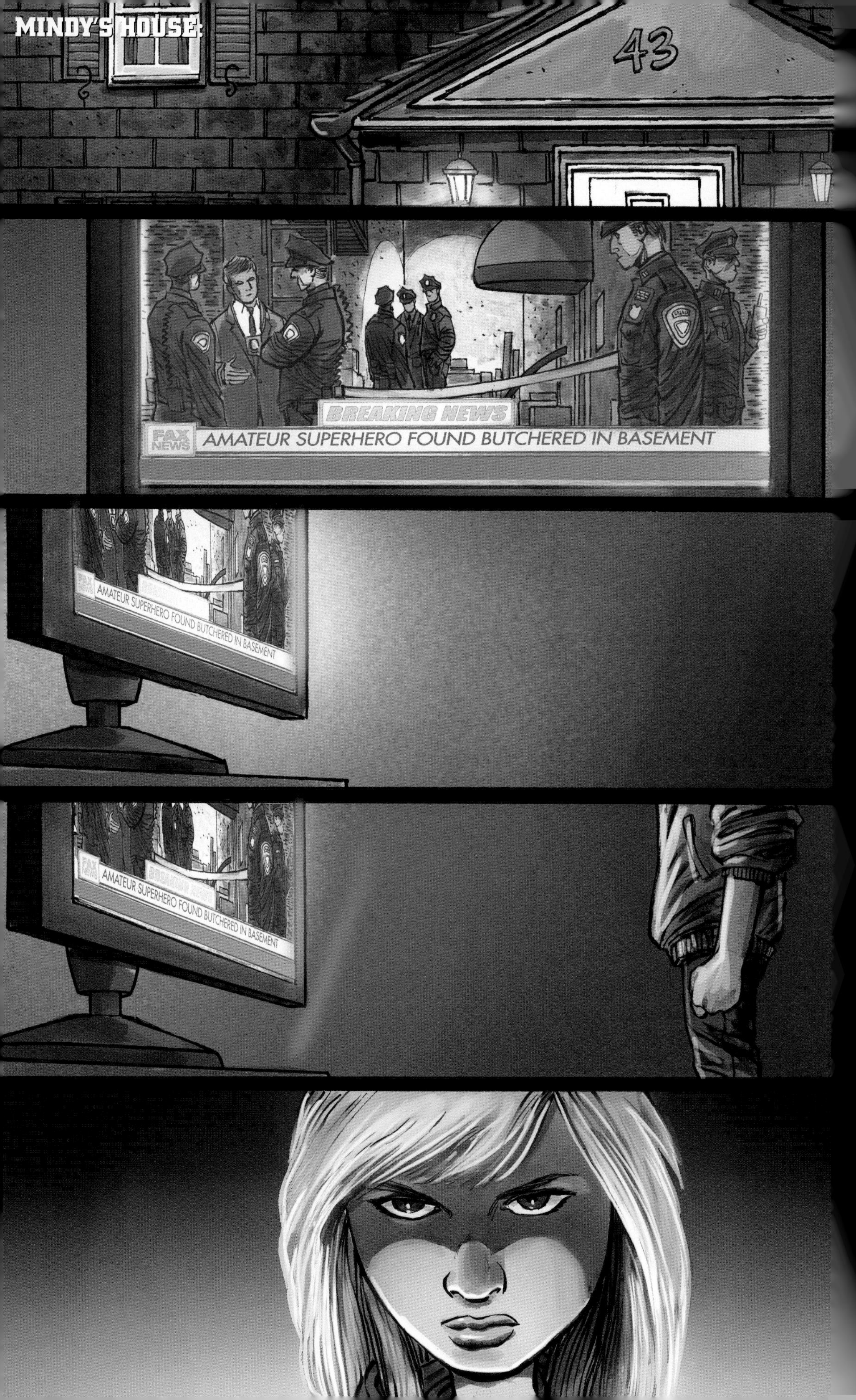
MINDY'S HOUSE:
43
BREAKING NEWS
FAX NEWS
AMATEUR SUPERHERO FOUND BUTCHERED IN BASEMENT
FAX NEWS
AMATEUR SUPERHERO FOUND BUTCHERED IN BASEMENT
AMATEUR SUPERHERO FOUND BUTCHERED IN BASEMENT

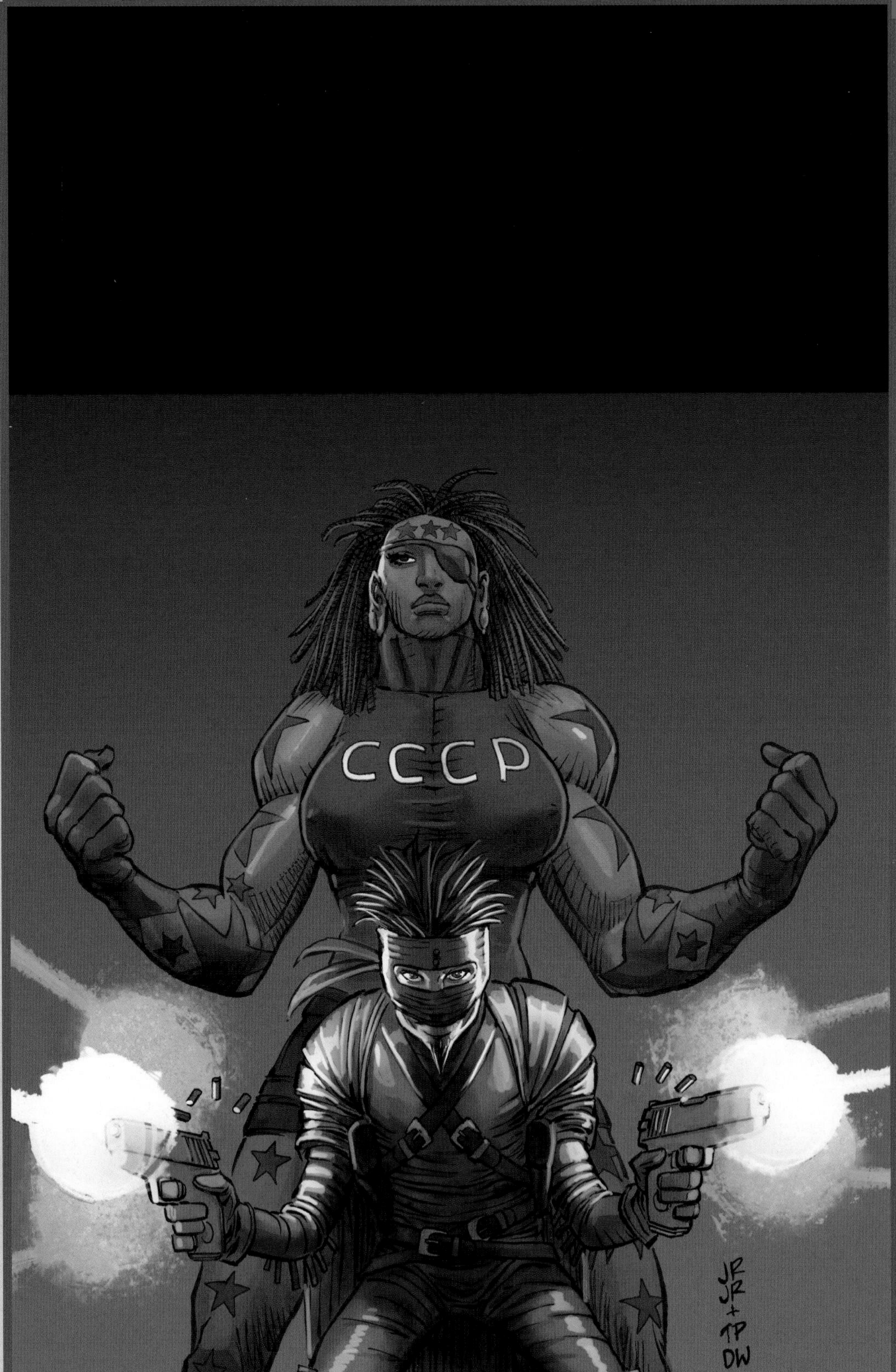
CCCP
JR JR + TP DW

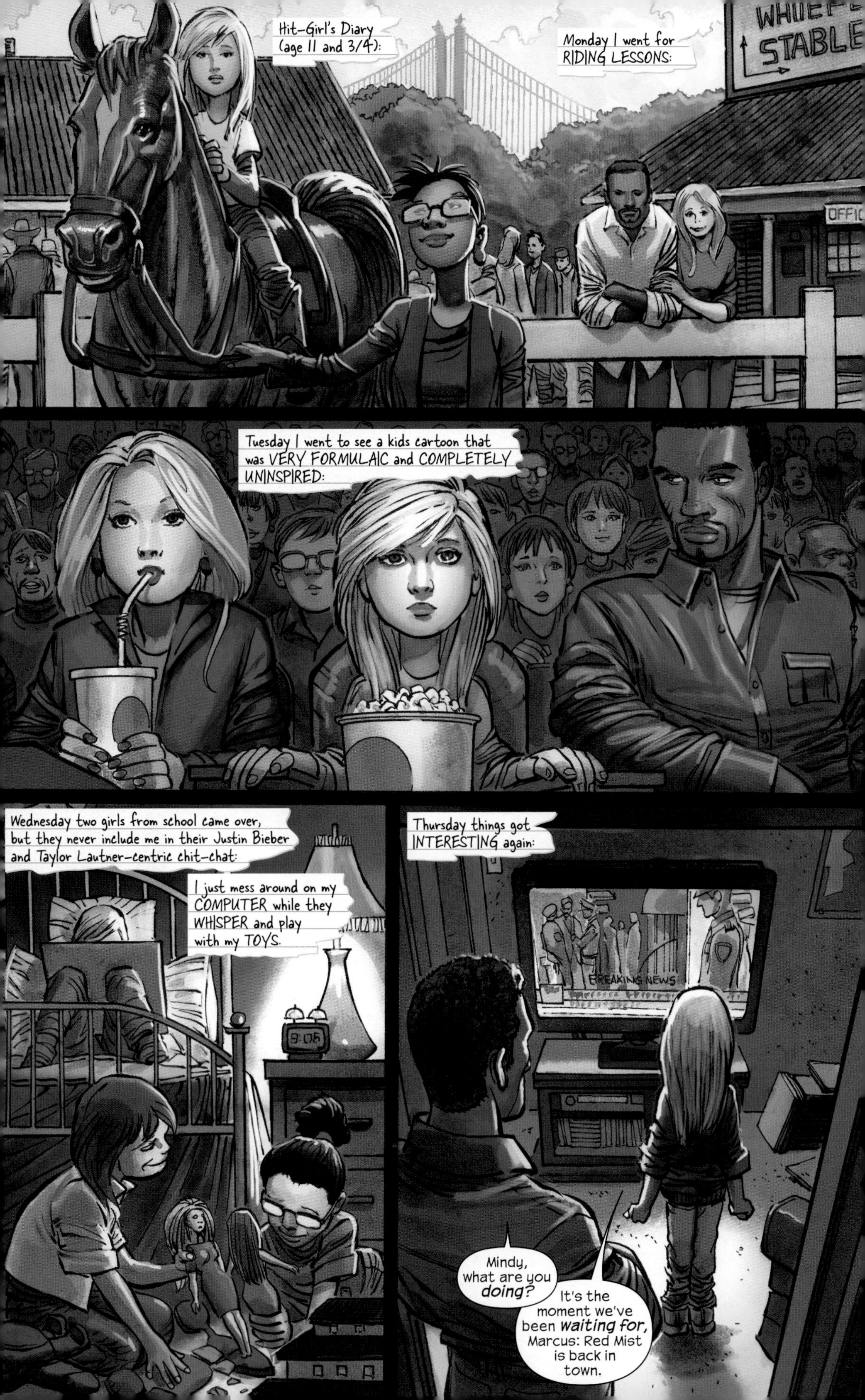
WHEELER STABLE
OFFIC
Hit-Girl's Diary (age 11 and 3/4):
Monday I went for RIDING LESSONS:
Tuesday I went to see a kids cartoon that was VERY FORMULAIC and COMPLETELY UNINSPIRED:
Wednesday two girls from school came over, but they never include me in their Justin Bieber and Taylor Lautner-centric chit-chat:
I just mess around on my COMPUTER while they WHISPER and play with my TOYS.
9:05
Thursday things got INTERESTING again:
BREAKING NEWS
Mindy, what are you doing?
It's the moment we've been waiting for, Marcus: Red Mist is back in town.

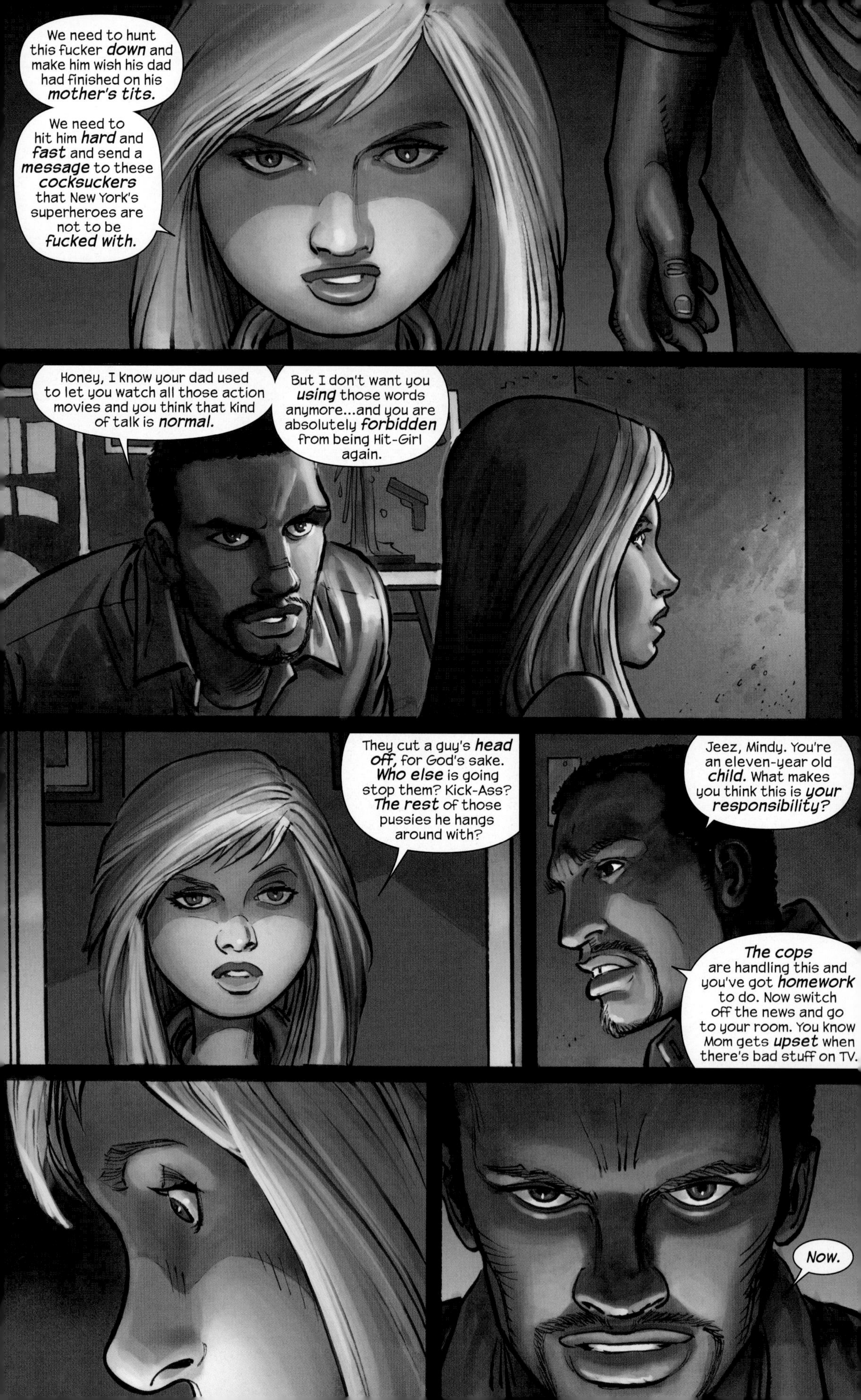
We need to hunt this fucker down and make him wish his dad had finished on his mother's tits.
We need to hit him hard and fast and send a message to these cocksuckers that New York's superheroes are not to be fucked with.
Honey, I know your dad used to let you watch all those action movies and you think that kind of talk is normal.
But I don't want you using those words anymore...and you are absolutely forbidden from being Hit-Girl again.
They cut a guy's head off, for God's sake. Who else is going stop them? Kick-Ass? The rest of those pussies he hangs around with?
Jeez, Mindy. You're an eleven-year old child. What makes you think this is your responsibility?
The cops are handling this and you've got homework to do. Now switch off the news and go to your room. You know Mom gets upset when there's bad stuff on TV.
Now.

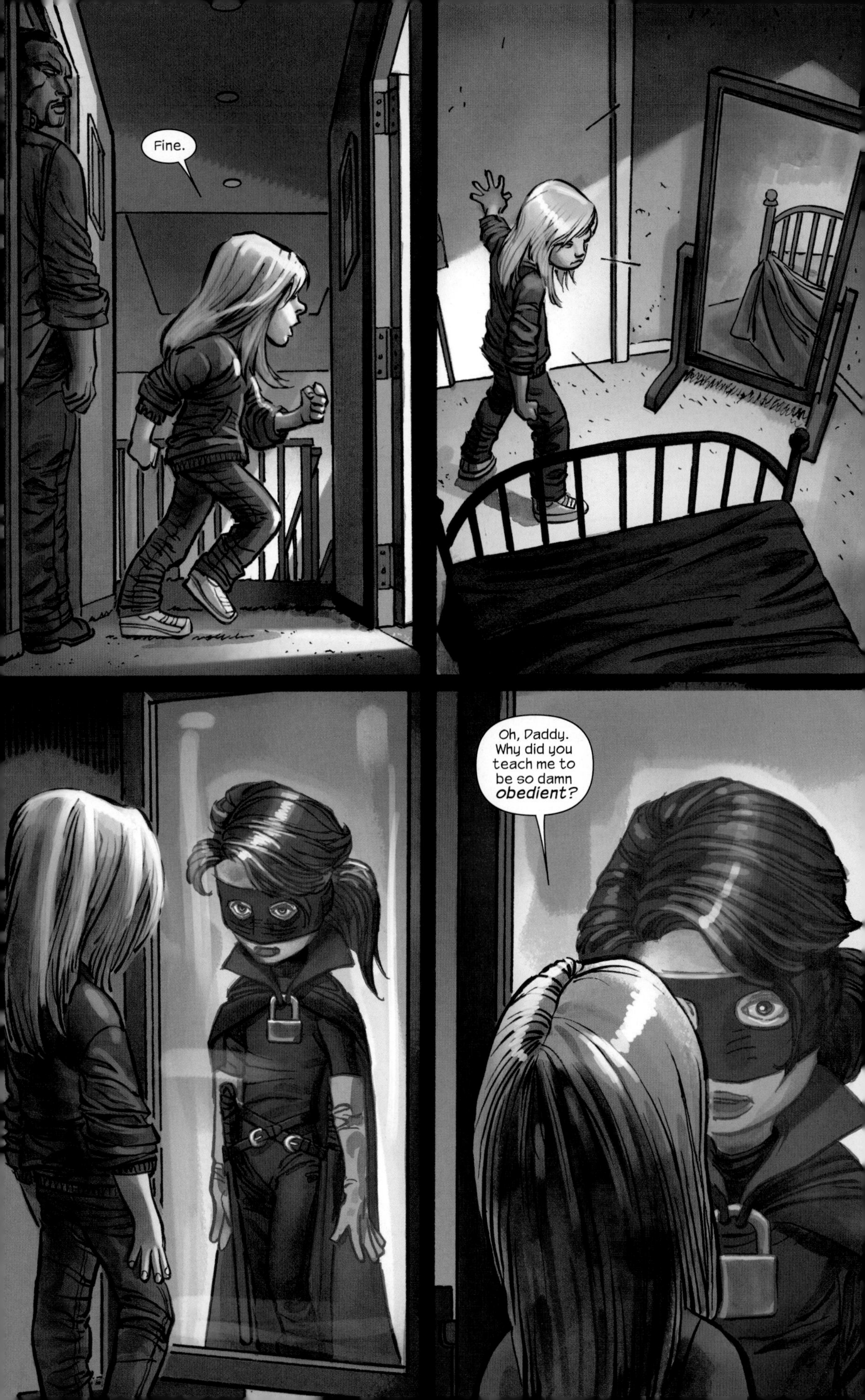
Fine.
Oh, Daddy. Why did you teach me to be so damn *obedient*?

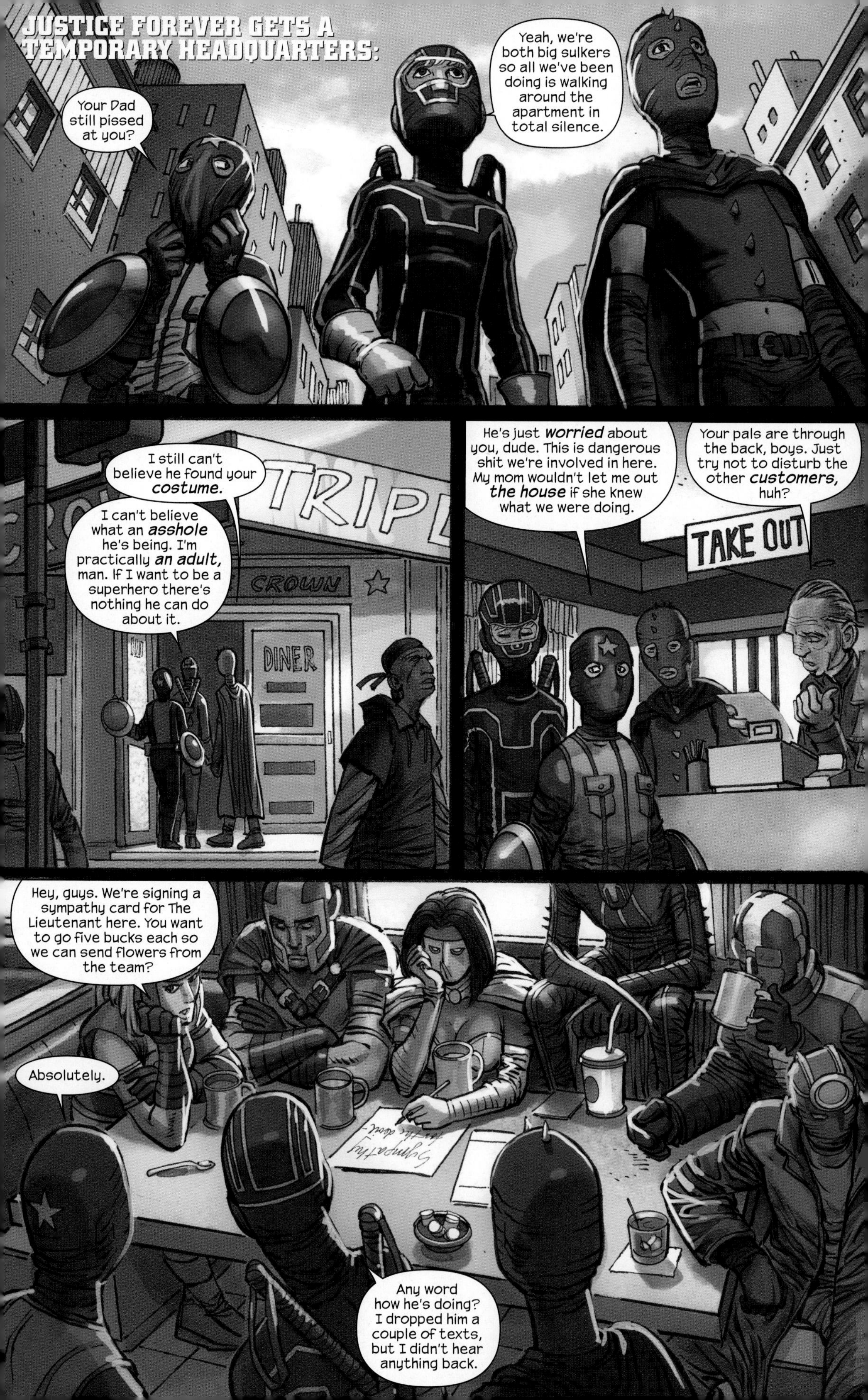
JUSTICE FOREVER GETS A TEMPORARY HEADQUARTERS:
Your Dad still pissed at you?
Yeah, we're both big sulkers so all we've been doing is walking around the apartment in total silence.
I still can't believe he found your costume.
I can't believe what an asshole he's being. I'm practically an adult, man. If I want to be a superhero there's nothing he can do about it.
TRIPL
CROWN
DINER
He's just worried about you, dude. This is dangerous shit we're involved in here. My mom wouldn't let me out the house if she knew what we were doing.
Your pals are through the back, boys. Just try not to disturb the other customers, huh?
TAKE OUT
Hey, guys. We're signing a sympathy card for The Lieutenant here. You want to go five bucks each so we can send flowers from the team?
Absolutely.
Any word how he's doing? I dropped him a couple of texts, but I didn't hear anything back.

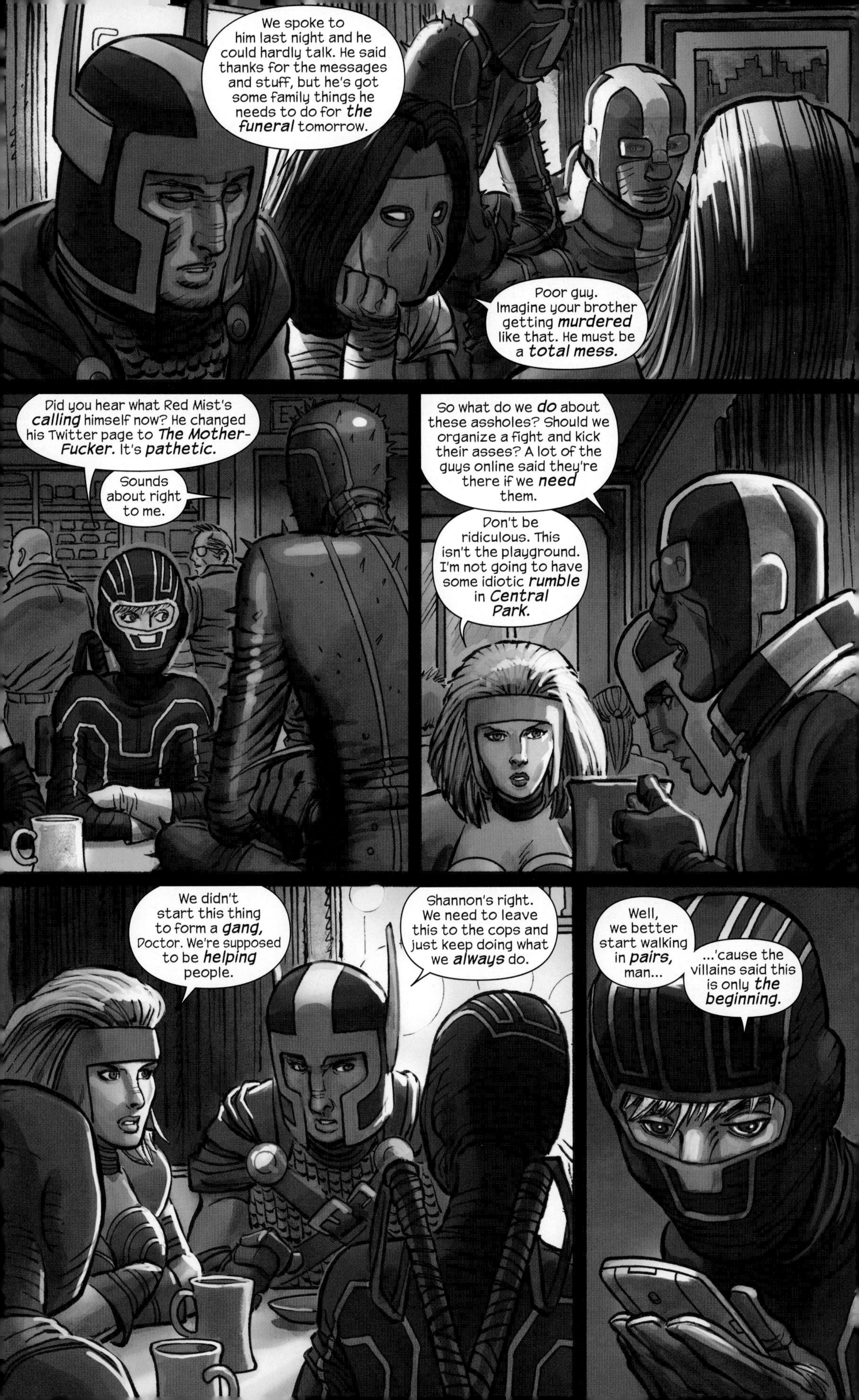
We spoke to him last night and he could hardly talk. He said thanks for the messages and stuff, but he's got some family things he needs to do for the funeral tomorrow.
Poor guy. Imagine your brother getting murdered like that. He must be a total mess.
Did you hear what Red Mist's calling himself now? He changed his Twitter page to The Mother-Fucker. It's pathetic.
Sounds about right to me.
So what do we do about these assholes? Should we organize a fight and kick their asses? A lot of the guys online said they're there if we need them.
Don't be ridiculous. This isn't the playground. I'm not going to have some idiotic rumble in Central Park.
We didn't start this thing to form a gang, Doctor. We're supposed to be helping people.
Shannon's right. We need to leave this to the cops and just keep doing what we always do.
Well, we better start walking in pairs, man...
...'cause the villains said this is only the beginning.

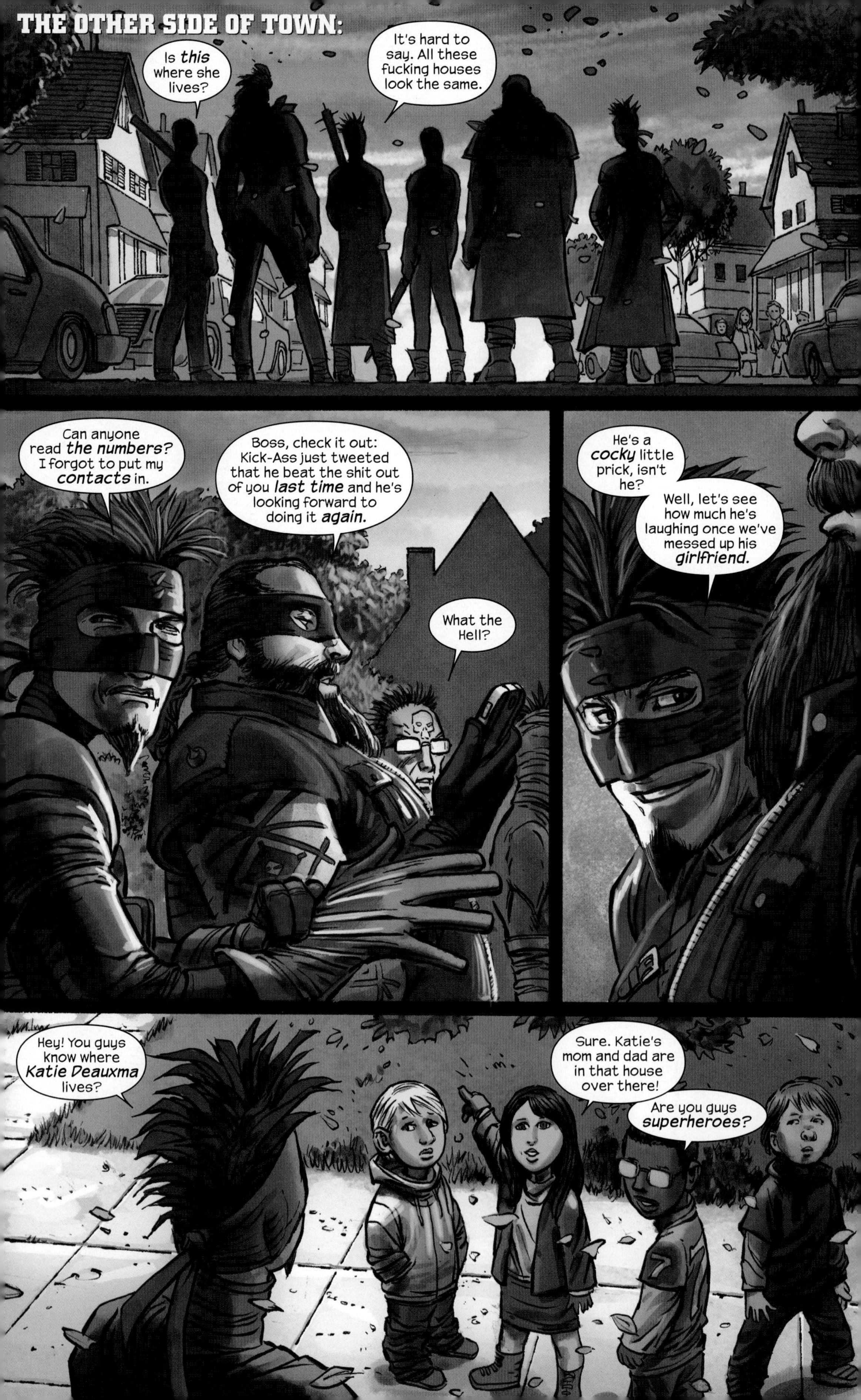
THE OTHER SIDE OF TOWN:
Is this where she lives?
It's hard to say. All these fucking houses look the same.
Can anyone read the numbers? I forgot to put my contacts in.
Boss, check it out: Kick-Ass just tweeted that he beat the shit out of you last time and he's looking forward to doing it again.
What the Hell?
He's a cocky little prick, isn't he?
Well, let's see how much he's laughing once we've messed up his girlfriend.
Hey! You guys know where Katie Deauxma lives?
Sure. Katie's mom and dad are in that house over there!
Are you guys superheroes?

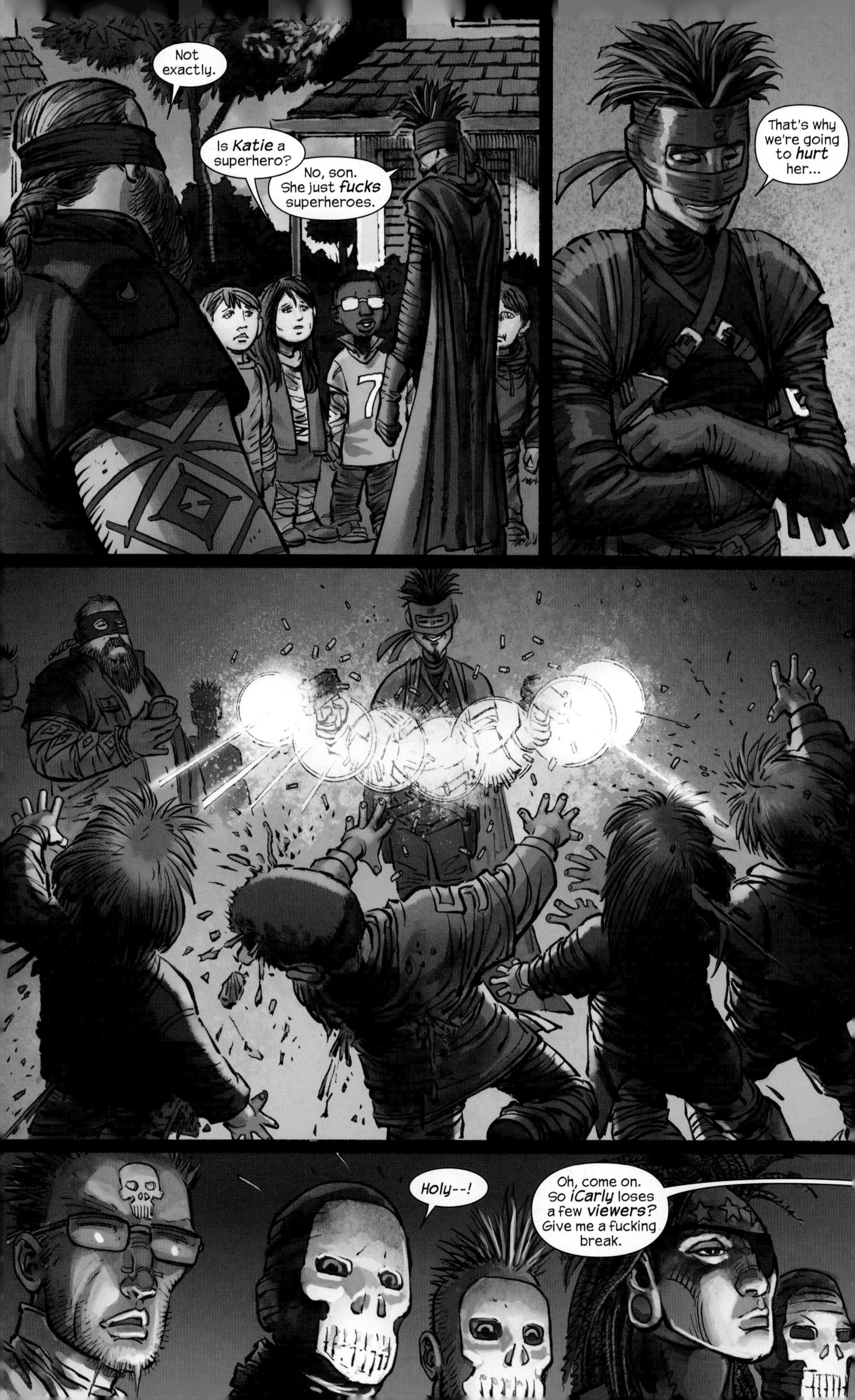
Not exactly.
Is Katie a superhero?
No, son. She just fucks superheroes.
That's why we're going to hurt her...
Holy--!
Oh, come on. So iCarly loses a few viewers? Give me a fucking break.

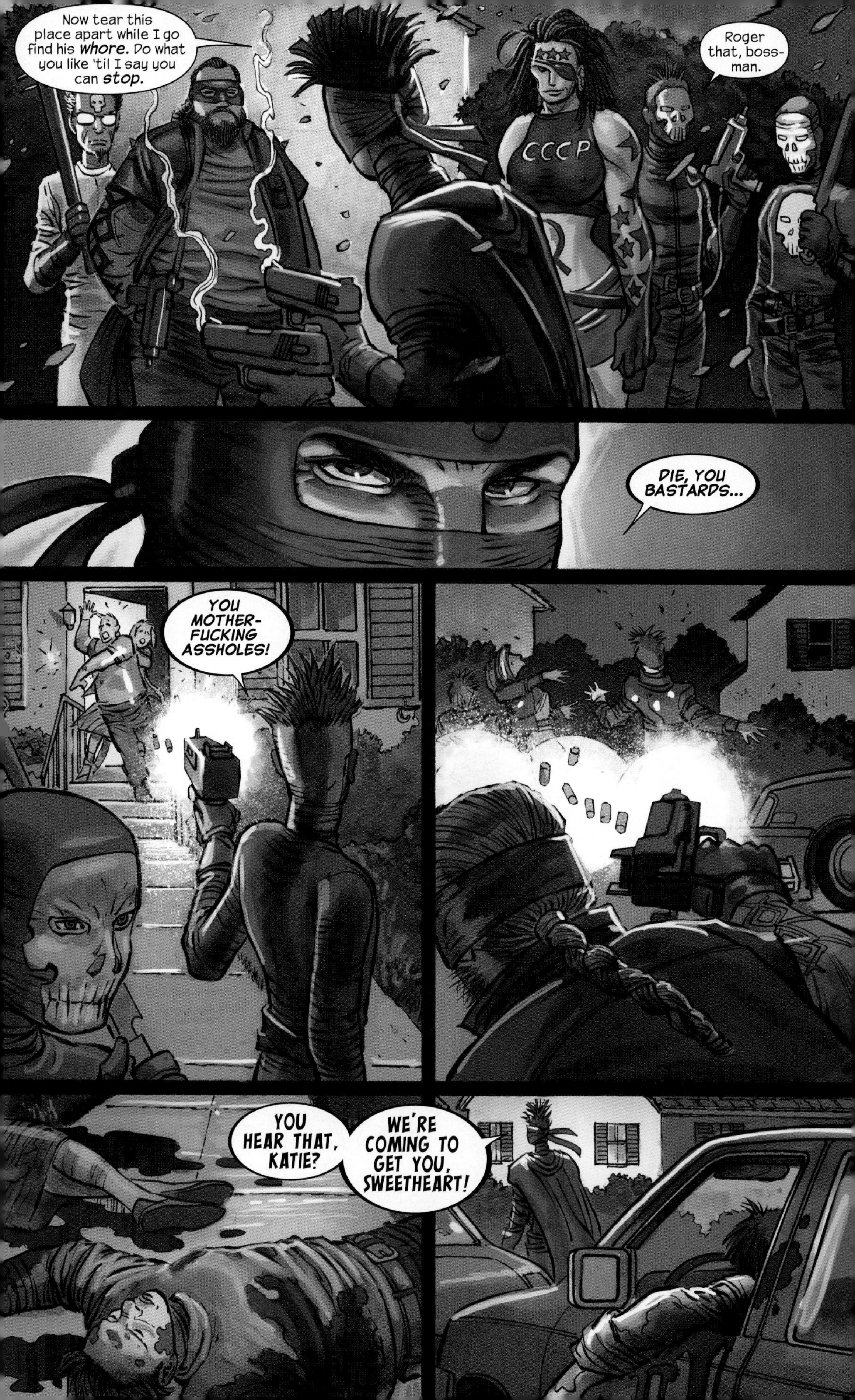
Now tear this place apart while I go find his whore. Do what you like 'til I say you can stop.
Roger that, boss-man.
DIE, YOU BASTARDS...
YOU MOTHER-FUCKING ASSHOLES!
YOU HEAR THAT, KATIE?
WE'RE COMING TO GET YOU, SWEETHEART!

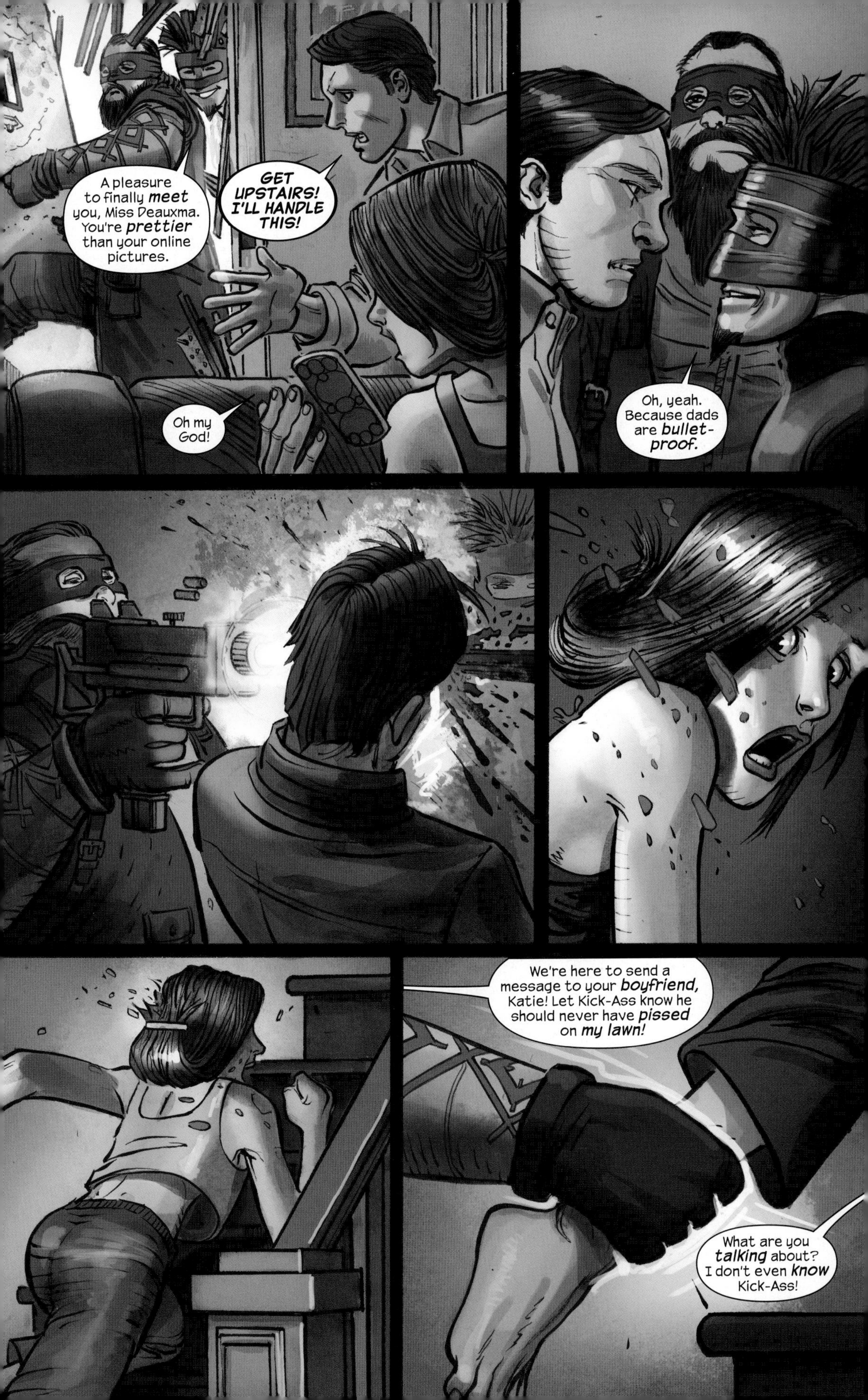
A pleasure to finally meet you, Miss Deauxma. You're prettier than your online pictures.
GET UPSTAIRS! I'LL HANDLE THIS!
Oh my God!
Oh, yeah. Because dads are bullet-proof.
We're here to send a message to your boyfriend, Katie! Let Kick-Ass know he should never have pissed on my lawn!
What are you talking about? I don't even know Kick-Ass!

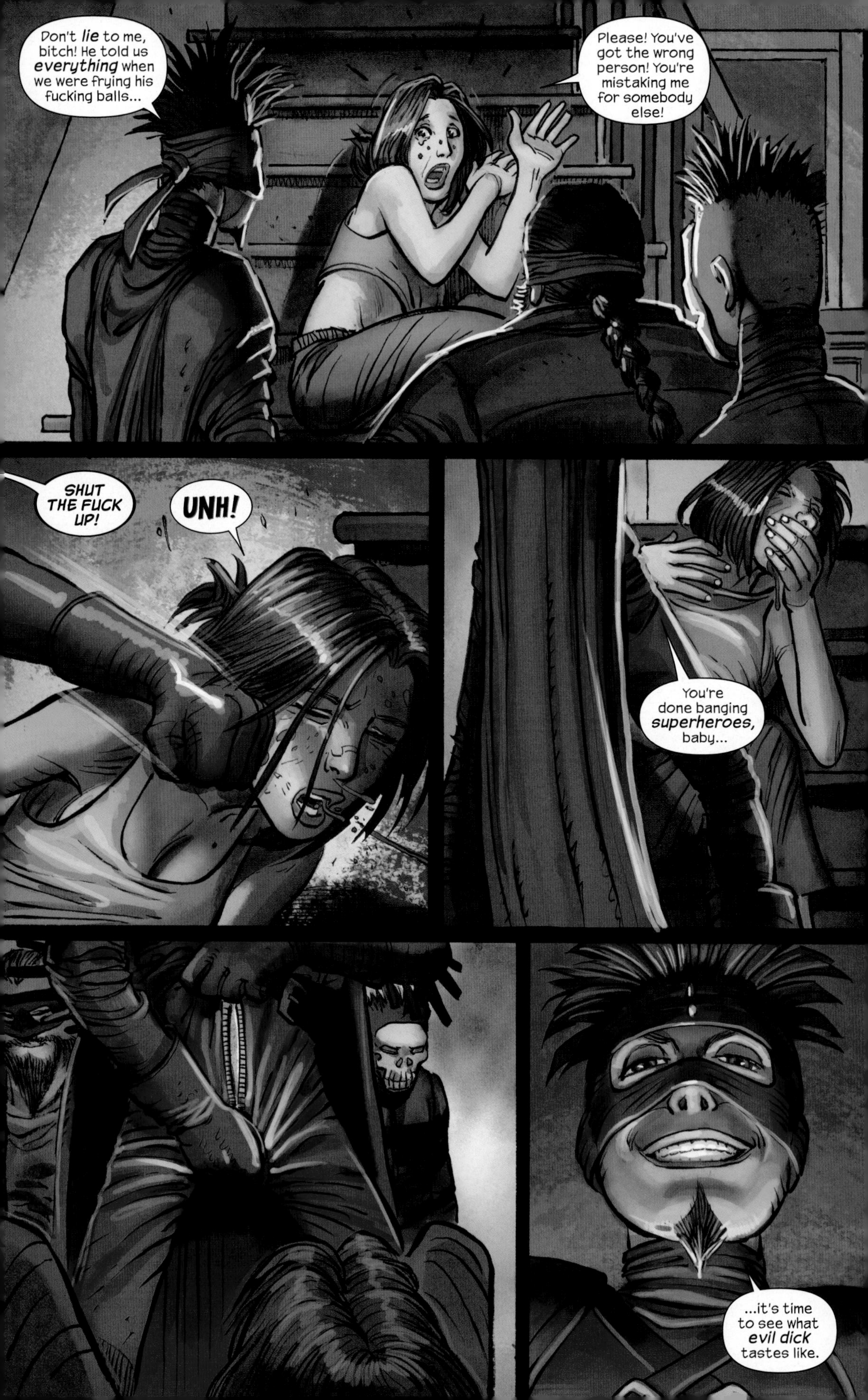
Don't *lie* to me, bitch! He told us ***everything*** when we were frying his fucking balls...
Please! You've got the wrong person! You're mistaking me for somebody else!
SHUT THE FUCK UP!
UNH!
You're done banging ***superheroes,*** baby...
...it's time to see what ***evil dick*** tastes like.

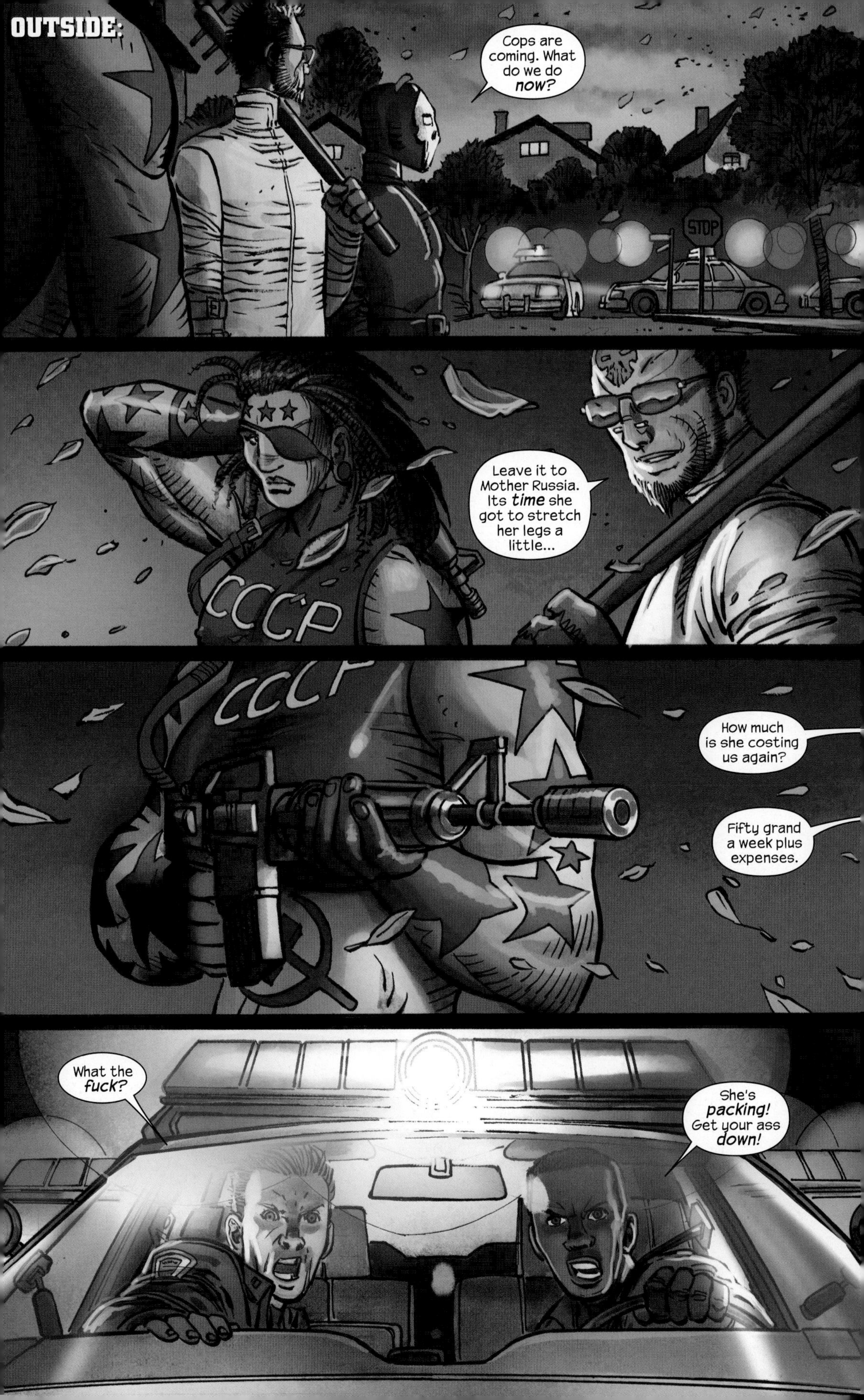
OUTSIDE:
Cops are coming. What do we do *now?*
Leave it to Mother Russia. Its *time* she got to stretch her legs a little...
How much is she costing us again?
Fifty grand a week plus expenses.
What the *fuck?*
She's *packing!* Get your ass *down!*

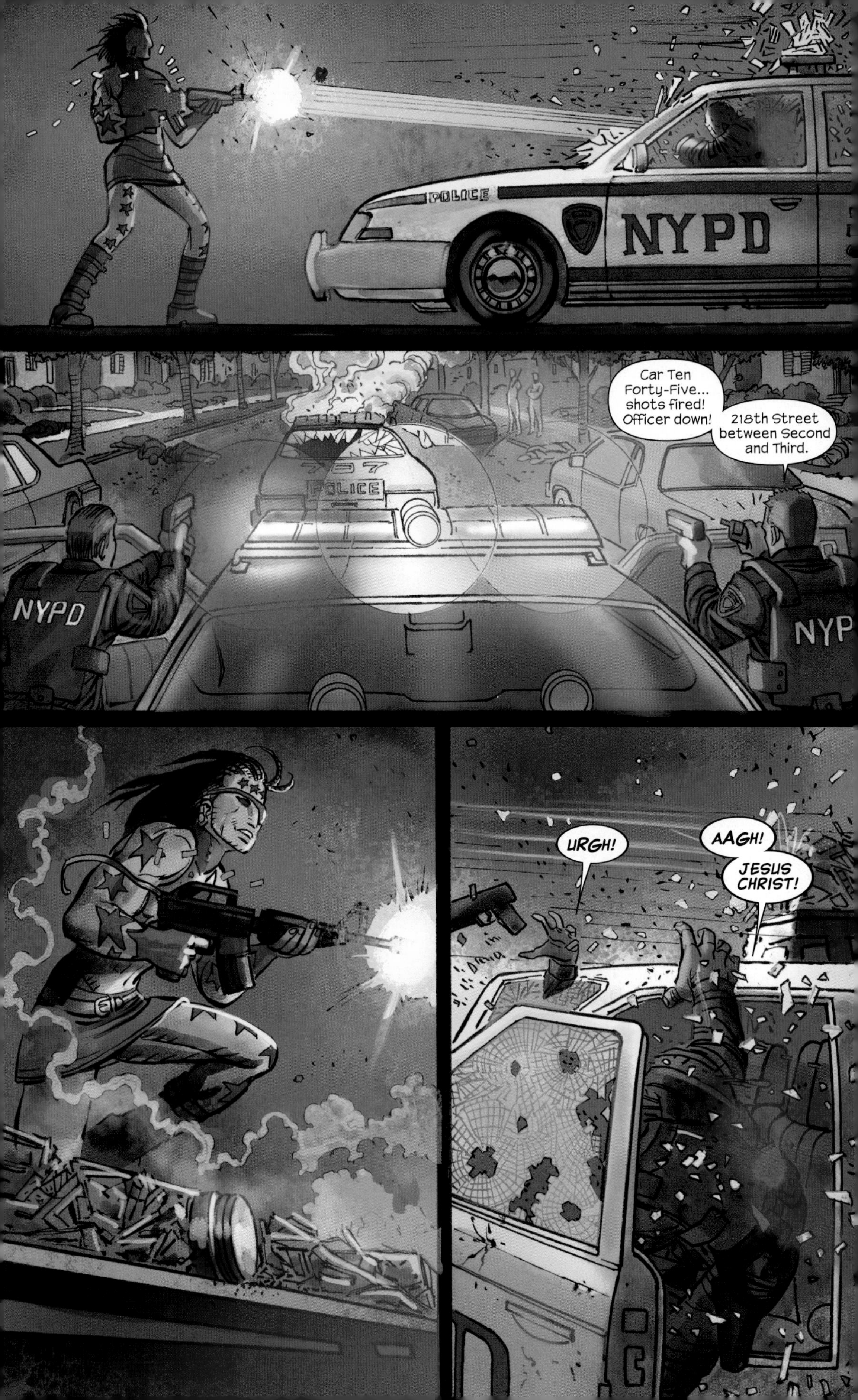
POLICE
NYPD
POLICE
NYPD
NYP
Car Ten Forty-Five... shots fired! Officer down!
218th Street between Second and Third.
URGH!
AAGH!
JESUS CHRIST!

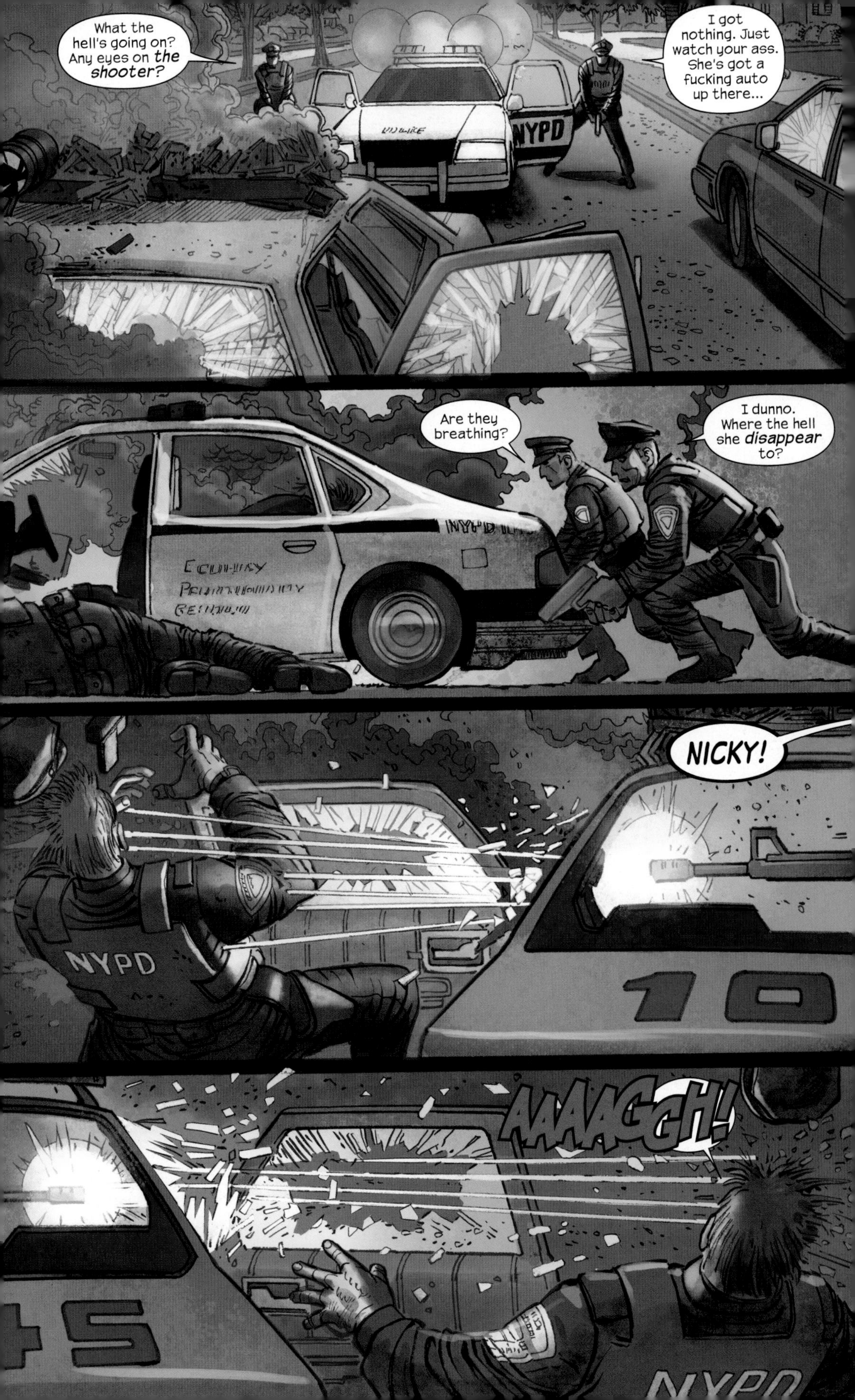
What the hell's going on? Any eyes on *the shooter?*
I got nothing. Just watch your ass. She's got a fucking auto up there...
NYPD
Are they breathing?
I dunno. Where the hell she *disappear* to?
NYPD
NICKY!
NYPD
10
AAAAGGH!
45
NYPD

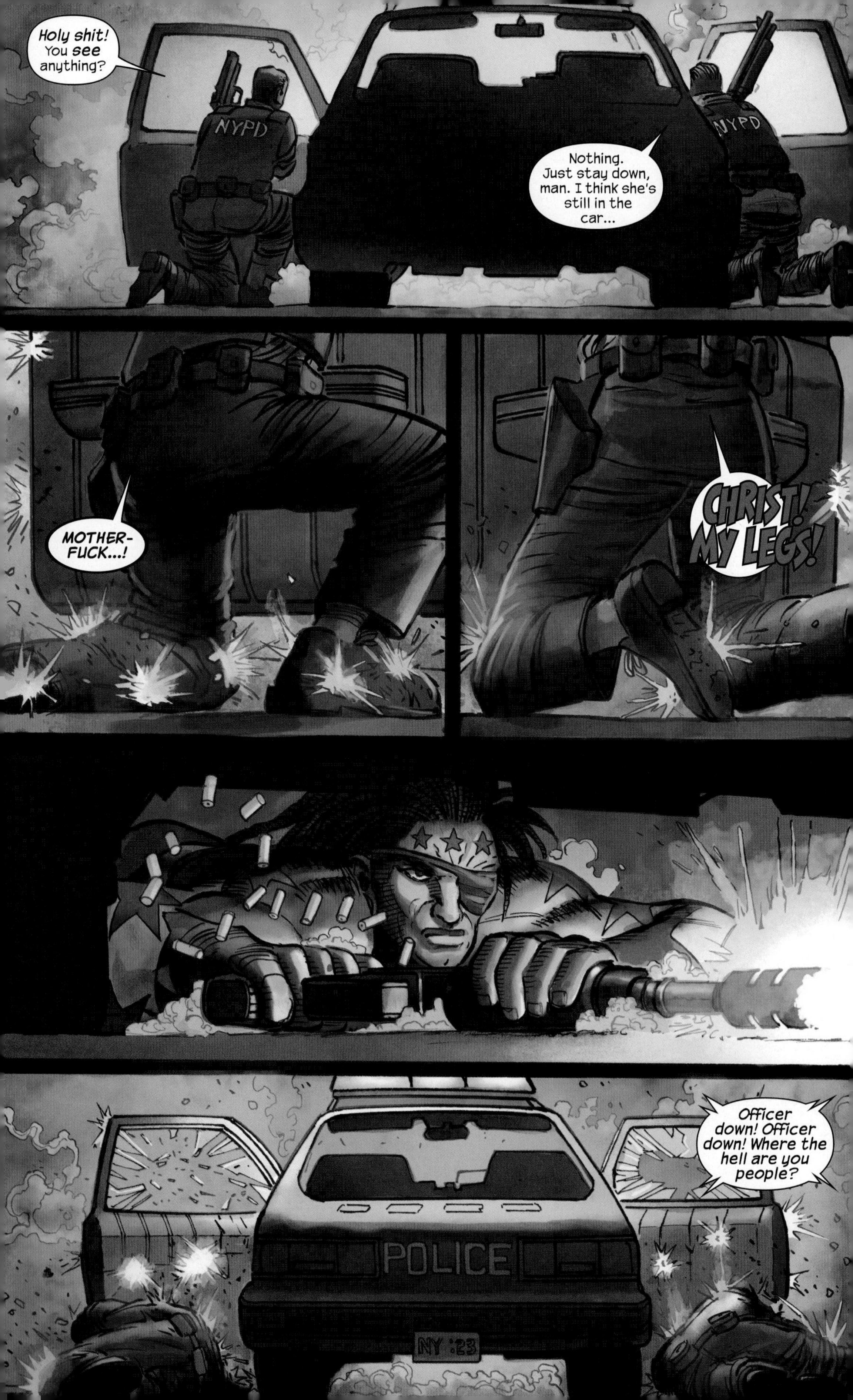
Holy shit! You see anything?
Nothing. Just stay down, man. I think she's still in the car...
MOTHER-FUCK...!
CHRIST! MY LEGS!
Officer down! Officer down! Where the hell are you people?
POLICE
NY 23

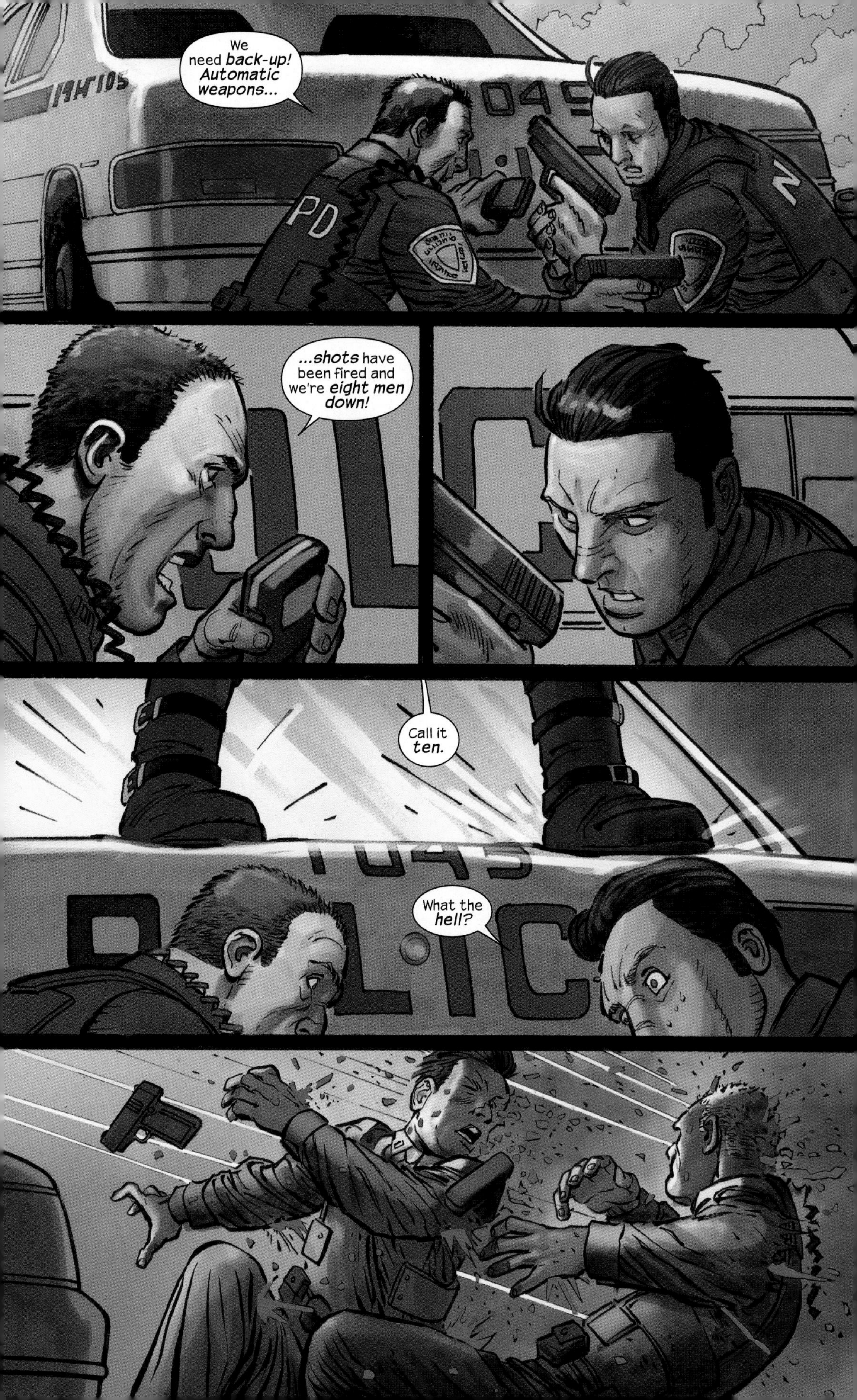
We need back-up! Automatic weapons...
...shots have been fired and we're eight men down!
Call it ten.
What the hell?

Wow! What a friggin' *mess!*

Where the hell did they *go?* How can a gang just *disappear?*

All they have to do is take off their *masks,* Tom. Who's going to recognize them once they're back in their *street-clothes?*

Hospital's saying twenty-seven *dead* and over eighty *injured.* What the hell is *going on* out there?

I'll tell you what's going on: us closing these goddamn freaks *down.*

The Feds have traced the IP addresses from all their Facebook and Twitter accounts. We've got *five hundred men* hitting these nuts all at the *same time.*

125117

DETAIN LIST

Why's Kick-Ass on the list? That crew he's running with isn't a part of this shit.

Just get out there and *nail* these punks, huh? I want everyone with *tights* in their closet in here for *questioning.*

Oh, yeah? Well, I wouldn't be so sure, Marcus. His *old best friend* was a superhero too and now he's shooting *toddlers* in the face.

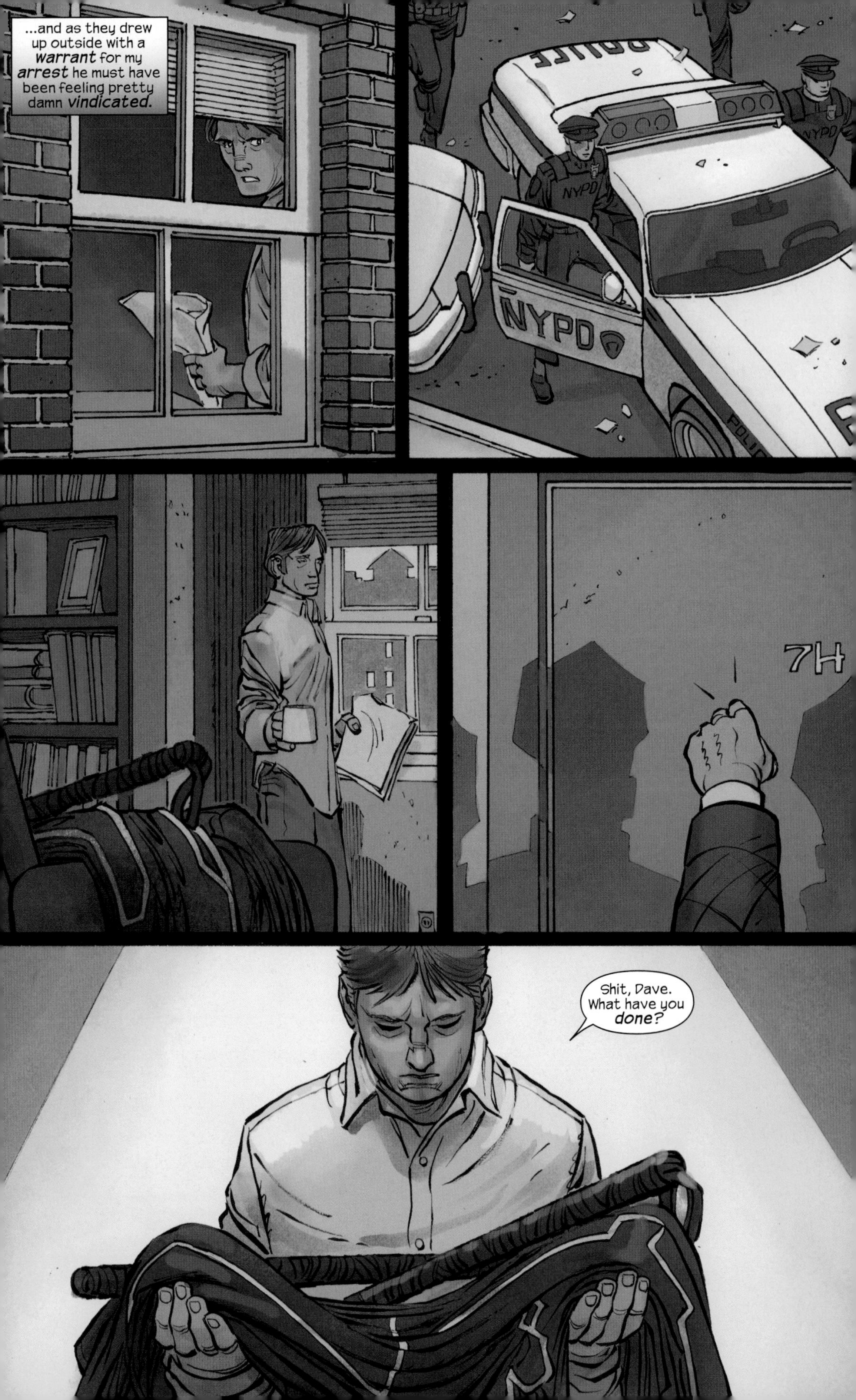
...and as they drew up outside with a warrant for my arrest he must have been feeling pretty damn vindicated.
NYPD
NYPD
POLICE
NYPD
7H
Shit, Dave. What have you done?

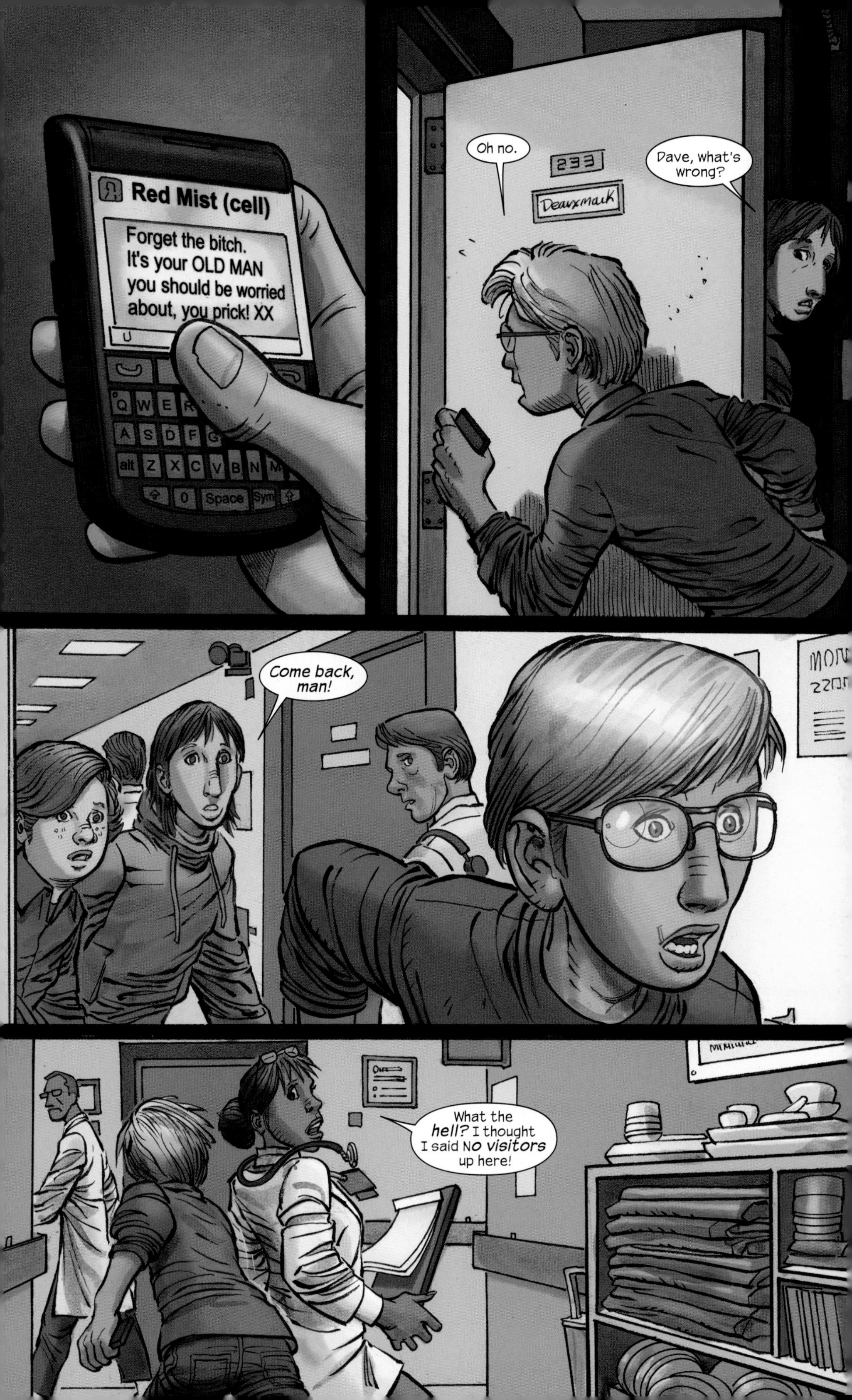
Red Mist (cell)
Forget the bitch. It's your OLD MAN you should be worried about, you prick! XX
Oh no.
233
Deauxmauk
Dave, what's wrong?
Come back, man!
What the *hell?* I thought I said N*o visitors* up here!

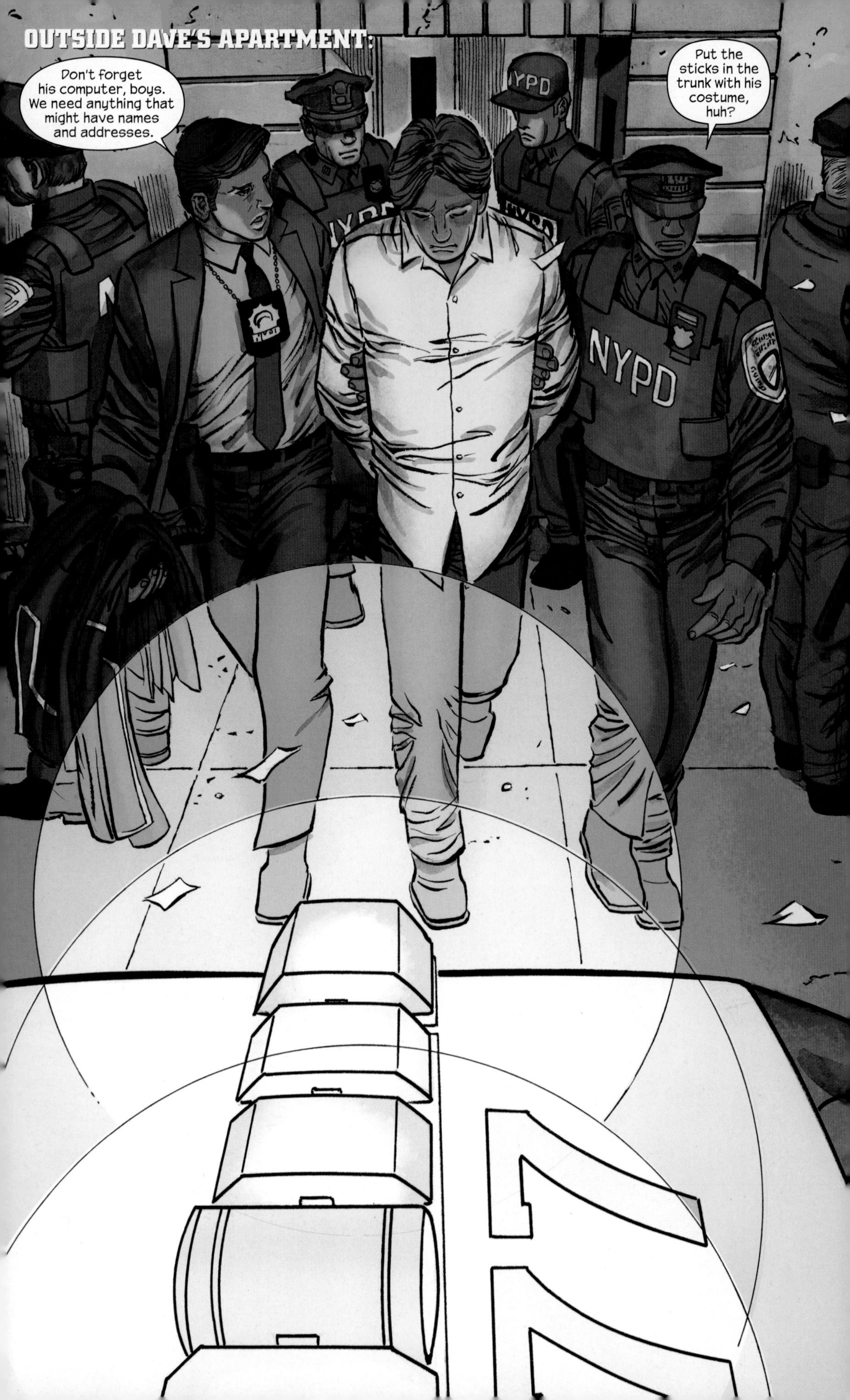
OUTSIDE DAVE'S APARTMENT:
Don't forget his computer, boys. We need anything that might have names and addresses.
Put the sticks in the trunk with his costume, huh?
NYPD
NYPD
NYPD
NYPD

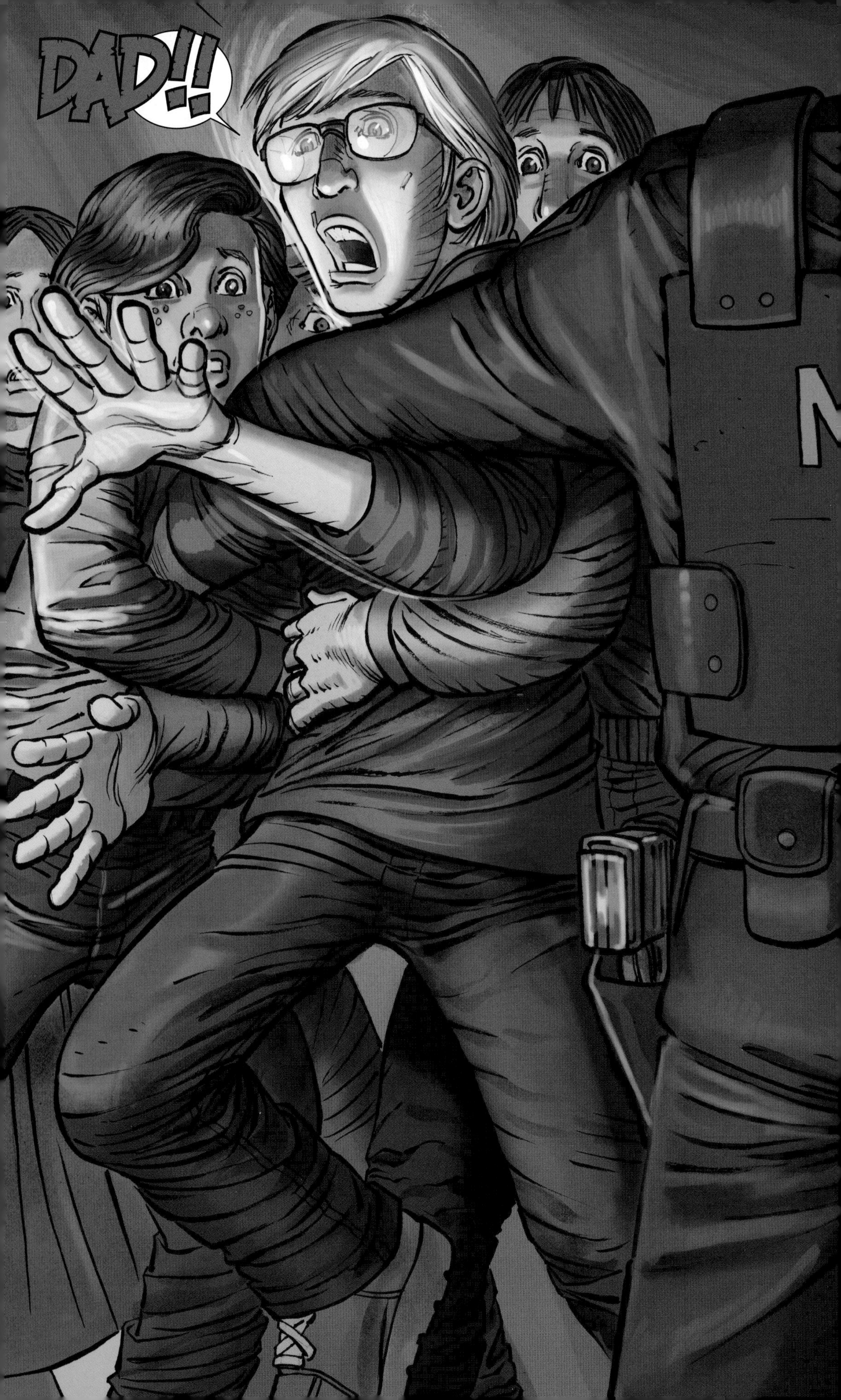
DAD!!!

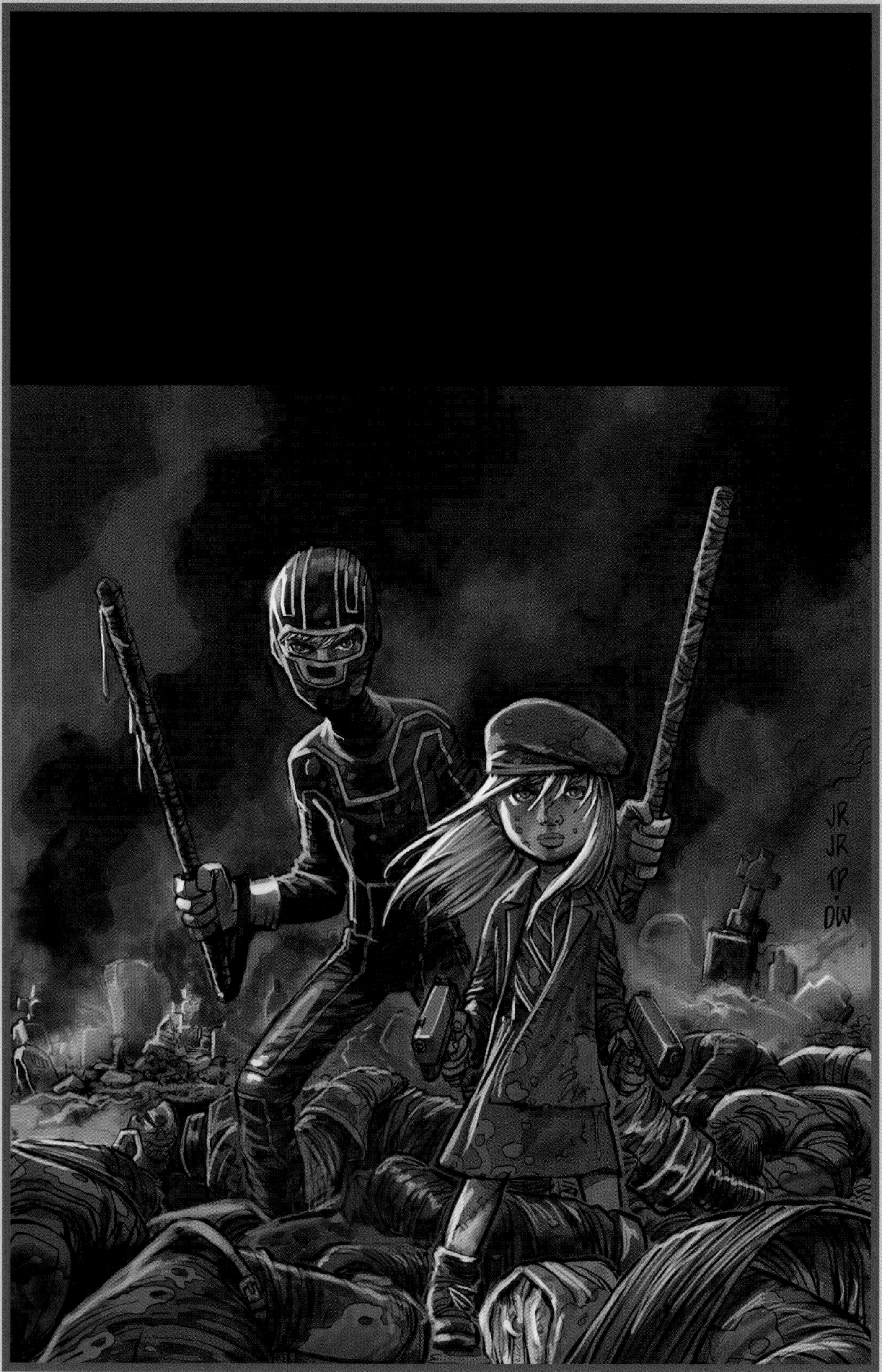
JR JR TP DW

RIKERS ISLAND:

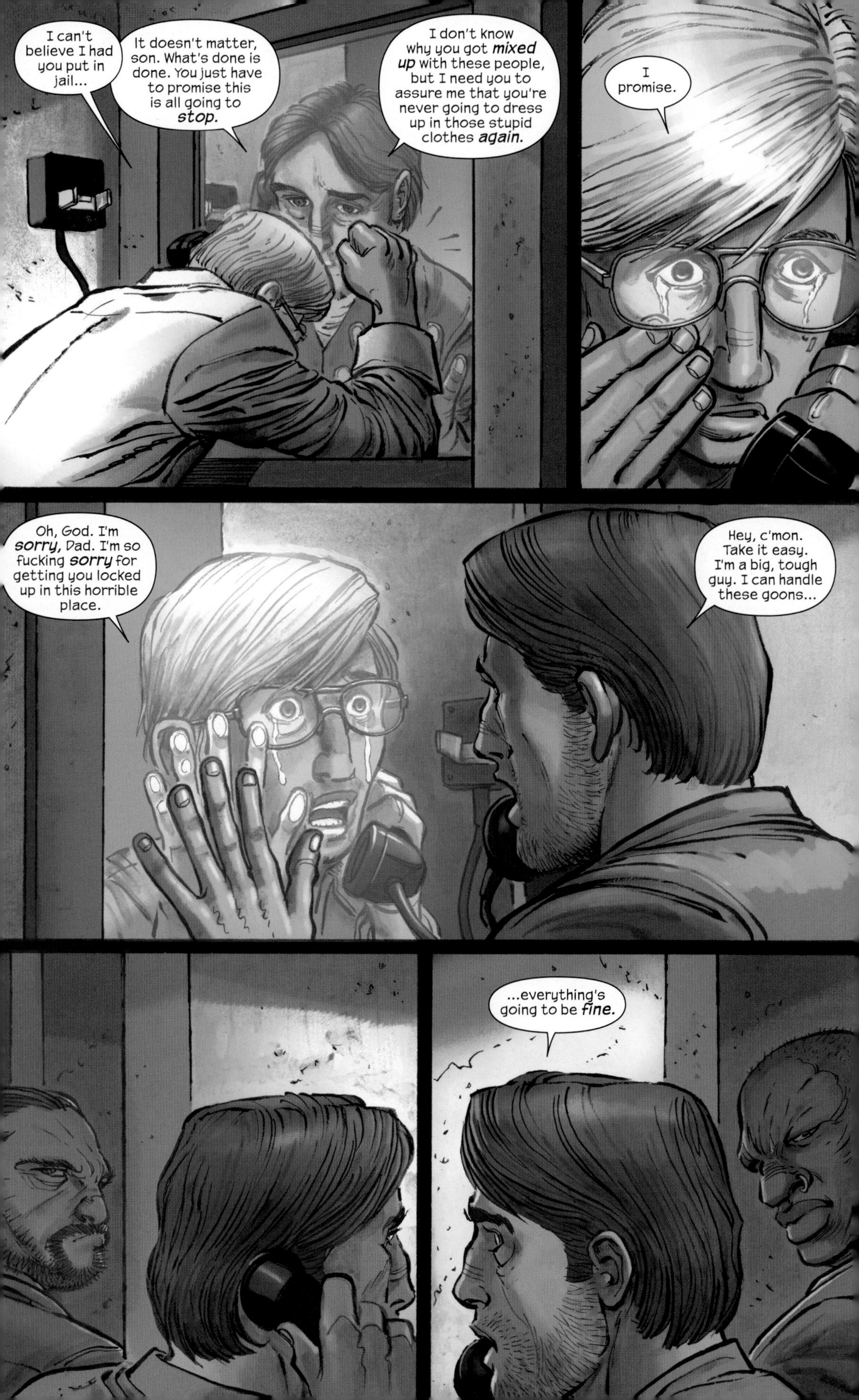
I can't believe I had you put in jail...
It doesn't matter, son. What's done is done. You just have to promise this is all going to *stop.*
I don't know why you got *mixed up* with these people, but I need you to assure me that you're never going to dress up in those stupid clothes *again.*
I promise.
Oh, God. I'm *sorry,* Dad. I'm so fucking *sorry* for getting you locked up in this horrible place.
Hey, c'mon. Take it easy. I'm a big, tough guy. I can handle these goons...
...everything's going to be *fine.*

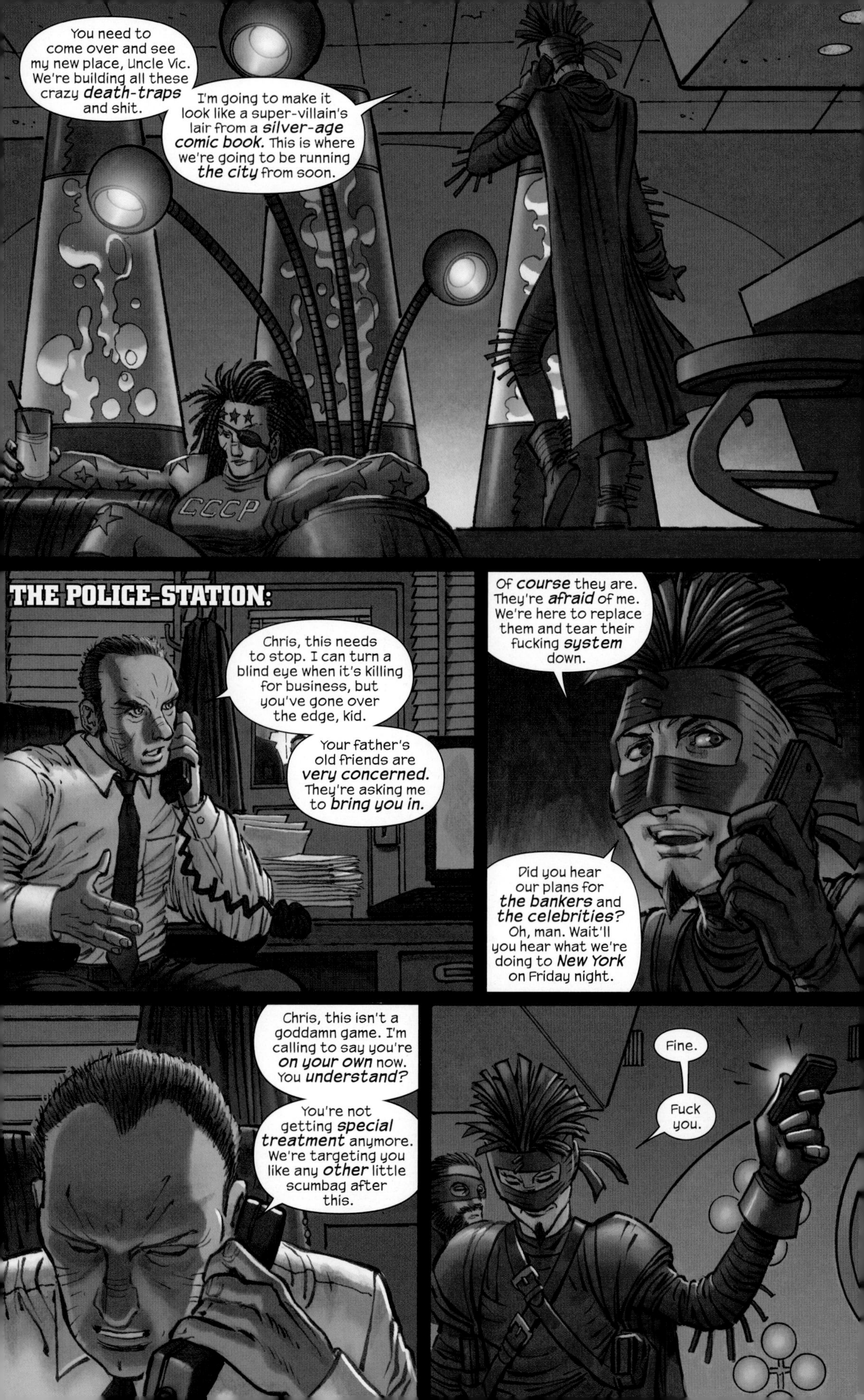
You need to come over and see my new place, Uncle Vic. We're building all these crazy death-traps and shit.
I'm going to make it look like a super-villain's lair from a silver-age comic book. This is where we're going to be running the city from soon.
CCCP
THE POLICE-STATION:
Chris, this needs to stop. I can turn a blind eye when it's killing for business, but you've gone over the edge, kid.
Your father's old friends are very concerned. They're asking me to bring you in.
Of course they are. They're afraid of me. We're here to replace them and tear their fucking system down.
Did you hear our plans for the bankers and the celebrities? Oh, man. Wait'll you hear what we're doing to New York on Friday night.
Chris, this isn't a goddamn game. I'm calling to say you're on your own now. You understand?
You're not getting special treatment anymore. We're targeting you like any other little scumbag after this.
Fine.
Fuck you.

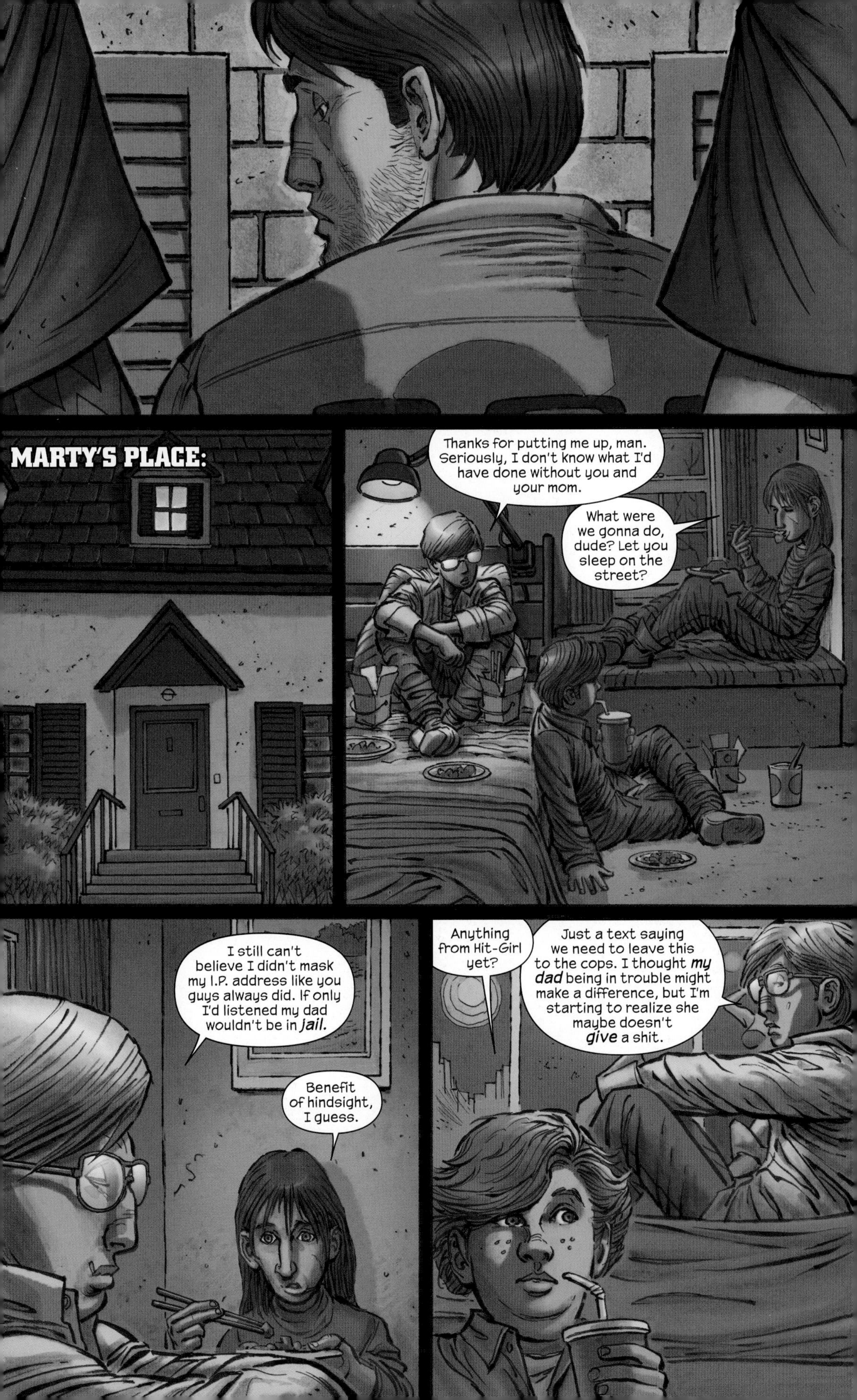
MARTY'S PLACE:
Thanks for putting me up, man. Seriously, I don't know what I'd have done without you and your mom.
What were we gonna do, dude? Let you sleep on the street?
I still can't believe I didn't mask my I.P. address like you guys always did. If only I'd listened my dad wouldn't be in *jail.*
Benefit of hindsight, I guess.
Anything from Hit-Girl yet?
Just a text saying we need to leave this to the cops. I thought *my dad* being in trouble might make a difference, but I'm starting to realize she maybe doesn't *give* a shit.

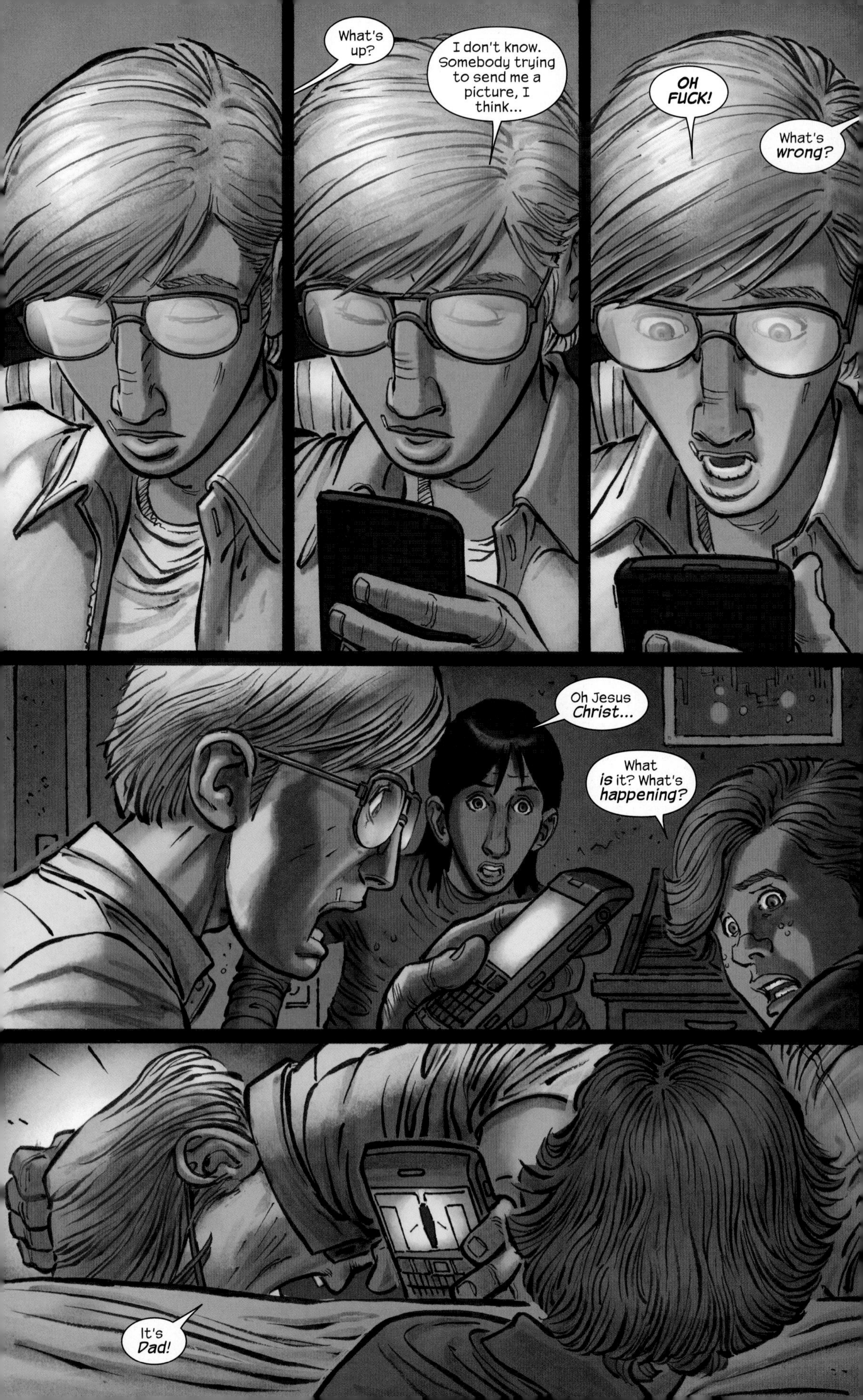
What's up?
I don't know. Somebody trying to send me a picture, I think...
OH FUCK!
What's wrong?
Oh Jesus Christ...
What is it? What's happening?
It's Dad!

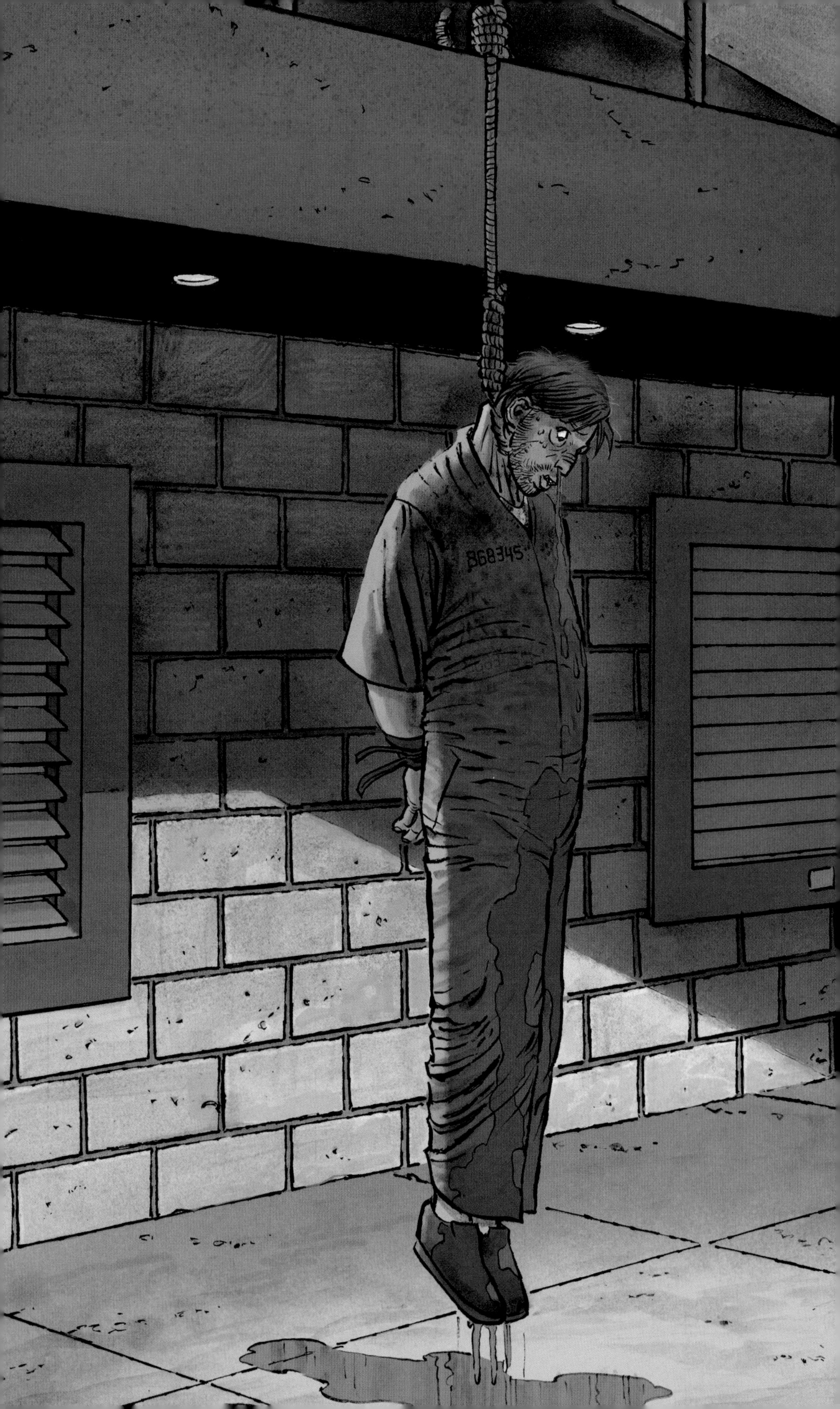
868345

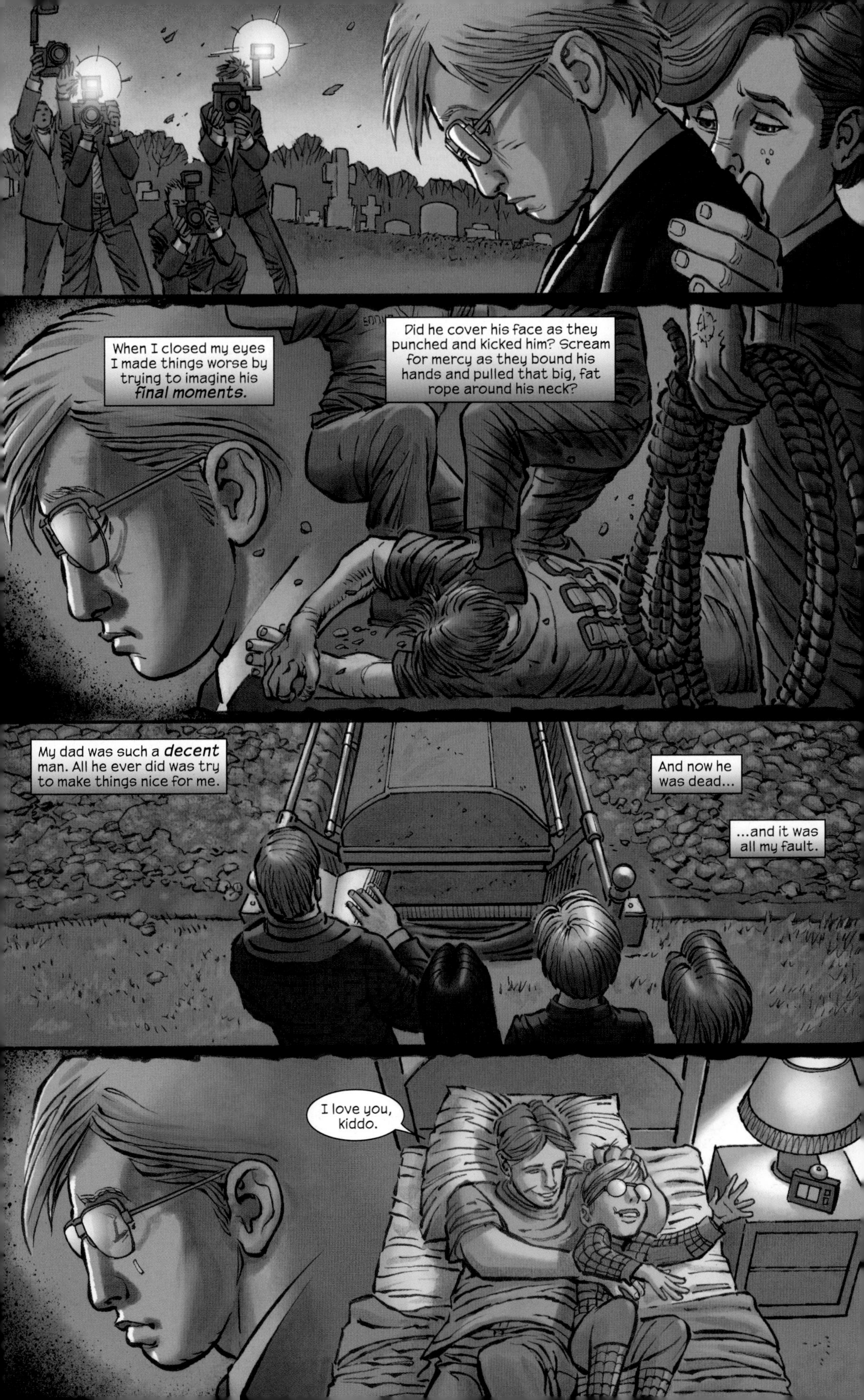
When I closed my eyes I made things worse by trying to imagine his final moments.
Did he cover his face as they punched and kicked him? Scream for mercy as they bound his hands and pulled that big, fat rope around his neck?
My dad was such a decent man. All he ever did was try to make things nice for me.
And now he was dead...
...and it was all my fault.
I love you, kiddo.

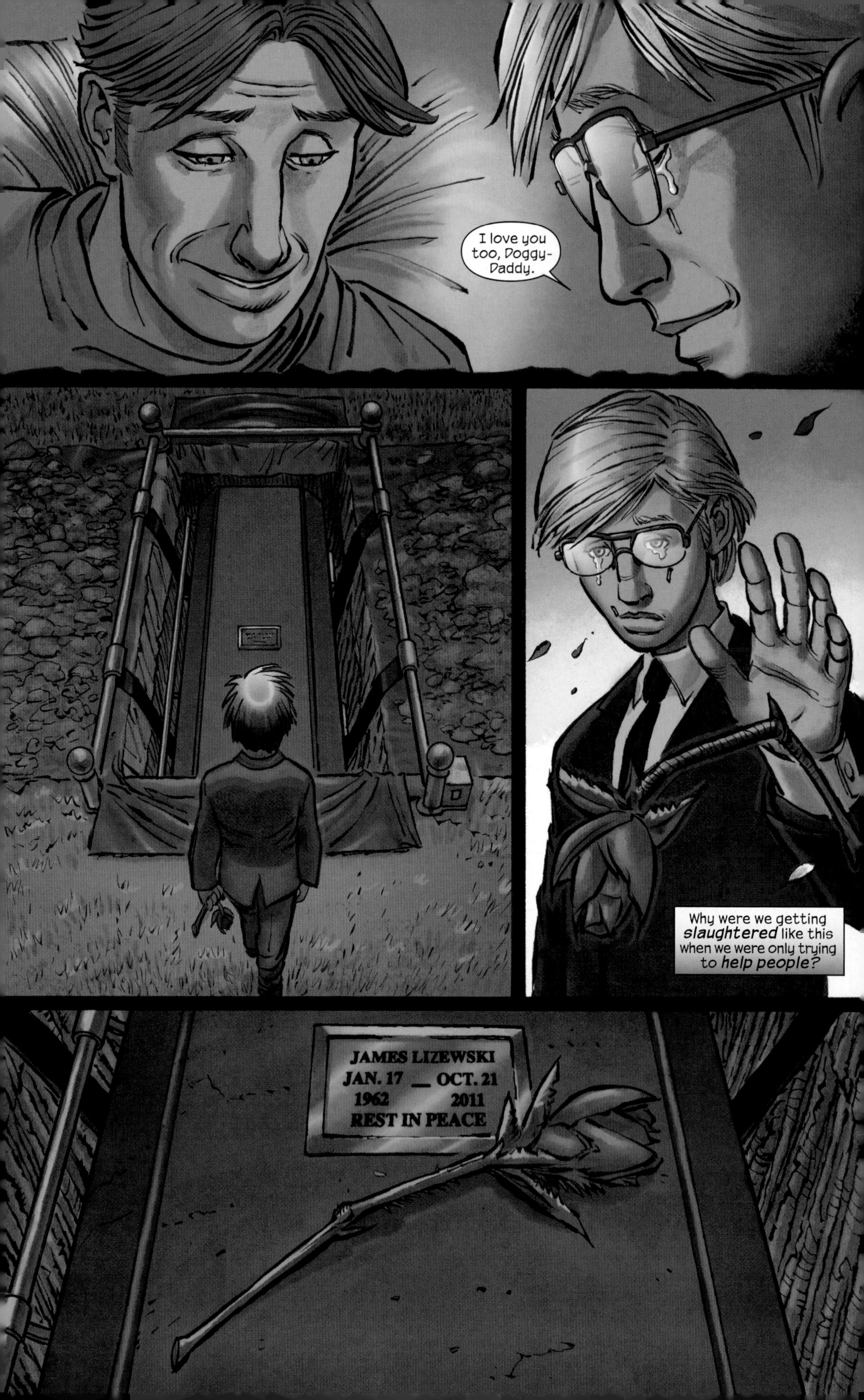
I love you too, Doggy-Daddy.
Why were we getting slaughtered like this when we were only trying to help people?
JAMES LIZEWSKI
JAN. 17 _ OCT. 21
1962 2011
REST IN PEACE

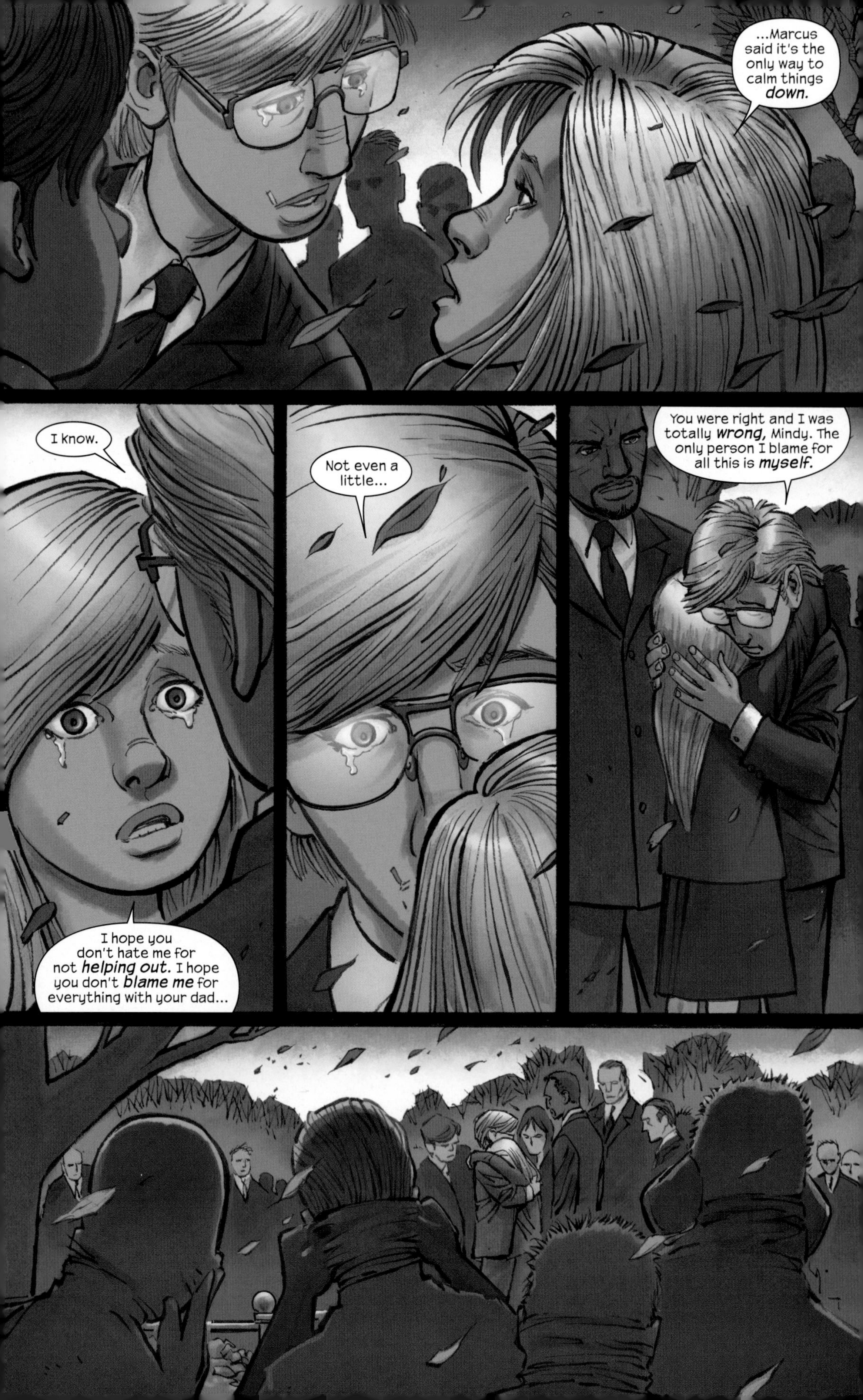
...Marcus said it's the only way to calm things *down.*
I know.
I hope you don't hate me for not *helping out.* I hope you don't *blame me* for everything with your dad...
Not even a little...
You were right and I was totally *wrong,* Mindy. The only person I blame for all this is *myself.*

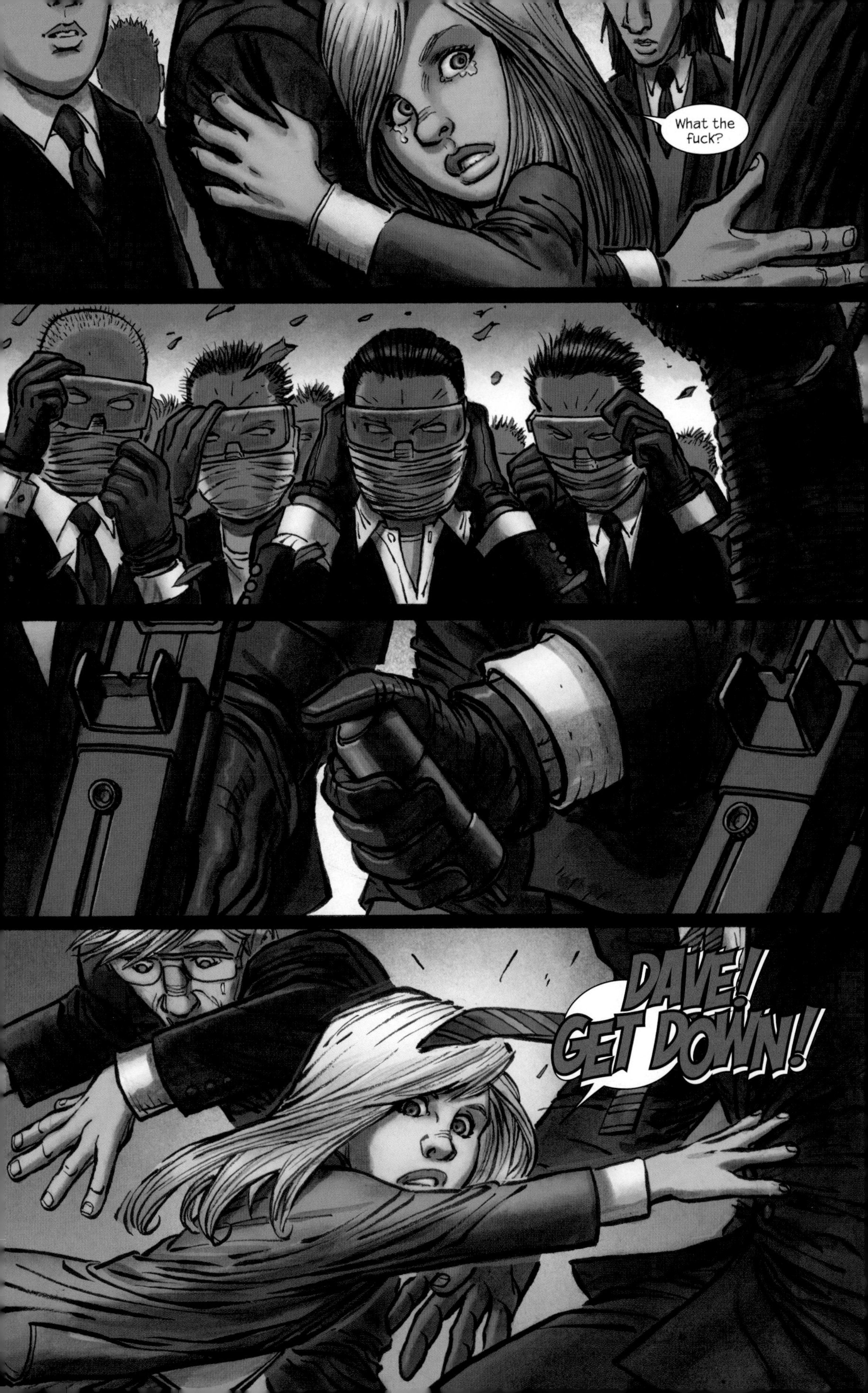
What the fuck?
DAVE! GET DOWN!

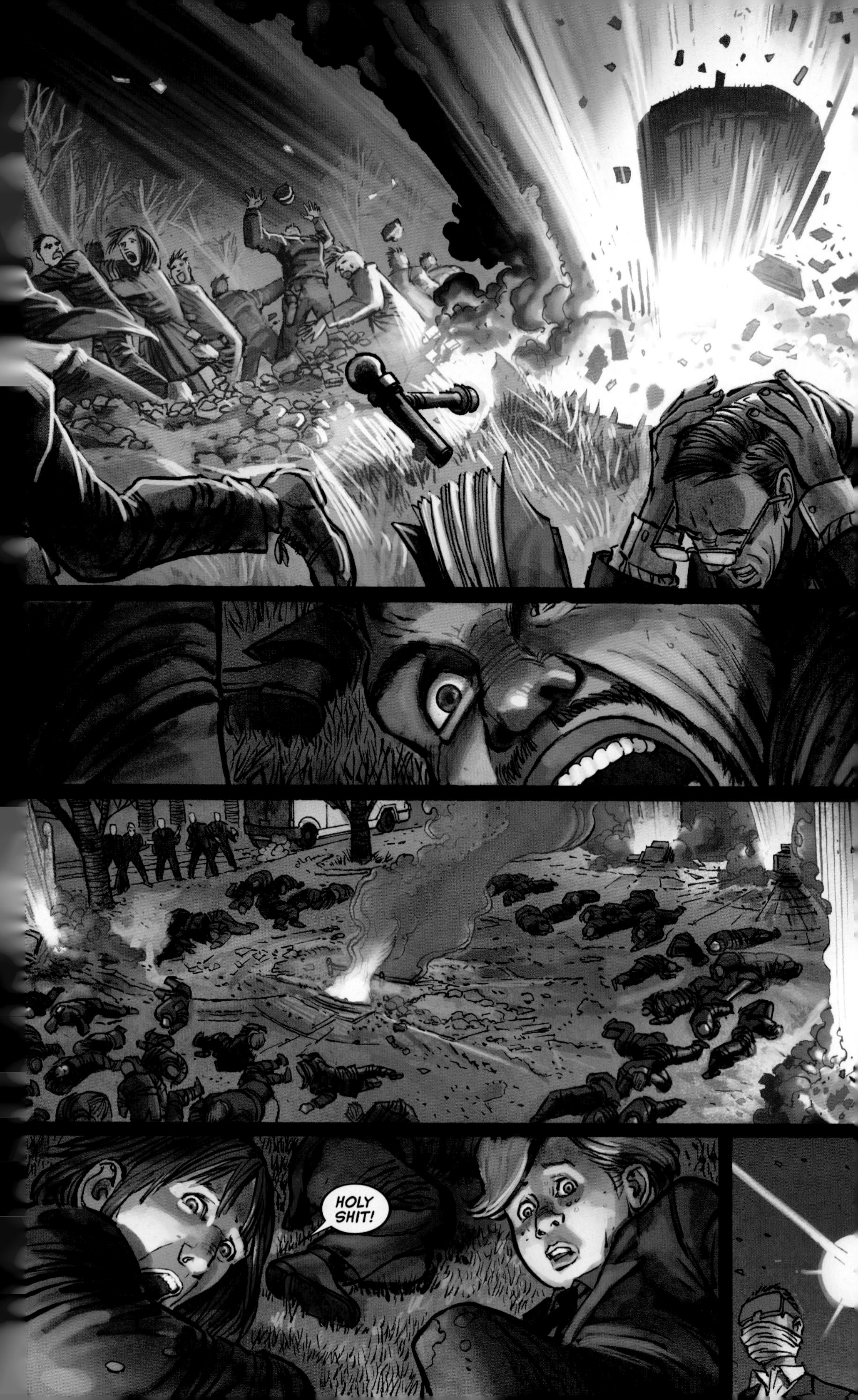
HOLY SHIT!

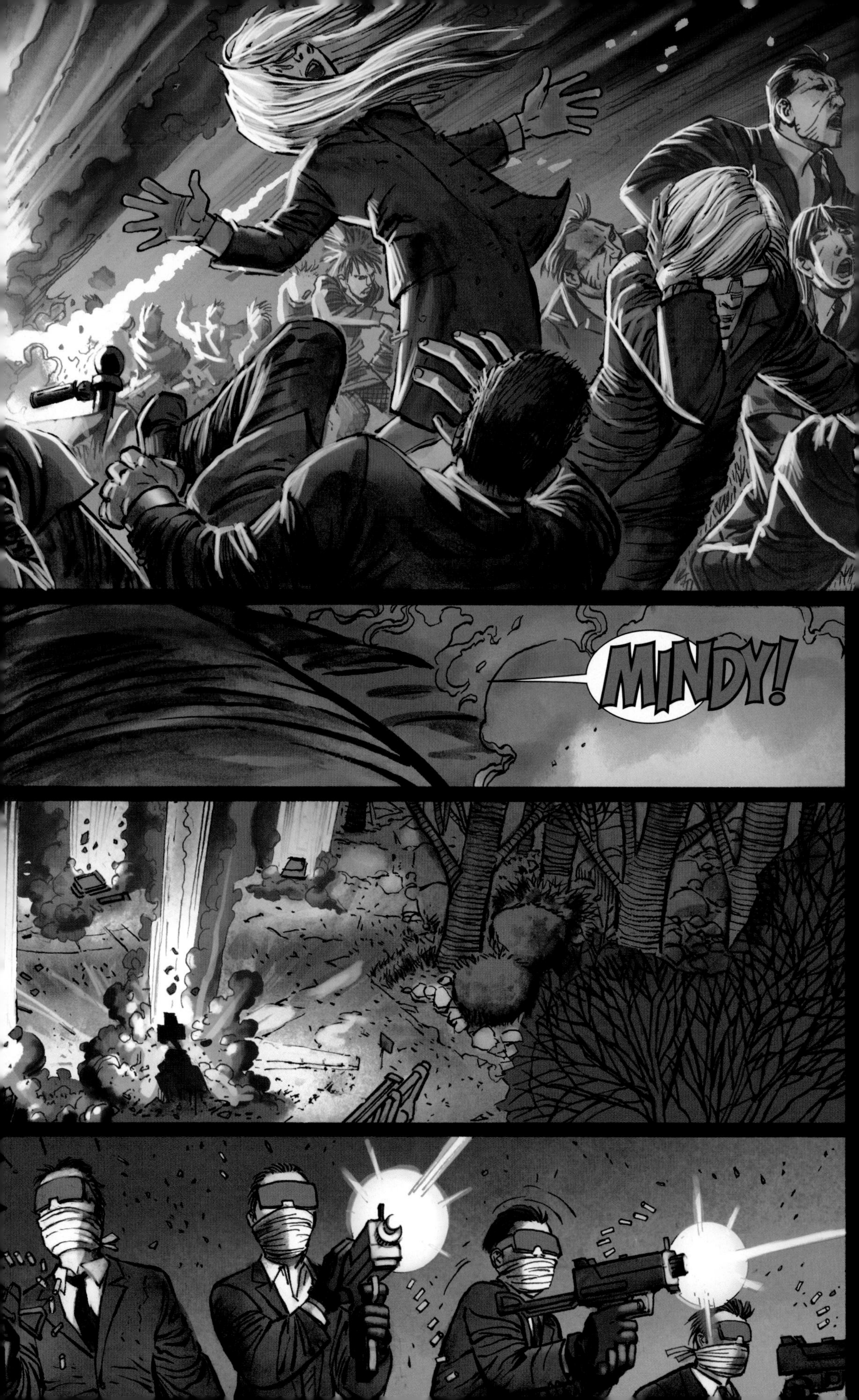
MINDY!

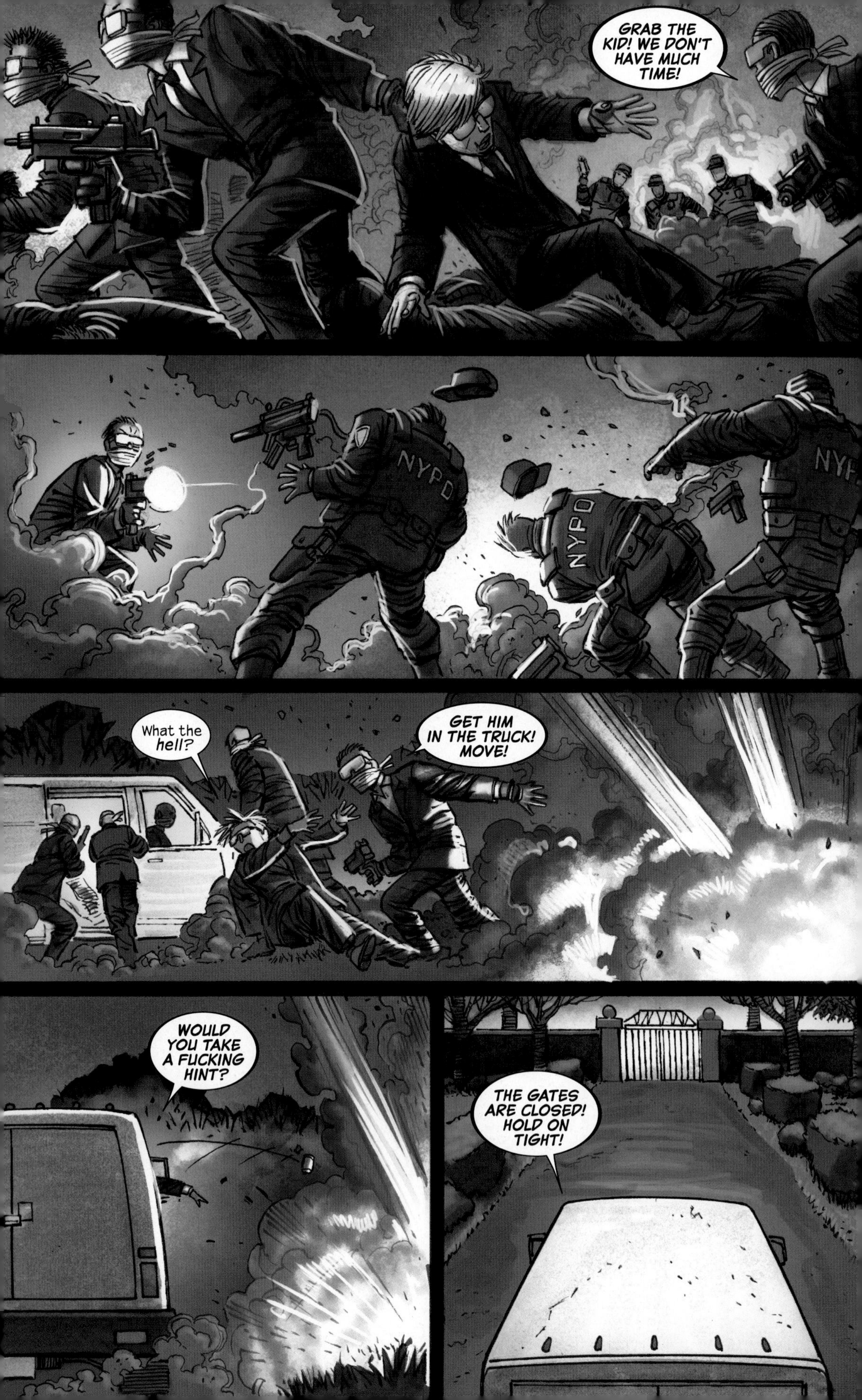
GRAB THE KID! WE DON'T HAVE MUCH TIME!
NYPD
NYPD
NYP
What the hell?
GET HIM IN THE TRUCK! MOVE!
WOULD YOU TAKE A FUCKING HINT?
THE GATES ARE CLOSED! HOLD ON TIGHT!

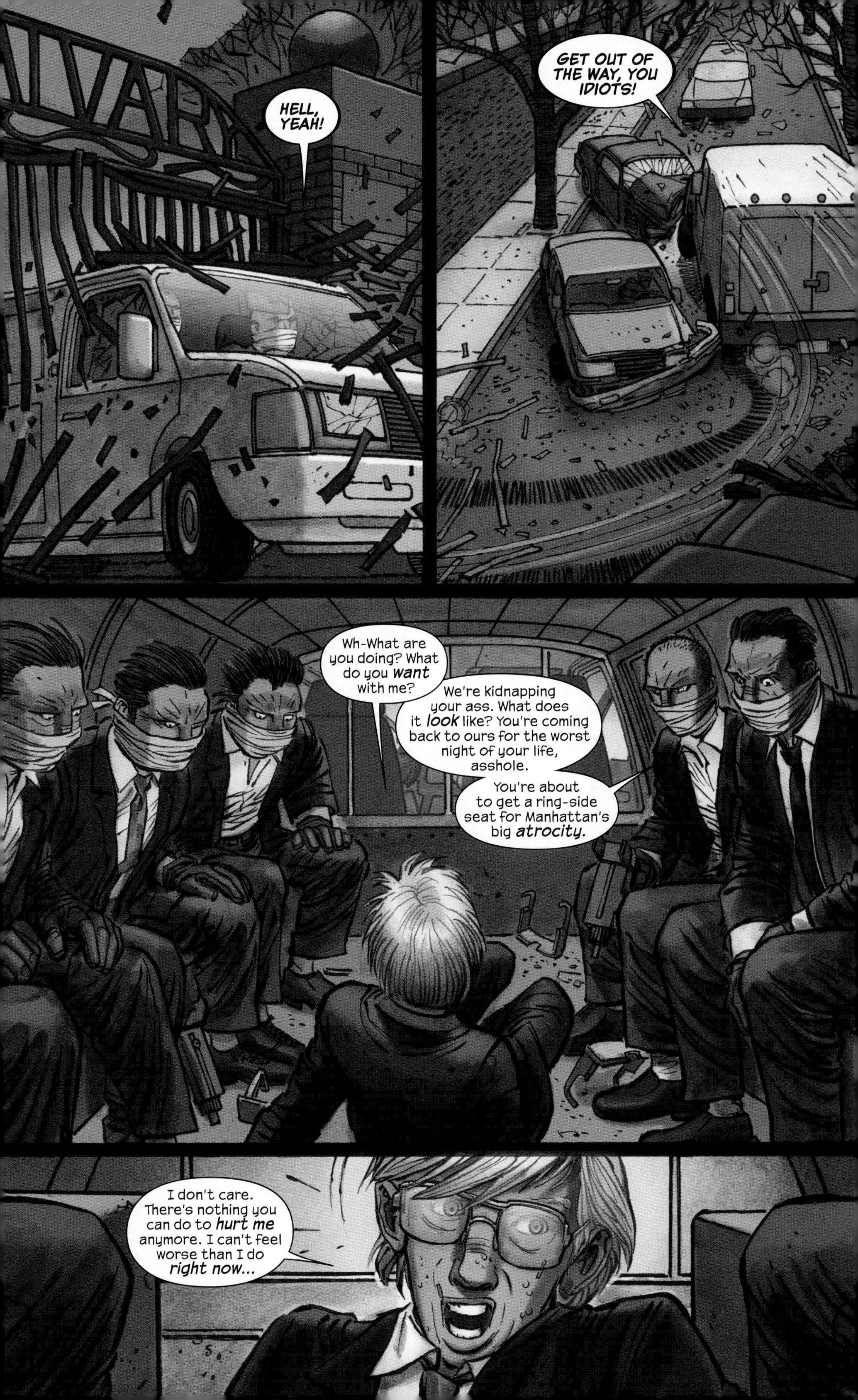
HELL, YEAH!
GET OUT OF THE WAY, YOU IDIOTS!
Wh-What are you doing? What do you *want* with me?
We're kidnapping your ass. What does it *look* like? You're coming back to ours for the worst night of your life, asshole.
You're about to get a ring-side seat for Manhattan's big *atrocity*.
I don't care. There's nothing you can do to *hurt me* anymore. I can't feel worse than I do *right now...*

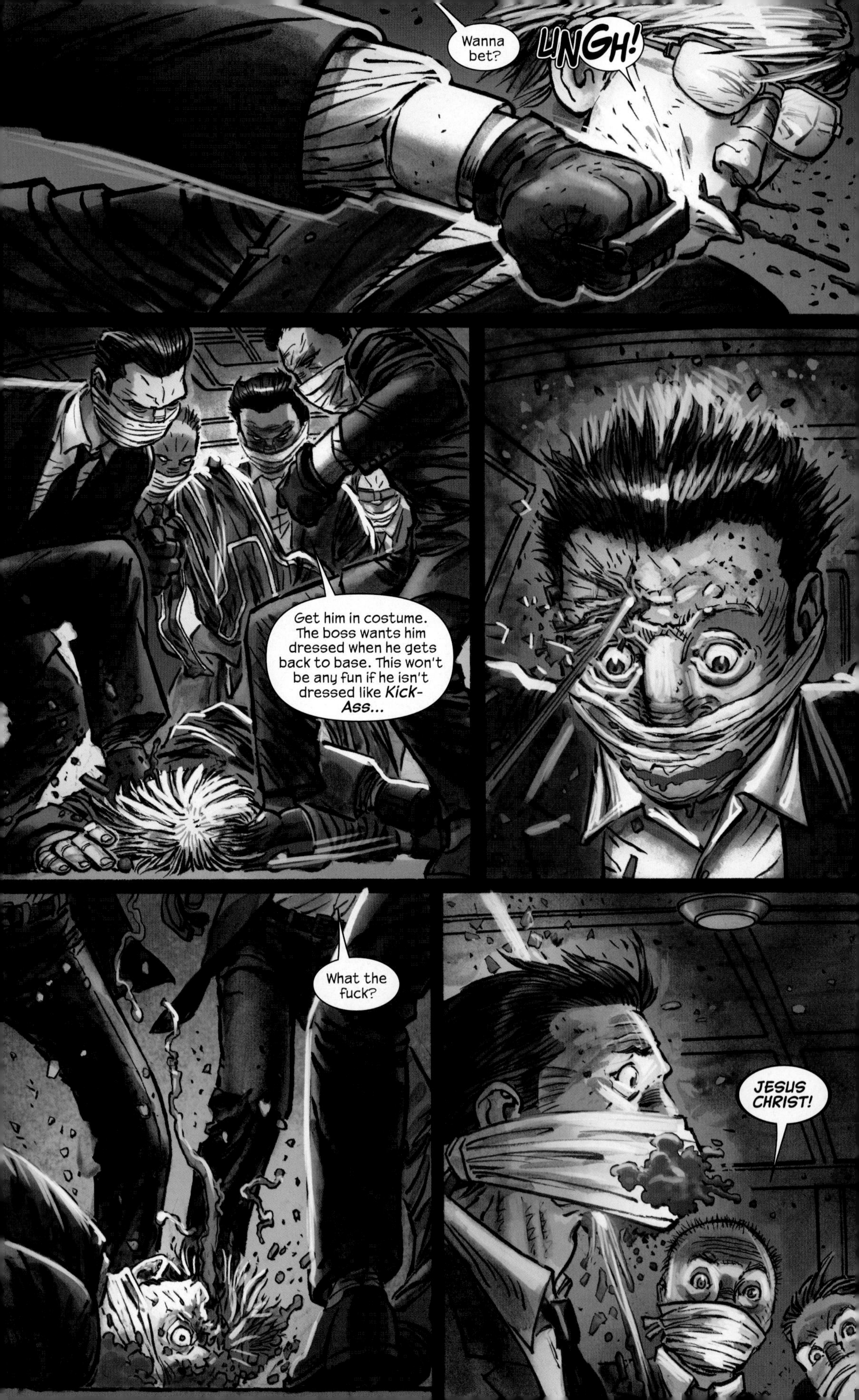
Wanna bet?
UNGH!
Get him in costume. The boss wants him dressed when he gets back to base. This won't be any fun if he isn't dressed like Kick-Ass...
What the fuck?
JESUS CHRIST!

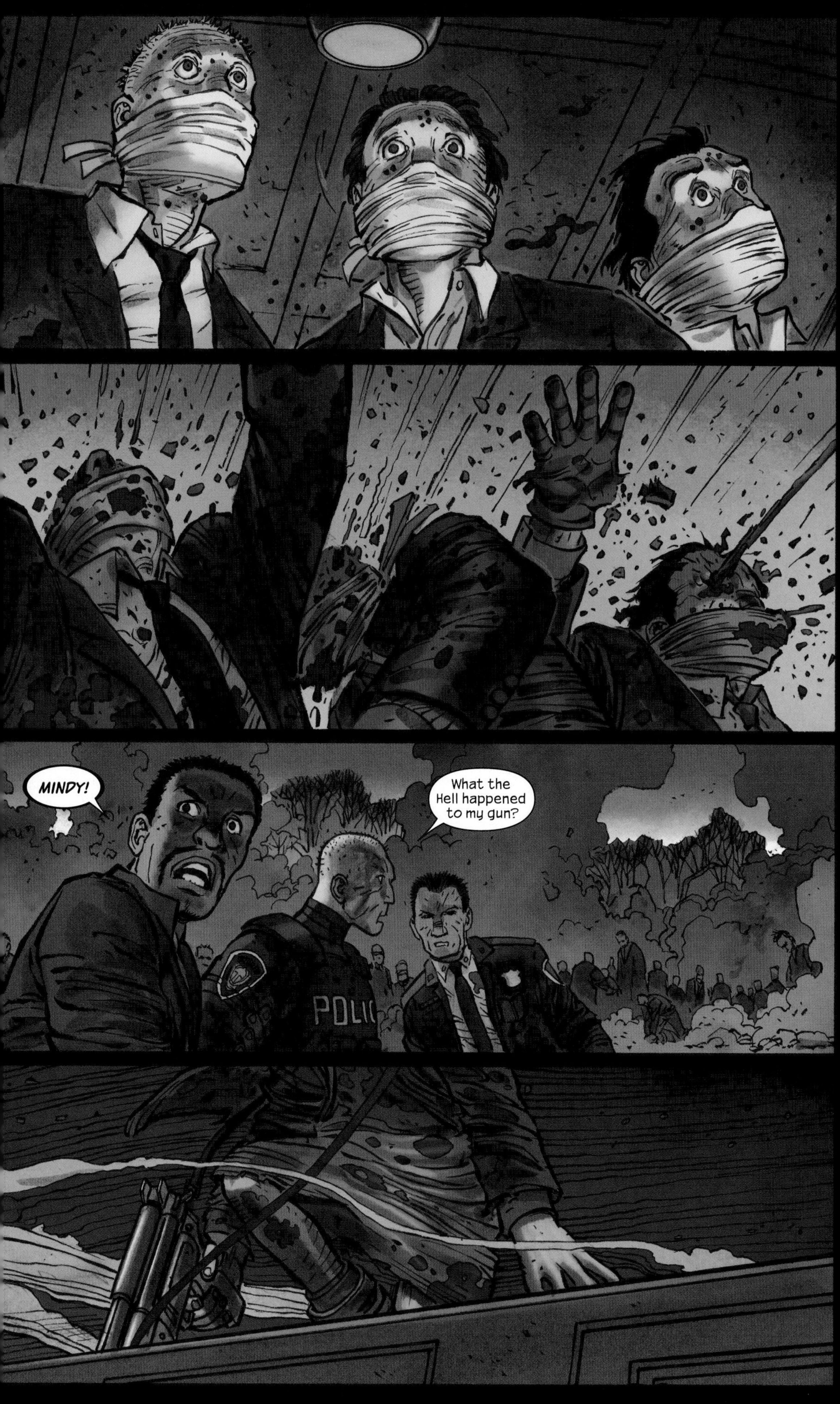
MINDY!
What the Hell happened to my gun?
POLIC

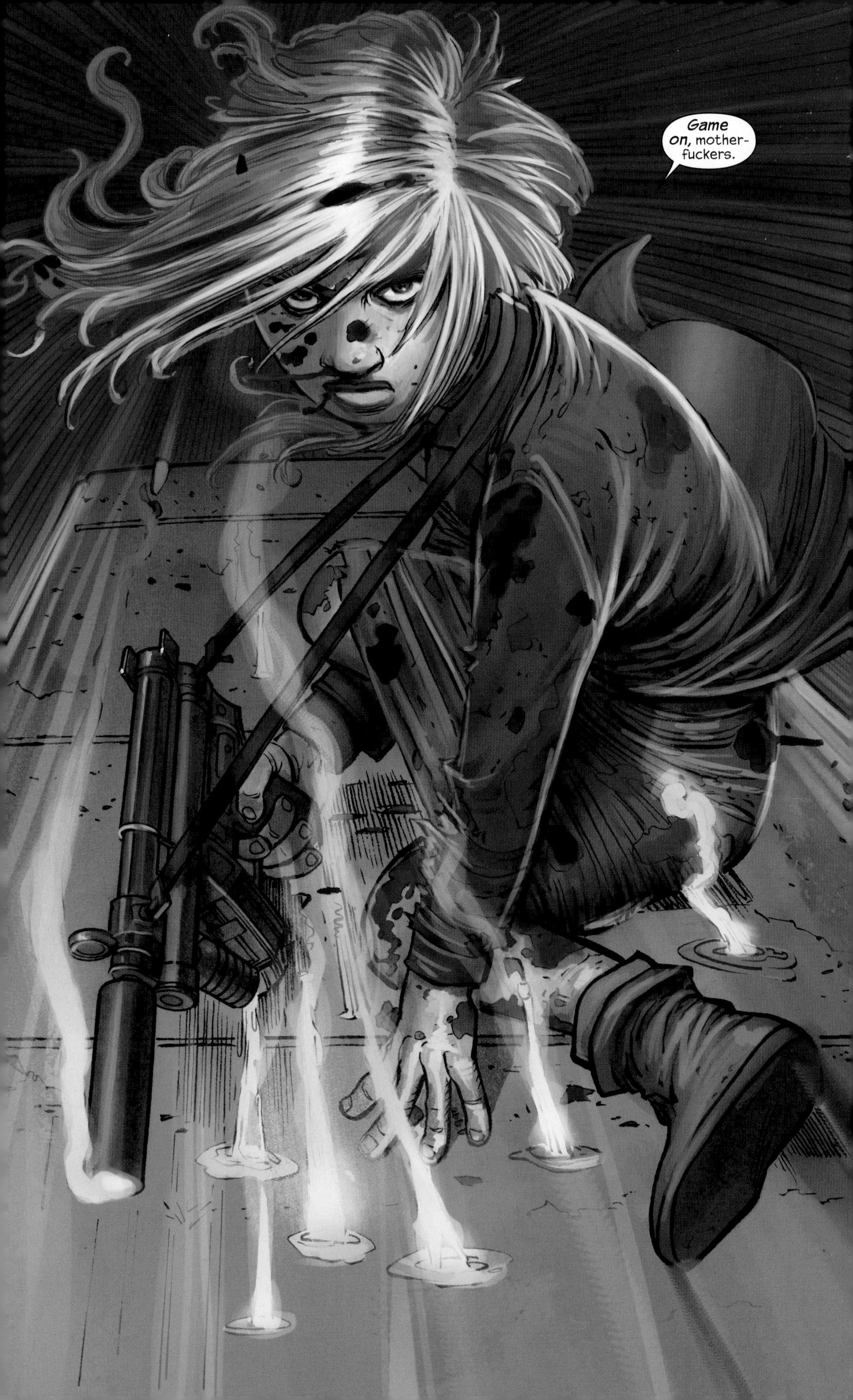
Game on, mother-fuckers.

SIX

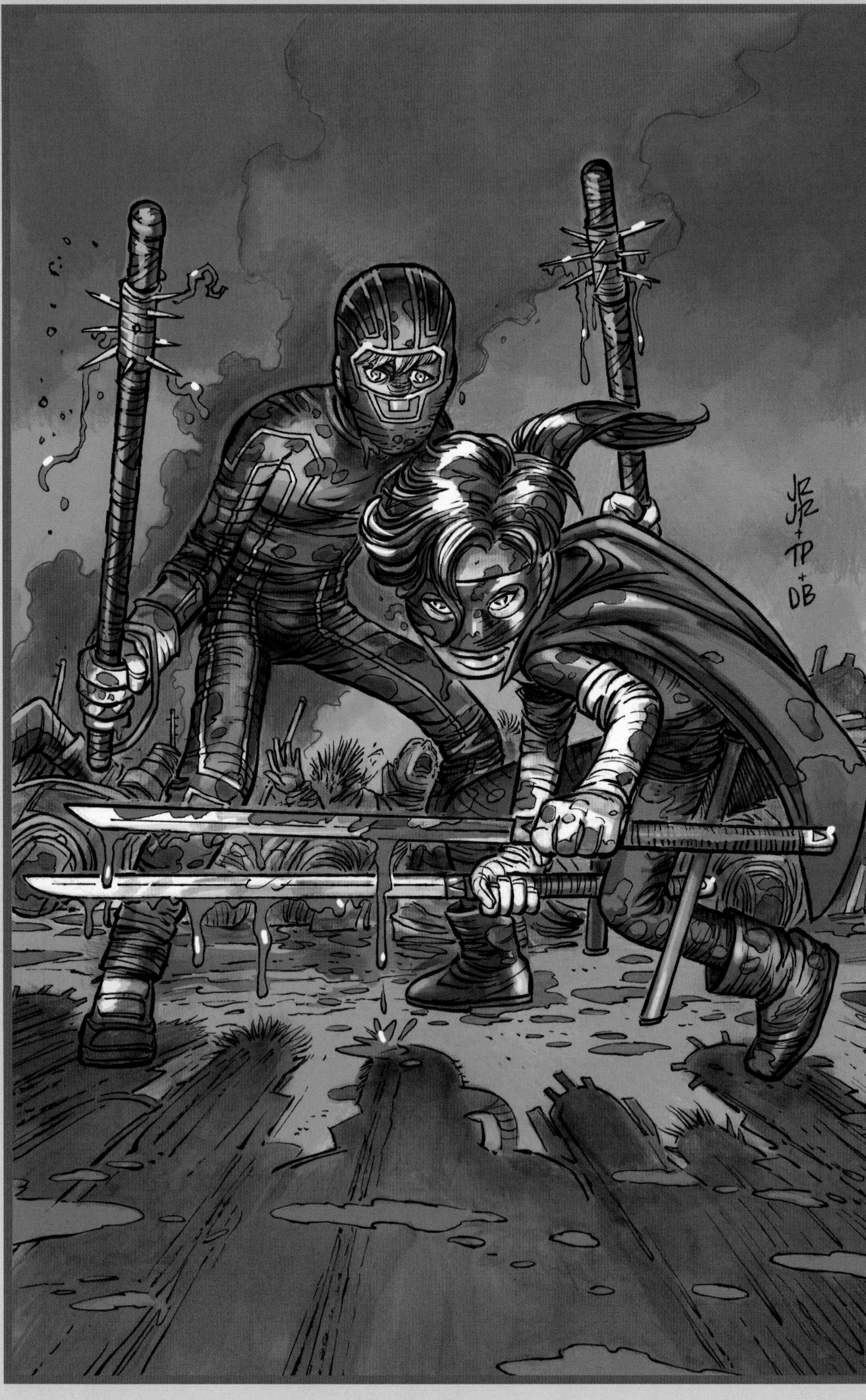
JR JR + TP + DB

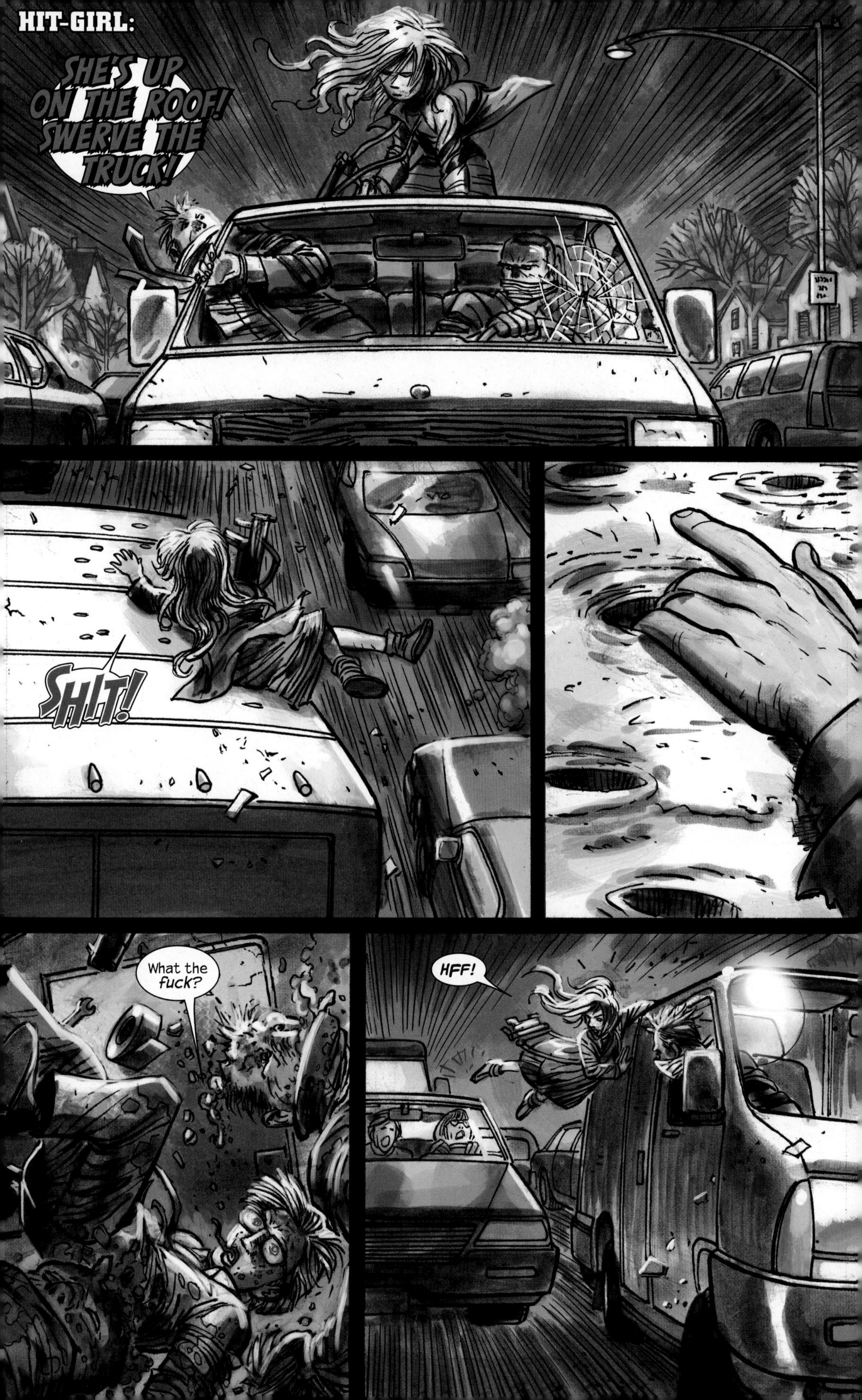
HIT-GIRL:
SHE'S UP ON THE ROOF! SWERVE THE TRUCK!
SHIT!
What the fuck?
HFF!

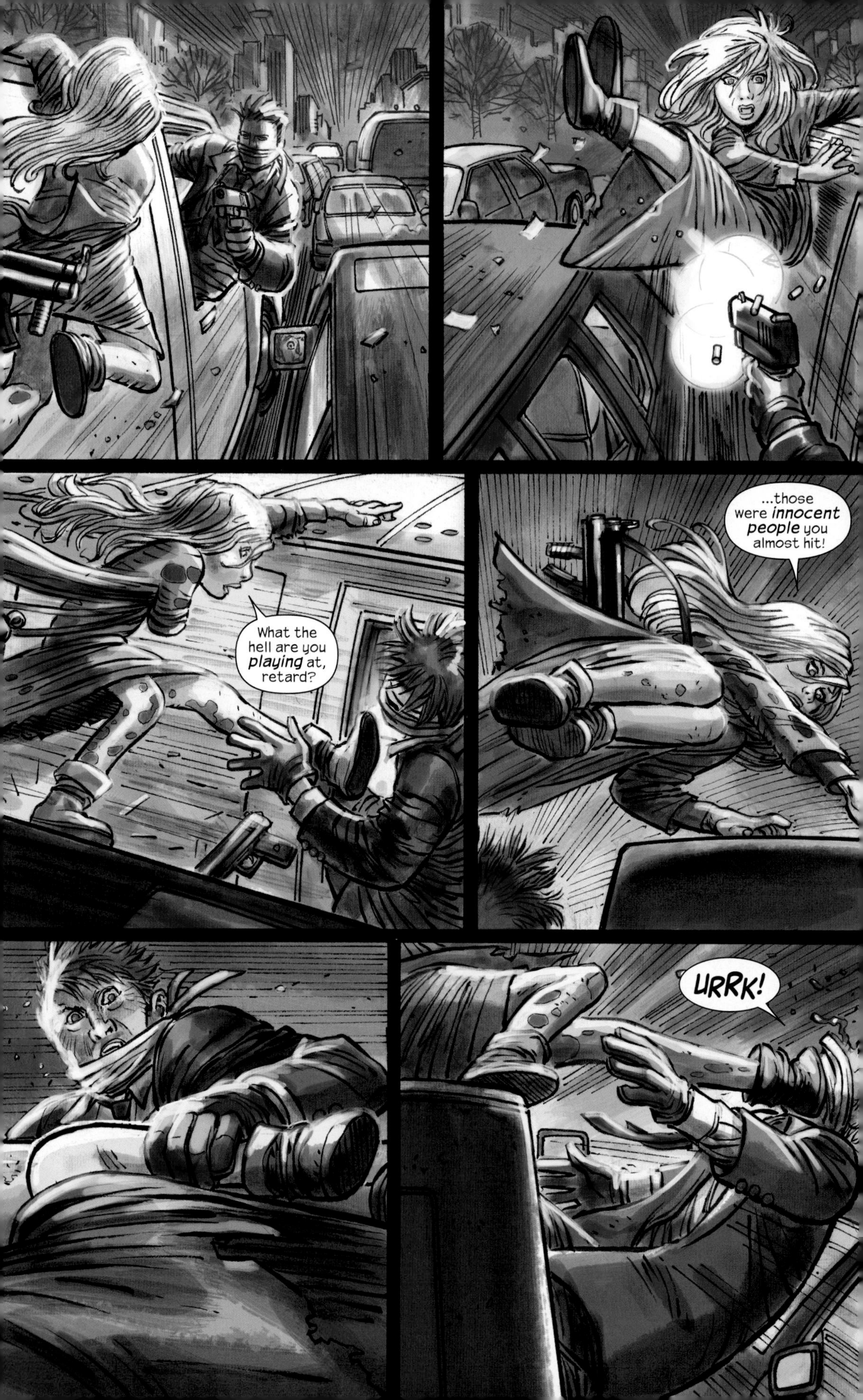
What the hell are you *playing* at, retard?
...those were *innocent people* you almost hit!
URRK!

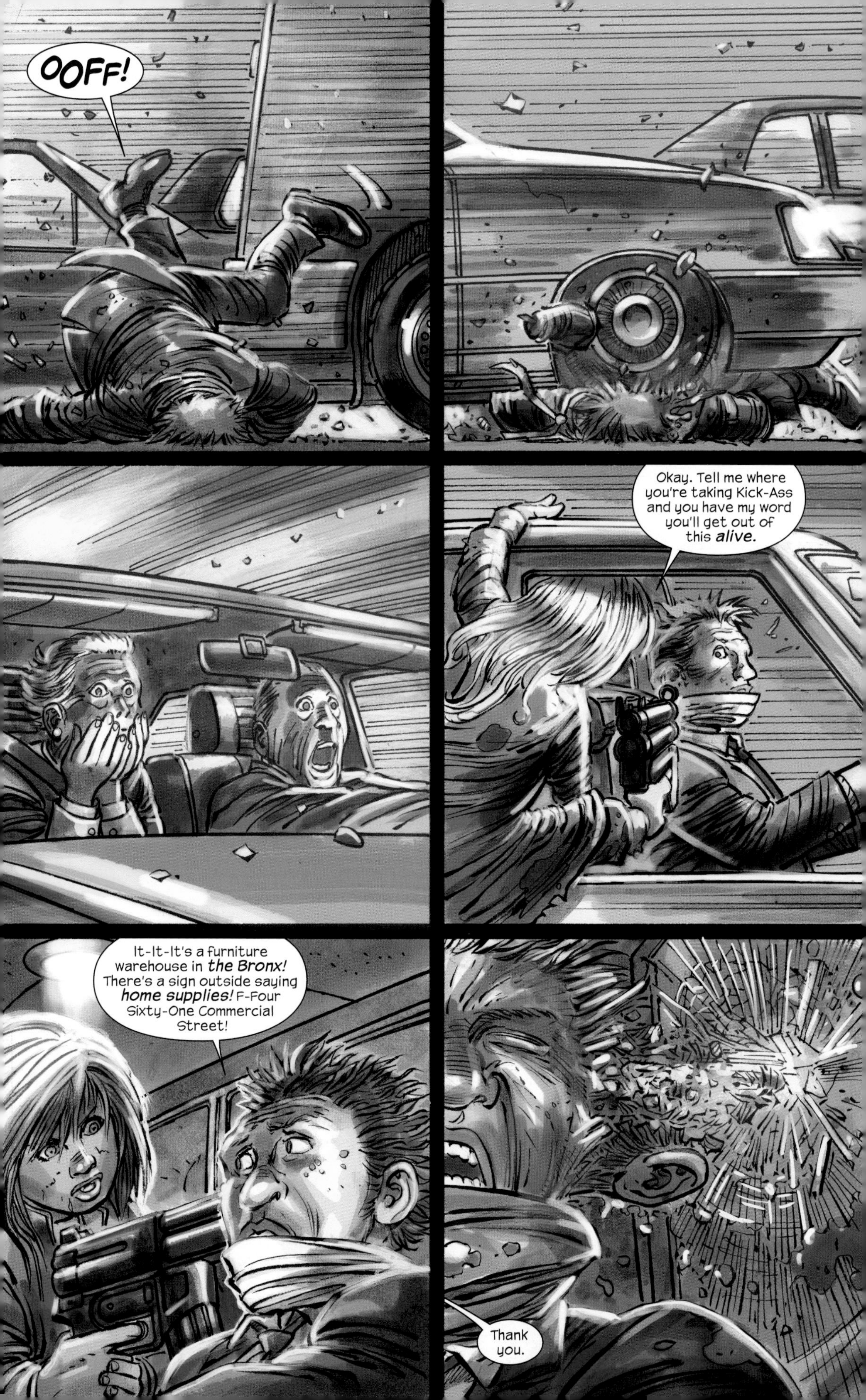
OOFF!
Okay. Tell me where you're taking Kick-Ass and you have my word you'll get out of this *alive.*
It-It-It's a furniture warehouse in *the Bronx!* There's a sign outside saying *home supplies!* F-Four Sixty-One Commercial Street!
Thank you.

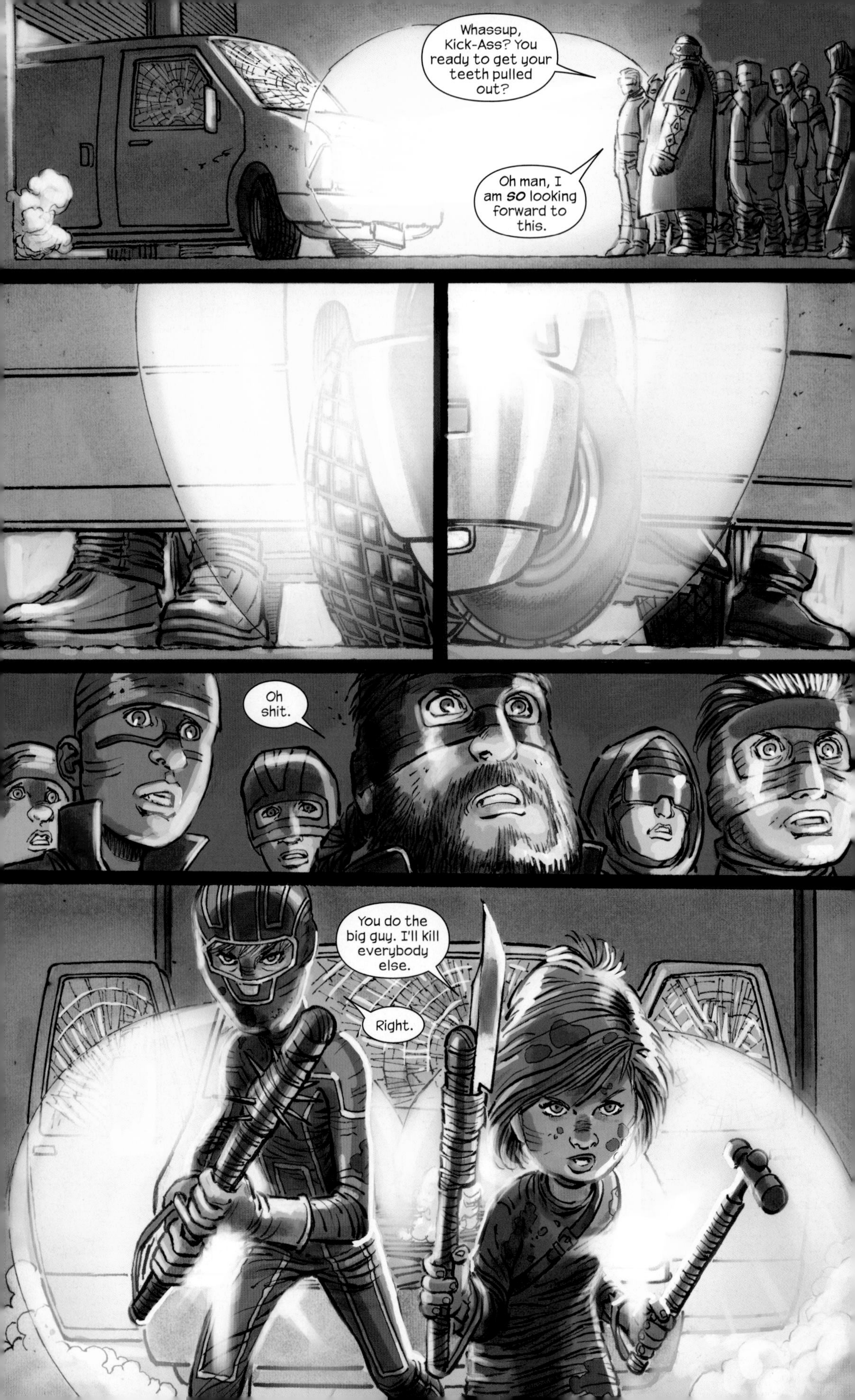
Whassup, Kick-Ass? You ready to get your teeth pulled out?
Oh man, I am SO looking forward to this.
Oh shit.
You do the big guy. I'll kill everybody else.
Right.

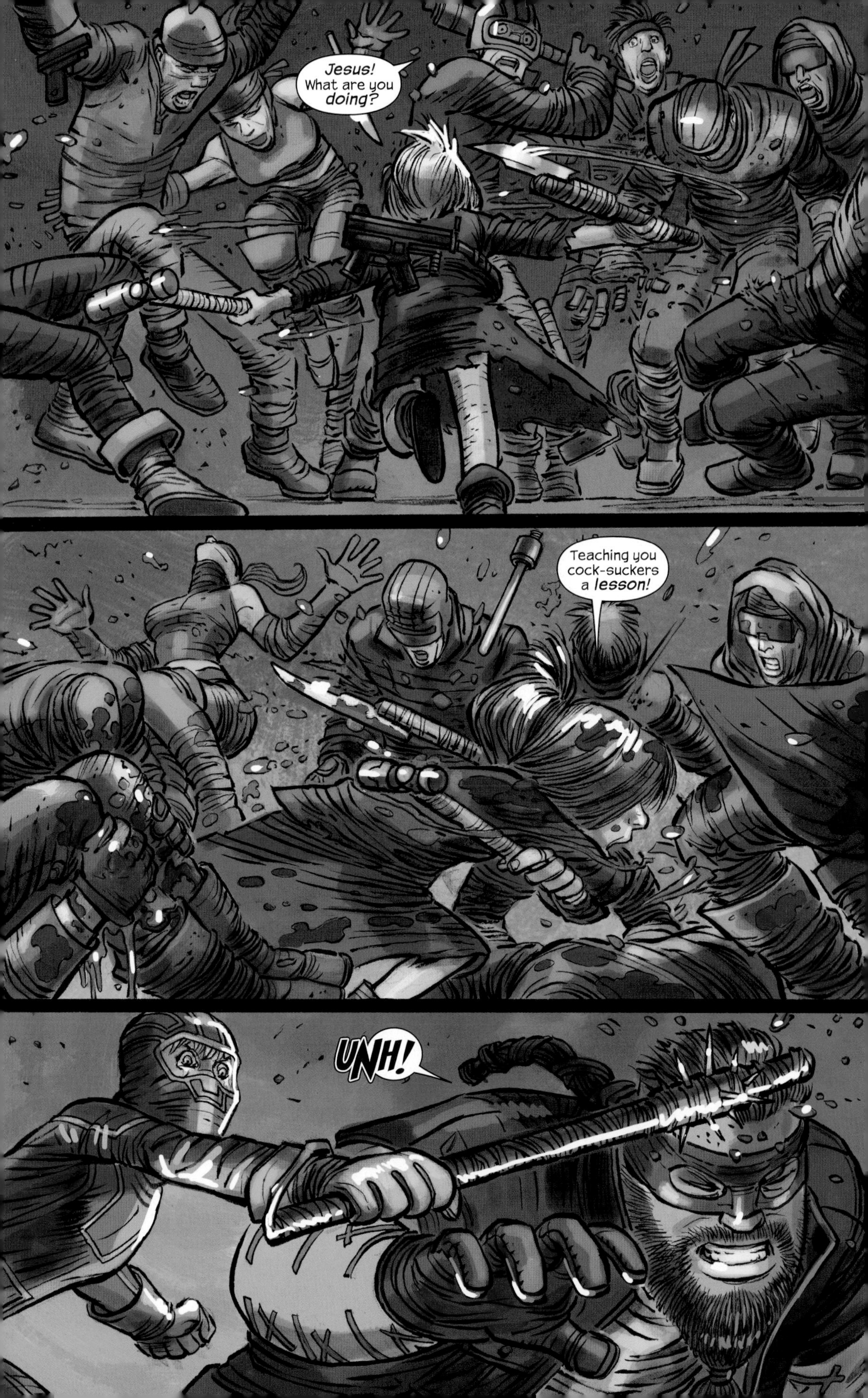
Jesus! What are you doing?
Teaching you cock-suckers a lesson!
UNH!

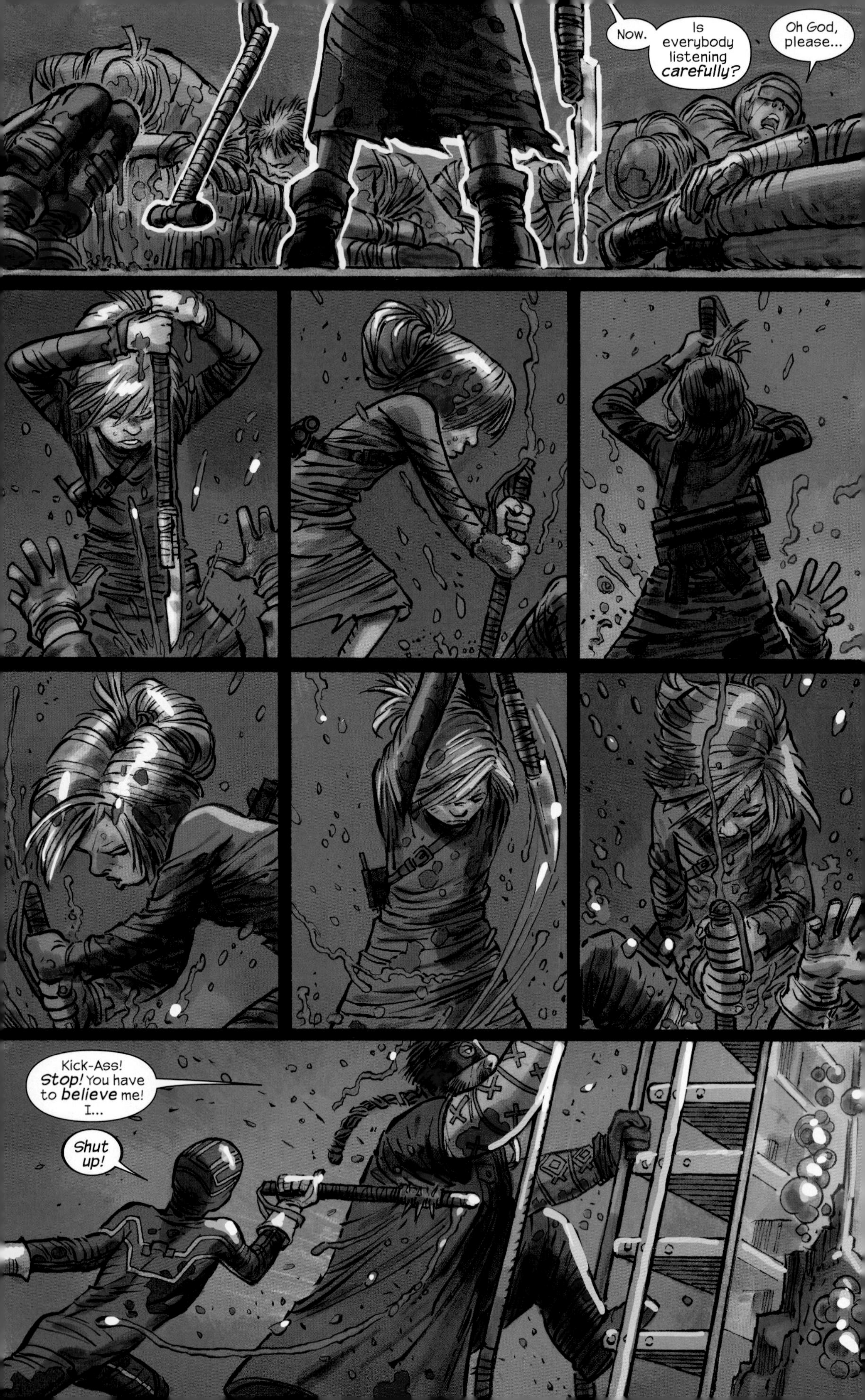
Now.
Is everybody listening carefully?
Oh God, please...
Kick-Ass! Stop! You have to believe me! I...
Shut up!

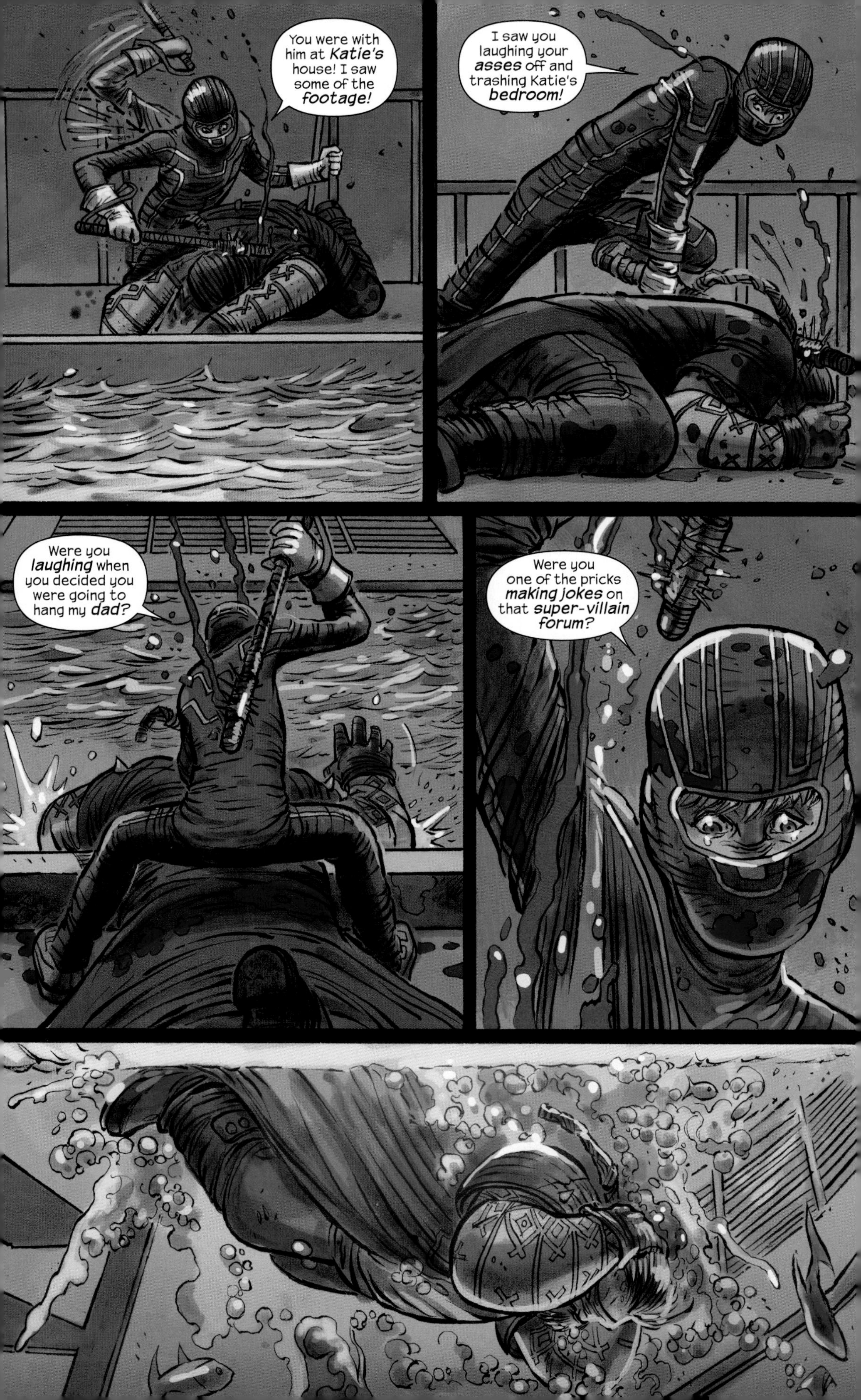
You were with him at Katie's house! I saw some of the footage!
I saw you laughing your asses off and trashing Katie's bedroom!
Were you laughing when you decided you were going to hang my dad?
Were you one of the pricks making jokes on that super-villain forum?

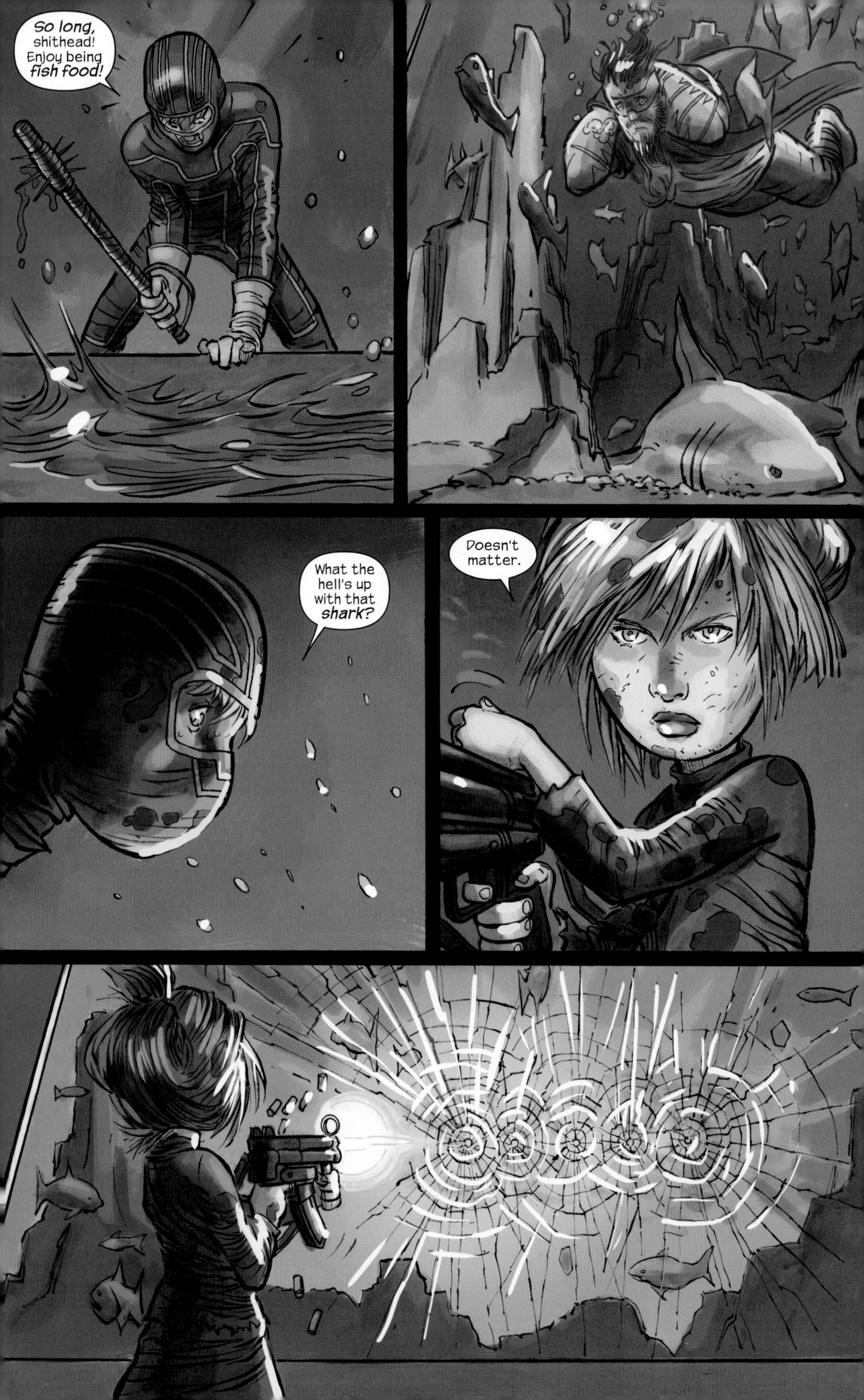
So long, shithead! Enjoy being fish food!
What the hell's up with that shark?
Doesn't matter.

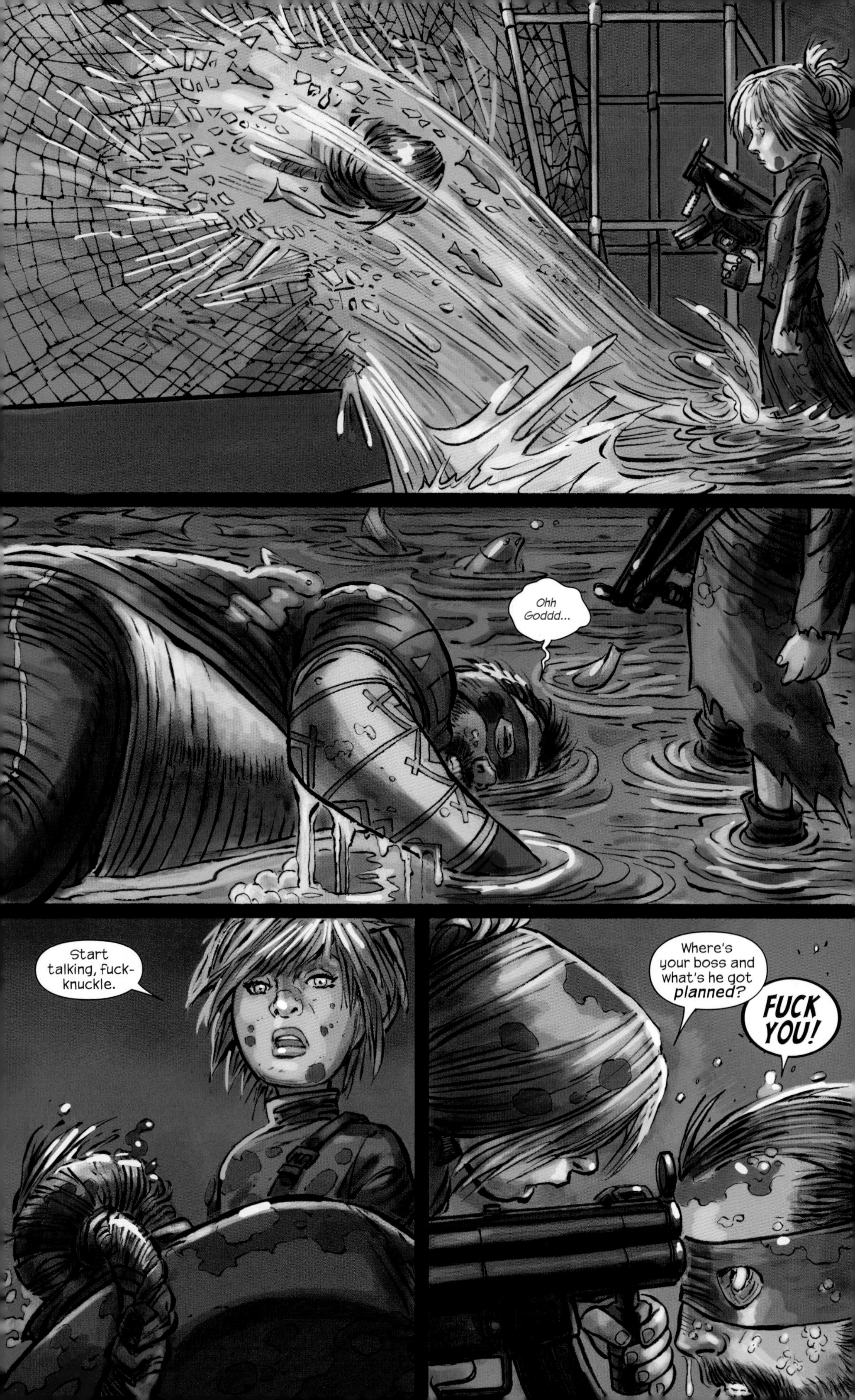
Ohh Goddd...
Start talking, fuck-knuckle.
Where's your boss and what's he got *planned*?
FUCK YOU!

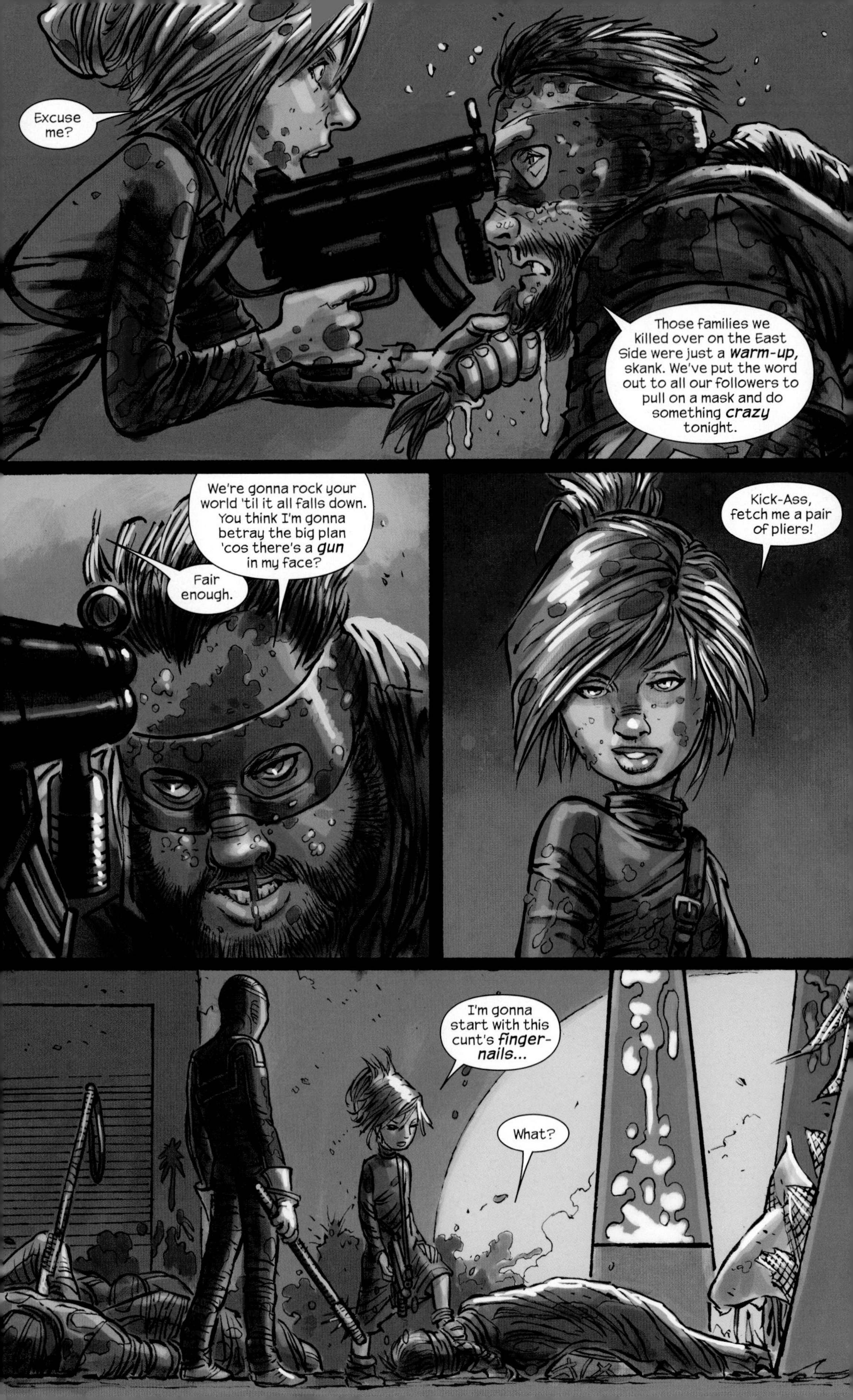
Excuse me?
Those families we killed over on the East Side were just a warm-up, skank. We've put the word out to all our followers to pull on a mask and do something crazy tonight.
We're gonna rock your world 'til it all falls down. You think I'm gonna betray the big plan 'cos there's a gun in my face?
Fair enough.
Kick-Ass, fetch me a pair of pliers!
I'm gonna start with this cunt's finger-nails...
What?

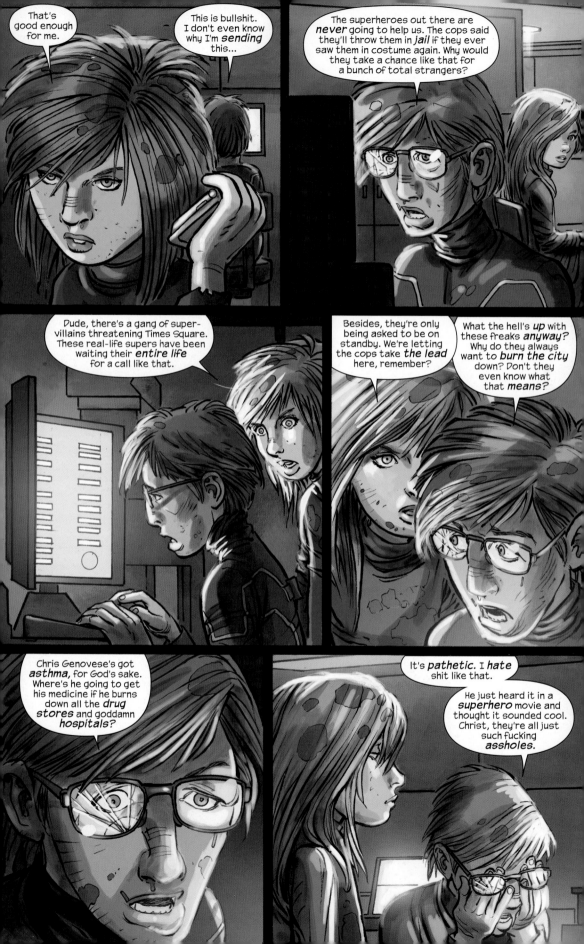

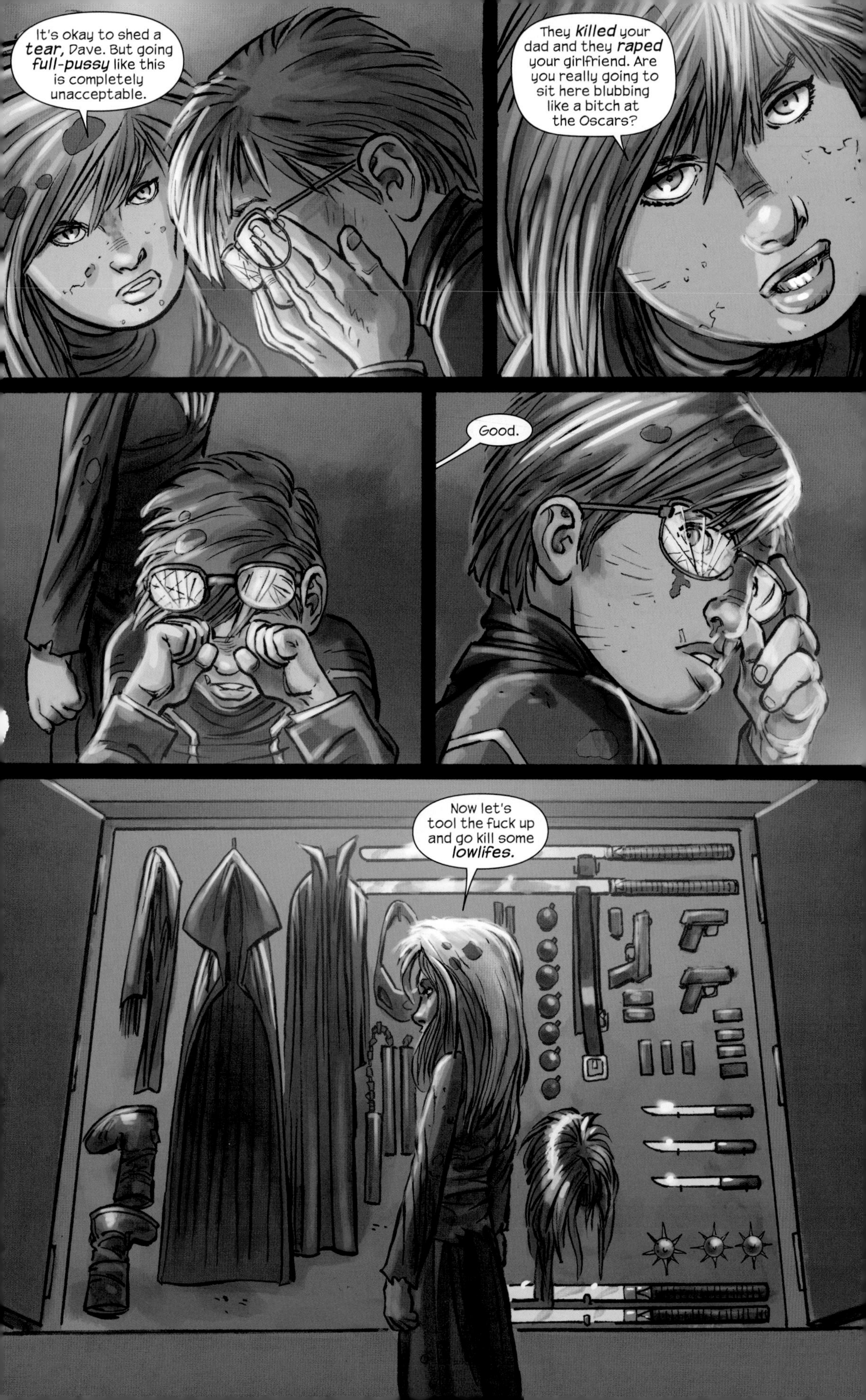
It's okay to shed a tear, Dave. But going full-pussy like this is completely unacceptable.
They killed your dad and they raped your girlfriend. Are you really going to sit here blubbing like a bitch at the Oscars?
Good.
Now let's tool the fuck up and go kill some lowlifes.

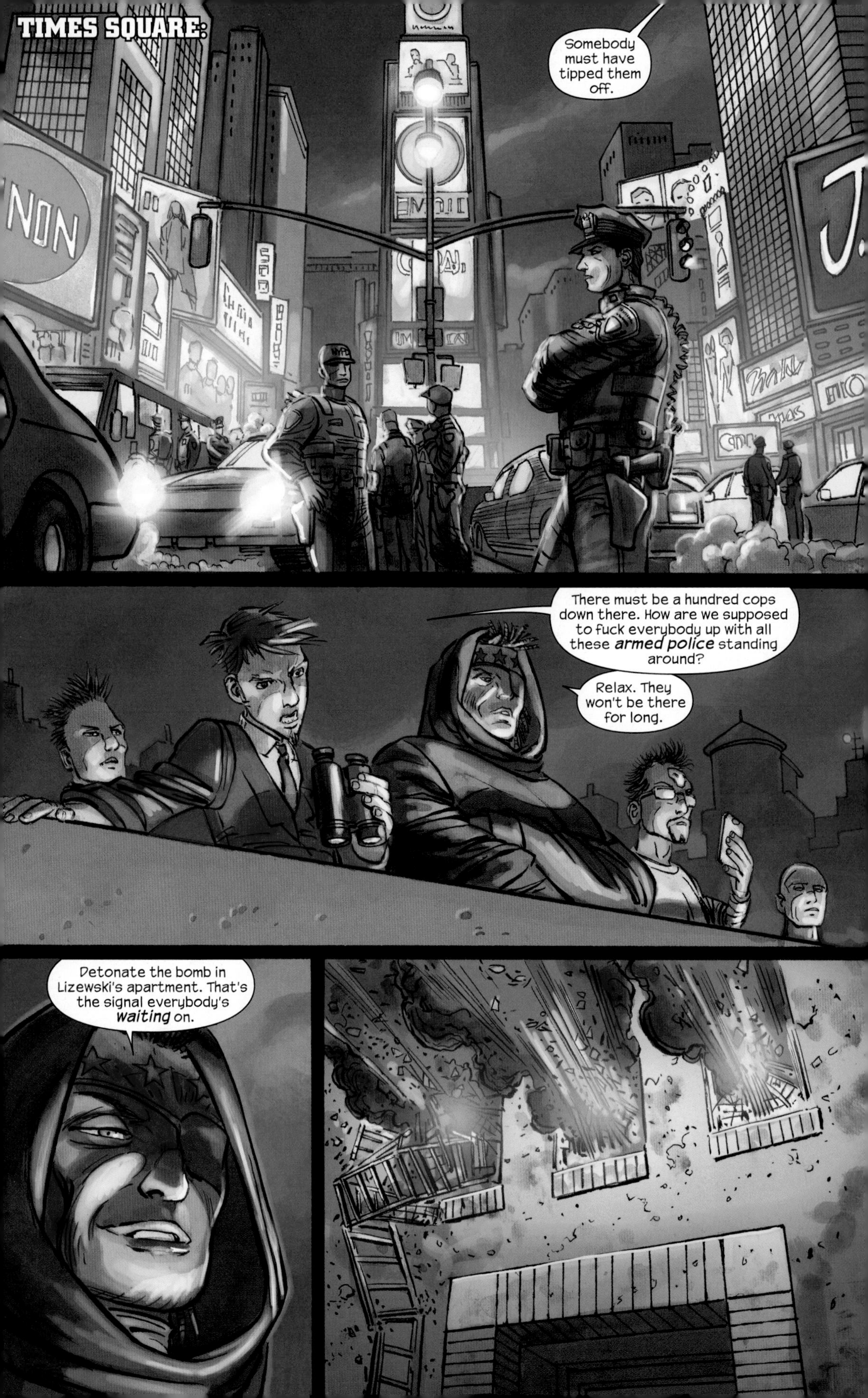
TIMES SQUARE:
Somebody must have tipped them off.
There must be a hundred cops down there. How are we supposed to fuck everybody up with all these *armed police* standing around?
Relax. They won't be there for long.
Detonate the bomb in Lizewski's apartment. That's the signal everybody's *waiting* on.

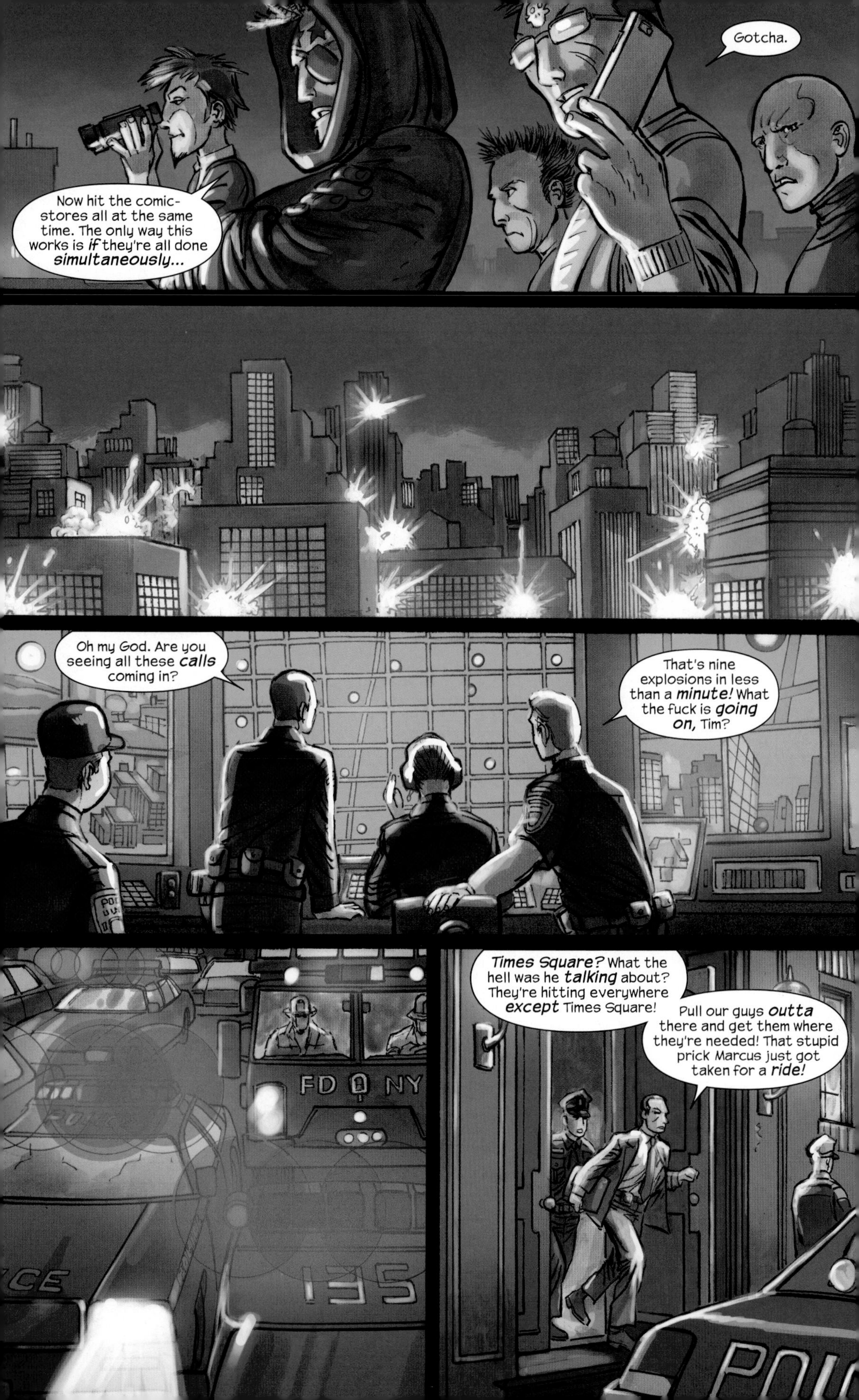
Gotcha.
Now hit the comic-stores all at the same time. The only way this works is *if* they're all done *simultaneously...*
Oh my God. Are you seeing all these *calls* coming in?
That's nine explosions in less than a *minute!* What the fuck is *going on,* Tim?
FD NY
135
Times Square? What the hell was he *talking* about? They're hitting everywhere *except* Times Square!
Pull our guys *outta* there and get them where they're needed! That stupid prick Marcus just got taken for a *ride!*

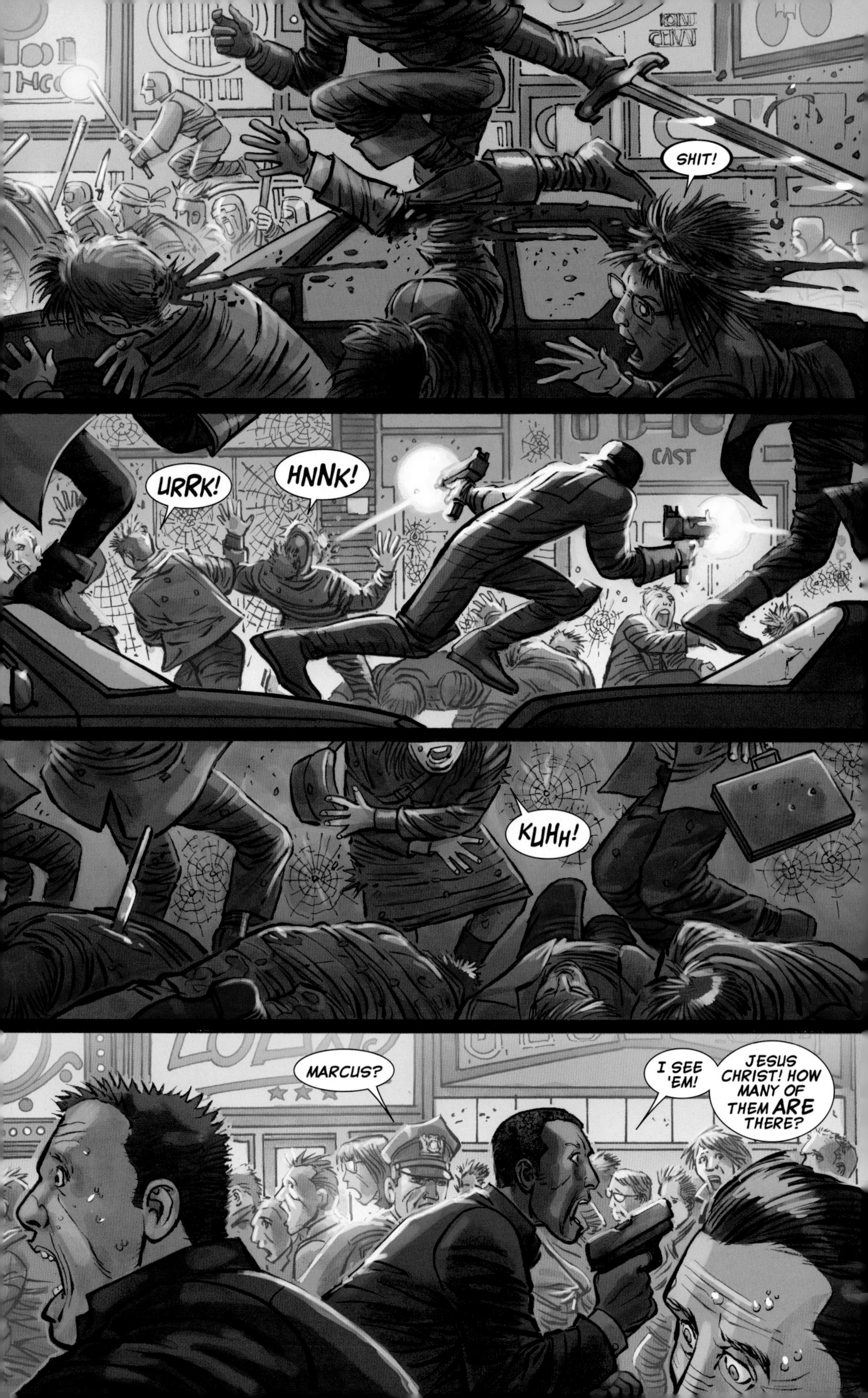
SHIT!
URRK!
HNNK!
KUHH!
MARCUS?
I SEE 'EM!
JESUS CHRIST! HOW MANY OF THEM ARE THERE?

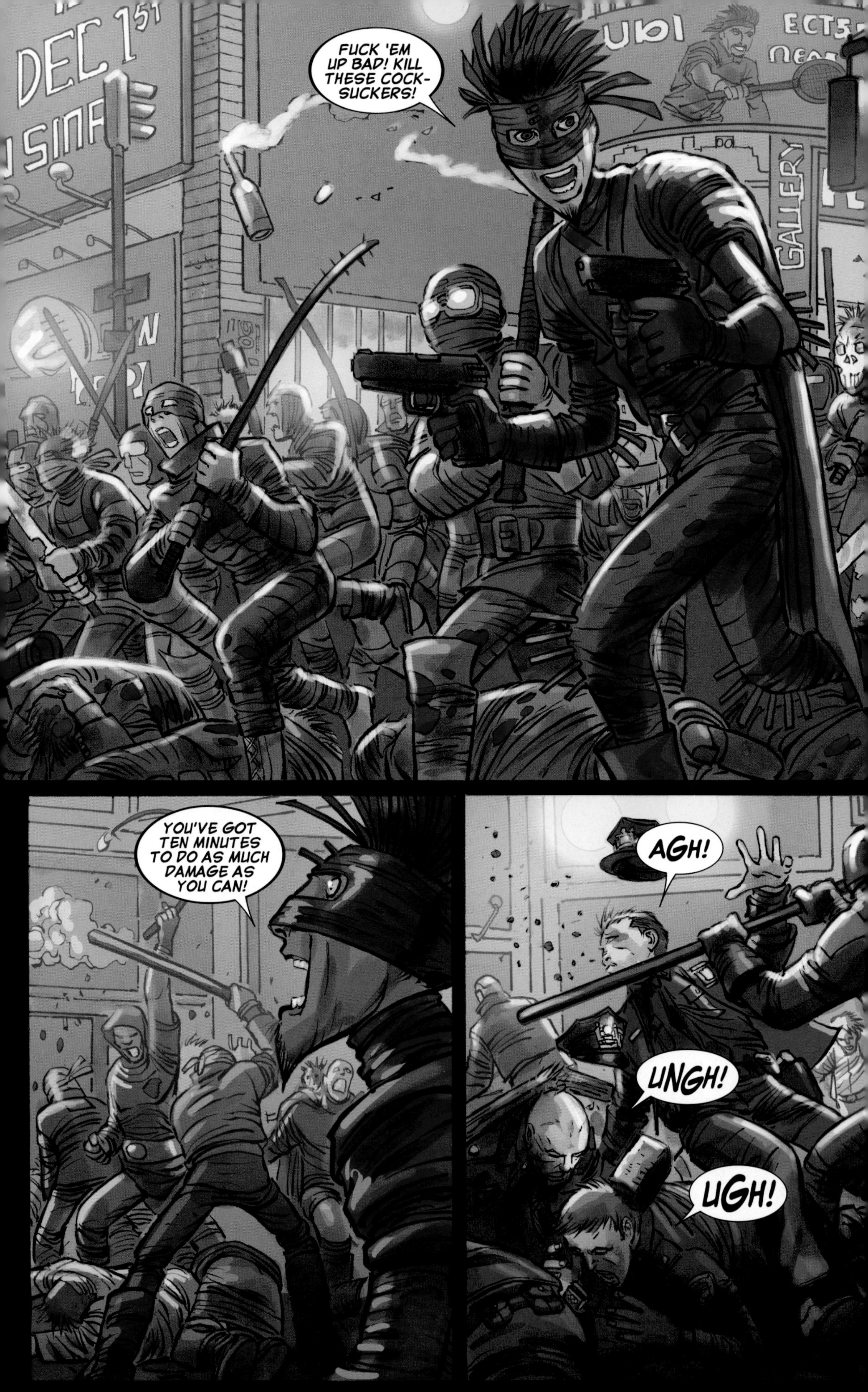
FUCK 'EM UP BAD! KILL THESE COCK-SUCKERS!
YOU'VE GOT TEN MINUTES TO DO AS MUCH DAMAGE AS YOU CAN!
AGH!
UNGH!
UGH!

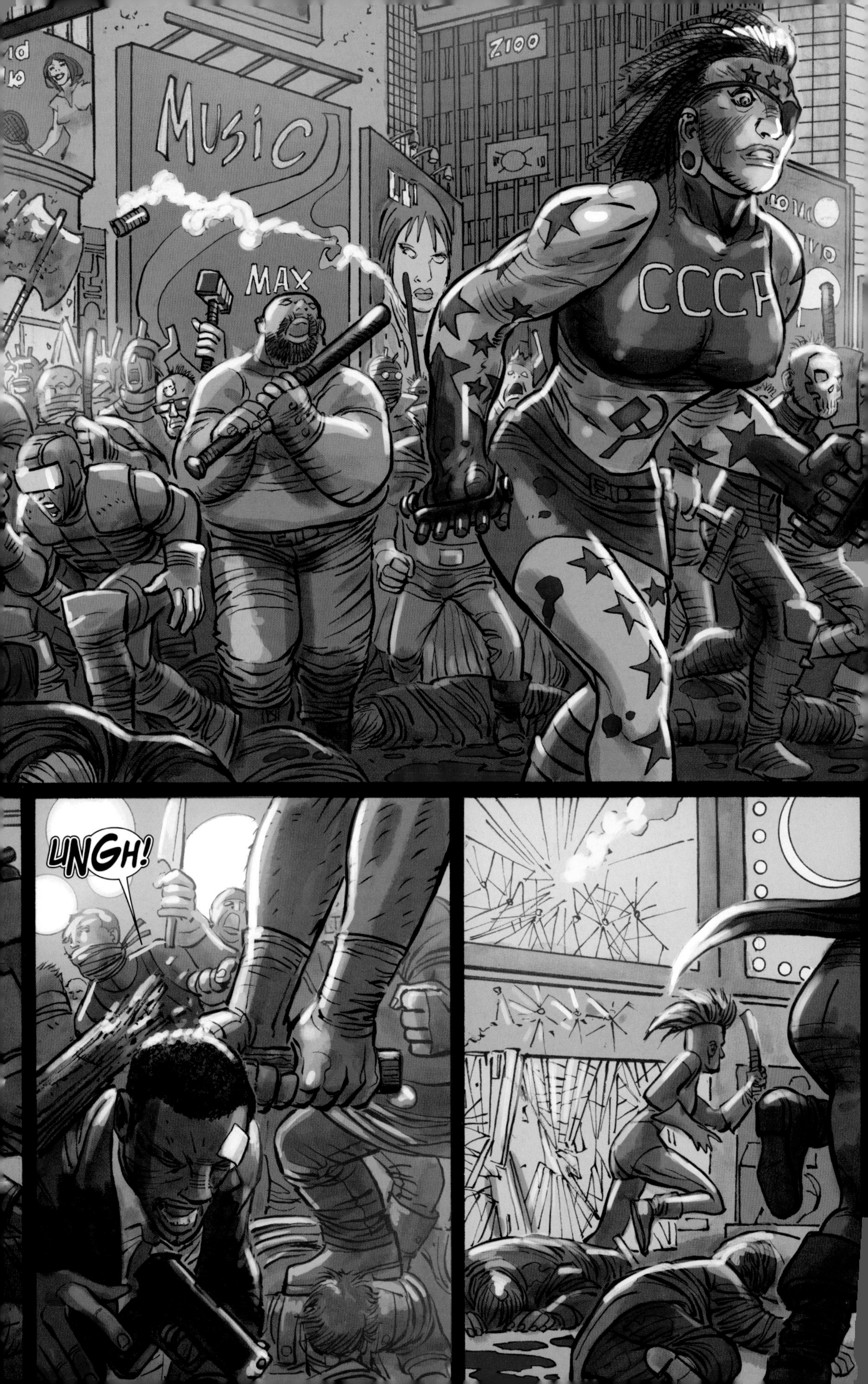
MUSIC
Z100
MAX
CCCP
UNGH!

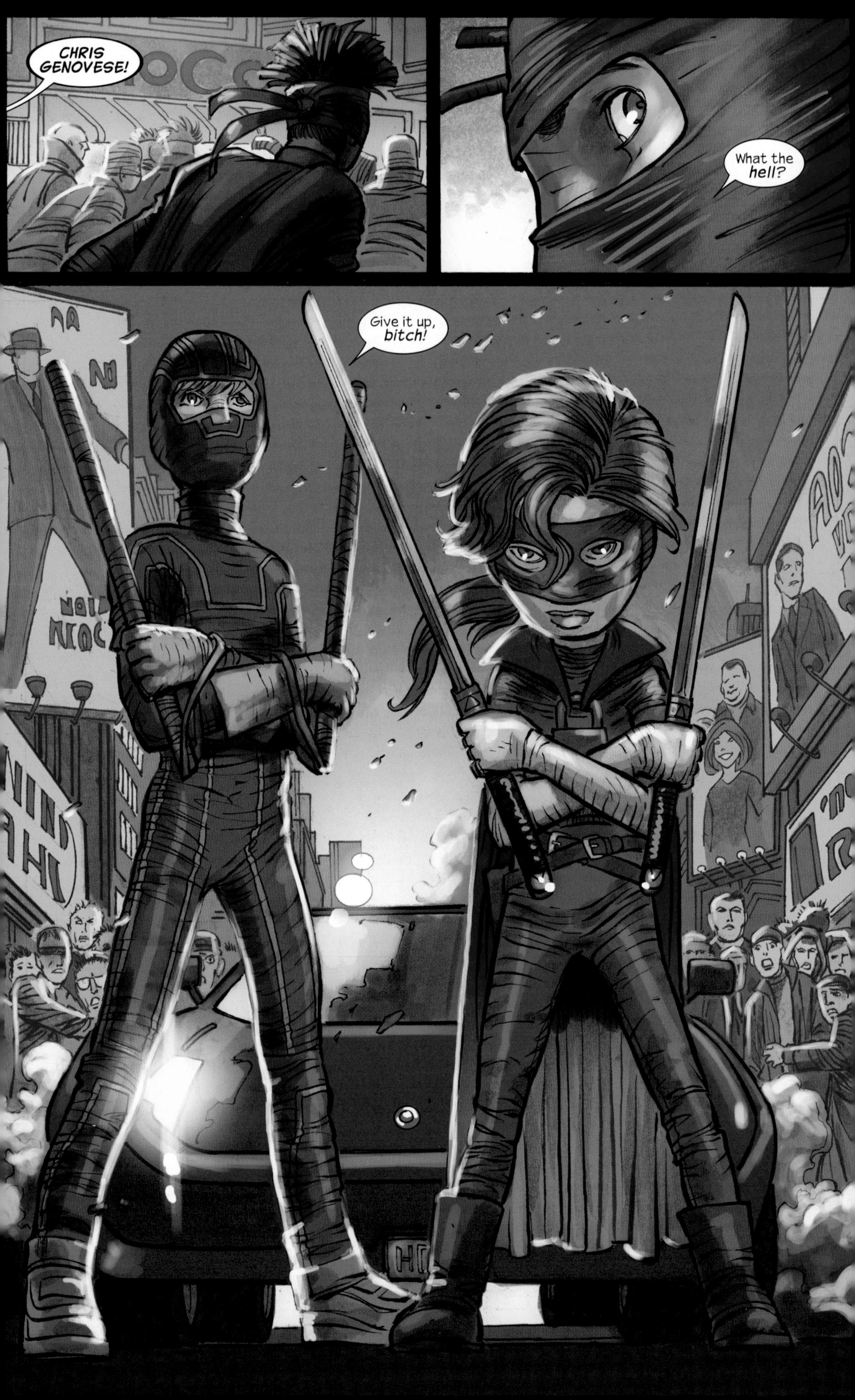
CHRIS GENOVESE!
What the hell?
Give it up, bitch!

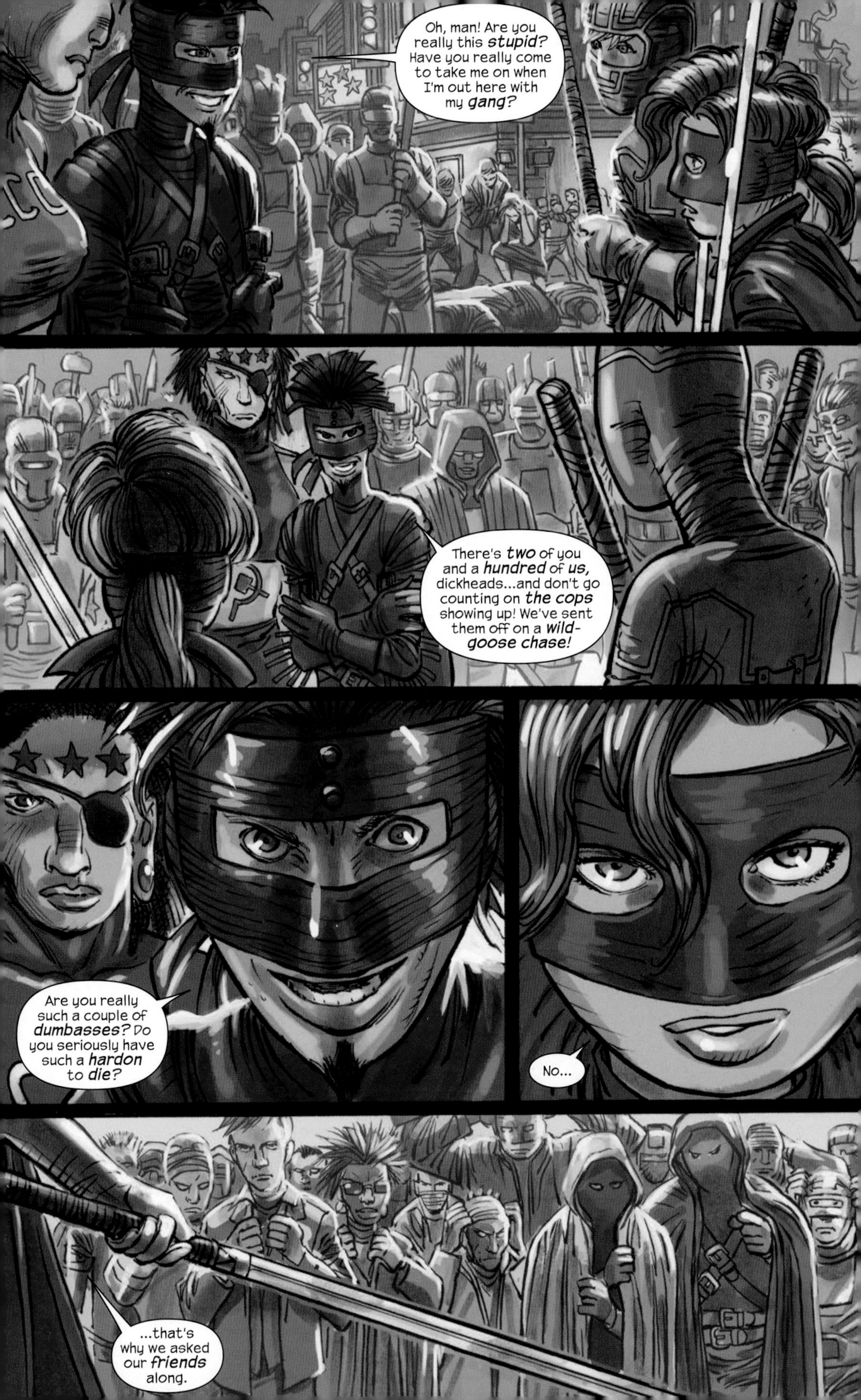
Oh, man! Are you really this *stupid*? Have you really come to take me on when I'm out here with my *gang*?
There's *two* of you and a *hundred* of *us*, dickheads...and don't go counting on *the cops* showing up! We've sent them off on a *wild-goose chase!*
Are you really such a couple of *dumbasses?* Do you seriously have such a *hardon* to *die*?
No...
...that's why we asked our *friends* along.

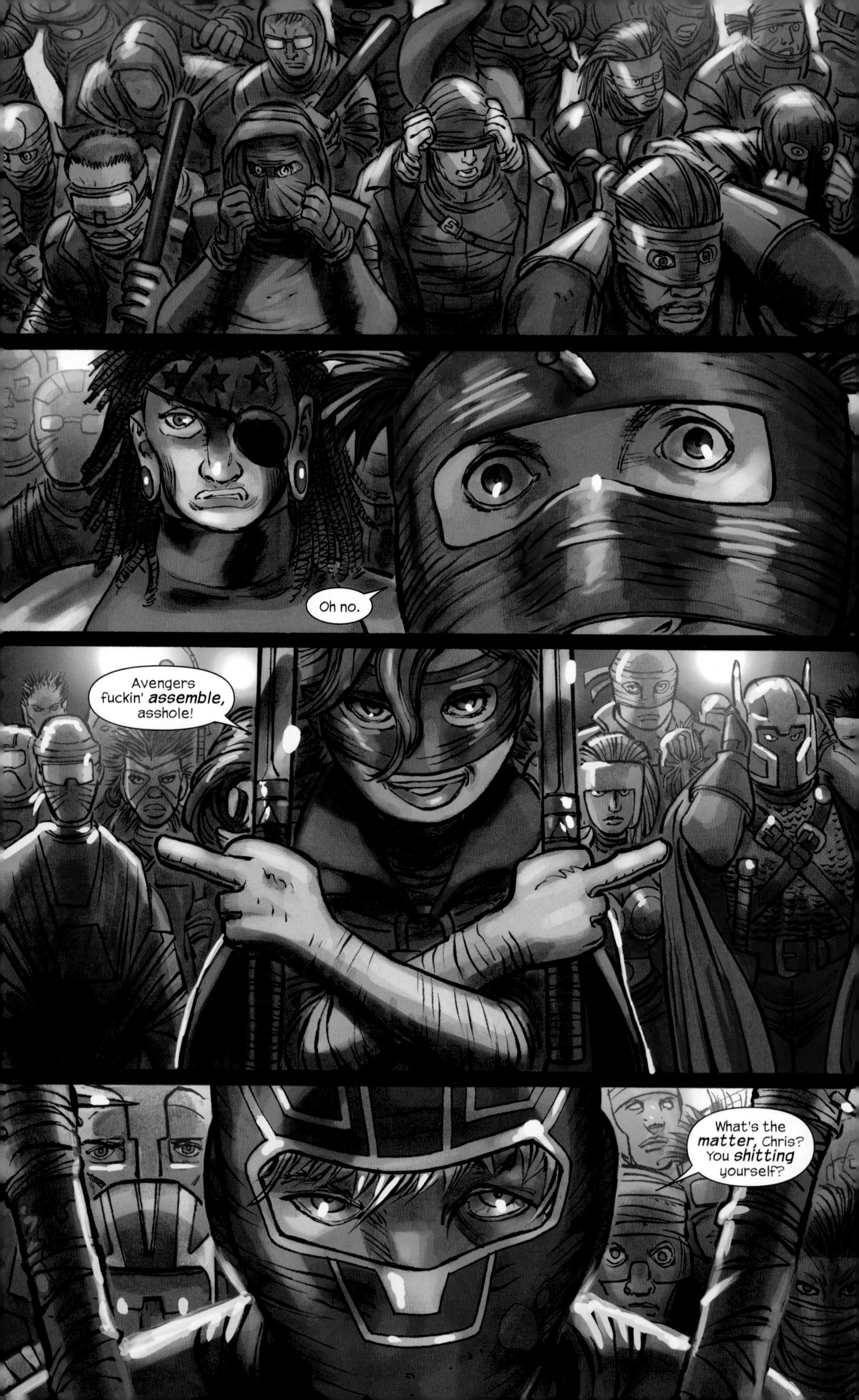
Oh no.
Avengers fuckin' assemble, asshole!
What's the matter, Chris? You shitting yourself?

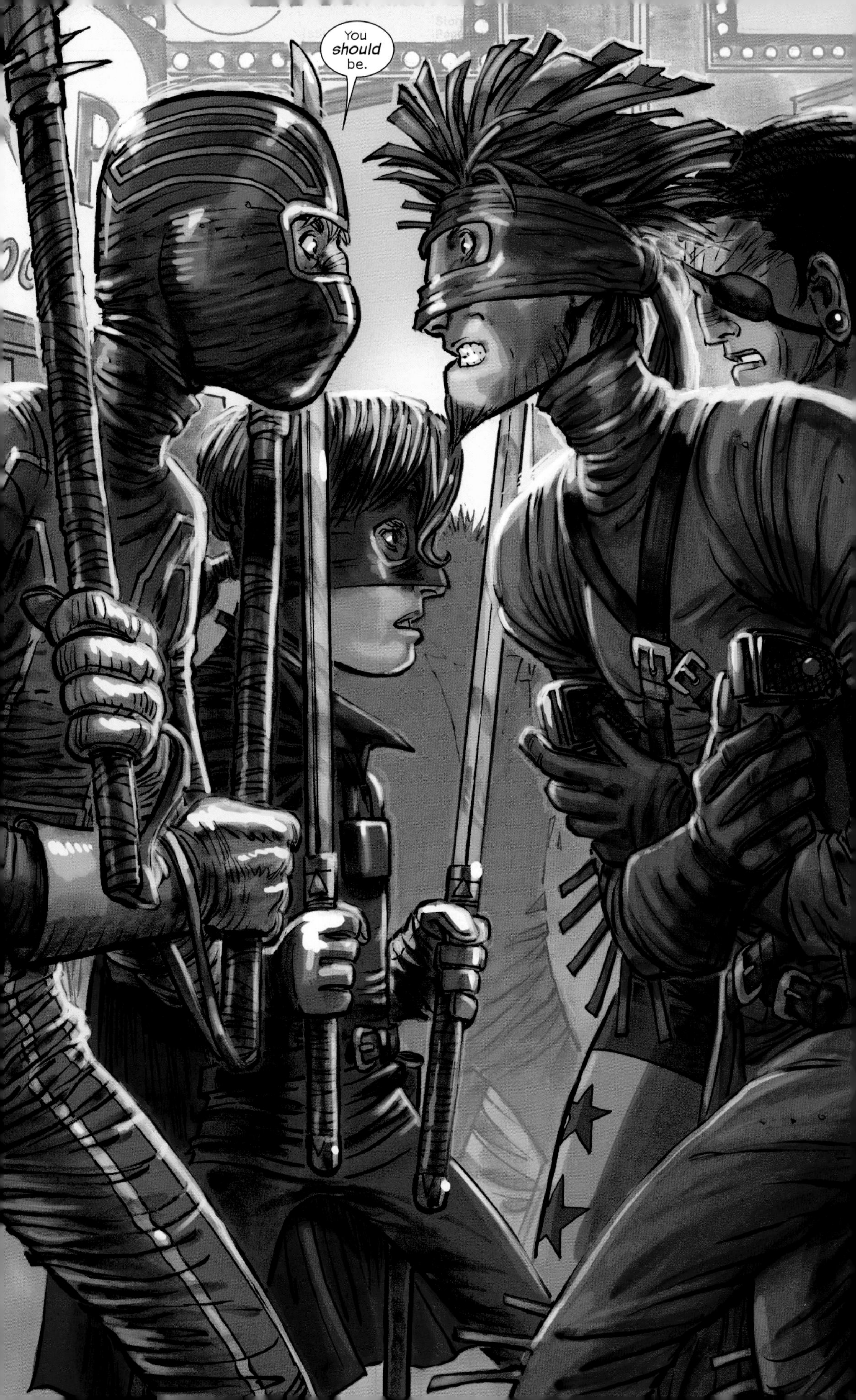
You should be.

SEVEN

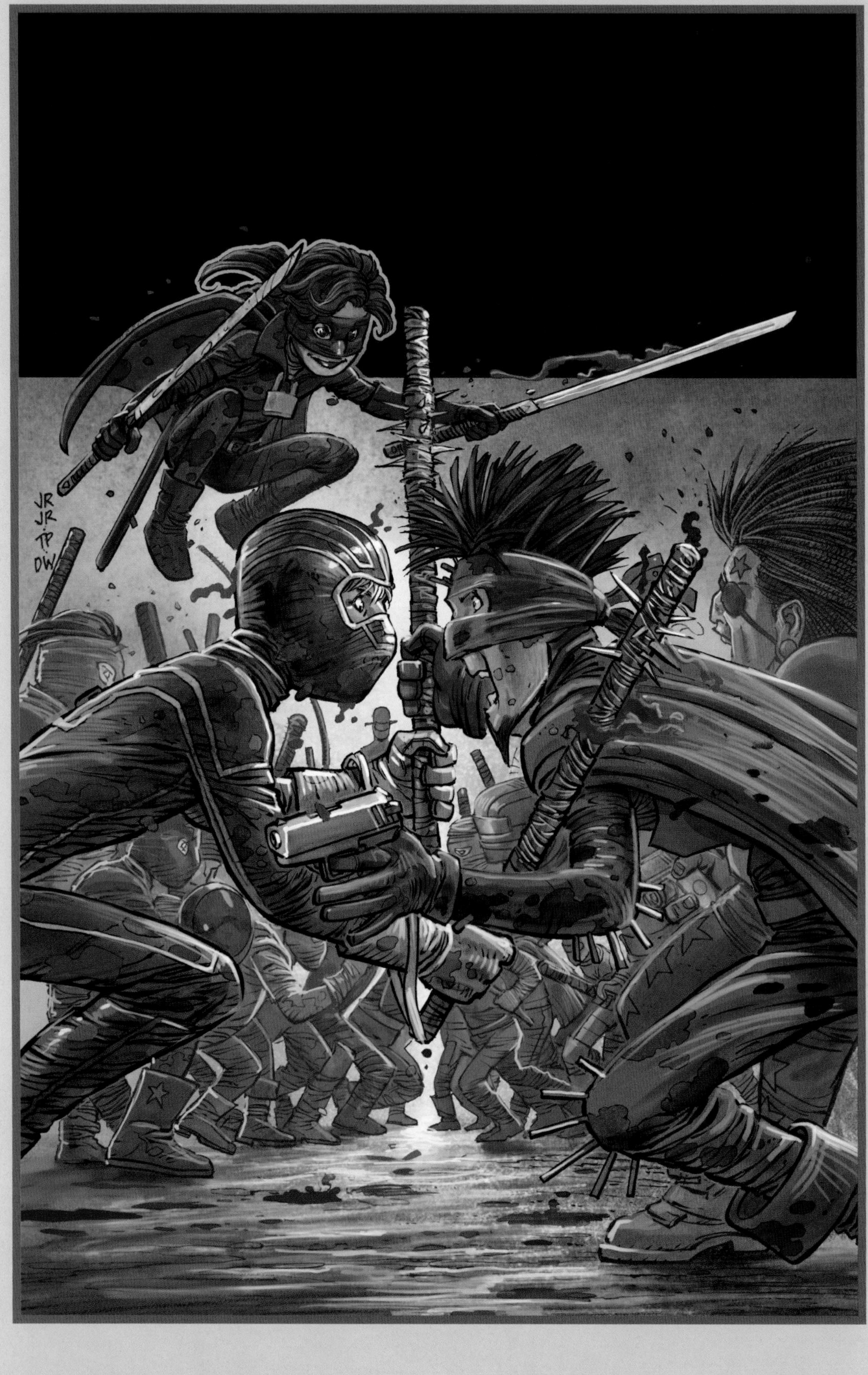
JR
JR
TP
DW

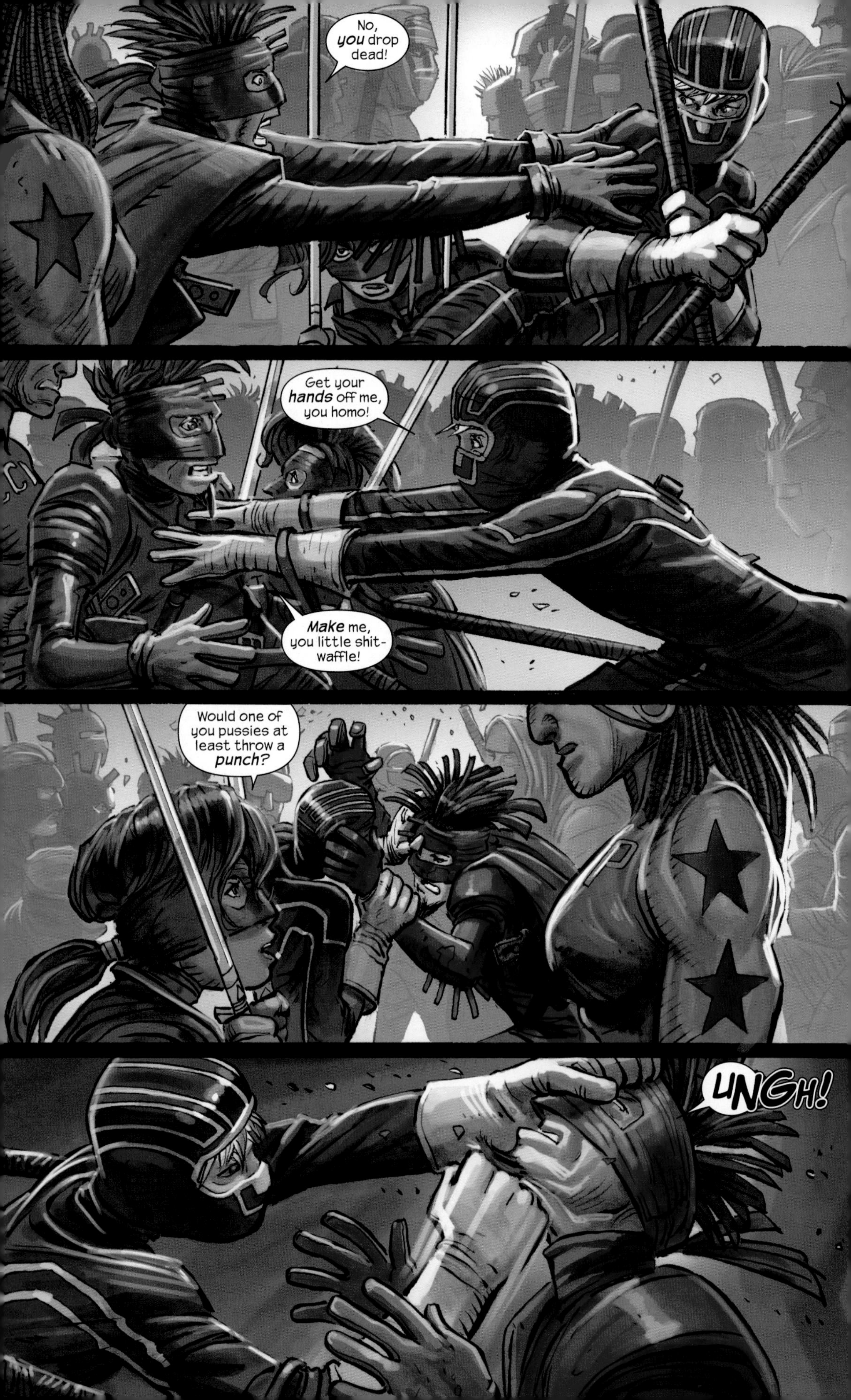
No, you drop dead!
Get your hands off me, you homo!
Make me, you little shit-waffle!
Would one of you pussies at least throw a punch?
UNGH!

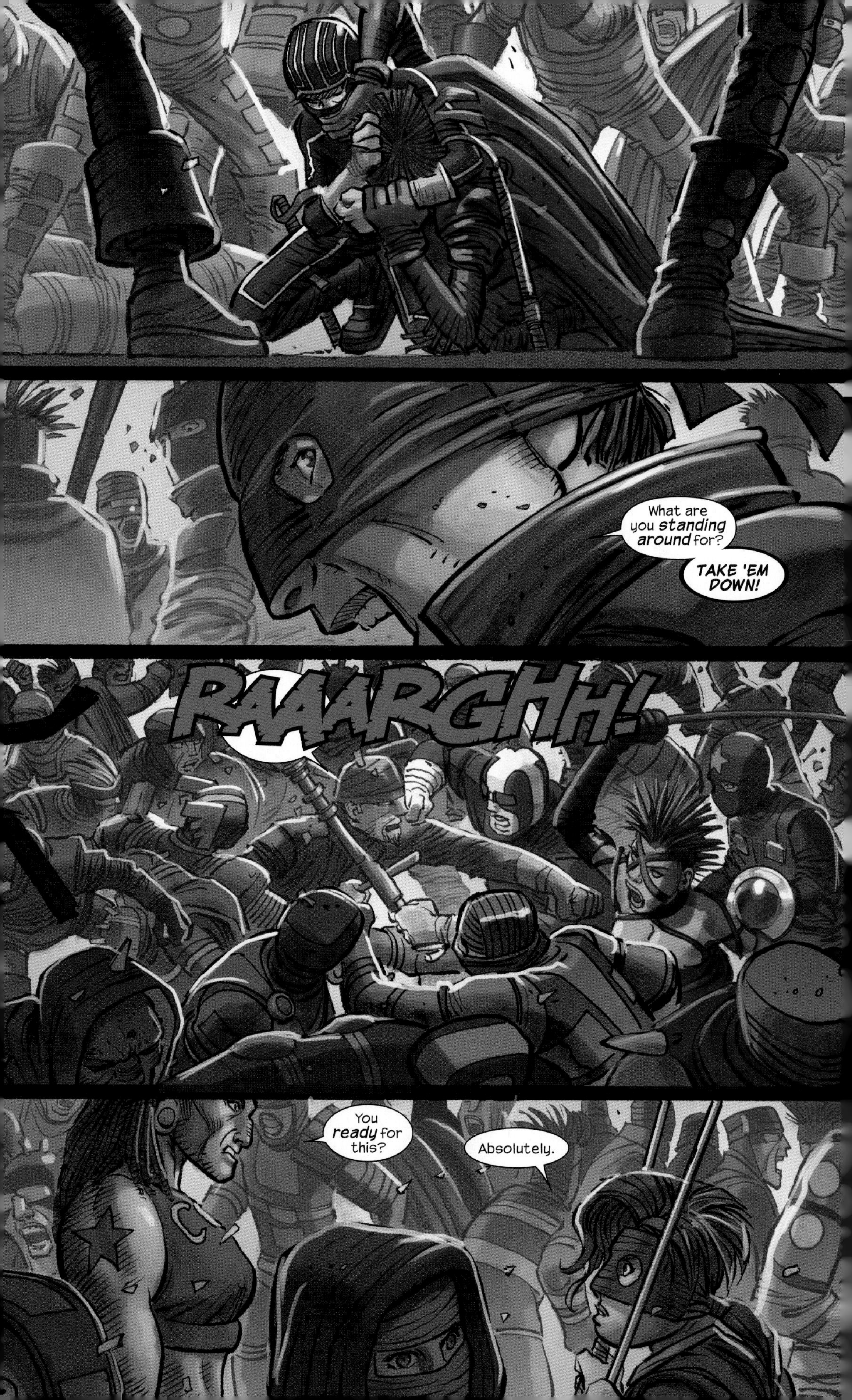
What are you **standing around** for?
TAKE 'EM DOWN!
RAAARGHH!
You **ready** for this?
Absolutely.

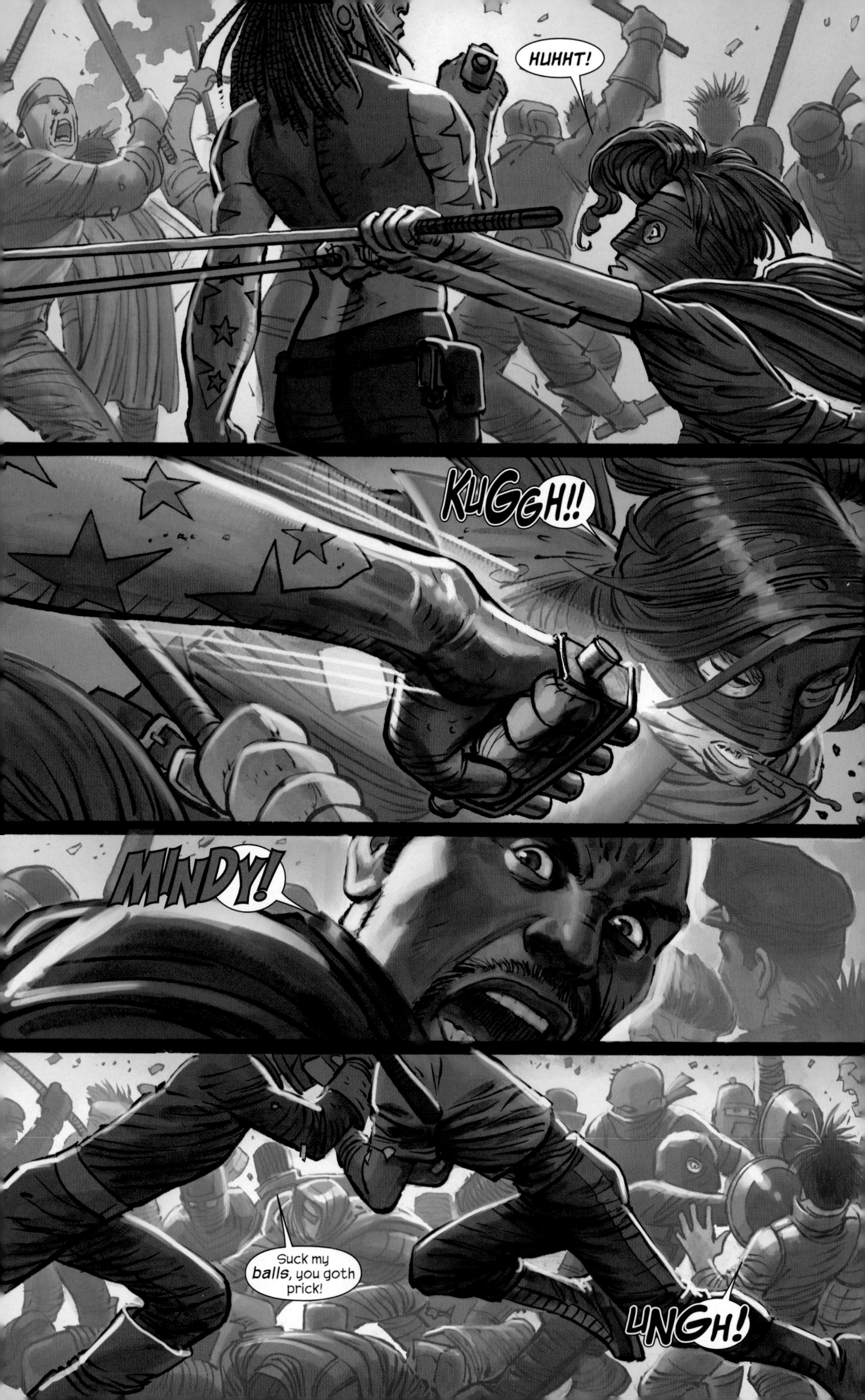
HUHHT!
KUGGH!!
MINDY!
Suck my *balls*, you goth prick!
UNGH!

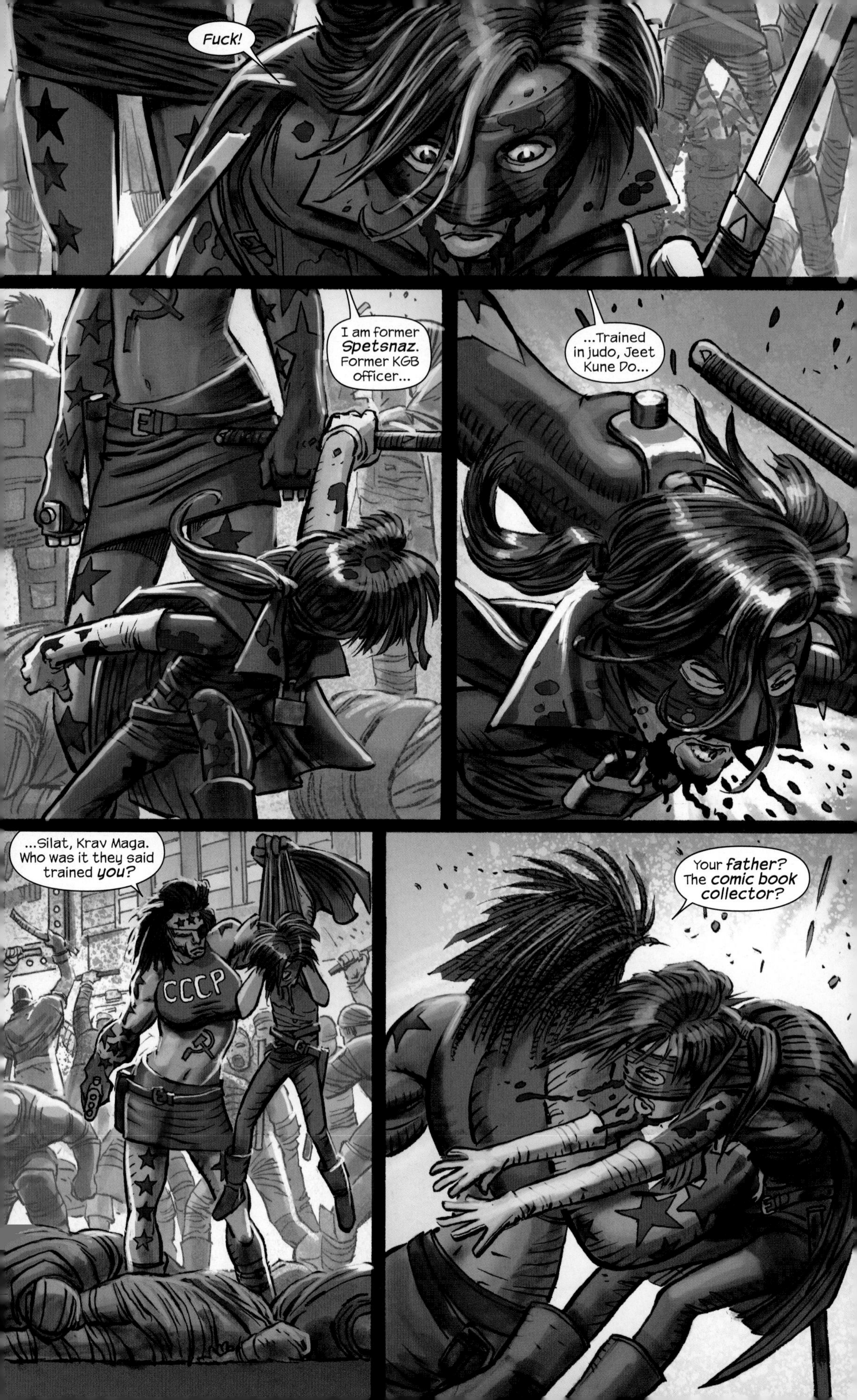

Fuck!
I am former Spetsnaz. Former KGB officer...
...Trained in judo, Jeet Kune Do...
...Silat, Krav Maga. Who was it they said trained you?
CCCP
Your father? The comic book collector?

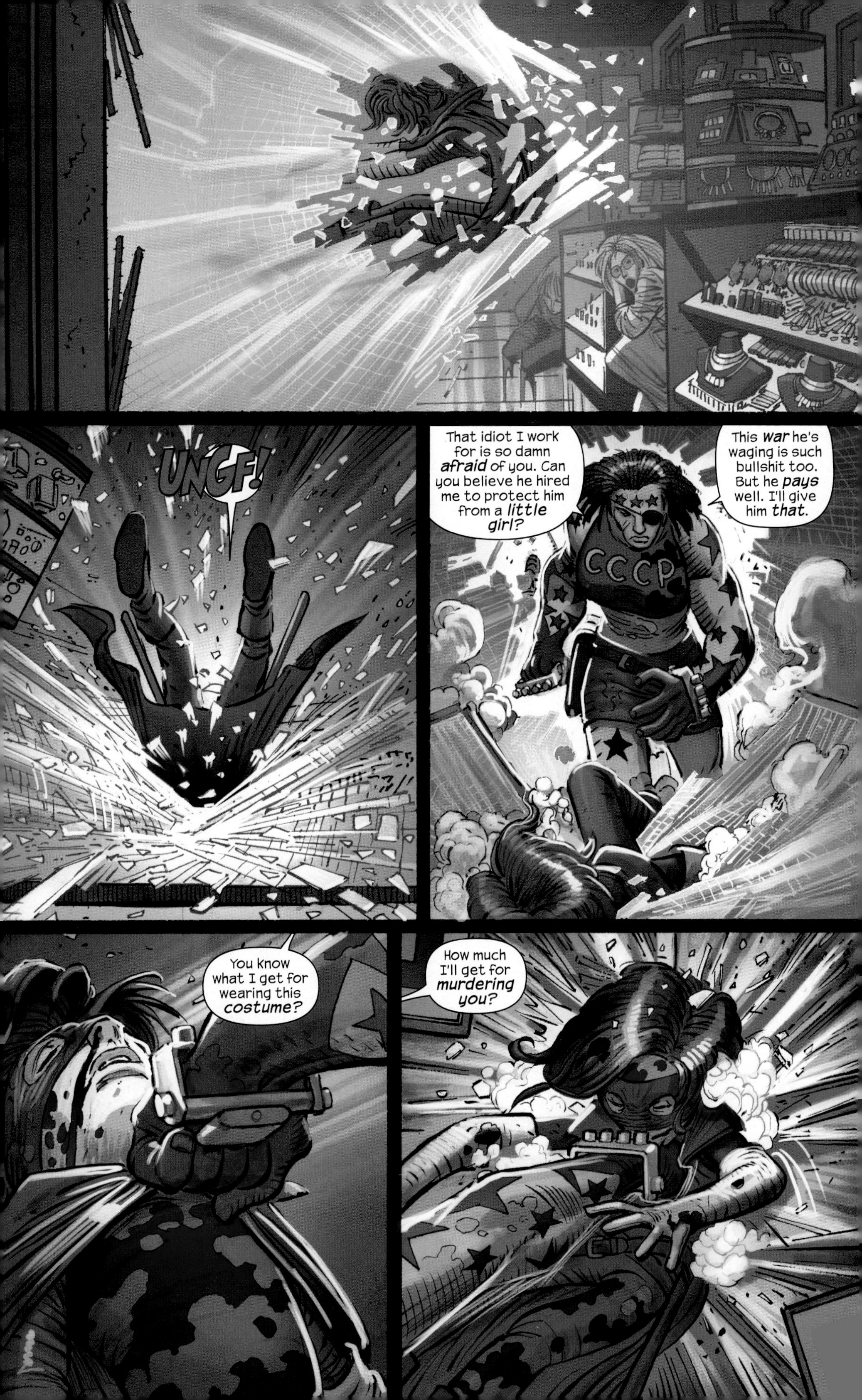
UNGF!
That idiot I work for is so damn *afraid* of you. Can you believe he hired me to protect him from a *little girl*?
This *war* he's waging is such bullshit too. But he *pays* well. I'll give him *that*.
You know what I get for wearing this *costume*?
How much I'll get for *murdering* you?

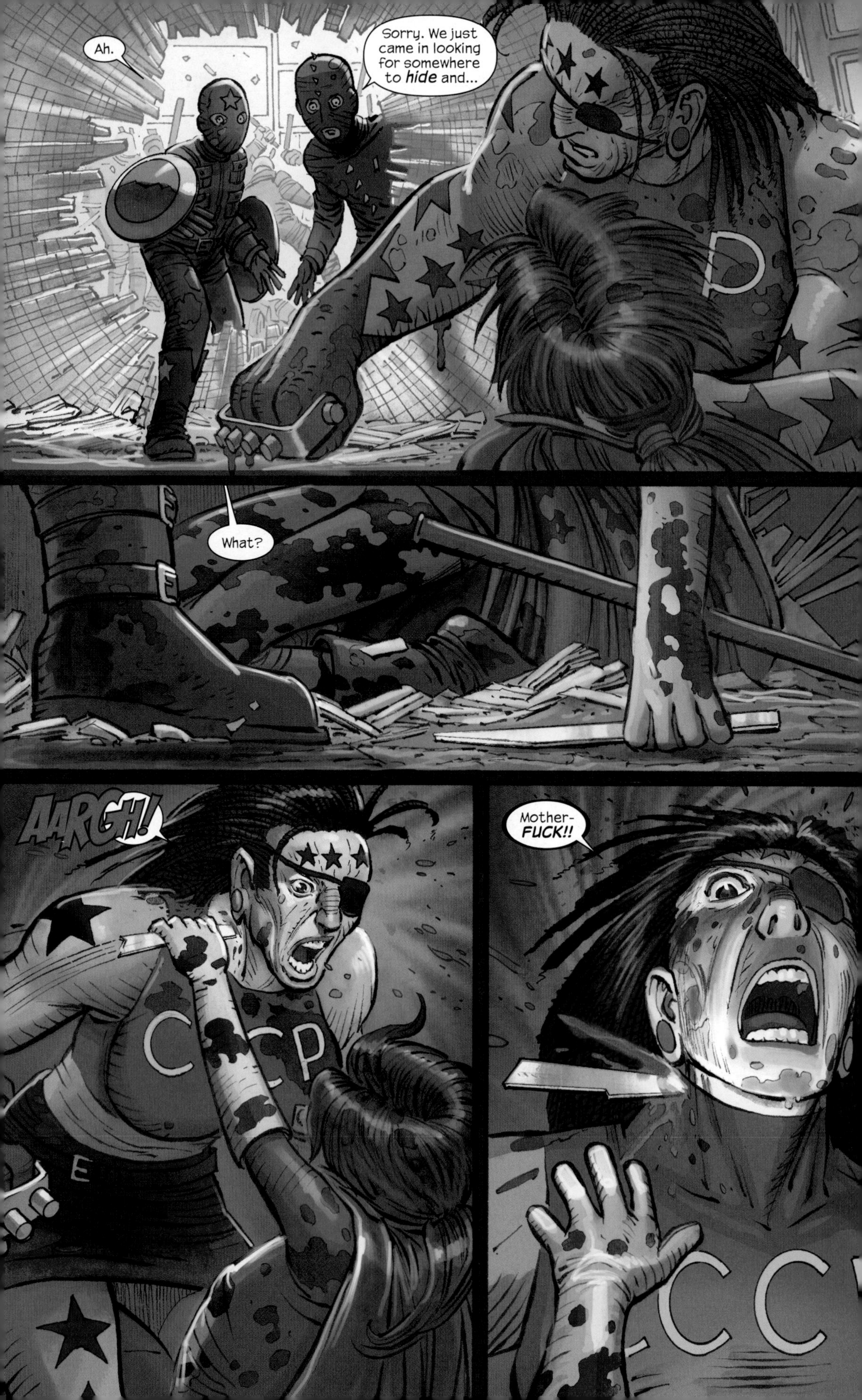

Ah.
Sorry. We just came in looking for somewhere to *hide* and...
What?
AARGH!
Mother-
FUCK!!

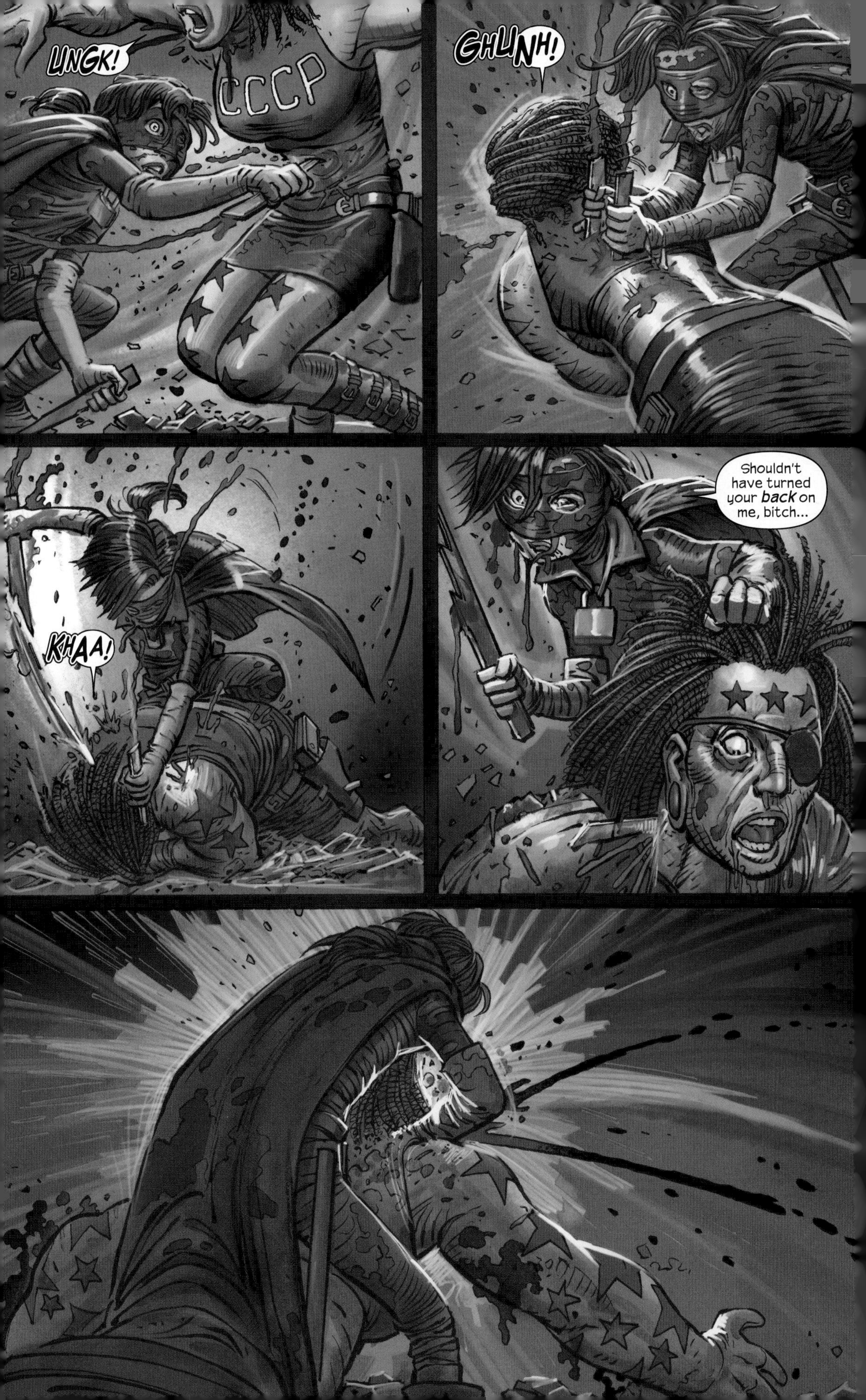
UNGK!
CCCP
GHLUNH!
KHAA!
Shouldn't have turned your *back* on me, bitch...

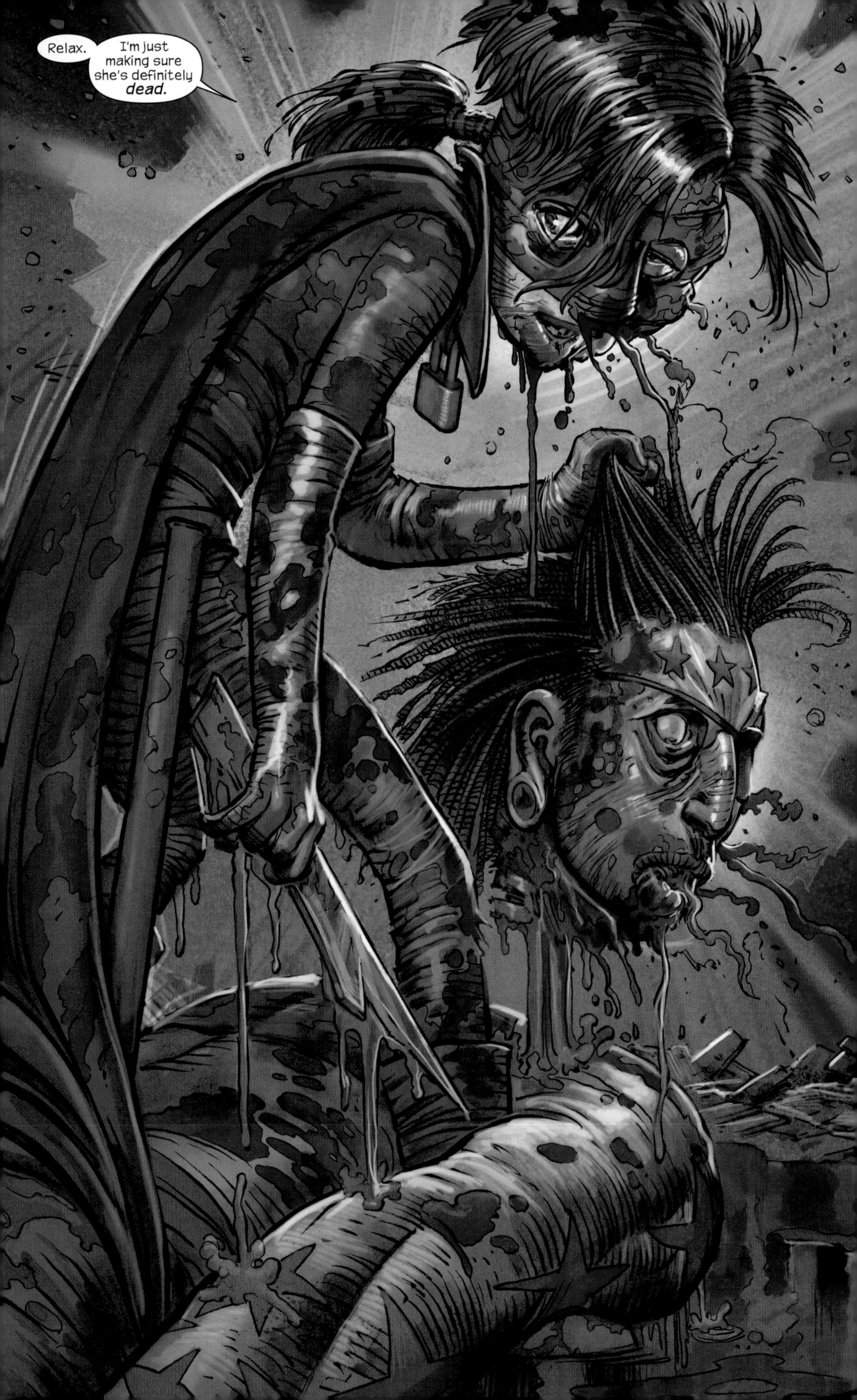
Relax.
I'm just making sure she's definitely *dead.*

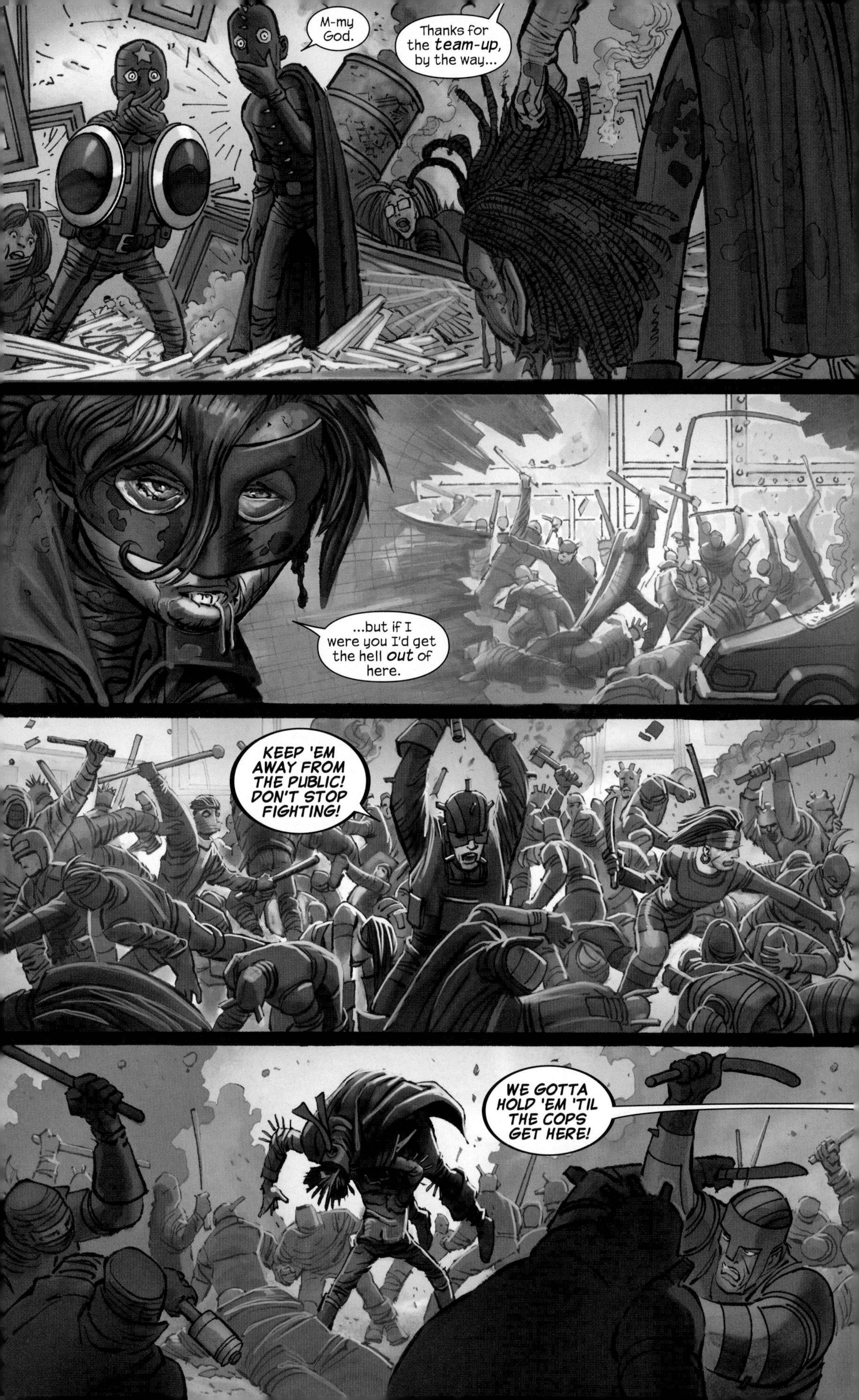
M-my God.
Thanks for the *team-up*, by the way...
...but if I were you I'd get the hell *out* of here.
KEEP 'EM AWAY FROM THE PUBLIC! DON'T STOP FIGHTING!
WE GOTTA HOLD 'EM 'TIL THE COPS GET HERE!

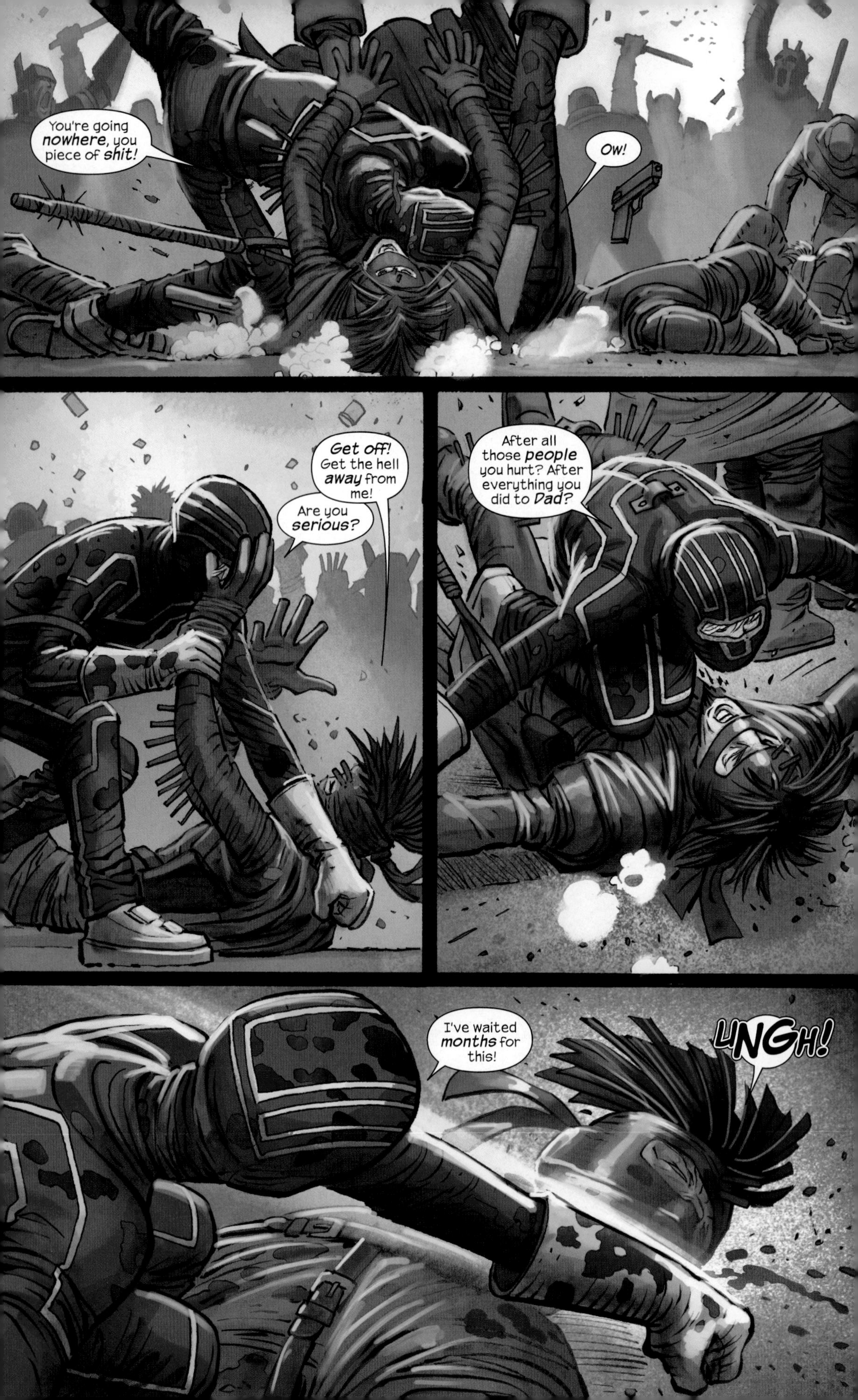

You're going nowhere, you piece of shit!
Ow!
Get off! Get the hell away from me!
Are you serious?
After all those people you hurt? After everything you did to Dad?
I've waited months for this!
UNGH!

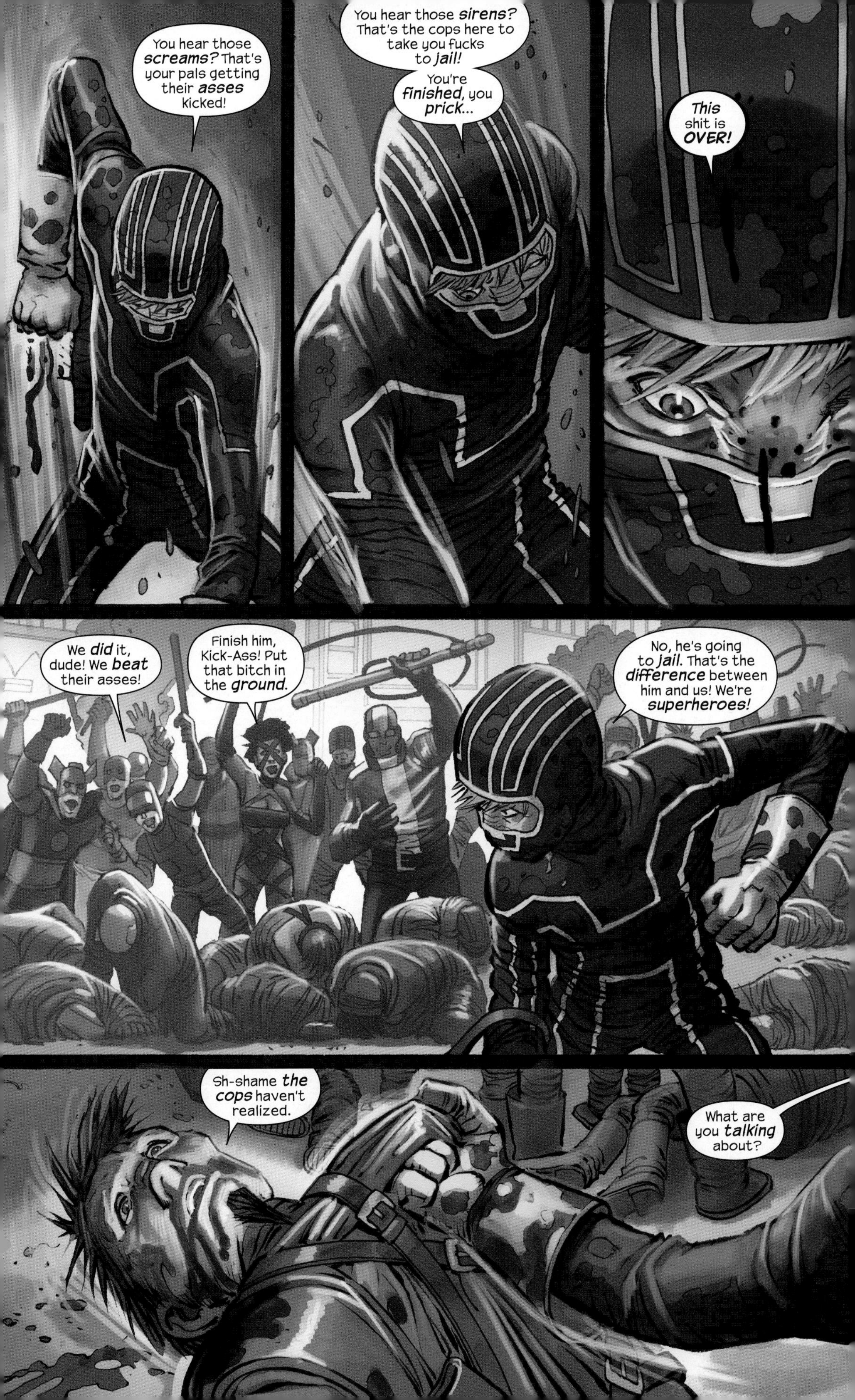
You hear those *screams?* That's your pals getting their *asses* kicked!
You hear those *sirens?* That's the cops here to take you fucks to *jail!*
You're *finished*, you *prick*...
This shit is *OVER!*
We *did* it, dude! We *beat* their asses!
Finish him, Kick-Ass! Put that bitch in the *ground*.
No, he's going to *jail*. That's the *difference* between him and us! We're *superheroes!*
Sh-shame *the cops* haven't realized.
What are you *talking* about?

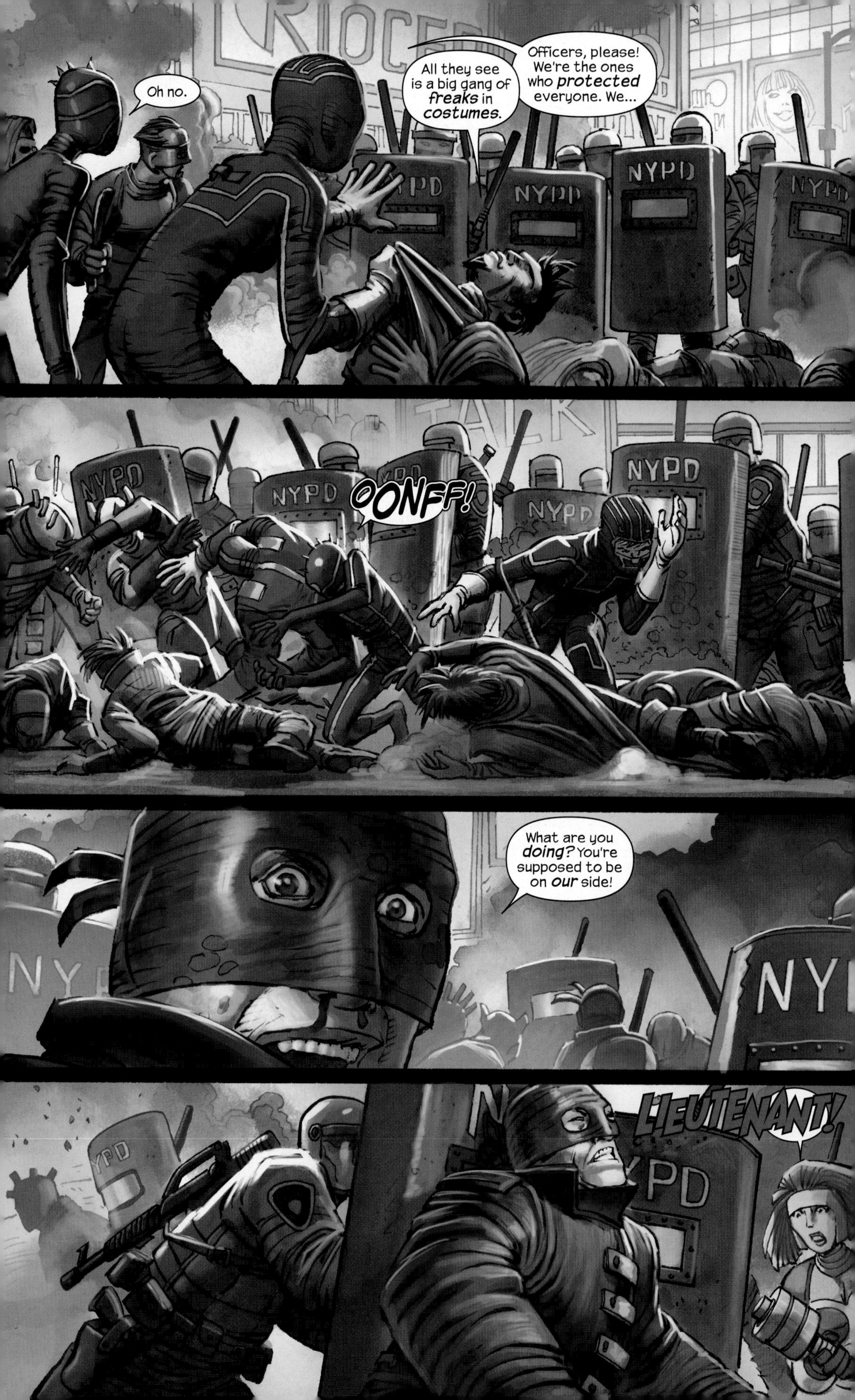
Oh no.
All they see is a big gang of *freaks* in *costumes*.
Officers, please! We're the ones who *protected* everyone. We...
OONFF!
What are you *doing?* You're supposed to be on *our* side!
LIEUTENANT!

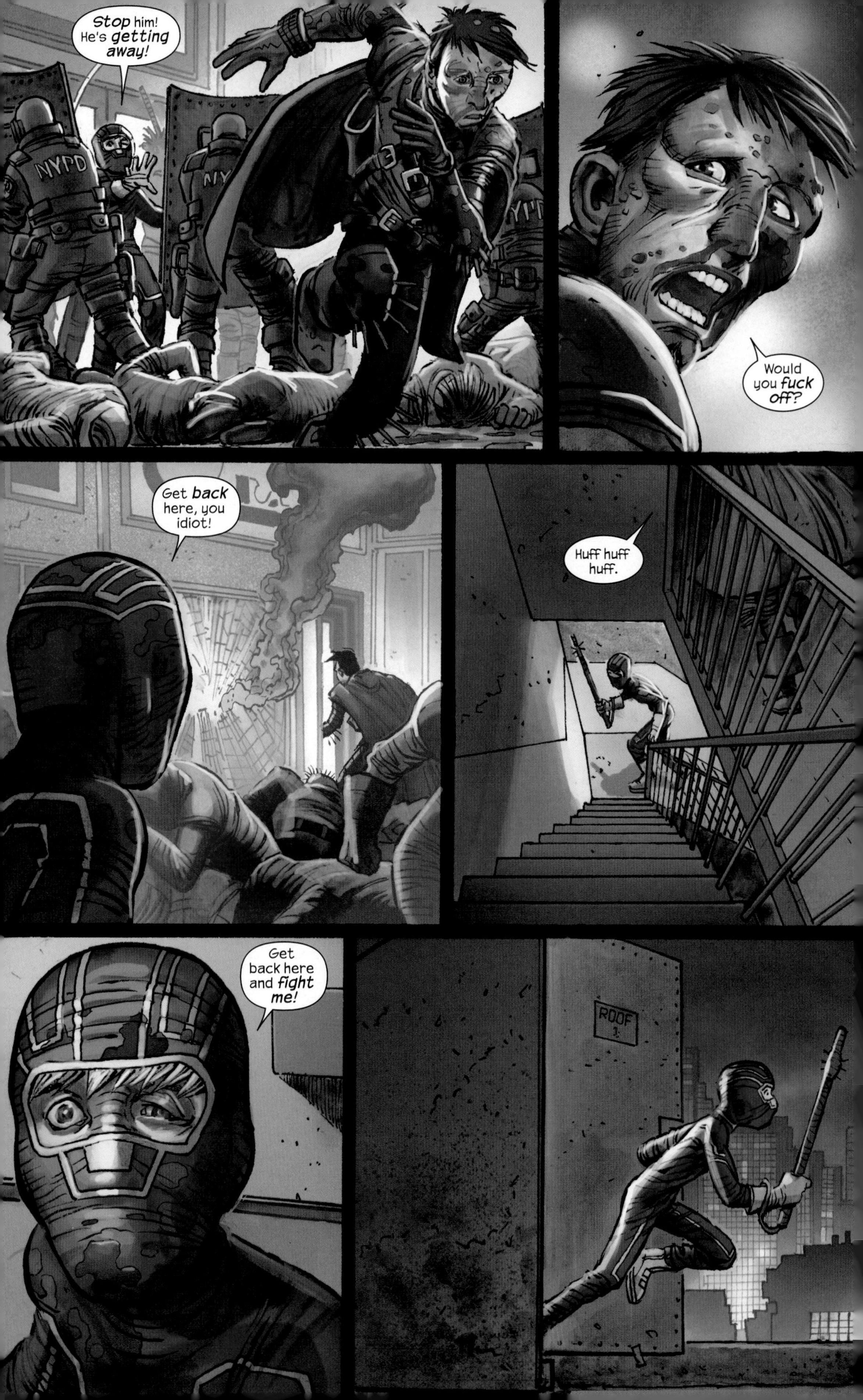
Stop him! He's getting away!
Would you fuck off?
Get back here, you idiot!
Huff huff huff.
Get back here and fight me!
ROOF

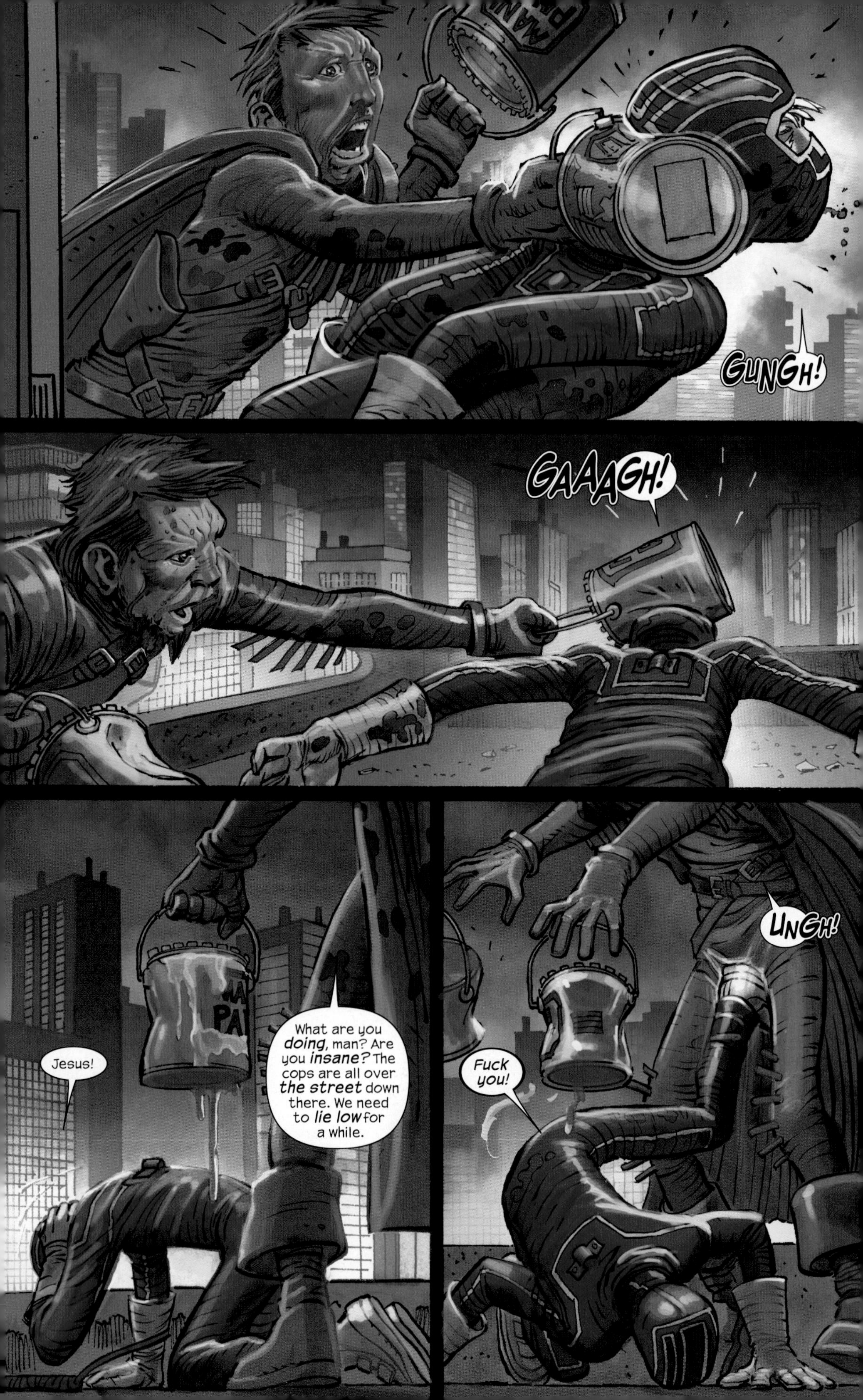
GUNGH!
GAAAGH!
Jesus!
What are you doing, man? Are you insane? The cops are all over the street down there. We need to lie low for a while.
UNGH!
Fuck you!

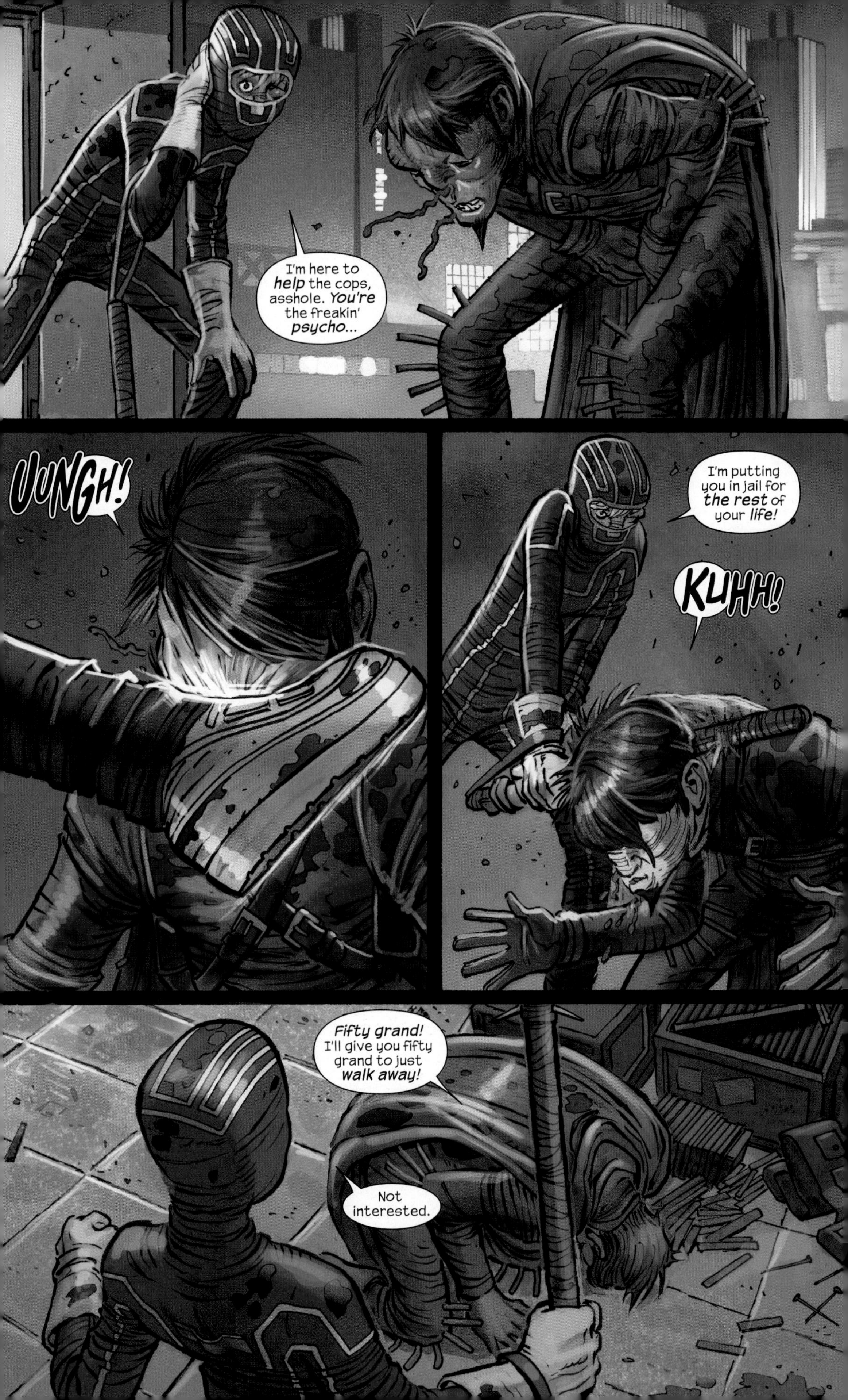

I'm here to *help* the cops, asshole. *You're* the freakin' *psycho...*
UUNGH!
I'm putting you in jail for *the rest* of your *life!*
KUHH!
Fifty grand! I'll give you fifty grand to just *walk away!*
Not interested.

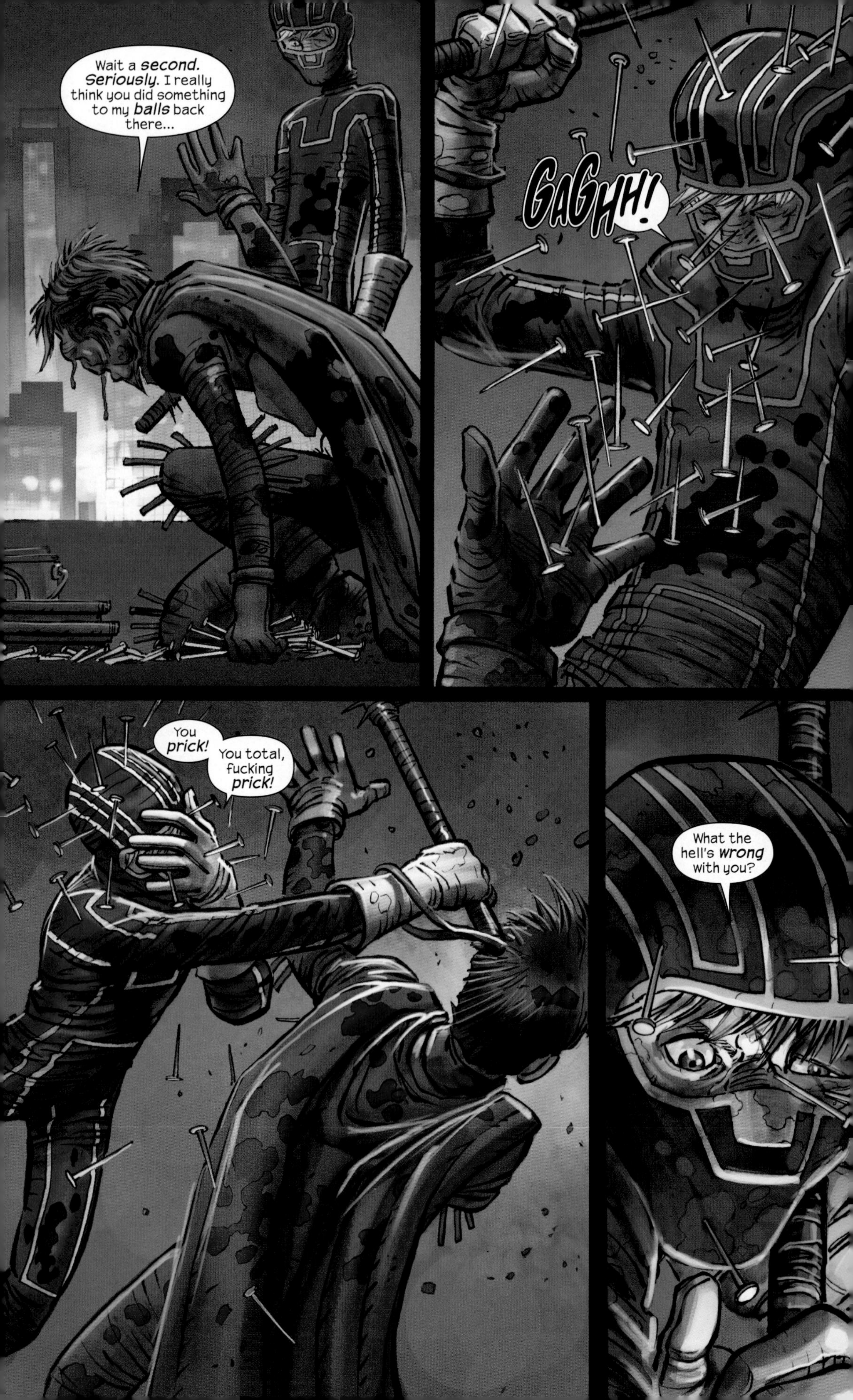

Wait a *second.* *Seriously.* I really think you did something to my *balls* back there...
GAGHH!
You *prick!*
You total, fucking *prick!*
What the hell's *wrong* with you?

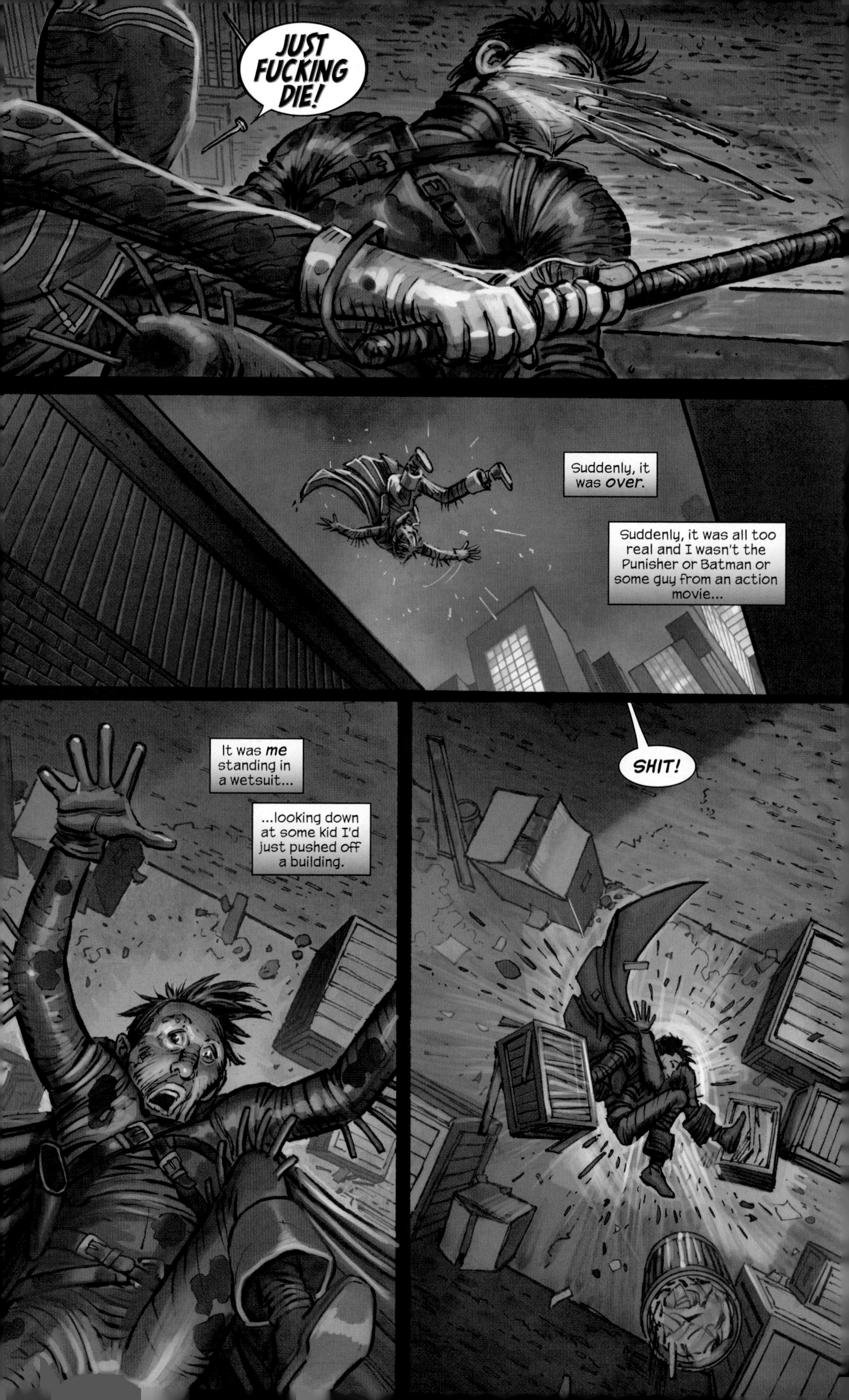
JUST FUCKING DIE!
Suddenly, it was over.
Suddenly, it was all too real and I wasn't the Punisher or Batman or some guy from an action movie...
It was me standing in a wetsuit...
...looking down at some kid I'd just pushed off a building.
SHIT!

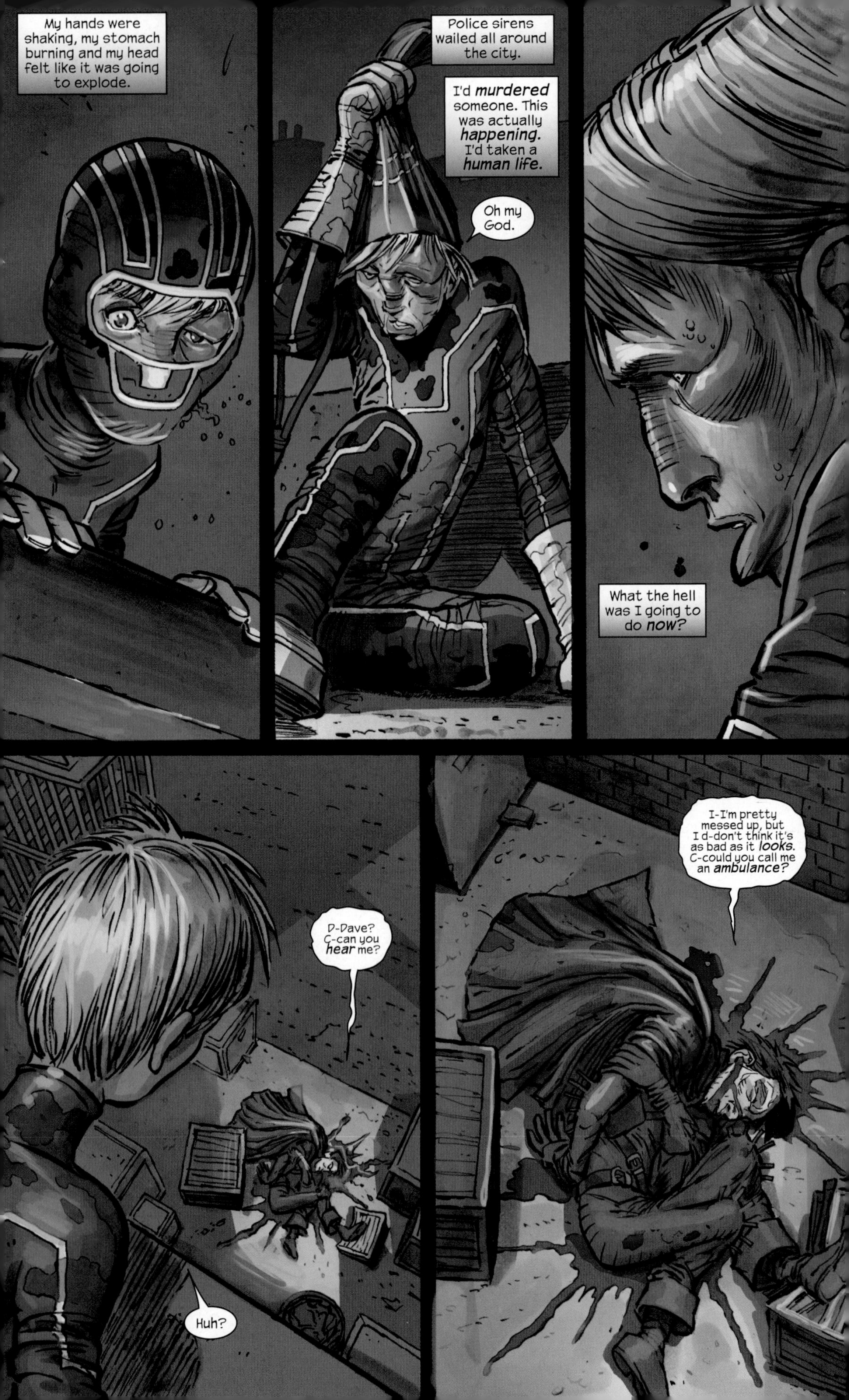

My hands were shaking, my stomach burning and my head felt like it was going to explode.
Police sirens wailed all around the city.
I'd *murdered* someone. This was actually *happening.* I'd taken a *human life.*
Oh my God.
What the hell was I going to do *now?*
D-Dave? C-can you *hear* me?
Huh?
I-I'm pretty messed up, but I d-don't think it's as bad as it *looks.* C-could you call me an *ambulance?*

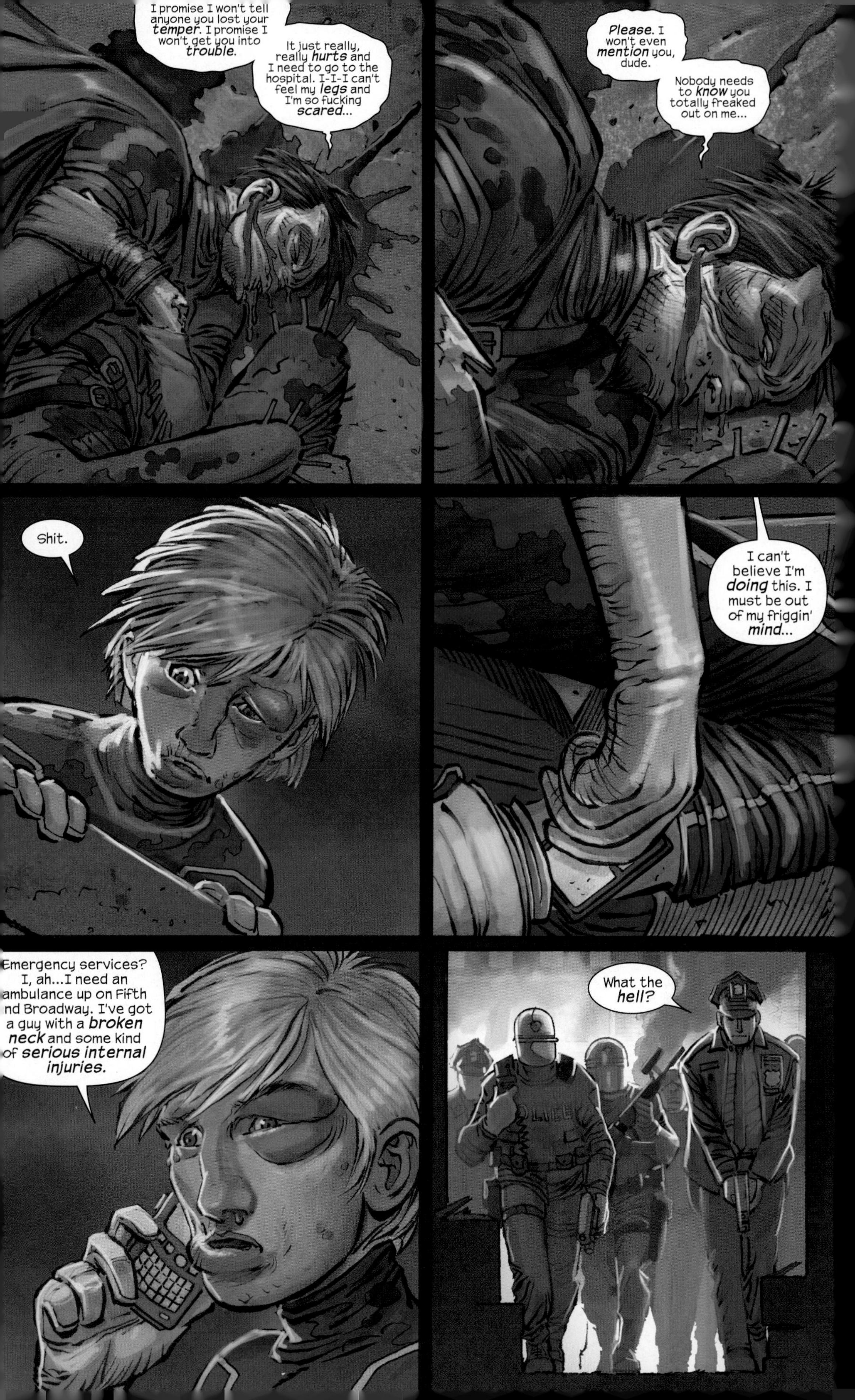
I promise I won't tell anyone you lost your temper. I promise I won't get you into trouble.
It just really, really hurts and I need to go to the hospital. I-I-I can't feel my legs and I'm so fucking scared...
Please. I won't even mention you, dude.
Nobody needs to know you totally freaked out on me...
Shit.
I can't believe I'm doing this. I must be out of my friggin' mind...
Emergency services? I, ah...I need an ambulance up on Fifth nd Broadway. I've got a guy with a broken neck and some kind of serious internal injuries.
What the hell?

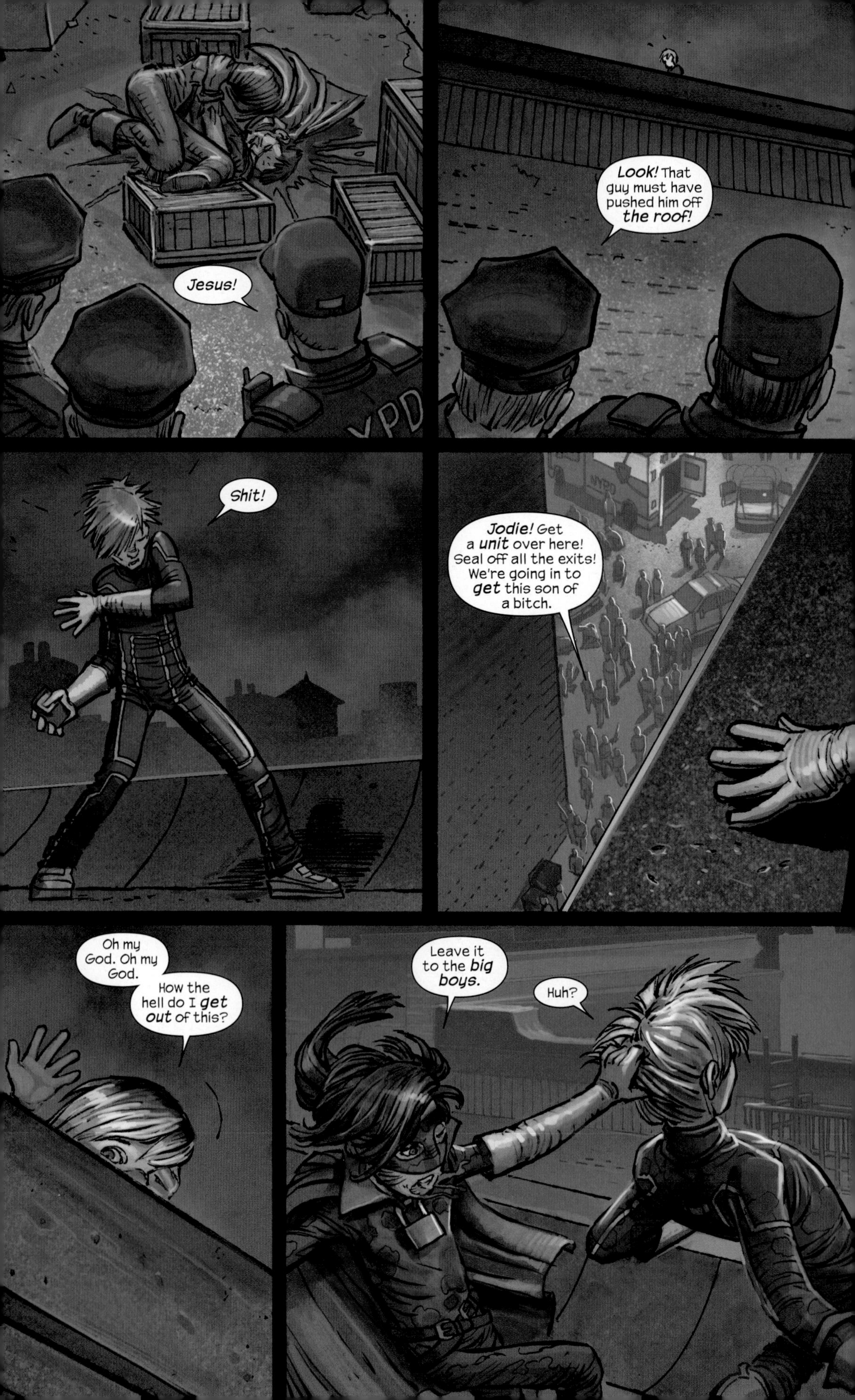
Jesus!
Look! That guy must have pushed him off the roof!
Shit!
Jodie! Get a unit over here! Seal off all the exits! We're going in to get this son of a bitch.
Oh my God. Oh my God.
How the hell do I get out of this?
Leave it to the big boys.
Huh?

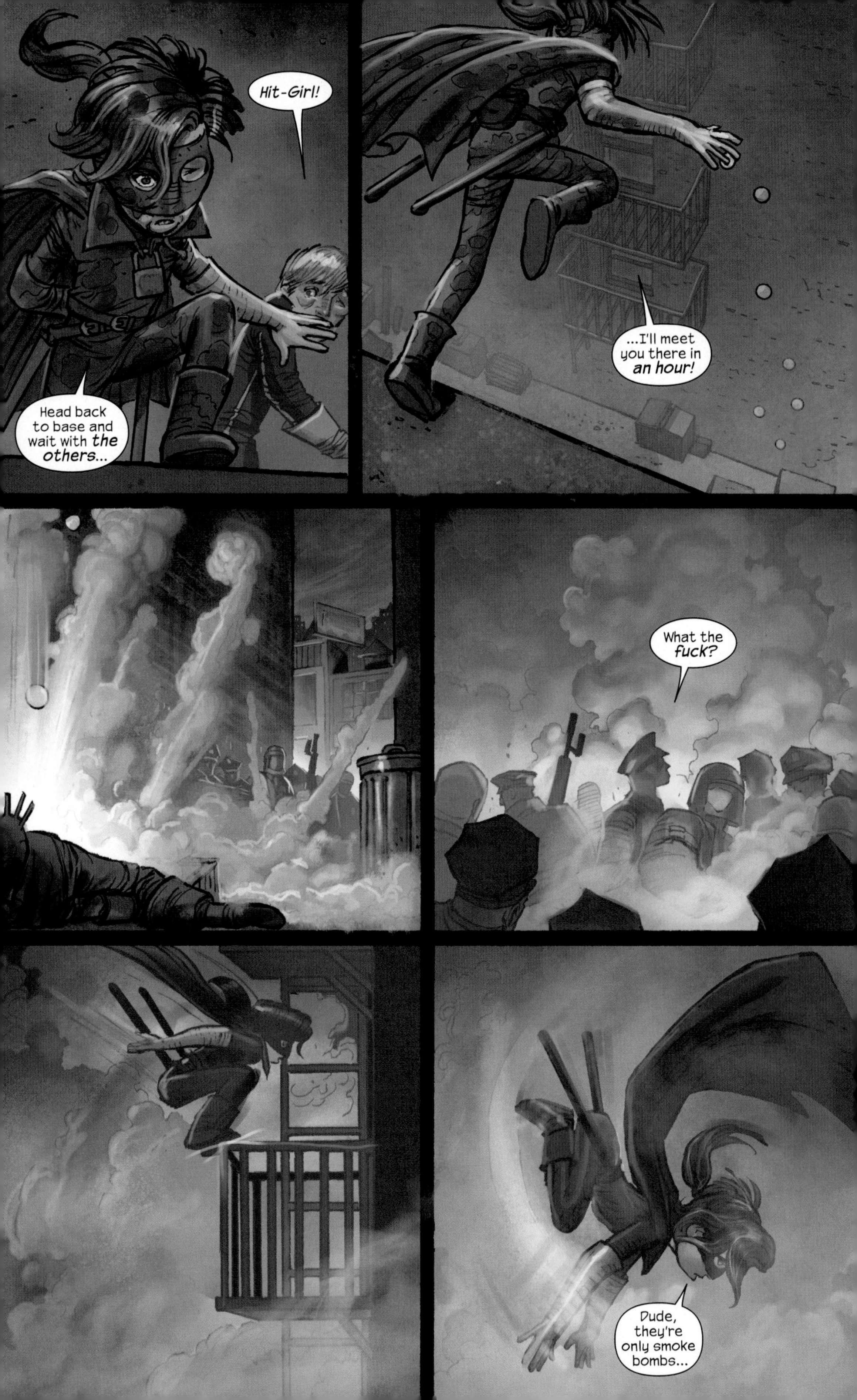
Hit-Girl!
Head back to base and wait with *the others*...
...I'll meet you there in *an hour!*
What the *fuck?*
Dude, they're only smoke bombs...

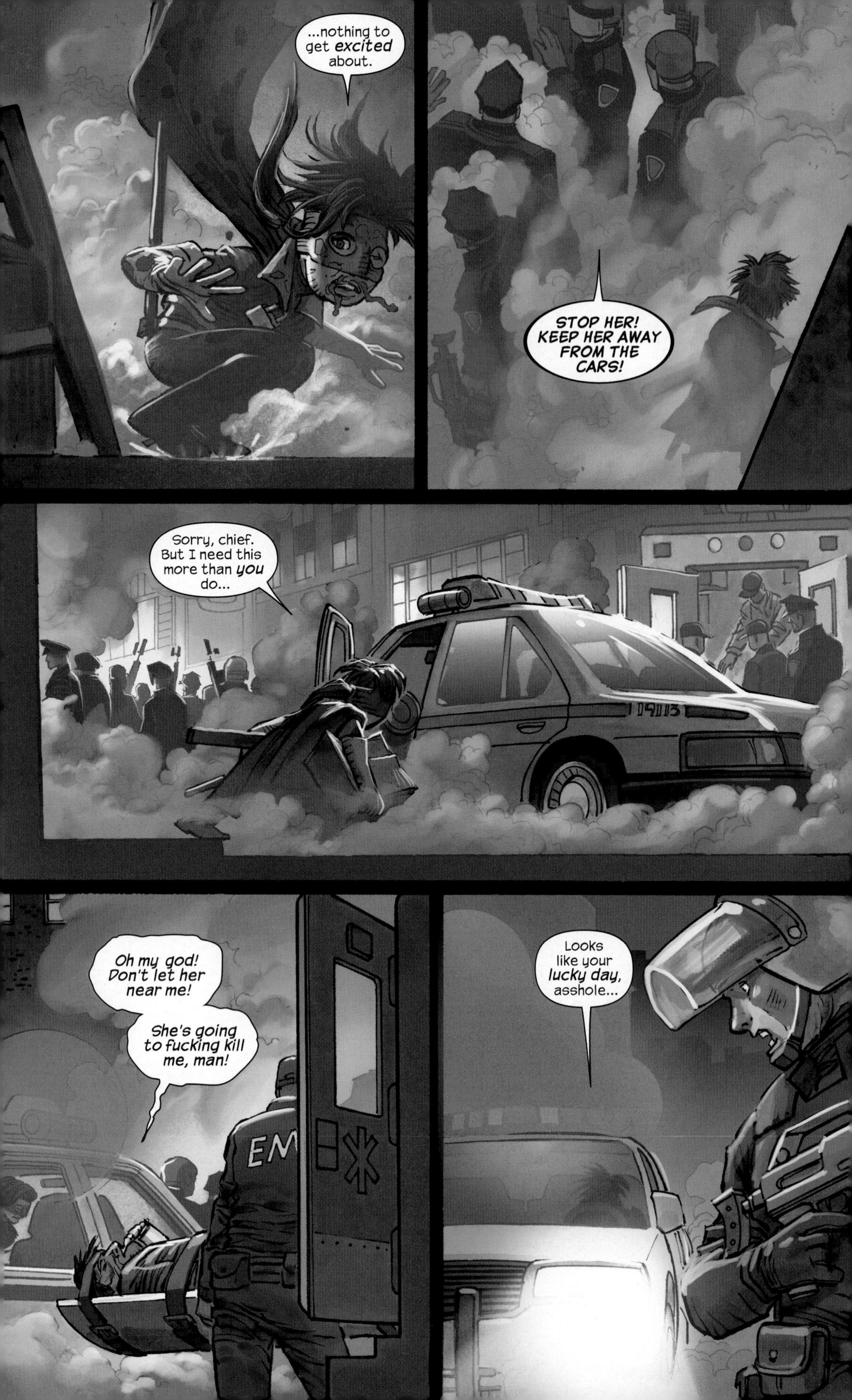
...nothing to get *excited* about.
STOP HER! KEEP HER AWAY FROM THE CARS!
Sorry, chief. But I need this more than *you* do...
19113
Oh my god! Don't let her near me!
She's going to fucking kill me, man!
EM
Looks like your *lucky day*, asshole...

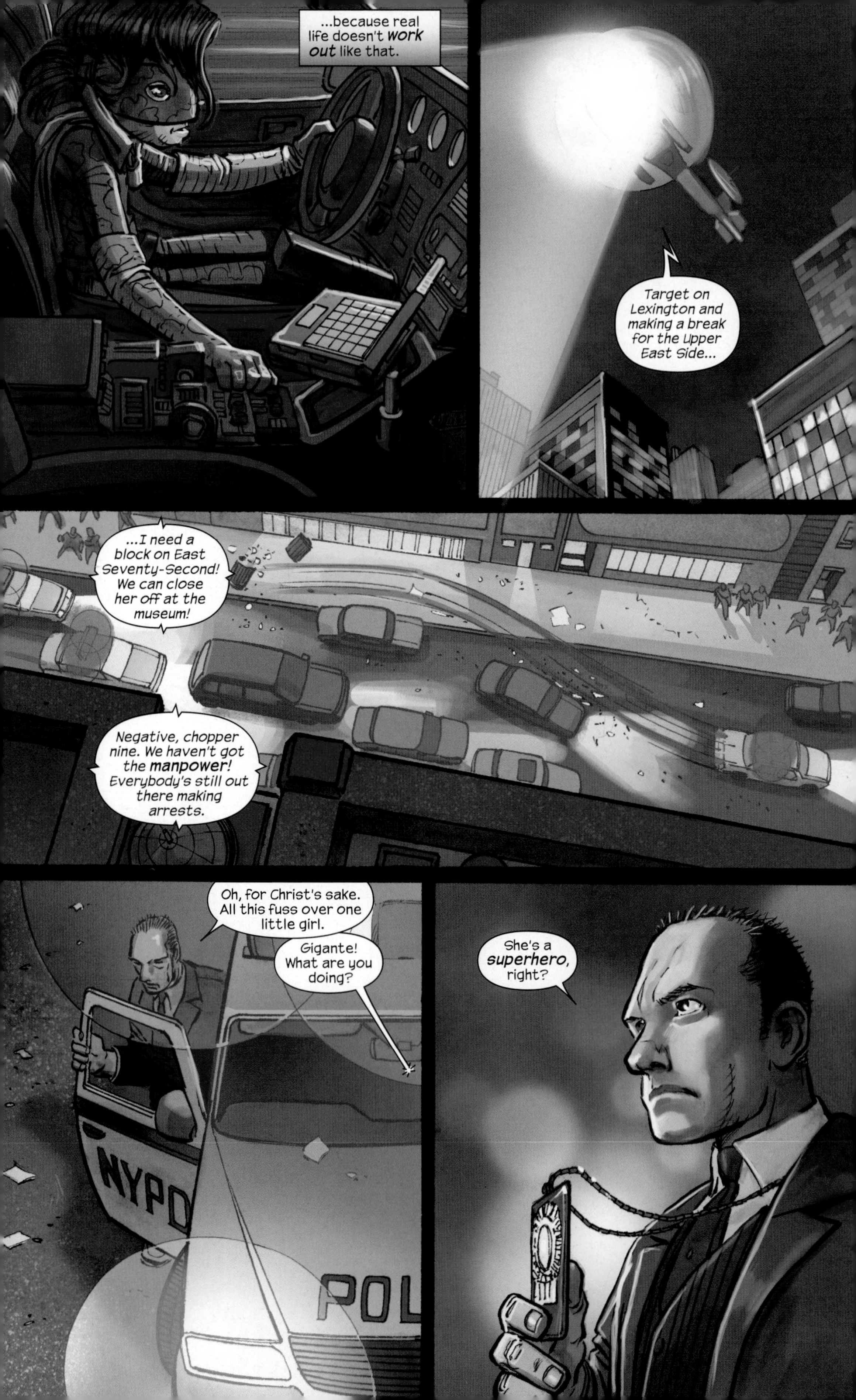
...because real life doesn't **work out** like that.
Target on Lexington and making a break for the Upper East Side...
...I need a block on East Seventy-Second! We can close her off at the museum!
Negative, chopper nine. We haven't got the **manpower!** Everybody's still out there making arrests.
Oh, for Christ's sake. All this fuss over one little girl.
Gigante! What are you doing?
NYPD
POL
She's a **superhero**, right?

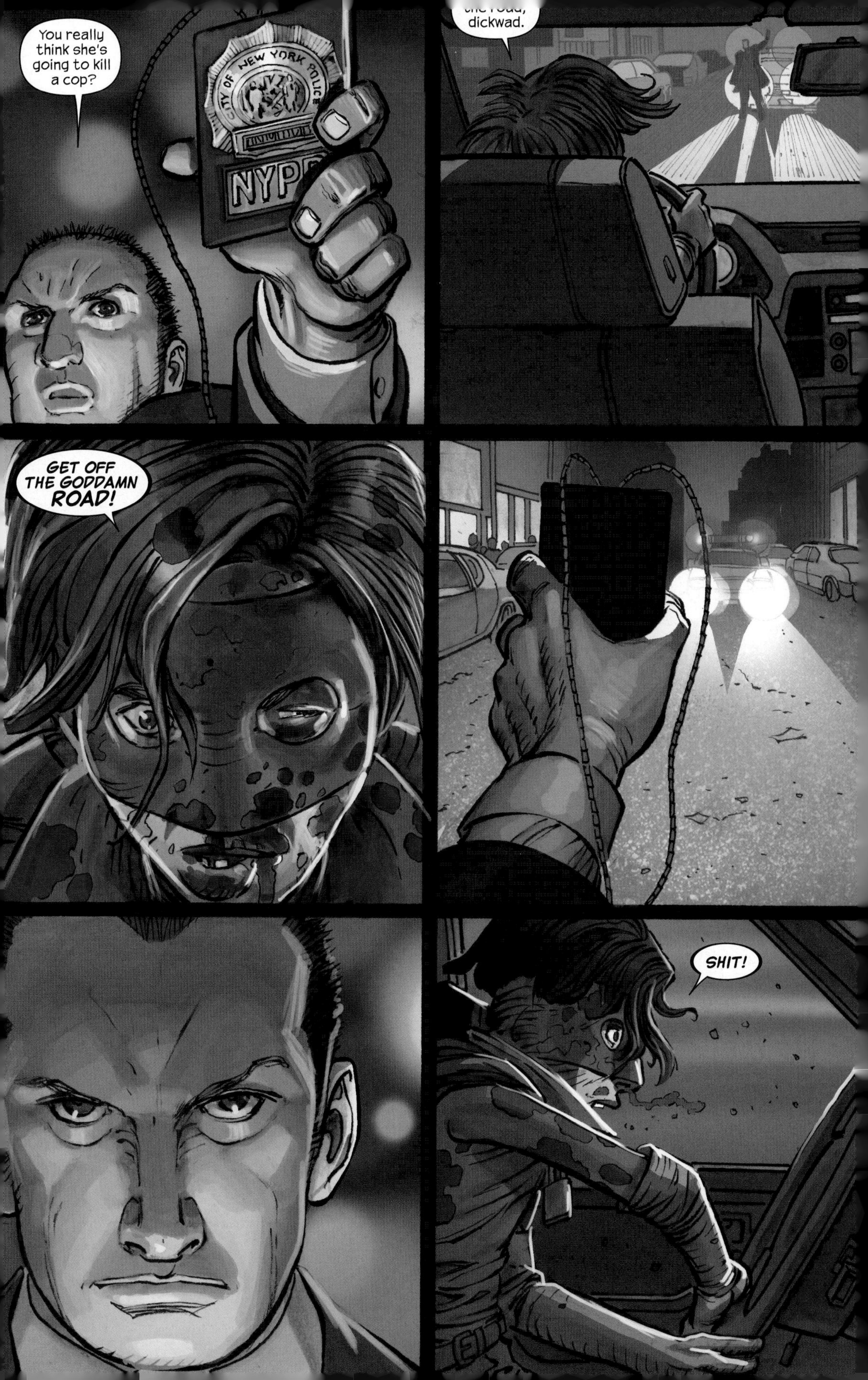

You really think she's going to kill a cop?
CITY OF NEW YORK POLICE
NYPD
dickwad.
GET OFF THE GODDAMN ROAD!
SHIT!

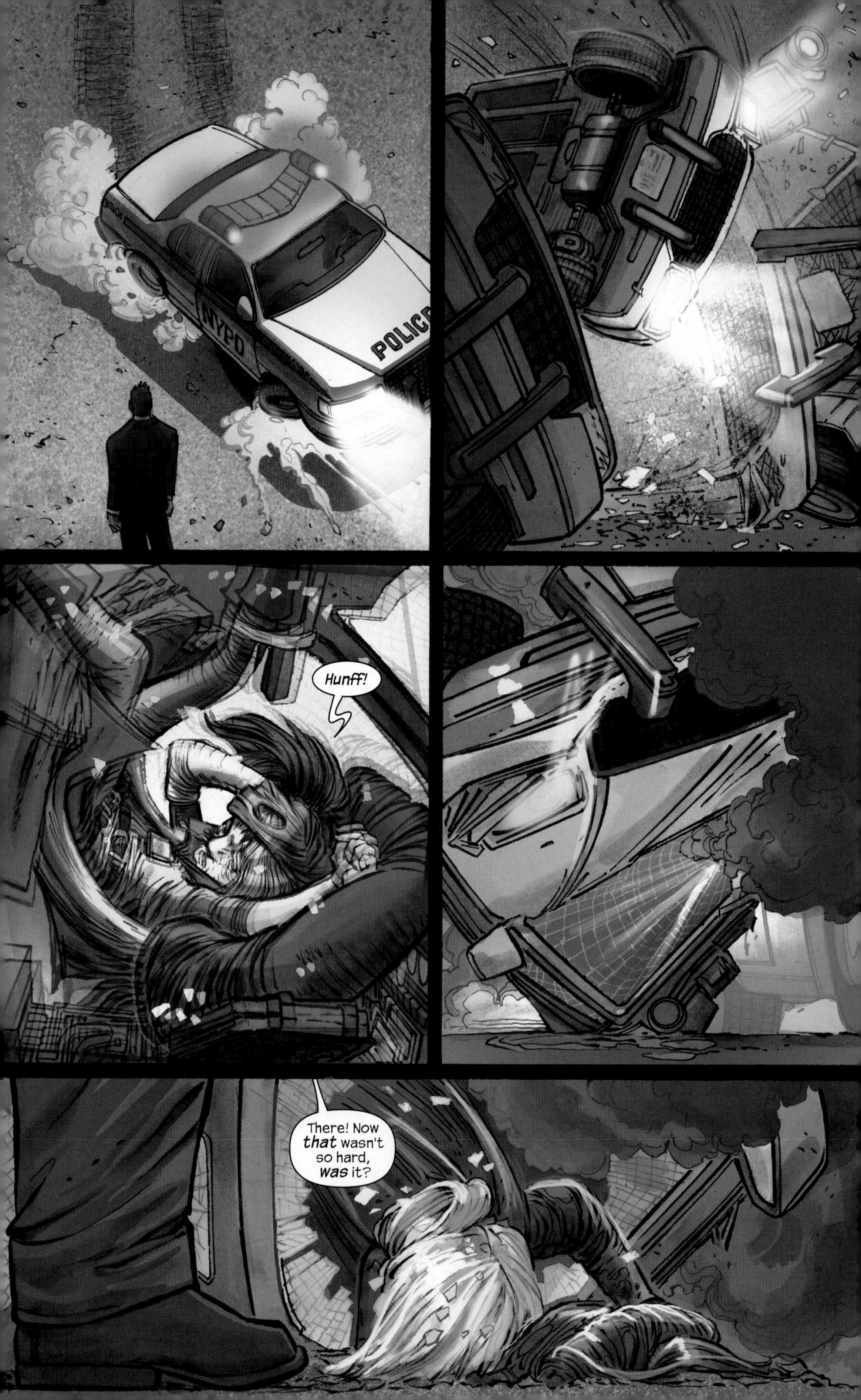
NYPO
POLICE
Hunff!
There! Now that wasn't so hard, was it?

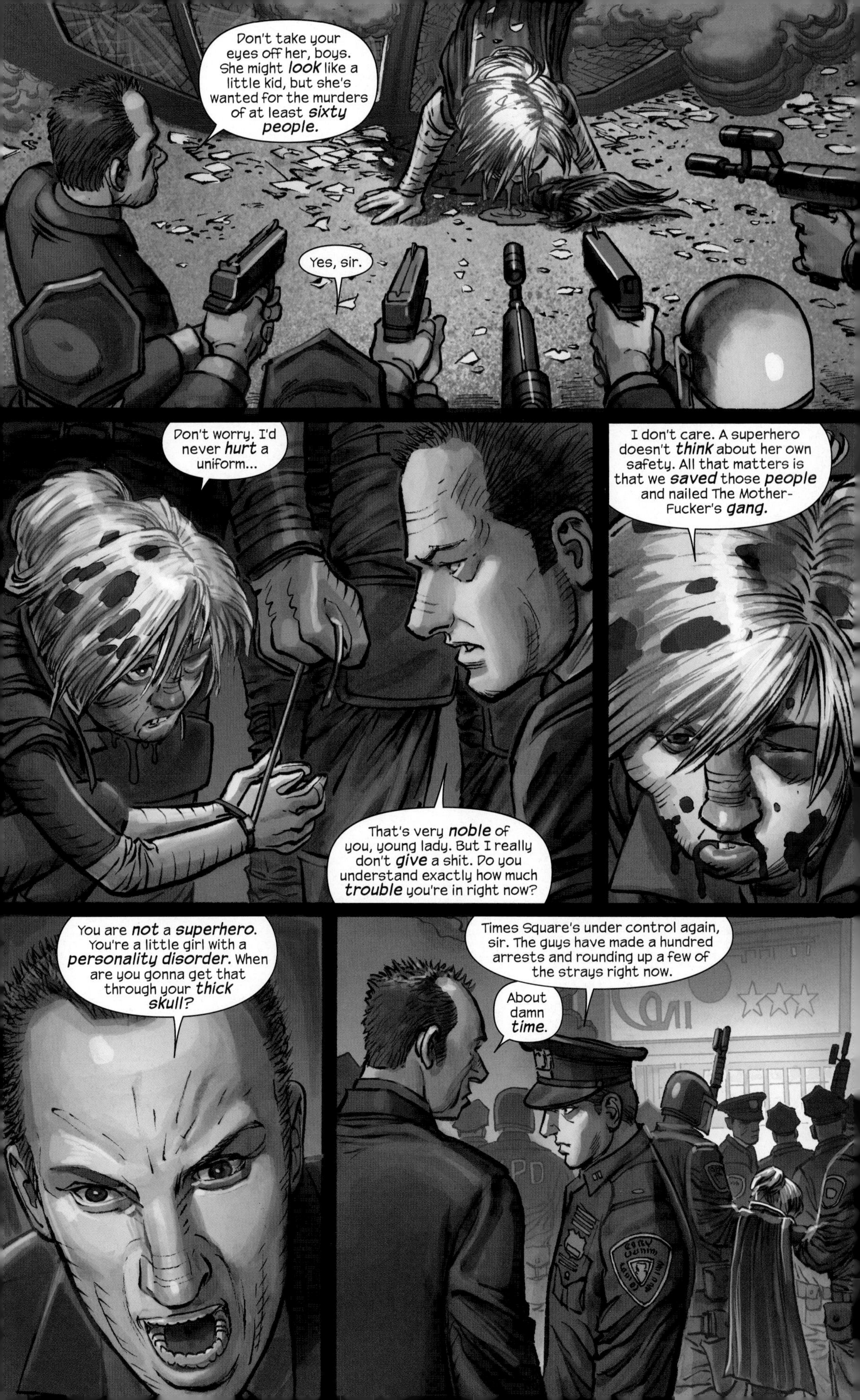
Don't take your eyes off her, boys. She might look like a little kid, but she's wanted for the murders of at least sixty people.
Yes, sir.
Don't worry. I'd never hurt a uniform...
That's very noble of you, young lady. But I really don't give a shit. Do you understand exactly how much trouble you're in right now?
I don't care. A superhero doesn't think about her own safety. All that matters is that we saved those people and nailed The Mother-Fucker's gang.
You are not a superhero. You're a little girl with a personality disorder. When are you gonna get that through your thick skull?
Times Square's under control again, sir. The guys have made a hundred arrests and rounding up a few of the strays right now.
About damn time.

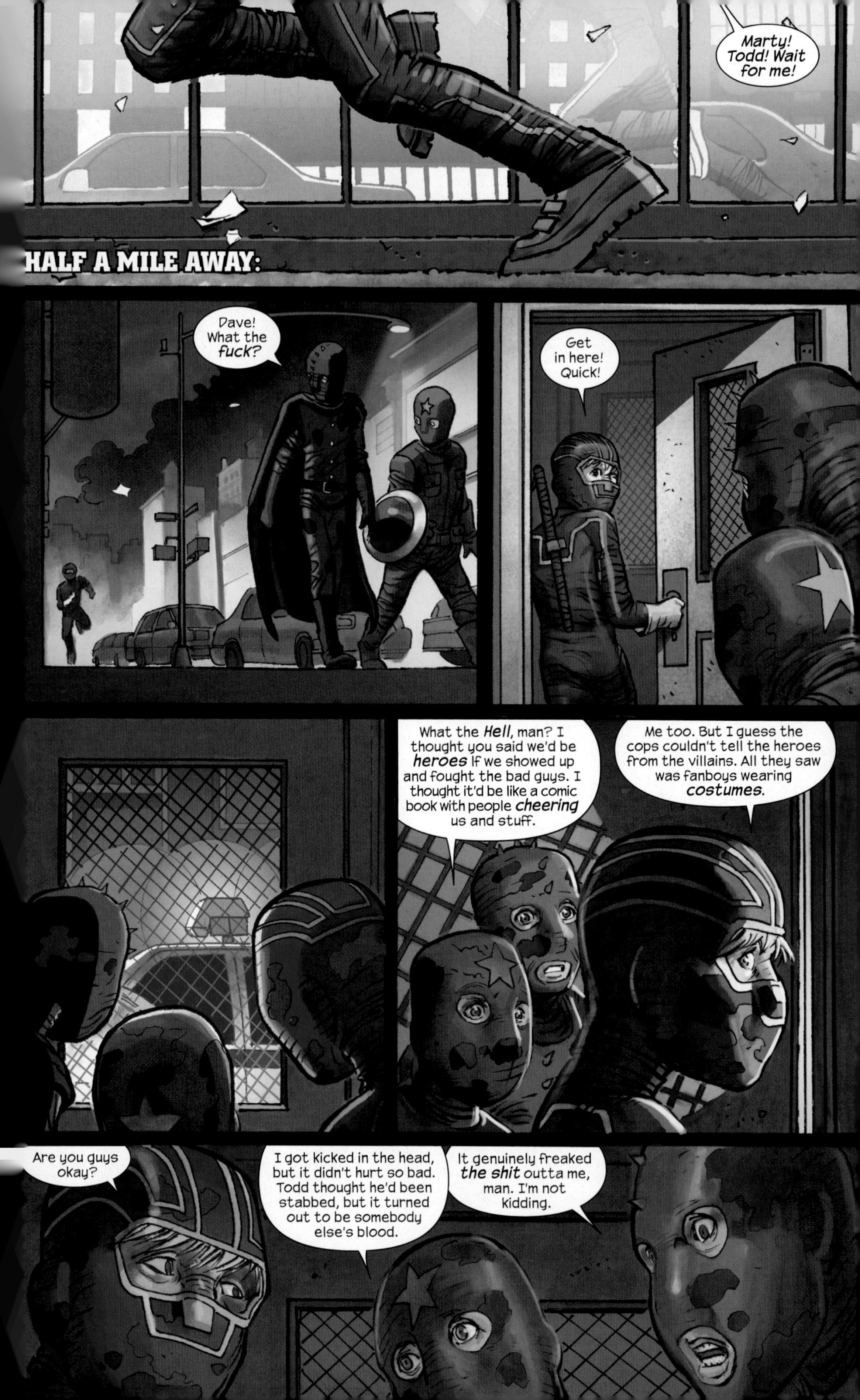

Marty! Todd! Wait for me!
HALF A MILE AWAY:
Dave! What the *fuck*?
Get in here! Quick!
What the *Hell*, man? I thought you said we'd be *heroes* if we showed up and fought the bad guys. I thought it'd be like a comic book with people *cheering* us and stuff.
Me too. But I guess the cops couldn't tell the heroes from the villains. All they saw was fanboys wearing *costumes*.
Are you guys okay?
I got kicked in the head, but it didn't hurt so bad. Todd thought he'd been stabbed, but it turned out to be somebody else's blood.
It genuinely freaked *the shit* outta me, man. I'm not kidding.

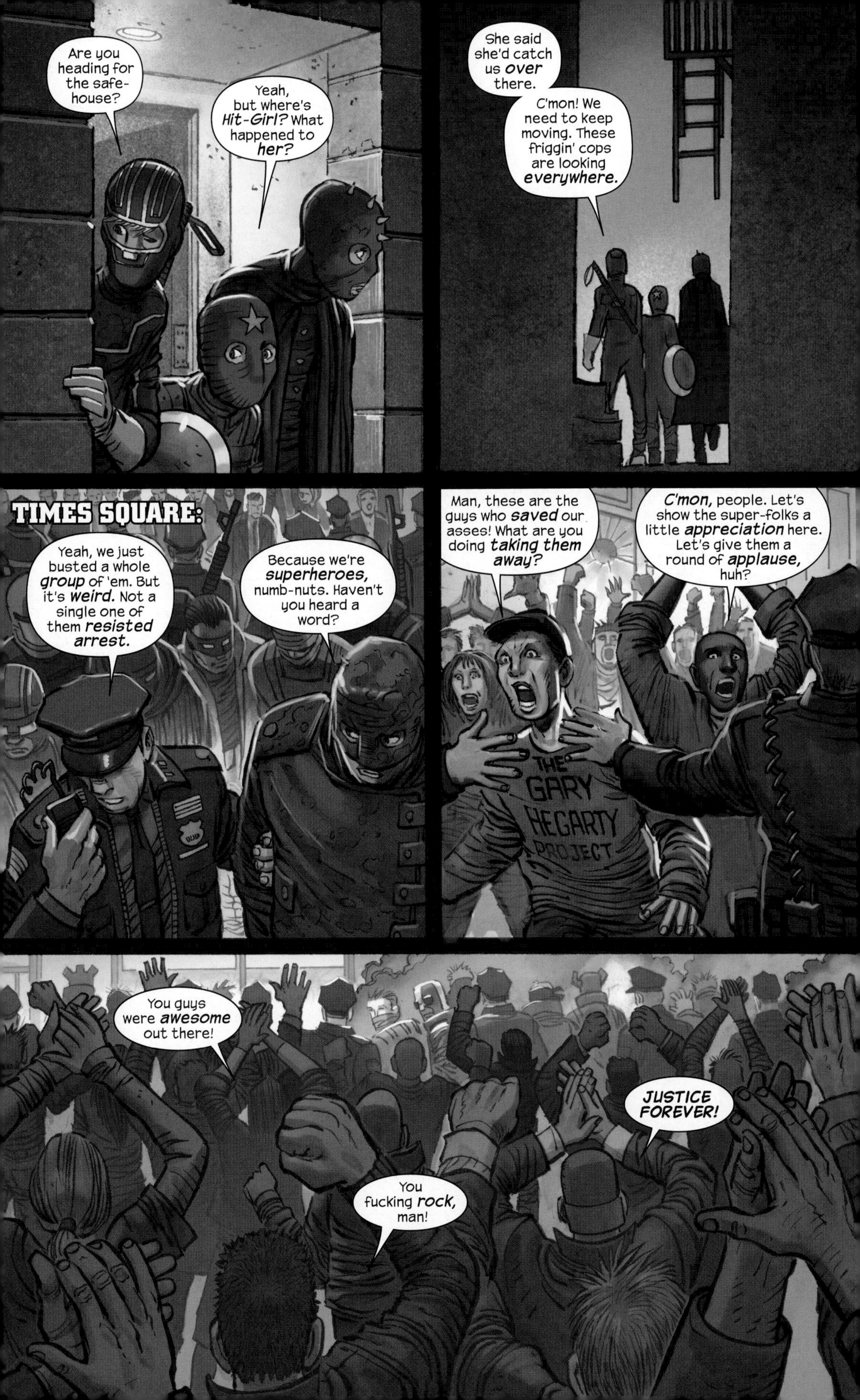
Are you heading for the safe-house?
Yeah, but where's Hit-Girl? What happened to her?
She said she'd catch us over there.
C'mon! We need to keep moving. These friggin' cops are looking everywhere.
TIMES SQUARE:
Yeah, we just busted a whole group of 'em. But it's weird. Not a single one of them resisted arrest.
Because we're superheroes, numb-nuts. Haven't you heard a word?
Man, these are the guys who saved our asses! What are you doing taking them away?
C'mon, people. Let's show the super-folks a little appreciation here. Let's give them a round of applause, huh?
THE GARY HEGARTY PROJECT
You guys were awesome out there!
JUSTICE FOREVER!
You fucking rock, man!

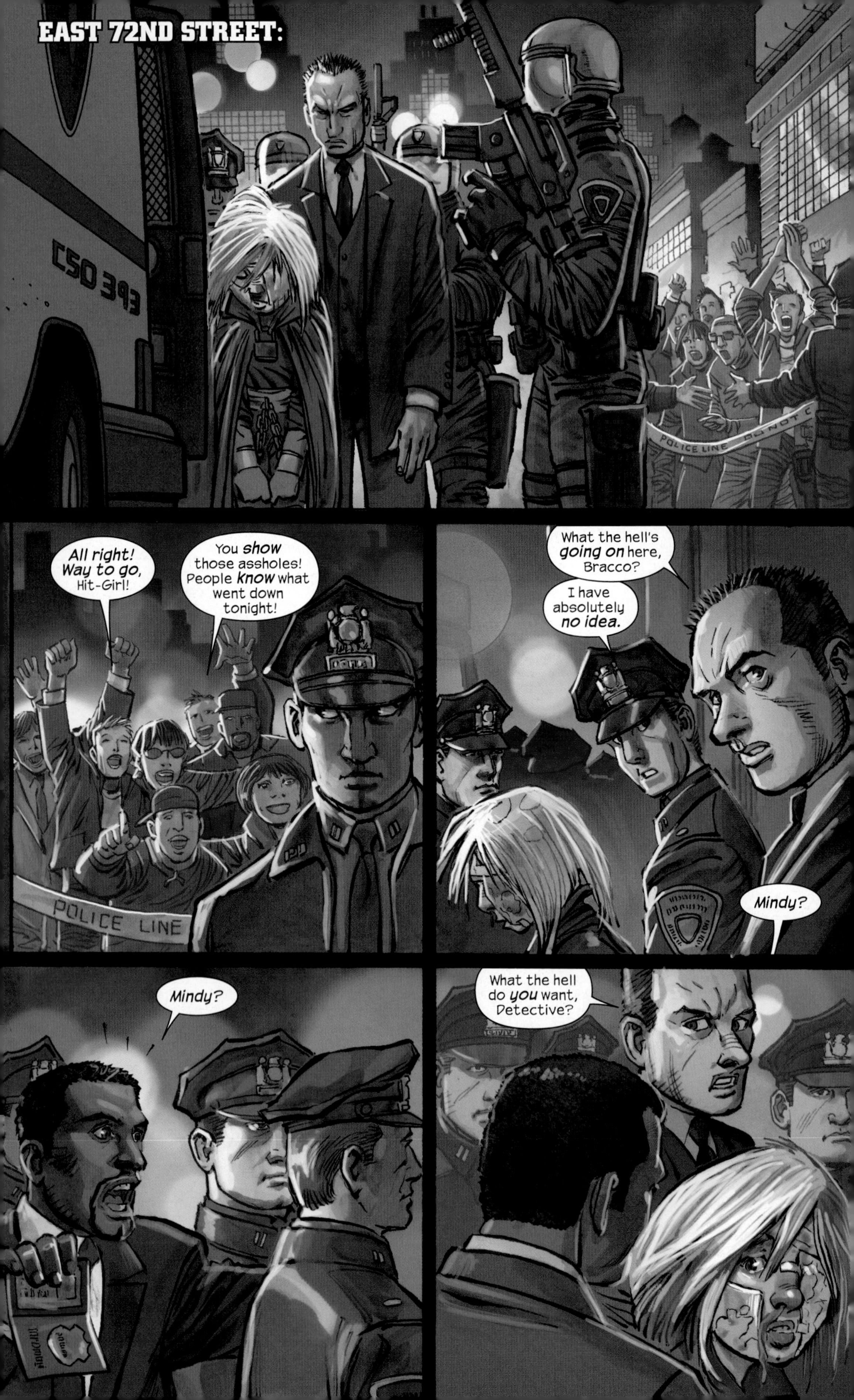
EAST 72ND STREET:
CSO 393
POLICE LINE DO NOT C
All right! Way to go, Hit-Girl!
You show those assholes! People know what went down tonight!
POLICE LINE
What the hell's going on here, Bracco?
I have absolutely no idea.
Mindy?
Mindy?
What the hell do you want, Detective?

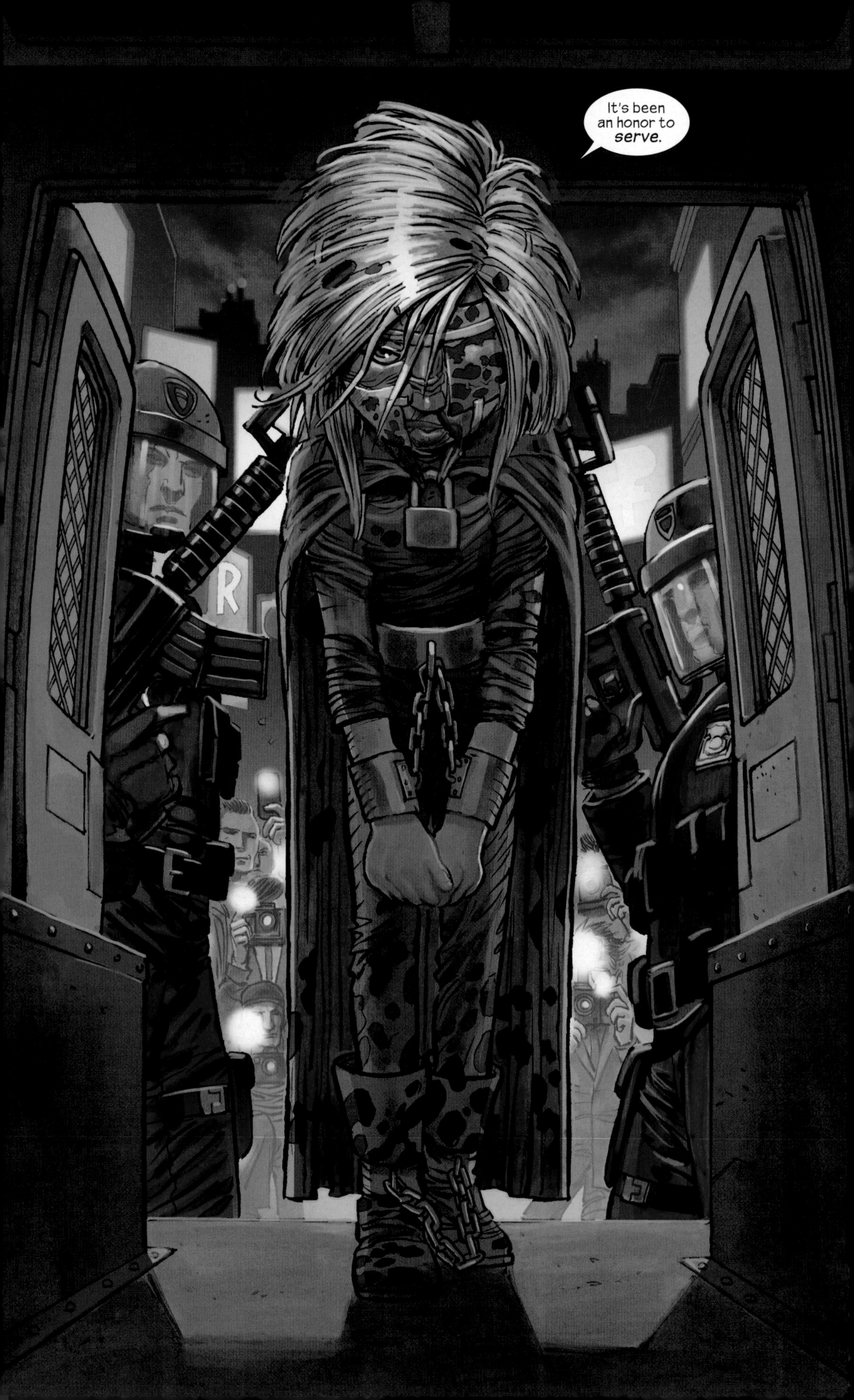
It's been an honor to *serve*.

END OF BOOK THREE

KICK

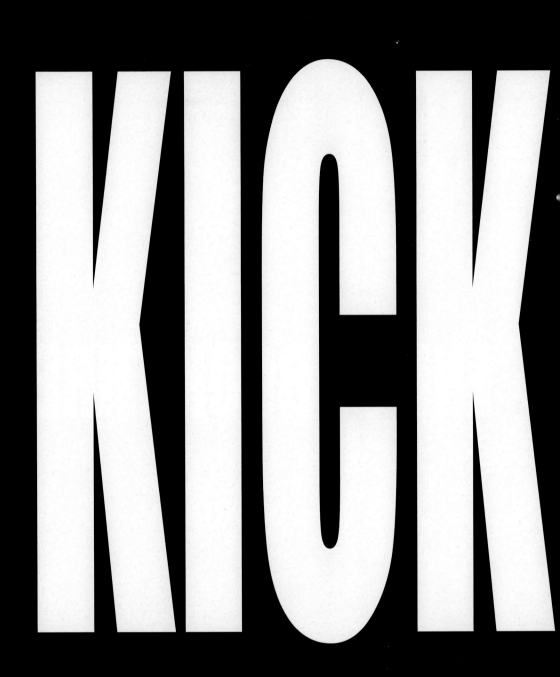

-ASS

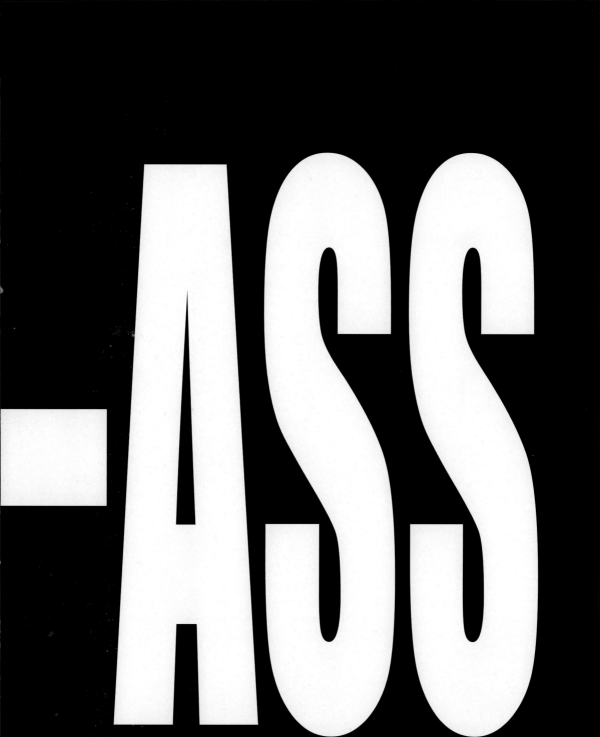

MARK MILLAR has been one of the key writers for Marvel Comics in the 21st century. Millar's first major contribution to Marvel was *Ultimate X-Men*, which achieved great creative and commercial success throughout his two-year run. Working with artist Bryan Hitch on *The Ultimates*, Millar surpassed his own success with that commercial and critical darling. Next, joining up with some of the industry's top creative talent, the Scottish writer took on two of Marvel's most iconic characters: Spider-Man and Wolverine. While working on creator-owned books like *Wanted*, turned into a Hollywood blockbuster staring Angelina Jolie, he penned *Civil War*, the epic miniseries that definitively reshaped the landscape of Marvel's heroes. More recently, Millar has reunited with Hitch on *Fantastic Four* and with *Civil War* artist Steve McNiven in both the pages of *Wolverine* and the upcoming *Nemesis*, as well as returning to the Ultimate Universe with *Ultimate Avengers*.

JOHN ROMITA JR. is a modern-day comic-art legend. A loyal Marvel artist since the late '70s, he has followed in his father's footsteps and helped keep the Romita name on the list of top-shelf talent. Timeless runs on *Iron Man, Uncanny X-Men, Amazing Spider-Man,* and *Daredevil* helped establish him as his own man artistically, and his art on *Wolverine* is arguably the decade's most explosive comic art—trumped perhaps only by his own work on the massive summer blockbuster event *World War Hulk*. JRJR has also paired with renowned writer Neil Gaiman for *The Eternals*, their reworking of the classic Marvel Comics characters, and has recently returned to *Amazing Spider-Man*; he will follow that up with another high-profile Marvel series.

TOM PALMER has worked as an illustrator in the advertising and editorial fields, but he has spent the majority of his career in comic books. His first assignment, fresh out of art school, was on *Doctor Strange*, and he has gone on to lend his inking talents to many of Marvel's top titles, including *X-Men, The Avengers, Tomb of Dracula*, and more recently *Punisher, Hulk,* and *Ghost Rider.* He lives and works in New Jersey.

DEAN WHITE is one of the comic industry's best and most sought-after color artists. Well-known for his work on titles such as *The Amazing Spider-Man, Punisher, Dark Avengers, Captain America, Black Panther, Wolverine* and countless more, Dean's envelope-pushing rendering and color palette bring a sense of urgency and power to every page he touches.

CHRIS ELIOPOULOS is a multiple award-winner for his lettering, having worked on dozens of books during the twenty years he's been in the industry—including Erik Larsen's *Savage Dragon*, for which he hand-lettered the first 100 issues. Along with his success as a letterer, he also publishes his own strip *Misery Loves Sherman*, wrote and illustrated the popular *Franklin Richards: Son of a Genius* one-shots, and writes Marvel's *Lockjaw and the Pet Avengers* series.

AUBREY SITTERSON began his comics career as an intern at Marvel Comics, and went on to edit fan-favorite runs on *The Irredeemable Ant-Man, Ghost Rider* and more, before taking the plunge to write and edit comics freelance. Since then, he has edited *Kick-Ass, The Walking Dead* and other hit books, while writing comics for Marvel, DC, Image, Oni Press and Viz Media. Find him on the internet at aubreysitterson.com.

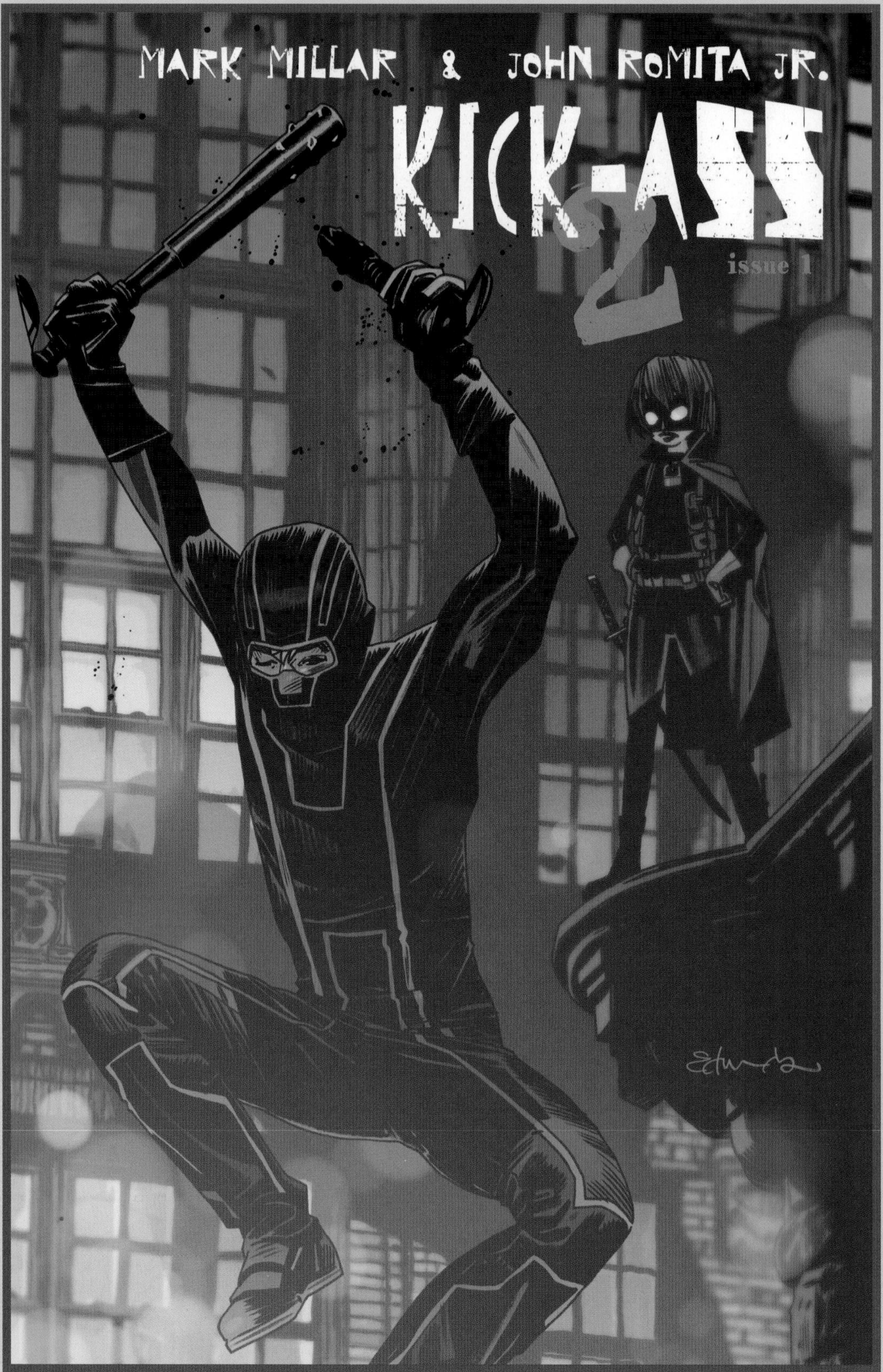
MARK MILLAR & JOHN ROMITA JR.
KICK-ASS 2
issue 1

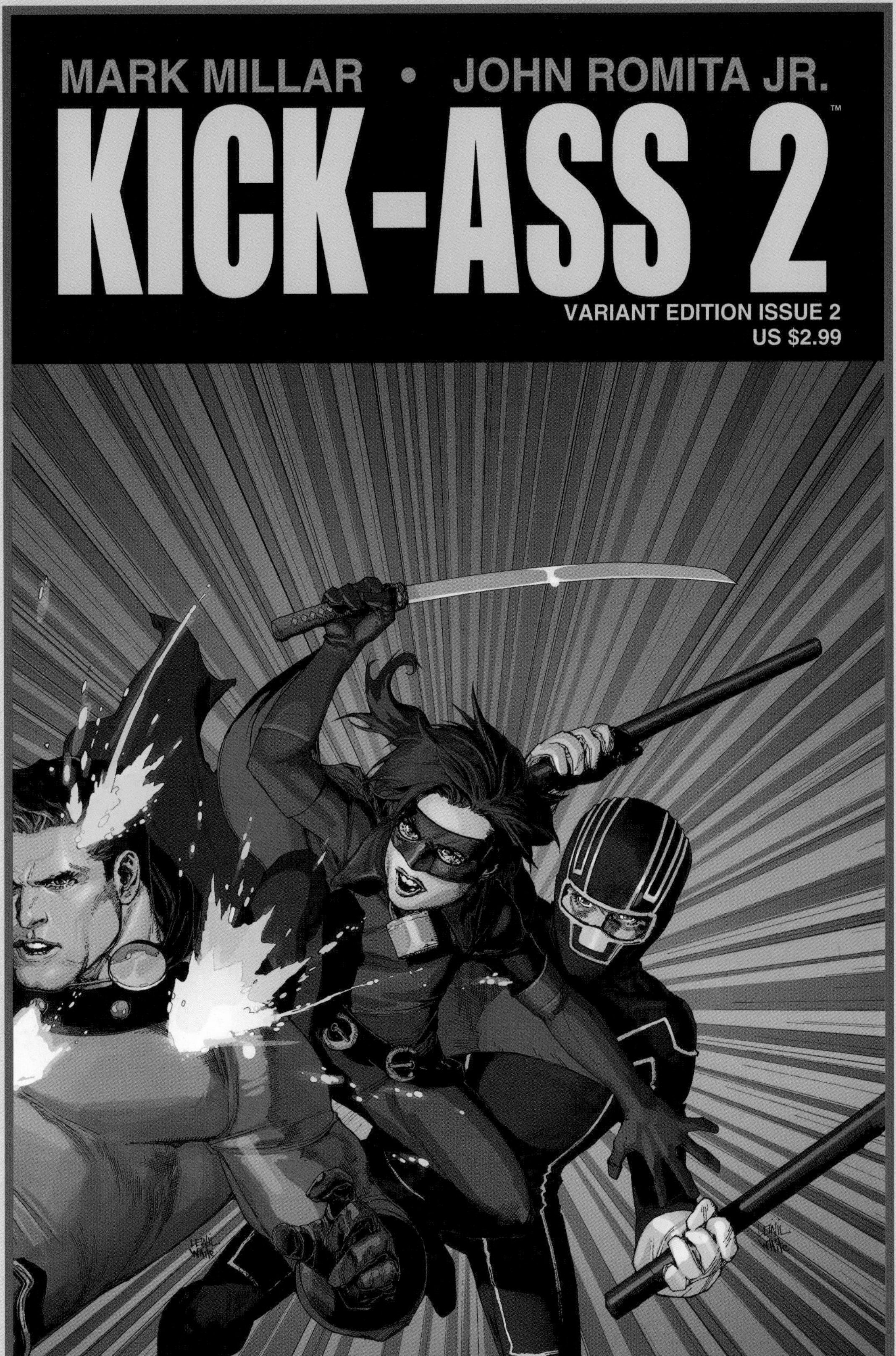
MARK MILLAR • JOHN ROMITA JR.
KICK-ASS 2™
VARIANT EDITION ISSUE 2
US $2.99

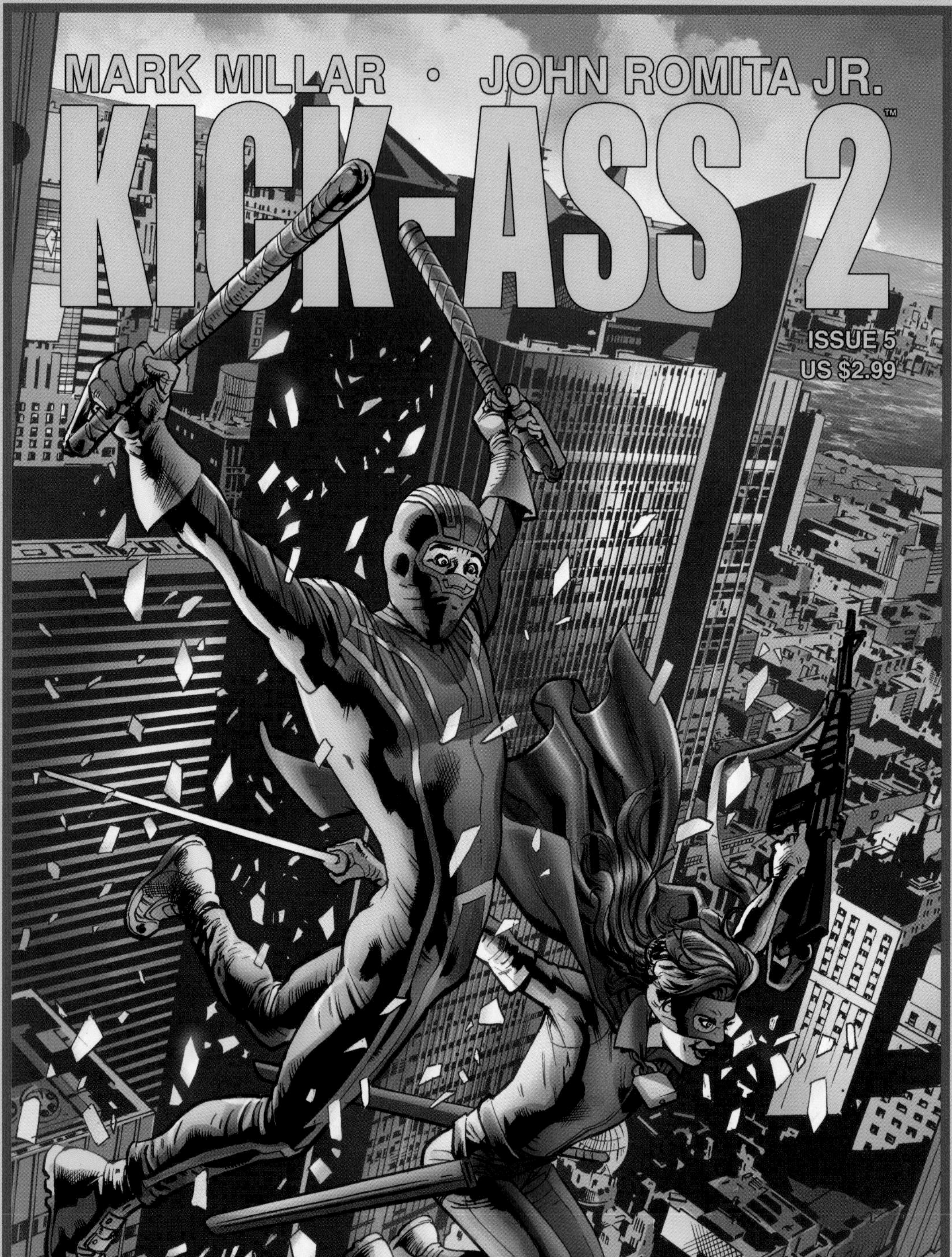

MARK MILLAR · JOHN ROMITA JR.
KICK-ASS 2™
ISSUE 5
US $2.99

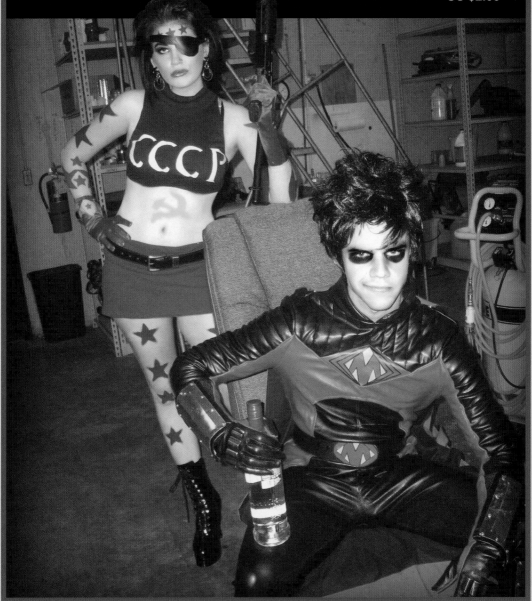

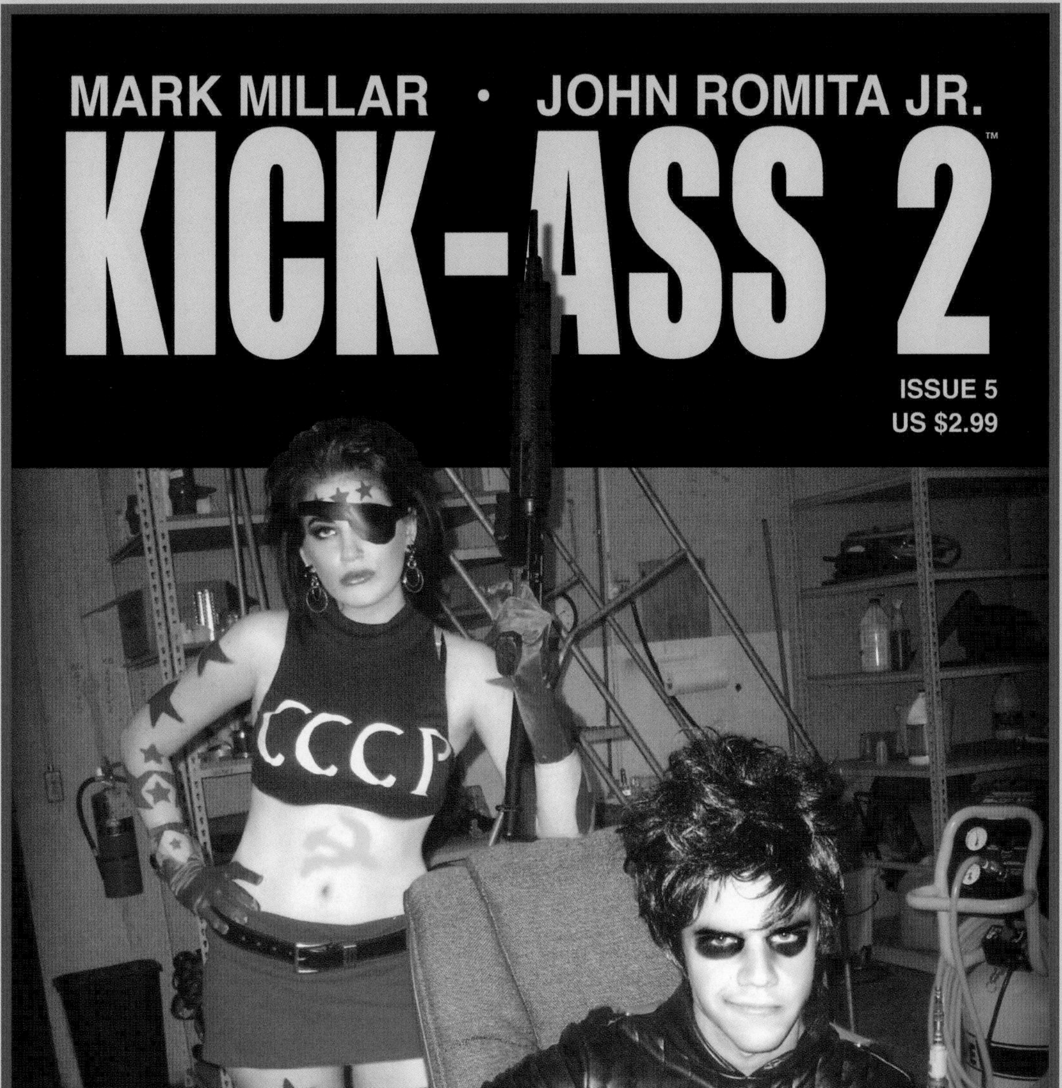
MARK MILLAR · JOHN ROMITA JR.
KICK-ASS 2™
ISSUE 5
US $2.99
CCCP

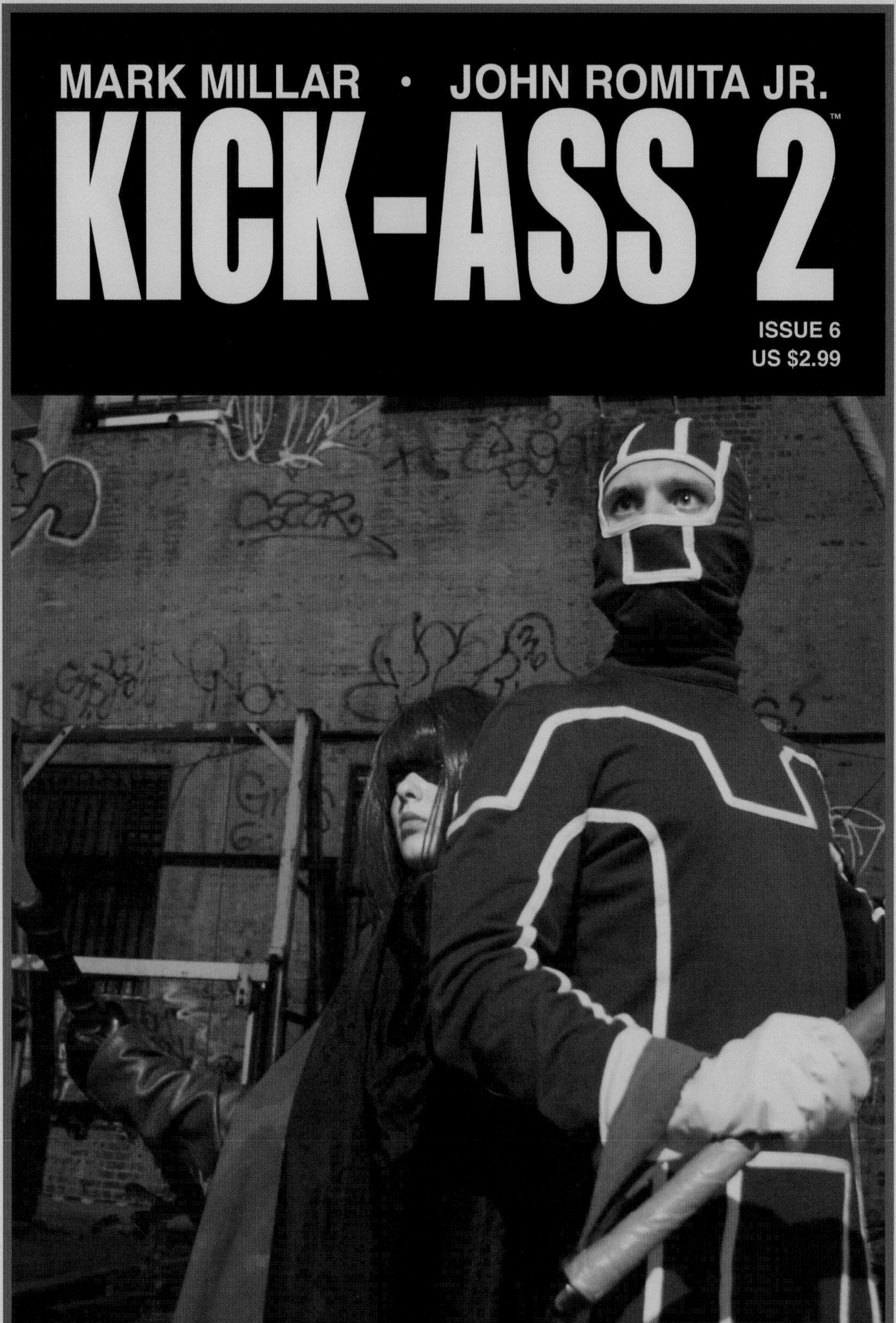
MARK MILLAR · JOHN ROMITA JR.
KICK-ASS 2™
ISSUE 6
US $2.99

SEVEN (PHOTO VARIANT)

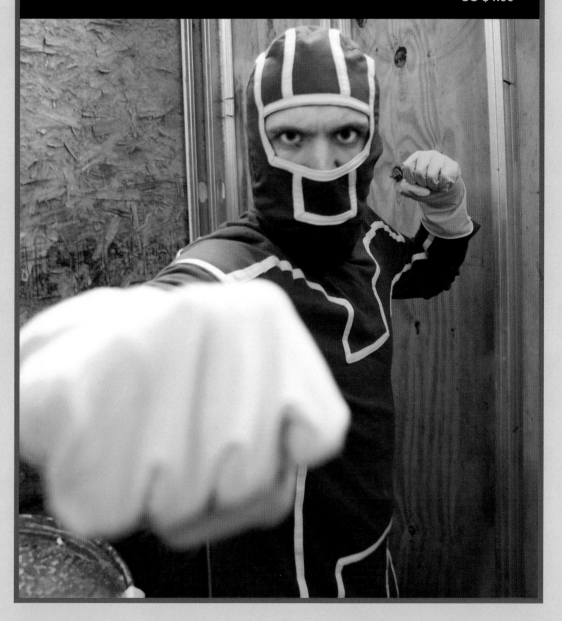

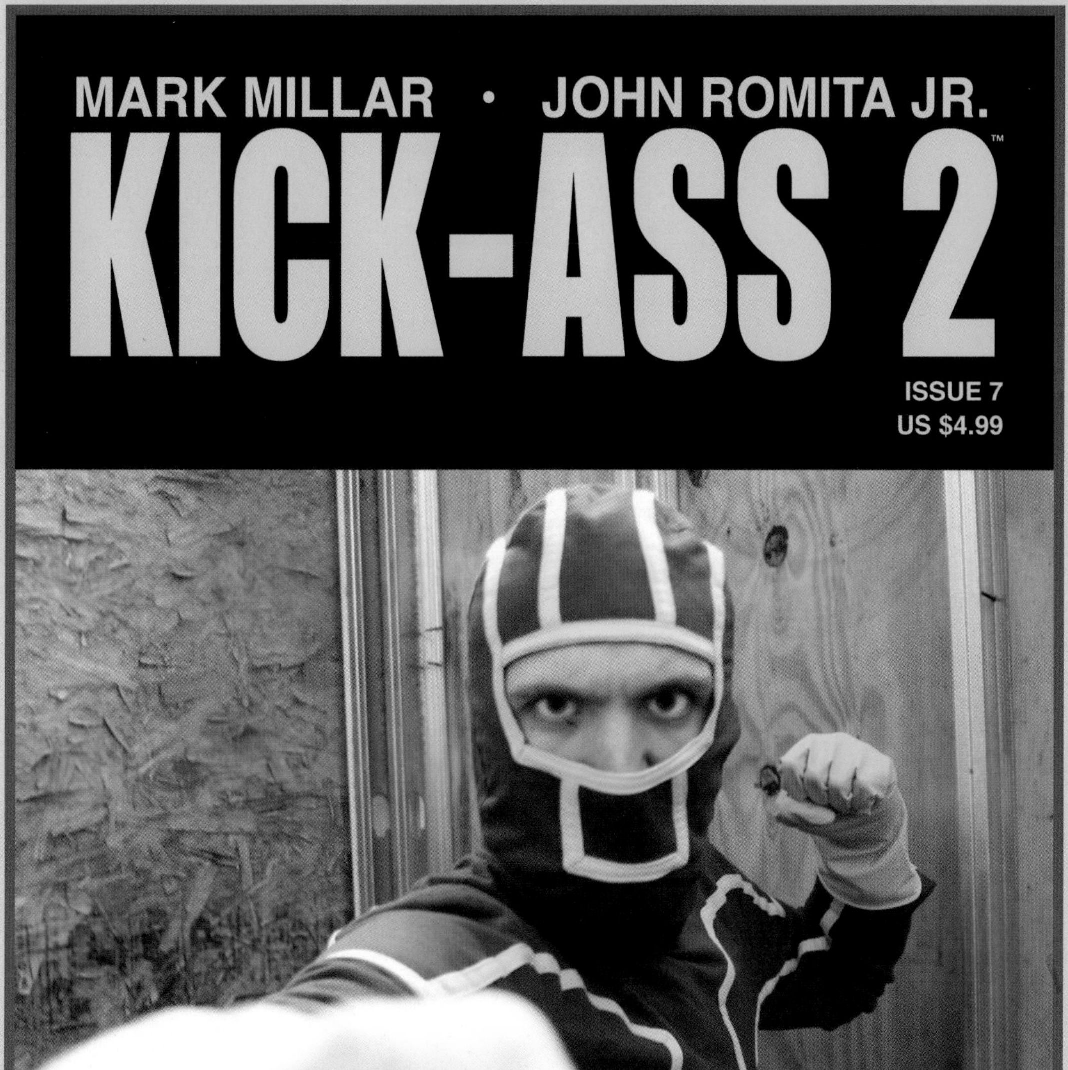
MARK MILLAR · JOHN ROMITA JR.
KICK-ASS 2™
ISSUE 7
US $4.99

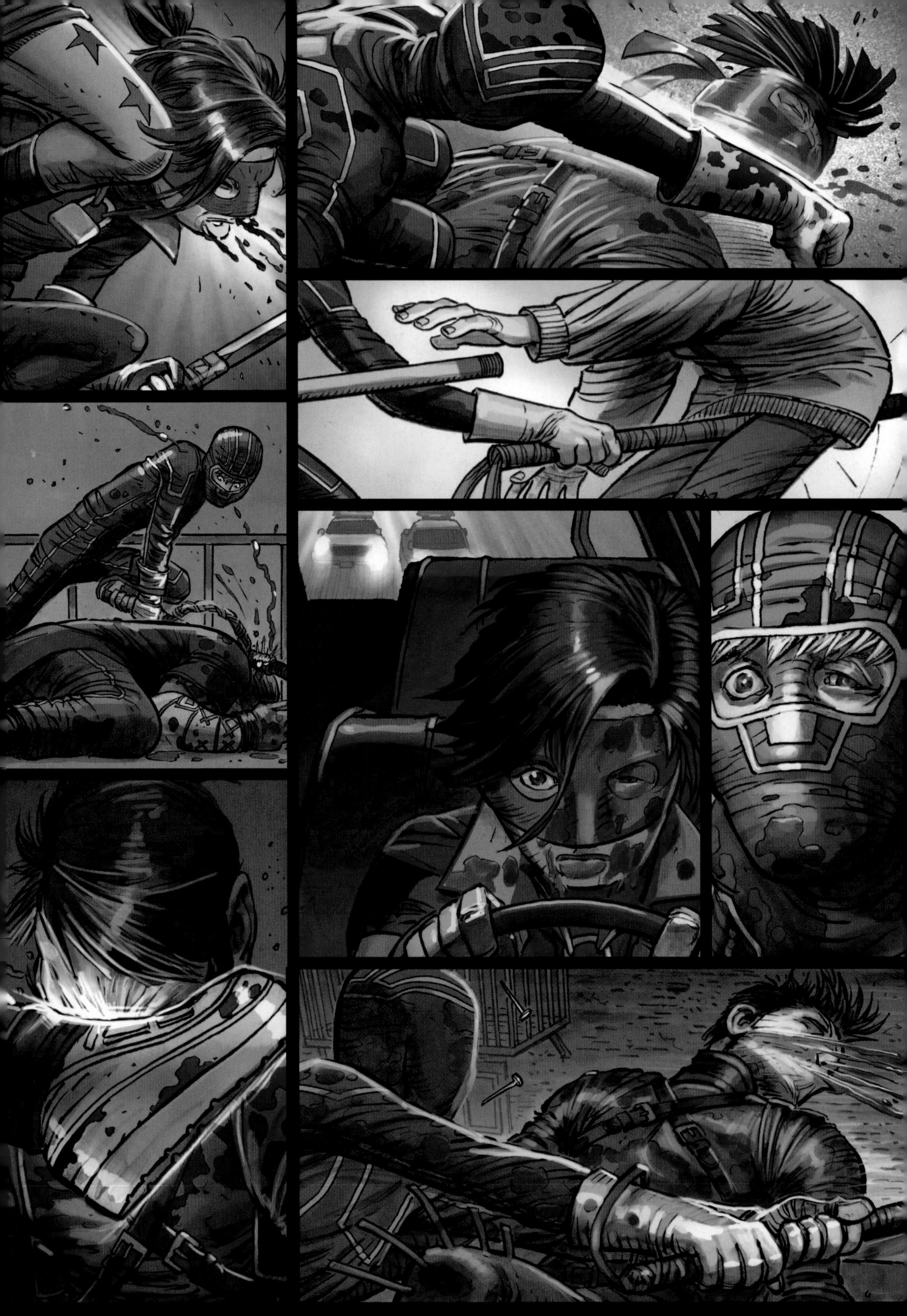

KICK-ASS'S GREATEST HITS

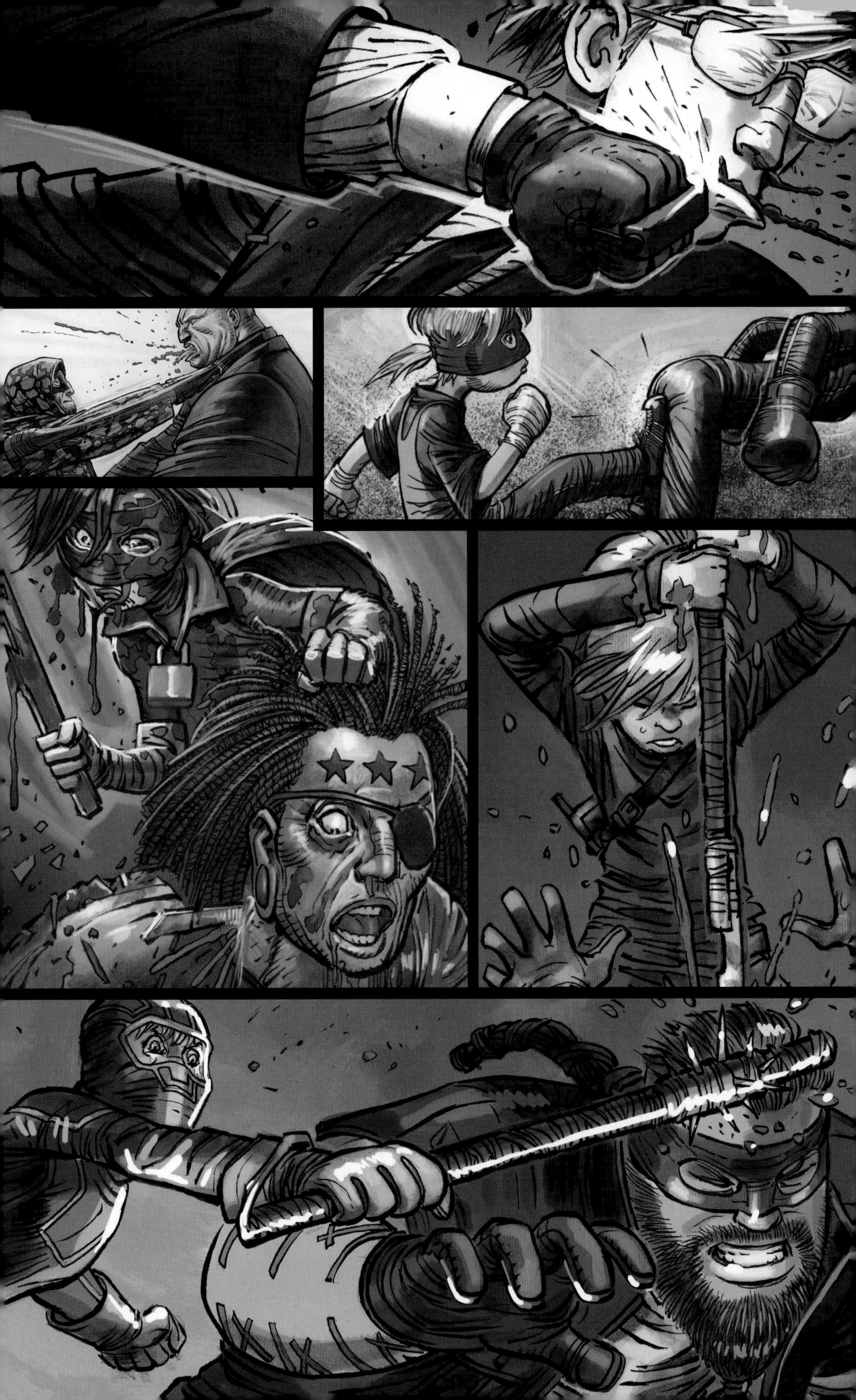

OTHER BOOKS FROM

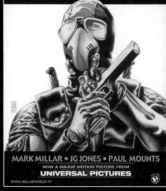
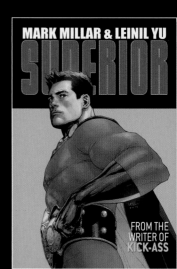
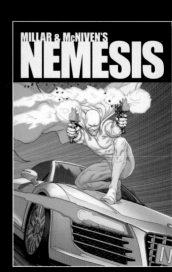

KICK-ASS
NOW A MAJOR MOTION PICTURE!
MARK MILLAR
JOHN ROMITA JR.

AVAILABLE NOW

MARK MILLAR • JOHN ROMITA JR.
HIT-GIRL

AMERICAN
JESUS
BOOK ONE : CHOSEN
MARK MILLAR ❖ PETER GROSS

AVAILABLE NOW

MARK MILLAR DAVE GIBBONS
the SECRET SERVICE
1
$2.99

MARK MILLAR & LEINIL YU
SUPER CROOKS
ISSUE ONE $2.99
There are too many Superheroes in America.
Let's go somewhere else...

BUY THEM ALL!

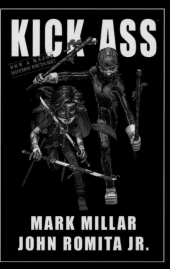

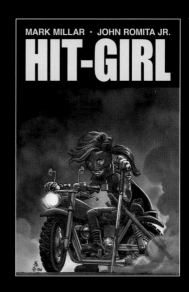

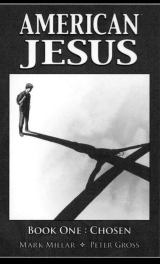

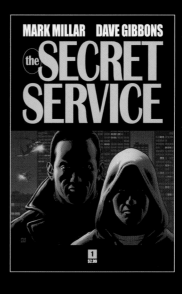

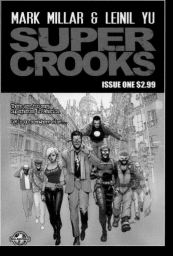

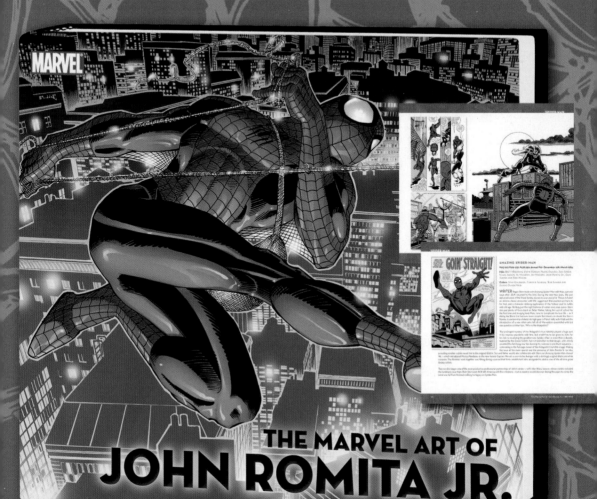

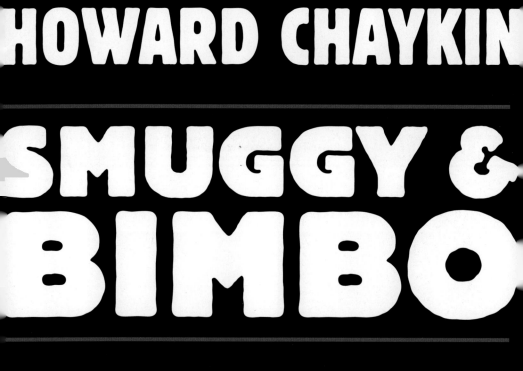

COMING IN 2013

JOHN ROMITA, JR.
HOWARD CHAYKIN

SMUGGY &
BIMBO

WITH A TITLE LIKE THAT, IT HAS TO BE GREAT!

KICK-ASS READING ORDER

PART ONE

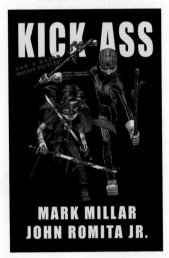

KICK-ASS

NOW A MAJOR MOTION PICTURE

MARK MILLAR
JOHN ROMITA JR.

PART TWO

MARK MILLAR · JOHN ROMITA JR.

HIT-GIRL

PART THREE

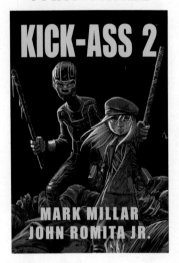

KICK-ASS 2

MARK MILLAR
JOHN ROMITA JR.

PART FOUR

PART FIVE